SHEET METAL

shop practice

Notice the varieties of operations which take place in this large sheet metal shop.

SHEET METAL
shop practice

LEROY F. BRUCE
Formerly Teacher of Sheet Metal Work,
Jefferson High School, Rochester, New York;

Instructor in Sheet Metal, Air Conditioning,
and Welding, Vocational School, Rochester, New York

LEO A. MEYER
Assistant Dean of Instruction,
Chabot College, San Leandro, California;

Formerly Instructor in Vocational Sheet Metal
and Apprentice Sheet Metal Classes,
Bakersfield College, Bakersfield, California

AMERICAN TECHNICAL SOCIETY   CHICAGO, ILLINOIS

PREFACE

Few persons not directly connected with it can imagine the importance which sheet metals play in their everyday lives. Sheet metal's numerous advantages make its use desirable in many products used in the home, factory, office, on the farm, and in transportation of all kinds.

Rolled sheet iron production dates back to the 17th Century, but massproduced steels and other metals have been comparatively recent developments. Much of this growth has been the result of the introduction of methods by which steel and other metals may be economically produced.

Moreover, discoveries in the field of metallurgy are increasing this growth at a rapid rate. As we entered the Nuclear and Space Ages, the new metals and metal alloys developed as a result of the requirements of those technologies have still further expanded the need of the sheet metal worker for fundamental and basic information.

Sheet Metal Shop Practice is significant in that it satisfies such needs by presenting information in such a way as to progressively develop the necessary skills required of sheet metal workers. At the same time, this information is so ordered as to make each chapter a complete unit of work.

This third edition incorporates the suggestions of many instructors. It reflects the results of a careful analysis of the book's use and its testing by many thousands of students. For example, since the sheet metal worker generally works from patterns or may even adapt such patterns to suit particular applications, an understanding of the basic methods by which such patterns are developed is as vital as a knowledge of the tools and machines used to produce a finished object from such a pattern.

It is equally important to put this understanding into practice and, for that reason, work projects in this revised edition have been increased in number and variety over previous editions. The projects are designed both to carry through operations previously learned and to add new elements presented in each chapter. They are spotted throughout the text and thereby serve as guides by which progress and understanding may be measured.

Some of the major additions to this revised edition include new chapters on plastics and exotic metals. Fabrication processes by which plastics are produced use many of the same techniques employed in conventional metal working and this field is rapidly expanding. The exotic metals developed to meet new needs in our complex technologies require that the sheet metal worker be aware of what some of these metals are. Therefore, both plastics and exotic metals are two of the areas with which the sheet metal worker will have to become familiar in at least general terms.

In addition, the chapters dealing with pattern developments have been completely updated and amplified because of their importance to much of the work done by the sheet metal worker. Drawings in these chapters and in all others are in conformity with accepted industrial drawing practices.

The authors wish to take this opportunity to thank all those individuals, organizations, and companies for their assistance in this revised edition of *Sheet Metal Shop Practice*. They also wish to extend a special word of thanks to Mrs. J. A. Scott for her contributions in typing and readying the manuscript.

Leroy Bruce and Leo Meyer are also the authors of a number of textbooks, booklets, and technical journal articles on sheet metal-related subjects. In addition, they bring to this text the combined practical experience of more than 50 years of teaching sheet metal in vocational and apprentice programs.

THE PUBLISHERS

CONTENTS

OPPORTUNITIES UNLIMITED

What are the places open to you as a sheet metal craftsman? What are some of the uses to which sheet metal is put in the modern world? What are the fundamental areas of sheet metal shop practice with which you must be familiar in order to become a craftsman in the field?

What are the potentials awaiting you as a qualified sheet metal worker in the United States today? The range of opportunities are as wide as your abilities and they will carry you as far as the amount of work you are willing to invest in your future. Sheet metal crafts are vital to expanding American industry. As the possessor of a much needed and wanted vocational skill, the sheet metal worker is assured of employment and good wages anywhere in the United States.

Naturally, the specific area in which you choose to make use of your training will depend to some extent on your particular interests. The field is wide and varied. Are your interests in aviation and Space Age technology? The trained sheet metal worker plays an essential part in civilian and military aeronautical demands as well as those brought about by the Space Age.

Would you like to go into business for yourself? Sheet metal contracting and estimating offer you many important opportunities. You can become a qualified sheet metal draftsman, coppersmith, welder or whatever you feel utilizes your potential in the most productive and interesting way for you. Your future achievements depend on you!

As you can see, the breadth of activities possible for you within the sheet metal field is very great. Though the uses of sheet metal are too numerous to list here, some of the major industries in which it is obvious that sheet metal plays an important part are heating and air conditioning, roofing, aircraft, shipbuilding, freight cars, refrigeration, steel furniture, cabinets and restaurant and cafeteria installations.

Federal Government buildings, in-

Figure 1. Workers are shown installing an air conditioning duct system. Notice the extensive use of sheet metal in fabricating the ducts.

cluding the White House are roofed with sheet metal which adds beauty as well as fire resistance. The most modern of America's new office buildings employ sheet metal extensively in their complex heating and air conditioning systems. A typical example of such a system is shown in Fig. 1. Sheet metal applications exist in nearly every automobile, plane, ship and train built in the United States.

The term *sheet metal* generally applies to metals and alloys in sheets rolled to thicknesses ranging from approximately $\frac{1}{64}$ inch to approximately $\frac{1}{8}$ inch. Chapter 4 will acquaint you with the various metals used in sheet metal work and their properties along with the gage system of measurement.

Whatever area of sheet metal work you eventually specialize in, a thorough knowledge of sheet metal fundamentals is indispensable. These essentials in the trade will be pre-

sented to you in succeeding chapters.

Sheet metal work can be roughly divided into five phases: planning and layout, fabrication, assembly, installation and, finally, repair and maintenance.

Chapter 2 will introduce you to the tools and machinery with which you will work and will explain their functions.

Planning and layout work is concerned with the steps by which a flat piece of sheet metal is formed into the finished article. Specifically, through the use of tools and methods explained in Chapters, 5, 11, 12, 13, 14, and 15, patterns are traced or drawn on the flat sheet of metal in order to serve as a guide for the operations to follow. Drafting, layout, and pattern development must be done with care and accuracy.

The flat sheet metal with the layout on it is fabricated through a number

Figure 2. Workman shown here trims metal with a squaring shears.

Figure 3. Adjustable bar folder is used by this workman to make locks in metal sheets.

of different operations. These steps vary from job to job. Some of the more common ones are *cutting,* explained in Chapter 5, *turning, burring,* and *raising,* explained in Chapter 9, *folding, edging,* and *making seams,* explained in Chapter 7, *forming, grooving, crimping,* and *beading,* explained in Chapter 8, and *notching patterns* explained in Chapter 12. Figs. 2, 3 and 4 show some of these operations being performed by a sheet metal worker.

Next, individual articles or parts, now shaped and formed, are connected as specified. Such connections may be made in a number of ways. For example, they may be *punched, drilled* or *riveted,* as explained in Chapter 6; or they may be *soldered,* which is explained in Chapter 10.

Installation, and repair and maintenance require a good working knowledge of the product, and often involve connecting skills such as drilling, etc., hoisting and scaffolding work, finishing skills (using both hand and power

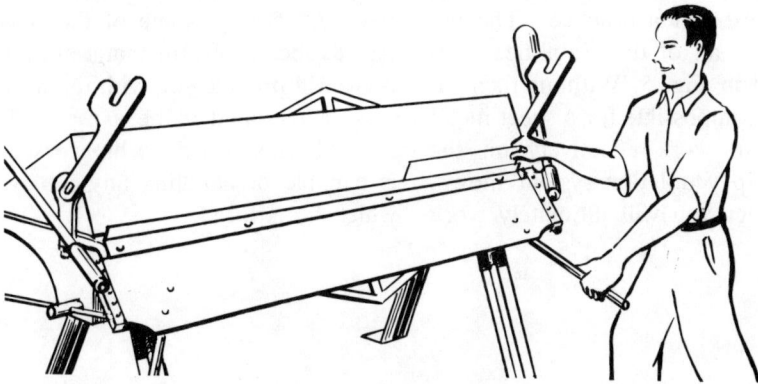

Figure 4. Metal bending brake used by this workman is employed to form edges in metal sheets.

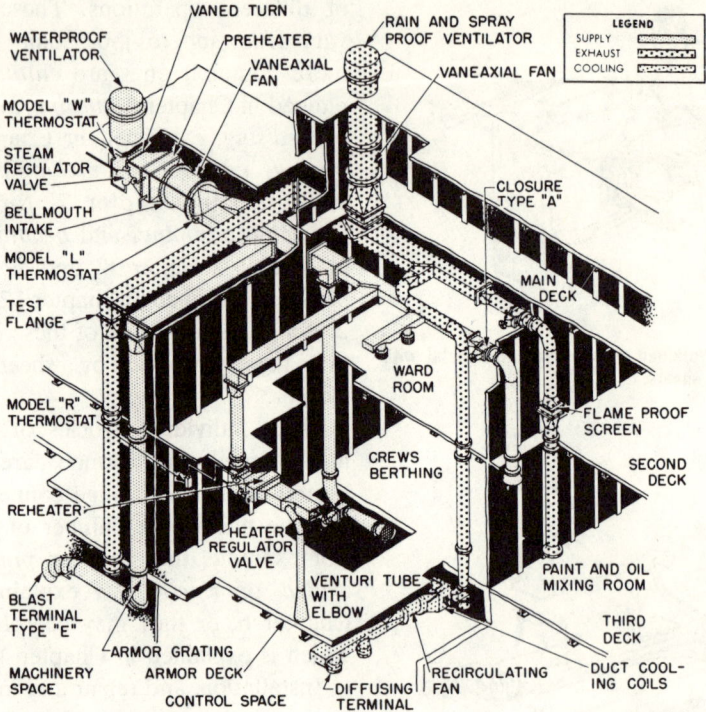

Figure 5. See the many uses for sheet metal fabricating processes in this naval ship ventilation system. Courtesy: Training Division, Department of the Navy.

tools such as buffers or chisels). They also require some understanding of basic construction practices. The necessity for all of these abilities is illustrated in Fig. 5. Without them, it would be impossible for a sheet metal worker to work effectively on the naval ship ventilation system shown.

Whether you will ultimately work with sheets of aluminum for aircraft "skins", sheet metal building materials, plastics, or some of the Space Age exotic metals, the material in this book will provide you with the necessary background to be a top craftsman who takes pride in his work and is capable of handling any job with which he is faced.

SHEET METAL WORKING TOOLS AND MACHINERY

What are the hand tools common to the sheet metal trade? What are the purposes of each of these tools? What are the basic machine tools used in sheet metal work? What operations are these machines designed to perform?

One of the characteristics of the skilled worker is the way in which he selects and uses the tools of his trade. For this reason, it is essential that you know how to select and properly use both the hand and machine tools of the sheet metal trade. You will find that when you do this, the quality of your work will improve, you will save valuable time, and your work will be easier. When you have completed reading this chapter and can associate the proper tool with the proper operation, you have taken the first step toward becoming a successful sheet metal craftsman.

Hand tools

Sheet metal hand tools are used to scribe or measure lines, perform layout operations and shape or cut metal. Some of the hand tools described in the following pages actually perform these operations, while others, such as stakes and some punches, serve as aids in performing them.

Scratch awls

There are three common types of scratch awls (also called scribers) as shown in Fig. 1. *All three awls perform the same function of marking lines on metals*. Lines are marked on metal for a variety of purposes in laying out patterns.

RING SCRATCH AWL. The ring scratch awl is made of one solid piece of steel approximately eight inches long with

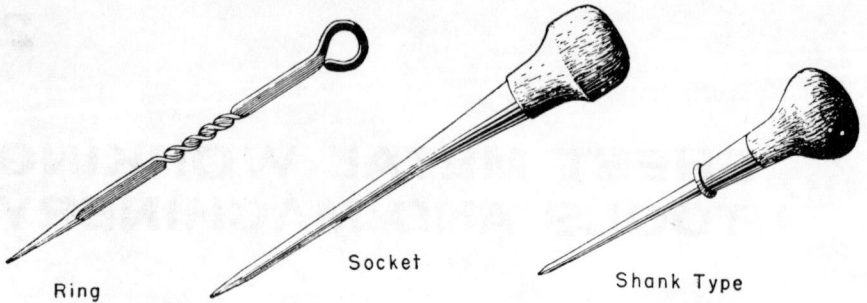

Ring   Socket   Shank Type

Figure 1. Commonly used scratch awls scribe lines on metal for a variety of purposes.

a tapered point on one end and a ring on the other.

SOCKET SCRATCH AWL. The socket scratch awl has a steel blade approximately five inches long, and is made with a replaceable wooden handle.

SHANK TYPE SCRATCH AWL. For general purposes, this shank type of scratch awl is preferred by most sheet metal mechanics since the steel blade passes through the handle, reinforcing the top.

Dividers

Dividers, such as the wing dividers, shown in Fig. 2, are made with each straight leg tapered to a needle point. These wing type dividers may be adjusted to any position by loosening the knurled screw, changing the distance between points, and then tightening the screw to retain the desired distance between points. Dividers are manufactured in a number of sizes

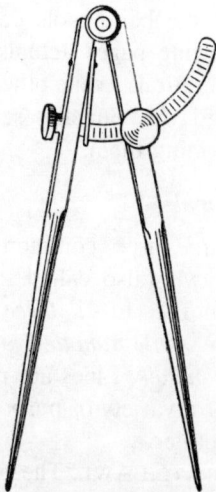

Figure 2. Wing dividers transfer dimensions and scribe arcs and circles.

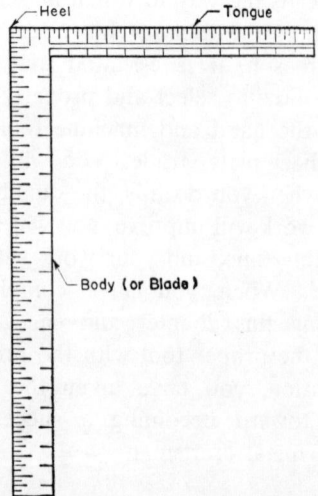

Heel   Tongue

Body (or Blade)

Figure 3. Steel squares are used for accuracy in transferring layouts.

and types and are used to space off equal distances, to divide lines into equal parts and to scribe arcs and circles.

Steel square

The steel square shown in Fig. 3 is invaluable for accurate layout work in pattern drafting since all layout must start from a square corner. The long arm of the square is known as the *body* (also called "blade"), and the short arm is called the *tongue*. Squares are manufactured in a number of sizes.

Trammel points

Trammel points (sometimes called a beam compass), shown in Fig. 4, are instruments used for drawing large circles, arcs, etc. They are manufactured in various types with two straight, removable legs tapered to needle points and attached to separate heads or holders. These heads or hold-

ers slide on wood or steel bars or beams, and are held in place by thumbscrews. Either of the points can be moved and often one point has a fine adjustment for more accurate setting. A special clamp for a pencil can be attached to one of the points.

Rules

Rule instruments are manufactured in a variety of lengths and types; each of which is designed for measuring or laying out different work.

FOLDING RULE. The six-foot-length folding rule is commonly used for taking job measurements in sheet metal work.

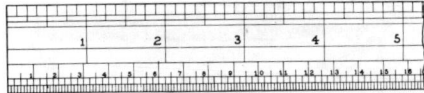

STEEL CIRCUMFERENCE RULE. The steel circumference rule, used much

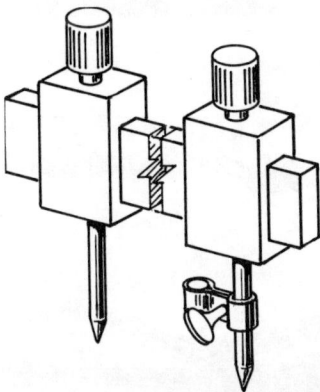

FOLDING RULE

CIRCUMFERENCE RULE

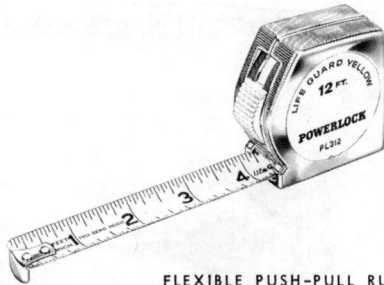

FLEXIBLE PUSH-PULL RULE

Figure 4. Trammel points, or beam compasses are normally in 2 or 4 foot lengths or multiples of those lengths and are used to draw large circles, arcs and similar shapes requiring accuracy.

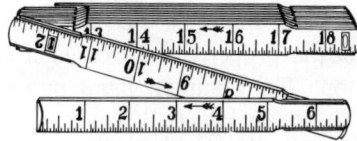

Figure 5. Folding, circumference, and tape rule instruments take measurements necessary for many sheet metal jobs.

like the common rule, is invaluable for laying out patterns. Its length is 36″ or 48″; the upper edge having a standard graduation of ⅛ inch. The lower edge is designed for finding the circumference of a cylinder. The reverse side of the rule contains information to aid the sheet metal worker including: the sizes of 60 objects such as pails, measures, cans, etc., with straight or flaring sides, flat or pitched top; liquid and dry measure in quarts, gallons and bushels.

TAPE RULE. The tape rule, either in 6 foot or 10 foot lengths is becoming popular for taking measurements of a job. The various types of rules are shown in Fig. 5.

Punches

Great care should be used in order to select the proper punch for each operation. The common hand punches are shown in Fig. 6.

PRICK PUNCH. Prick punches are made of tool steel and have a tapered point ground to approximately a 30 degree included angle. These punches are used for making small dents or indentations, and/or establishing points for dividers and trammel points.

CENTER PUNCH. Center punches are similar in design to the prick punch, except that the tapered point is ground to an angle of approximately 90 degrees. They are used primarily for marking the location of points and the centers of holes to be drilled. Such punches are manufactured in various sizes and may be purchased in sets.

Neither prick punches nor center punches should be used to punch holes. These are both intended for establishing points only.

SOLID PUNCH. Solid punches are used to punch small holes in light gage metal; these punches may also be purchased in sets of various sizes.

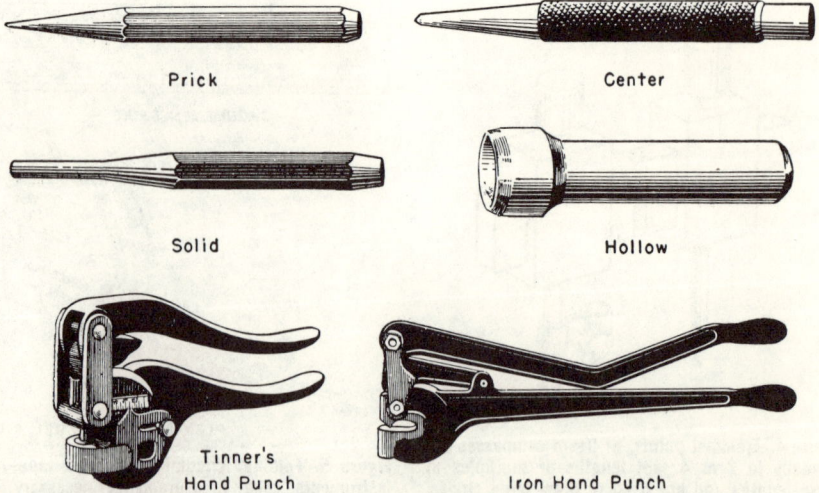

Prick

Center

Solid

Hollow

Tinner's
Hand Punch

Iron Hand Punch

Figure 6. Common types of punches employed to make round holes in sheet metal.

HOLLOW PUNCH. Hollow punches are used for cutting circular holes, ¼″ or larger from sheet metal. However, with the development of the modern turret punch described in Chapter 6, the hollow punch is used infrequently in the sheet metal shop. To avoid chipping the edges of the hollow punch, the sheet metal should be placed over a block of lead.

HAND LEVER PUNCHES. This type of punch is equipped with a die and a punch moved by levers. They are made in several different types, but the principle of operation is the same. The tinner's hand punch, used for punching small holes in light and medium weight metal, is furnished with punches and corresponding dies ranging in size from $\frac{1}{16}$ to $\frac{9}{32}$-inch. Each punch is $\frac{1}{64}$-inch larger than the next smaller punch; the size is marked on the punch to aid in punching holes of different sizes. The iron hand punch is used on heavier material, and is equipped with punches ranging from $\frac{3}{32}$ to $\frac{1}{2}$-inch. The punches and dies of both types are easily changed.

Hand groover

The hand groover shown in Fig. 7 is used when grooving a seam by hand. The end of the tool is recessed to fit over the lock, making the grooved seam. It is available in various sizes.

Rivet set

The rivet set, shown in Fig. 8, is made of tool steel. The deep hole in the bottom is used to draw a rivet through metal. The cup-shaped hole is used to form the finished head of

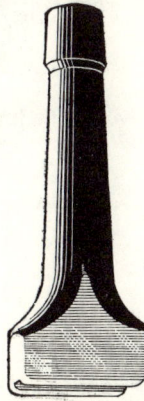

Figure 7. Hand groover.   Figure 8. Rivet set.

a rivet. The hole in the side is to release the burrs that are punched through the metal with the rivet. Rivet sets are manufactured in a variety of sizes.

Chisels

The various types of chisels shown in Fig. 9 are used for cutting and shaping metal.

FLAT COLD CHISEL. Sheet metal workers generally use this chisel more than the other types since it is used for cutting sheet metal, rivets, bolts, and in chipping operations.

CAPE CHISEL. Cape chisels are used for cutting grooves and keyways.

DIAMOND POINT CHISEL. These chisels are used for cutting V shaped grooves and for chipping corners.

ROUND NOSE CHISEL. Round nose chisels are used for roughing out the concave surfaces of corners, and also for cutting grooves.

Hammers

It is essential that sheet metal work-

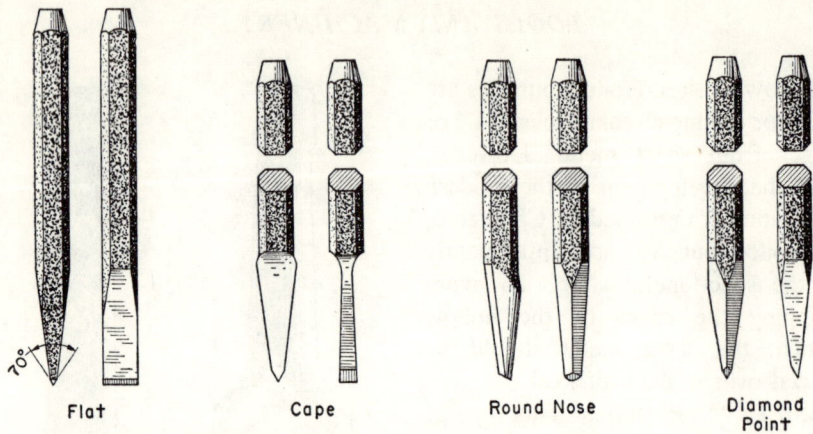

Figure 9. Common chisels used in the process of cutting and shaping metals.

Flat

Cape

Round Nose

Diamond Point

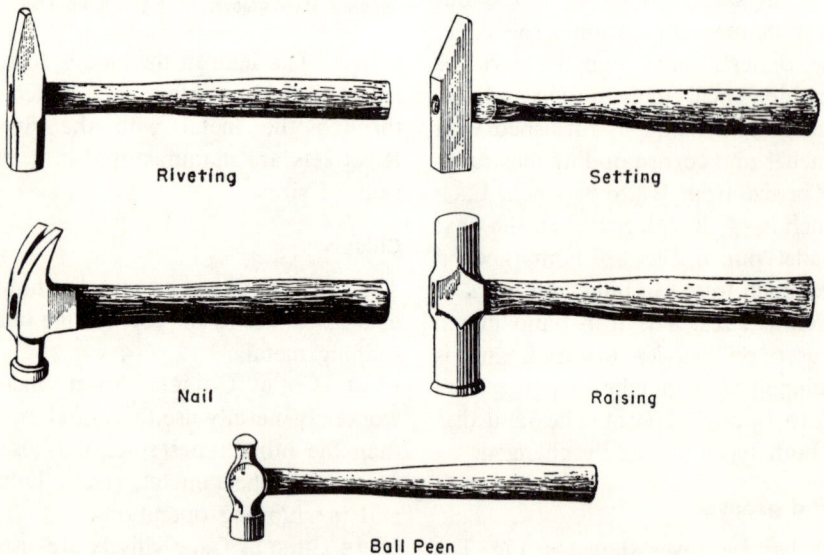

Riveting

Setting

Nail

Raising

Ball Peen

Figure 10. Sheet metal workers require a variety of hammer types.

ers have a variety of hammers. These should include the following: riveting hammers, setting hammers, ball peen or machinist's hammers, raising hammers, and nail hammers, all shown in Fig. 10. These hammers are manufactured in a variety of weights.

RIVETING HAMMER. The riveting hammer has a square, slightly curved face with beveled edges to prevent the head of the hammer from marking the metal. The peen side is double tapered and has a slightly rounded end.

SETTING HAMMER. The setting hammer has a square, flat face for flattening seams without damage to the metal. The single-tapered peen with

Figure 11. Mallet.

a beveled end is used for peening operations.

BALL PEEN HAMMER. The ball peen or machinist's hammer has a round, slightly curved face and round head. It is a general purpose hammer.

RAISING HAMMER. The raising hammer is one of a set of four hammers used in raising circular disks and ornaments for cornice work and many other raising and bumping operations.

COMMON NAIL HAMMER. The common nail hammer is not generally considered a sheet metal worker's tool, though it is very useful in this work and is employed for a variety of operations around the shop.

MALLET. The mallet is one of the most abused tools because it is often used to perform operations for which it is not designed. Mallets are properly used where steel hammers would deface the work. A good grade of hickory or hard fiber mallet, as shown in Fig. 11, will last a long time if used in the correct manner on proper materials.

Snips

Snips of various types, as shown in Fig. 12 are indispensable to the sheet metal worker. A brief description of blade types and the snips in most common use is given below so that the sheet metal student can select the best snips for a particular job.

BLADE TYPE. No matter what the purpose of the snips is, the blades are of two basic types—either *straight blade* or *combination blade*. Fig. 13 shows the difference between the straight and the combination blade. The cross sectional view of the two types shows that the straight blade has the face of the blade running straight up from the cutting edge, while the combination blade is curved back from the cutting edge. In use, the difference between the two is that the combination blade allows the metal to slide over the top blade when cutting curves, as shown in Fig. 14. The straight blade snips does not allow the metal to curve over the top blade in this manner and therefore the straight blade snips is best for cutting straight lines. However, straight blades, because of their design, have a greater amount of metal to strengthen them and therefore the blades can be made in a greater

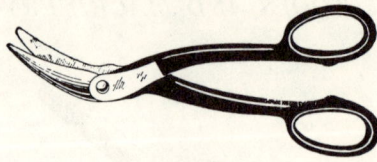

HAWK BILL

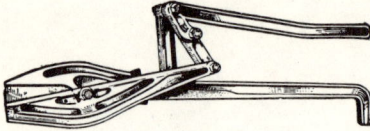

COMPOUND LEVER

BENCH

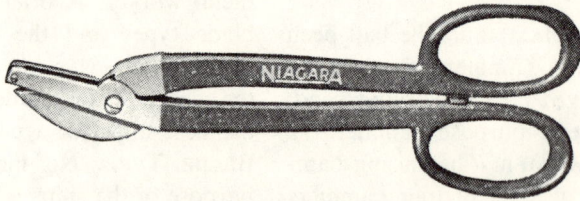

DOUBLE CUTTING

AIRPLANE SNIPS

BULLDOG

LEFT HAND

STRAIGHT

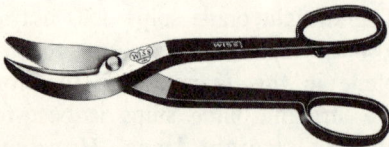

CIRCULAR

RIGHT HAND

Figure 12. Snips which are shown are those most commonly used in various sheet metal cutting operations. Courtesy: Bremil Mfg. Co.; J. Wiss & Sons Co.; Niagara Machine & Tool Works)

FACE STRAIGHT
FROM CUTTING EDGE

CROSS SECTION

STRAIGHT BLADE SNIPS

FACE CURVED BACK
FROM CUTTING EDGE

CROSS SECTION

COMBINATION BLADE SNIPS

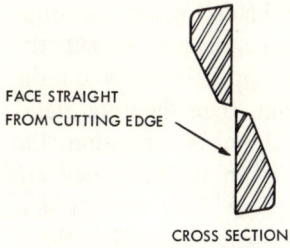

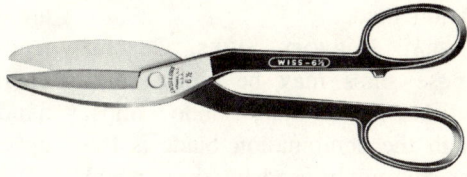

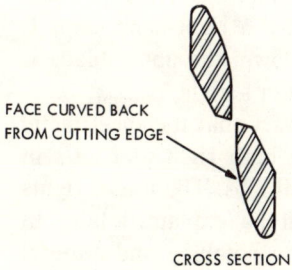

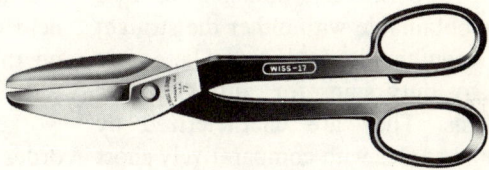

Figure 13. Straight and combination blades are the two most common types employed in sheet metal snips. Courtesy: J. Wiss & Sons Co.

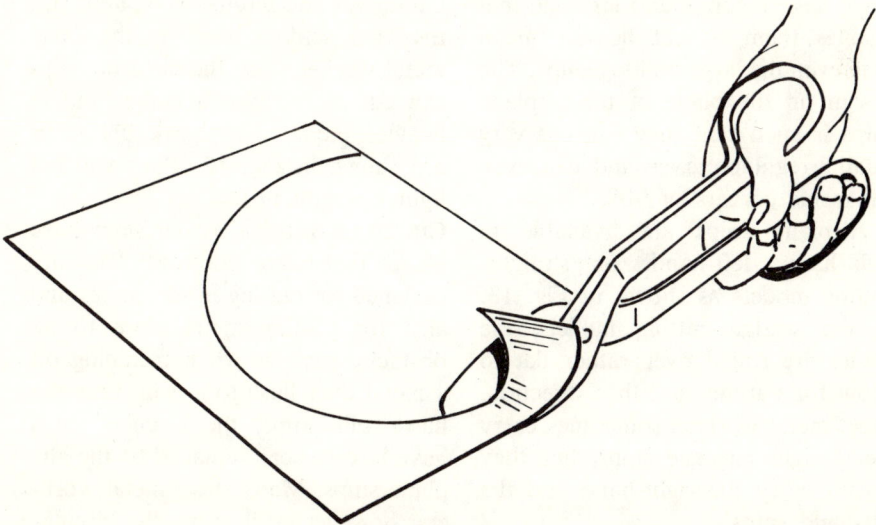

Figure 14. Combination snips blades permit metal to slide over top blades making it easier to cut curved edges. Straight blade snips are best used on sheet metal which is to be cut in a straight line.

length than is possible with the combination blade.

GENERAL PURPOSE SNIPS. General purpose snips may be either combination or straight blade snips, though the combination blade is the most commonly used by sheet metal workers. The snips are used for all routine cutting. General purpose snips are usually used on 26 gage or lighter.

BULLDOG SNIPS. Bulldog snips also are obtainable with either the straight or combination blade. These are heavy duty snips for cutting thicker metals. They are characterized by long handles with comparatively short blades for better leverage. Bulldogs are used for all general cutting on thicker metals.

AIRPLANE SNIPS. Fig. 12 also shows airplane or aviation snips. Though they are only 8 inches long, these snips have a compound leverage that enables them to cut heavier metal than even the large bulldog snips. The design on the blade of the airplane snips is such that they can cut very small irregular curves and can even cut inside corners of 90°.

Airplane snips are available in right-hand, left-hand, or straight-cutting models as shown in Fig. 13. In the straight-cutting models, the blades are rolled over rather flat to allow for cutting in either direction. Sheet metal workers sometimes carry the straight airplane snips, but they *always* carry the right-hand and the left-hand snips.

The right-hand and left-hand snips can be distinguished by the position of the upper blade. When the snips are held in a position to cut the metal, if the upper blade is on the operator's right, then they are right-hand snips. If, in this position, the upper blade is on the left, they are left-hand snips. A frequent question concerning this explanation is, "What if the snips are held upside down?" Observe the illustration of the aviation snips in Fig. 12. Here you can see that even if a right-hand snips is held upside down, the upper blade is on the operator's right.

It is necessary that the sheet metal worker carry both right and lefts in order to do all jobs. The use of rights and lefts will be explained later in the chapter on notching and cutting.

HAWK BILL SNIPS. Before the development of the airplane snips, the hawk bill and some of the other special-purpose snips were in wide use to cut curves and scrolls. Now, however, they are seldom used by the sheet metal worker since the airplane snips can cut as intricate a curve, and in heavier metal. The hawk bill snips are shown in Fig. 12. They will cut lighter weight metals.

CIRCULAR SNIPS. Circular snips have blades that curve sideways. They are designed for cutting inside circles and also for cutting metal close to an obstacle, such as when trimming off a metal duct flush to a wall. Like the hawk bill snips, the circular snips have largely been replaced by the airplane snips. Many sheet metal workers, however, still carry the circular snips for trimming off sheet metal which is flush with the wall.

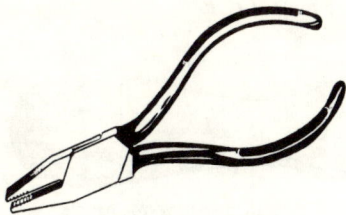

Flat-Nose Pliers

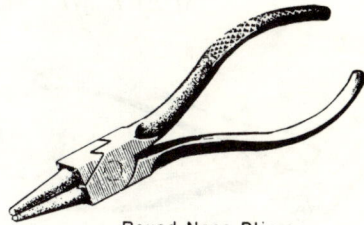

Round-Nose Pliers

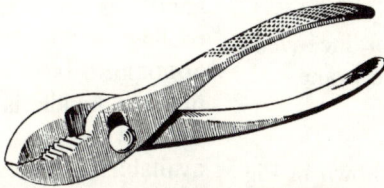

Combination Pliers (Slip-Joint)

Figure 15. Pliers such as these are used by the sheet metal worker to hold, cut, or bend his work.

BENCH SHEARS. Both the compound lever shears and the bench shears are designed to fasten onto the bench for heavy cutting. The bottom handle is bent at a right angle and is square in shape to fit into a square hole on a metal plate which bolts to the bench. These shears are two to three feet long and are used for cutting sheet metal which is $\frac{1}{16}$-inch thick, or more. With the development of the modern squaring shears and electric shears, these bench shears are no longer in common use.

DOUBLE CUTTING SNIPS. Double cutting snips are so called because they make two cuts at once to cut out a slit of metal $\frac{1}{8}''$ wide from the sheet. Double cuts are designed in this manner so that the right-hand and the left-hand pieces of metal being cut can lay flat. This makes these snips especially valuable in cutting off lengths of sheet metal pipe since neither side of the metal has to slide over the bottom blade as with conventional snips.

Pliers

Various types of pliers, as shown in Fig. 15, are used in sheet metal work for holding, cutting, and bending work.

FLAT-NOSE PLIERS. Flat-nose pliers have flat jaws with small grooves and are used for forming and holding work.

ROUND-NOSE PLIERS. Round-nose pliers have long jaws rounded on the outside, and are used in holding and forming the various shapes and patterns.

SLIP-JOINT COMBINATION PLIERS. Slip-joint combination pliers are constructed with an adjustable jaw. A screwdriver is sometimes formed at the end of one handle. These pliers are a general-purpose tool.

Handy seamer or tongs

The handy seamer or "tongs" shown in Fig. 16 is made of drop-forged steel with $3\frac{1}{2}''$ blades and an adjustable gage. This tool is used in seaming operations, and bending in situations

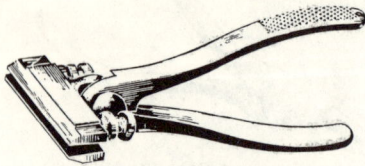

Figure 16. Handy seamer.

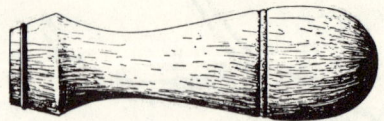

Figure 18. Soldering iron handle.

where it is impossible or inconvenient to bend metal on the brake.

Soldering irons

The soldering coppers, shown in Fig. 17, are commonly called "soldering irons" and are made of a forged copper bar or rod. The metal is fastened to a wooden handle by a rod or heavy twisted wires.

SQUARE POINTED SOLDERING IRON. The square pointed soldering iron is the ordinary soldering iron used for general soldering. The points of soldering irons are often forged to a particular shape to meet the requirements of different varieties of work.

BOTTOM SOLDERING IRON. The bottom soldering iron is used for soldering bottoms of objects such as pails, tanks, etc.

ROOFING SOLDERING IRON. The roofing soldering iron with shield and

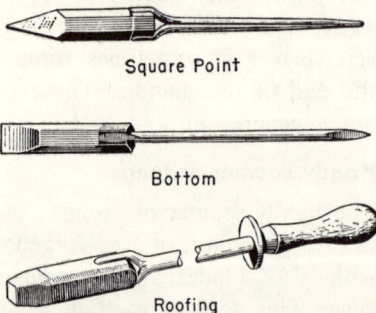

Square Point

Bottom

Roofing

Figure 17. Commonly used types of soldering irons.

handle is used for soldering metal roofing.

SOLDERING IRON HANDLES. A soldering iron handle is shown in Fig. 18. Both wood and fiber handles are available. The most popular handle is the screw-on type. This handle has a coarse thread in a steel insert inside the wood so that it will screw onto the tapered end of the soldering iron handle. Screw-on handles are more solid than the pound-on type and are less apt to work loose.

Hacksaws

There are two styles of hacksaw frames used by the sheet metal worker. These are shown in Fig. 19. The straight handle is usually preferred for fine work. Either type of frame is adjustable for various lengths of blades, eight to twelve inches in length. Tension is applied to the blade to make it taut by means of a wing nut on the pistol-grip type frame or by turning a threaded handle on the straight handle type.

Files

There are a number of files of various kinds and shapes. However, only the files generally used in the sheet metal trade will be described, see Fig. 20. Files are used to remove burrs from sheets of metal, to square the ends of band iron, to straighten uneven

Figure 19. Types of hacksaws.

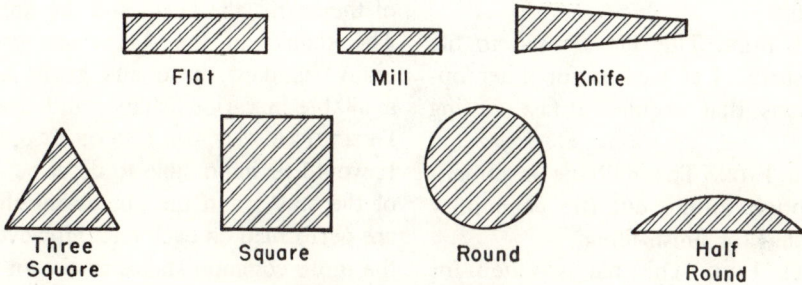

Figure 20. Shapes of commonly used files.

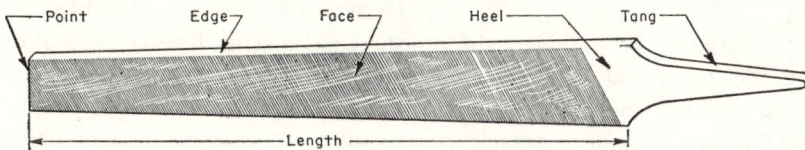

Figure 21. Parts of a file.

edges, and for various other operations that require a small amount of metal to be removed.

PARTS OF FILES. The parts of a file consist of the point, the edge, the face, the heel, and the tang, as shown in Fig. 21.

CUTS OF FILES. The single-cut files shown in *A* of Fig. 22 have a single set of teeth cut at an angle of 65 to 85 degrees. The double-cut files have two sets of teeth crossing each other, as shown in *B* of Fig. 22. Double-cut files are used for rough filing, since they remove material faster than do the single-cut files.

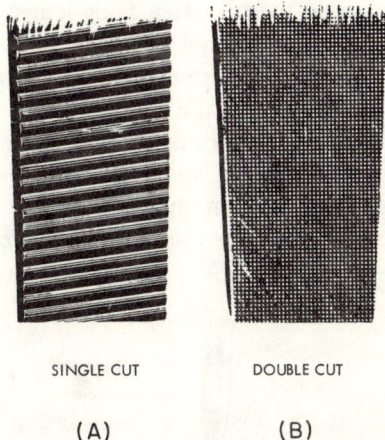

Figure 22. Single and double cut files are characterized by sets of teeth cut in the manner shown.

FILE HANDLES. File handles are usually made of wood and are designed to fit the hollow of the hand. A metal ferrule on the end of the handle prevents it from splitting.

A file card or brush with a scorer is used to remove particles which clog the file.

FLAT FILE. This file is used to file flat surfaces as well as for other operations that require a fast cutting file.

MILL FILE. The mill file is an all-purpose, single cut file especially adapted for finish filing.

KNIFE FILE. This file is suited for finishing the sharp corners of grooves and slots where other files would not fit.

THREE SQUARE FILE. The three square file (commonly called three cornered file) has angles of 60° and is used for filing internal angles, clearing out corners, etc.

Bench stakes

The metal worker often finds it necessary, when suitable machines are not available, to rivet, seam, form, or bend sheet metal objects over various types of steel anvils. The anvils are referred to as *stakes* and are designed to perform many operations for which machines are not available

or readily adaptable. The shank of each stake has a tapered point which fits the holes in the bench plate. These stakes are available in a variety of shapes and sizes.

PARTS OF A STAKE. The parts of a stake, as shown in Fig. 23, consist of the shank, the head, and the horn. The shanks of the stakes are generally standard; head and horns are available in various shapes and sizes.

DESCRIPTION OF AND USE OF STAKES. It would be impossible to describe all of the stakes and the operations that are performed on each one. However, the more common stakes as shown in Fig. 24 will be described along with some of the uses.

BLOWHORN STAKE. The blowhorn stake has a short, tapered horn at one end, and a long, tapered horn at the other. This stake is used in forming, riveting, or seaming tapered objects such as funnels, pitched covers, etc.

BEAKHORN STAKE. This stake has a thick, tapered horn at one end and rectangularly shaped horn at the other. It is used in forming, riveting, and seaming articles not suitable for the blowhorn stake.

CANDLEMOLD STAKE. The candlemold stake has two horns of different tapers, and is used in forming, riveting, and seaming long, flaring articles.

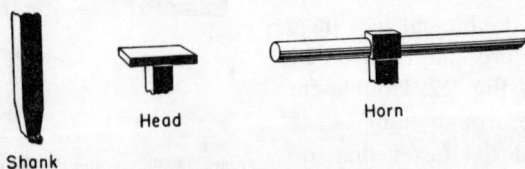

Head

Horn

Shank

Figure 23. Parts of a stake.

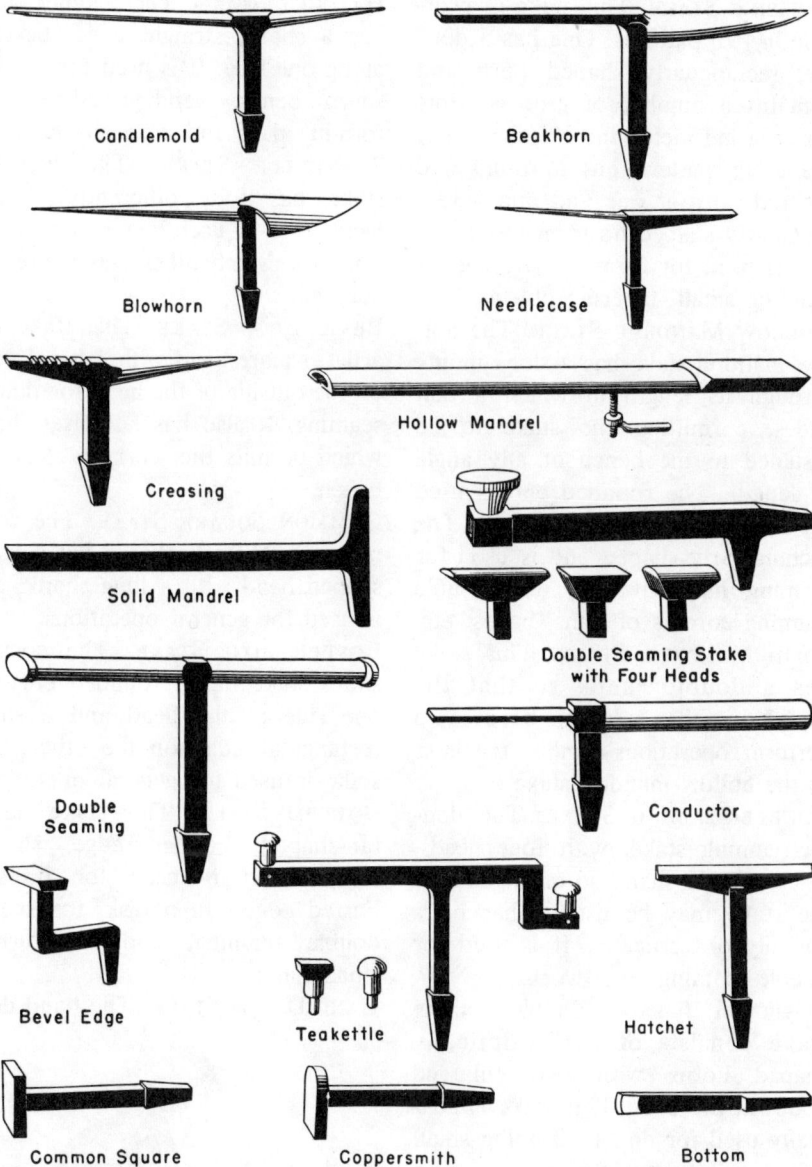

Figure 24. Common bench stakes used by the sheet metal worker.

NEEDLECASE STAKE. The needlecase stake has a small, tapered horn at one end, and a small, rectangular horn with a rounded beveled edge at the other. This stake is used for very fine hand work.

CREASING STAKE. This stake is available in two patterns. One has a double, rectanguarly shaped horn and contains a number of grooved slots for creasing metal and bending wire; the other pattern has a round and tapered horn at one end and a rectangularly shaped horn on the other, and is used for forming, riveting, or seaming small, tapering objects.

HOLLOW MANDREL STAKE. The hollow mandrel stake has a slot running through its length in which a bolt slides, permitting the stake to be fastened to the bench at any angle or length. The rounded end is used for riveting and seaming pipes. The rectangularly shaped end is used for forming laps, riveting, and double seaming corners of pans, boxes, etc.

SOLID MANDREL STAKE. This stake has a double shank so that the rounded or flat side can be used to perform operations similar to those of the hollow mandrel stake.

DOUBLE-SEAMING STAKE. The double-seaming stake, with four heads, has a double shank so arranged that the stake may be used either horizontally or vertically. It is used for double seaming large work.

Another type of double-seaming stake consists of two elliptically shaped horns with two enlarged knobs at the ends. This stake is generally used for double seaming small cylindrically shaped articles.

CONDUCTOR STAKE. The conductor stake has two cylindrical horns of different diameters and is used when forming, riveting, and seaming tubes and small-sized pipes.

HATCHET STAKE. The hatchet stake has a sharp, straight edge, beveled along one side. It is used for making sharp bends, bending edges, and forming pans and boxes by hand.

TEAKETTLE STAKE. The teakettle stake has four differently shaped heads and is useful in many operations for which other stakes are not adapted.

BEVEL-EDGE STAKE. This stake has a flat, square head with a bevel edge on the outside of the head for double seaming. It also has an offset shank which permits the work to clear the bench.

COMMON SQUARE STAKE. The common, square stake has a flat square-shaped head with a long shank, and is used for general operations.

COPPERSMITH STAKE. The coppersmith stake has a rounded edge on one side of the head and a sharp rectangular edge on the other. The stake is used for general operations.

BOTTOM STAKE. This stake has a fan-shaped, beveled edge, slightly rounded. It is used for dressing burred edges on a disk, for special double seaming, and for turning small flanges.

HAND DOLLY STAKE. The hand dolly

Figure 25. Hand dolly.

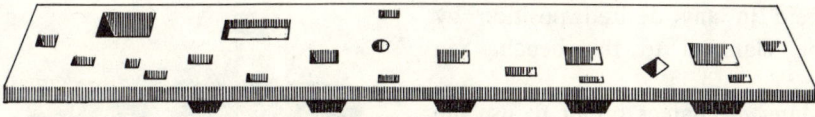

Figure 26. Bench plate.

stake, shown in Fig. 25 is designed with a flat face, two straight edges, one convex edge, and one concave edge. It is a handy stake for all general purposes such as bucking rivets and double seaming. Hand dolly stakes come in various shapes and sizes.

CARE OF STAKES. The condition of the stake has much to do with the workmanship of the finished job. If a stake has been roughened by punch marks or is chisel marked, the completed job will look rough and lacking in craftsmanship. Therefore, a stake should not be used to back up the work directly when prick punching or cutting with a cold chisel. A mallet should be used whenever possible when forming sheet metal by means of stakes.

Stakeholders

The most common holder used is the

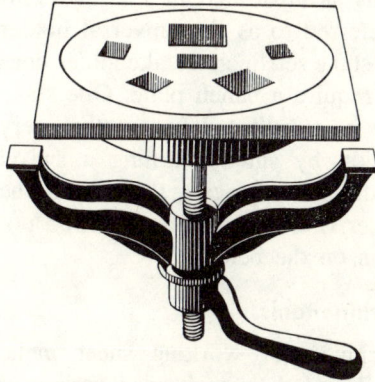

Figure 27. Revolving bench plate.

rectangularly shaped, cast iron bench plate, shown in Fig. 26, which is fastened to the bench with bolts. The tapered holes are conveniently arranged so the stakes may be used in different positions. (The smaller holes are used to support the bench snips.)

Another type of stakeholder consists of a revolving plate with tapered holes to support the stakes. This plate

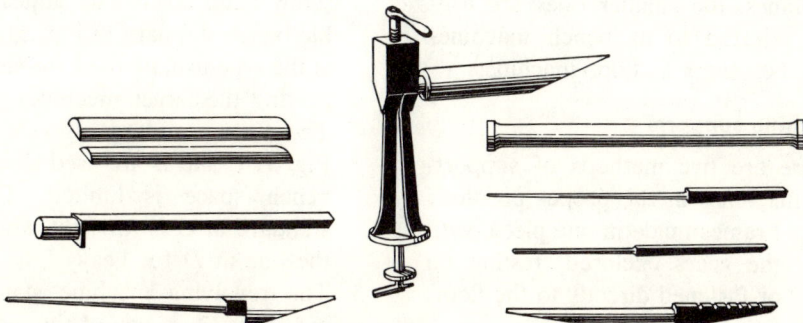

Figure 28. Universal stakeholder with a complete set of stakes.

is held in any desired position by being clamped to the bench. See Fig. 27.

Many mechanics prefer to use the stakeholder with a complete set of anvils as illustrated in Fig. 28. This is referred to as the universal holder and stake set. Such a stakeholder does not require a bench plate. One stake may be substituted for another very quickly by simply turning a swivel handle and replacing the stake. The holder is clamped to any desired position on the bench.

Machine tools

Machines for working sheet metal are designed to perform a variety of operations on straight and circular outlines, namely, forming, folding, bending, creasing, edging, grooving, double seaming, setting down, turning, burring, slitting, crimping, swedging, cutting, beading, wiring, punching, drilling, grinding, corrugating, and cutting metal disks.

Machines that are adapted for specific operations are available as either bench or floor models. However, to make it more convenient to discuss machines, the smaller ones are usually referred to as bench machines and the others as floor machines.

Machine supports

There are five methods of supporting machines in the proper position:
1. Frames made in one piece, with the gears enclosed, resting on or fastened directly to the floor. See Fig. 29.
2. Machines such as small form-

Figure 29. Machine housing complete with base. This model rests on the floor. Courtesy: Wysong & Miles Co.

ing machines, bar folders, such as the one shown in Fig. 30, etc., bolted directly to the bench.
3. Small rotary machines are held in position by bench standards. Fig. 31 *A* shows the regular standard that may be fastened securely to the bench by a screw hand lever. The adjustable bench standard in Fig. 31 *B* is the type usually used for supporting the larger machines.
4. The floor standards shown in Fig. 31 *C* and *D* are used where bench space is limited. The standard at *C* is for light work, the one at *D* for heavy.
5. The revolving machine standard, Fig. 32, is one of the most efficient. It has many features,

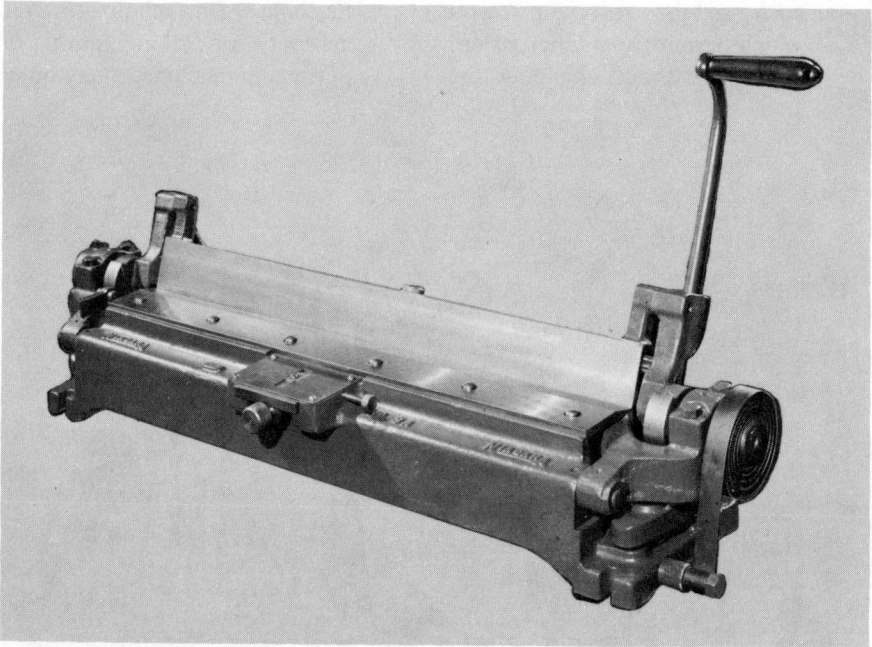

Figure 30. Adjustable bar folders, such as the one shown, may be fastened directly to the work bench. Courtesy: Niagara Machine & Tool Works.

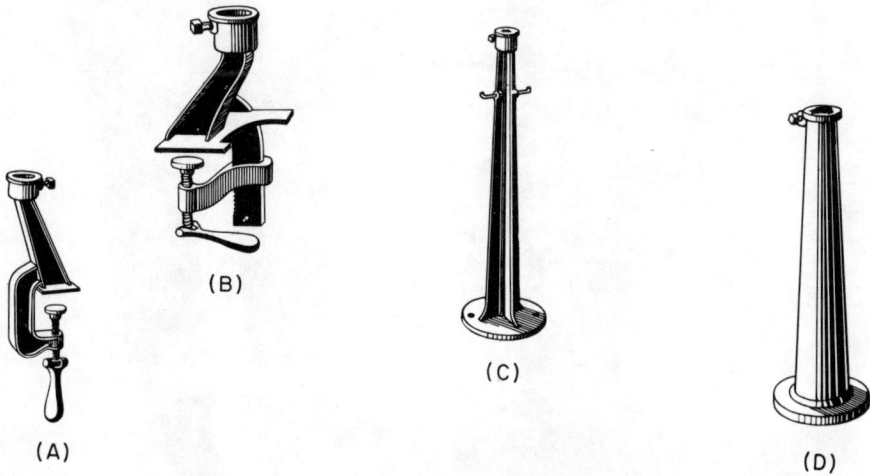

(A)

(B)

(C)

(D)

Figure 31. Standards such as these are used to support machines. The small machine (A) and adjustable machine (B) standards are used for bench work. Floor standards may be used for light work (C) or heavy work (D).

such as the revolving turret which permits four different operations without changing the machine. This eliminates the necessity of taking down or putting up machines many times

Figure 32. Revolving machine standard. Courtesy: Peck, Stow & Wilcox Co.

a day, thereby saving time and wear and tear.

Another great advantage is the lower turret which holds four machines. This saves valuable space and avoids breakage.

The upper brackets are for additional rolls.

Bench machines

The following so-called bench machines, which include the burring, turning, wiring, and edging machines, are somewhat similar. Each one is designed to perform a special operation and should be used according to the recommendation of the manufacturer. Operating these machines is not difficult; with a little practice each machine can be mastered in a satisfactory manner. The variety of operations of each machine will be described later.

Figure 33. Burring machine. Courtesy: Peck, Stow & Wilcox Co.

Figure 34. Turning machine. Courtesy: Niagara Machine & Tool Works.

BURRING MACHINE. The burring machine shown in Fig. 33 is used to turn burrs on circular disks such as bottoms and covers and also for preparing edges for double seaming cylindrically shaped articles.

TURNING MACHINE. The turning machine as seen in Fig. 34, while somewhat similar to the burring machine, differs in the sharpness of the edge it makes. A burring machine produces a sharp edge, while the turning machine makes a rounded edge for wiring operations, for bodies of cylinders, and for double seaming.

WIRING MACHINE. The machine, Fig. 35, is used to complete the metal edge around the wire after the seat to receive the wire has been prepared by the turning machine.

CRIMPING MACHINE. The crimping machine is designed for crimping and beading in one pass, or, by changing the rolls the machine may be used

Figure 35. Wiring machine. Courtesy: Niagara Machine & Tool Works.

Figure 37. Setting down machine. Courtesy: Peck, Stow & Wilcox Co.

Figure 36. Combination crimping and beading machine. Courtesy: Peck, Stow & Wilcox Co.

Figure 38. Double seaming machine. Courtesy: Peck, Stow & Wilcox Co.

for beading or crimping only. This machine is used also for crimping the small ends of pipes, flanges, etc. See Fig. 36.

SETTING-DOWN MACHINE. This machine, shown in Fig. 37, is used for setting down seams on containers of various shapes, thereby facilitating the operation in double seaming to do a better seaming job.

DOUBLE-SEAMING MACHINE. The double-seaming machine, Fig. 38, is used for double-seaming flat bottoms on straight or flared cylindrical pieces. It is recommended as a labor-saving device in cases where a number of double-seaming operations are required on projects such as waste cans, etc. and for production work.

GROOVING MACHINE. The grooving machine, as seen in Fig. 39, is used

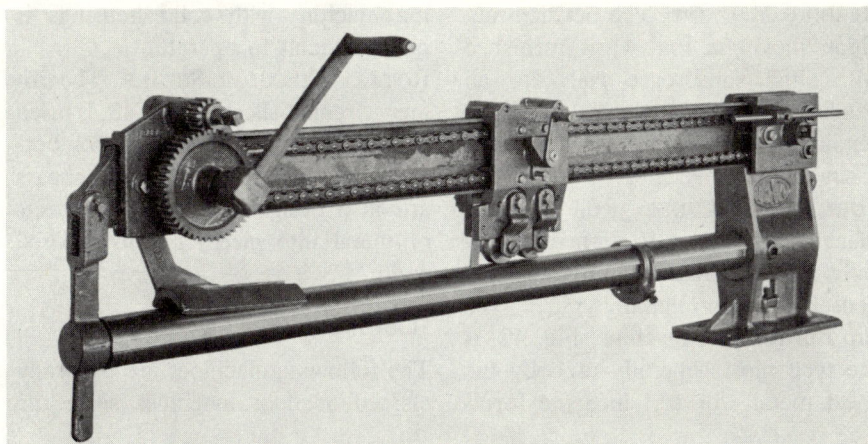

Figure 39. Grooving machine. Courtesy: Peck, Stow & Wilcox Co.

Figure 41. Beading machine with additional rolls. Courtesy: Peck, Stow & Wilcox Co.

Figure 40. Elbow edging machine with No. 1 rolls. Courtesy: Peck, Stow & Wilcox Co.

for grooving longitudinal seams in cylinders. This type of machine completes the seam by grooving and flattening in one operation of the carriage.

ELBOW EDGING MACHINE. The elbow edging machine, Fig. 40, is designed for turning the edges of elbows for tight or adjustable joints. The apron gage is generally used on the power machine. The sections for light gage elbows are creased on the ends to allow the section to enter the next corresponding section. Small, power elbow edging machines are used where large quantities are required, and are available with rolls of three types.

BEADING MACHINE. The beading machine shown in Fig. 41 is furnished with single and ogee rolls for all beading operations. Special rolls are obtainable when necessary and are easily interchangeable.

FORMING MACHINE. Roll forming machines are used to form cylindrically shaped articles and are indispensable when making pipe. The slip roll forming machine, Fig. 42, is the type most generally used by the sheet metal worker, since the forming machine with solid housings is more difficult to operate.

ROTARY CIRCULAR SHEARS. The rotary circular shears, Fig. 43 is used for cutting sheet metal disks for bottoms and tops of cans. These shears are also designed for slitting sheets of metal into pieces of any desired width.

Floor machines

The following machines are generally classed as floor machines since the

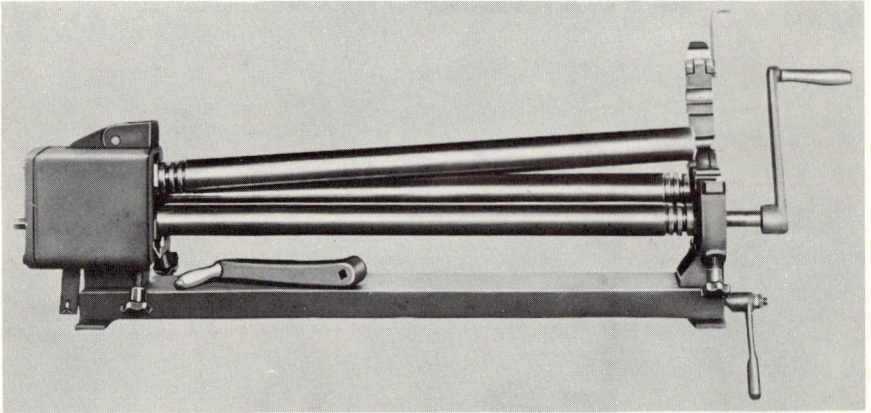

Figure 42. Slip roll forming machines are used by sheet metal workers to form cylindrical parts.

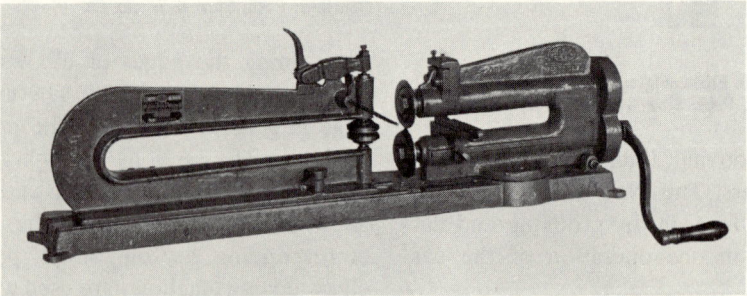

Figure 43. Rotary circular shears cut sheet metal bottoms and tops for cans. Courtesy: Peck, Stow & Wilcox Co.

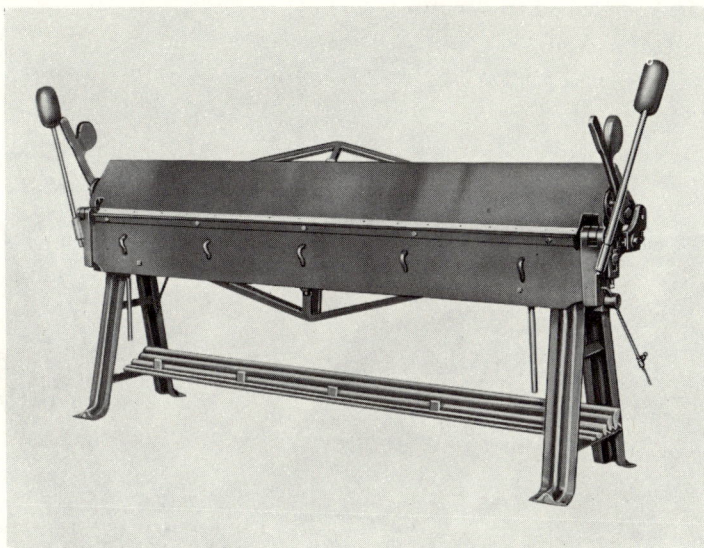

Figure 44. Cornice brakes are the metal bending machines principally used in the sheet metal shop. Courtesy: Deis & Krump Co.

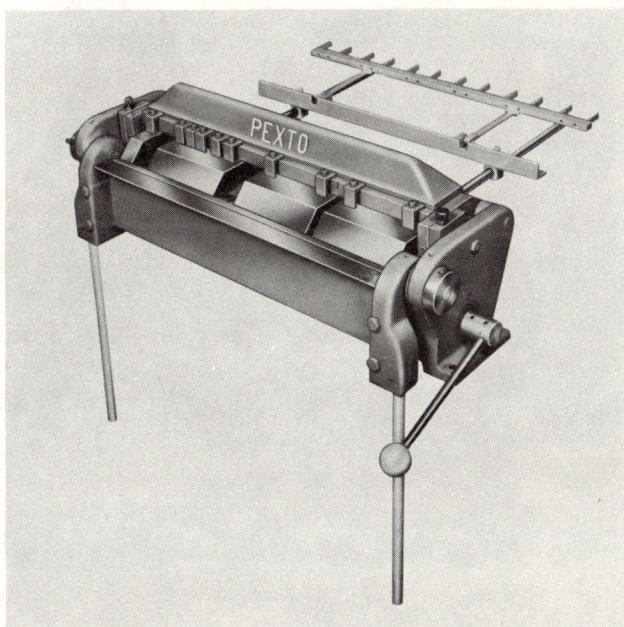

Figure 45. Pan brakes reach both sides of boxes or pans to bend the last side. Courtesy: Peck, Stow & Wilcox Co.

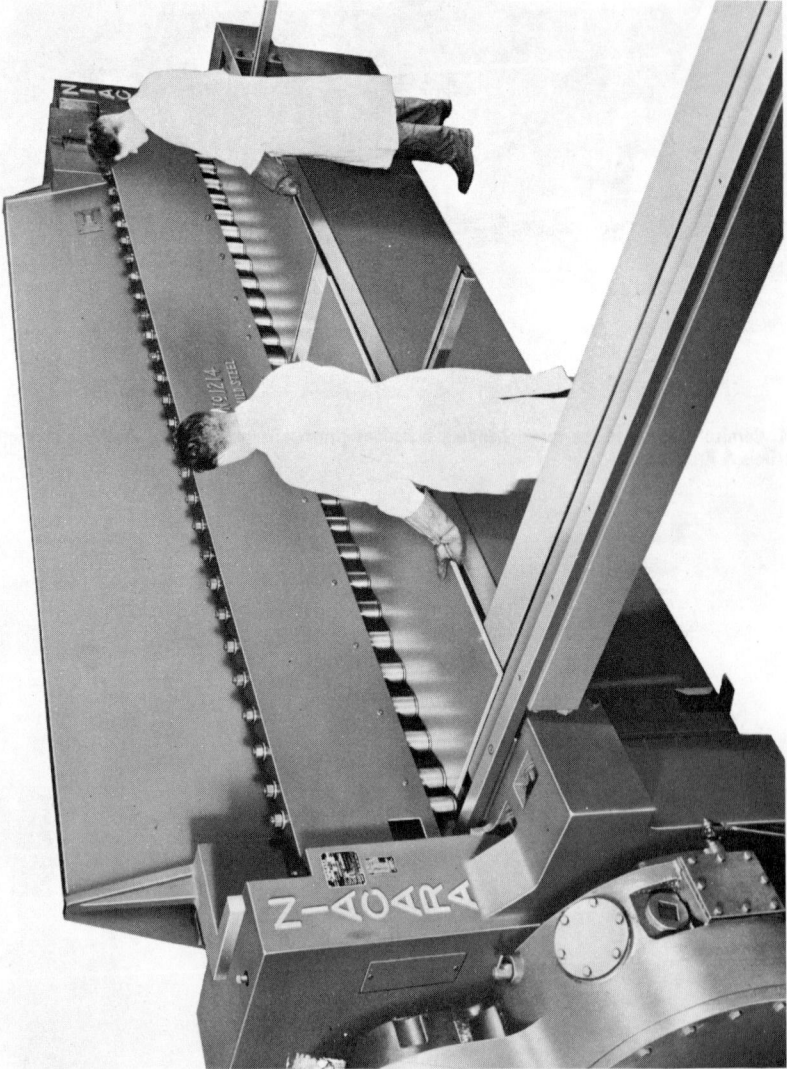

Figure 46. Power shears have greater speed and capacity than the foot powered squaring shears. Courtesy: Niagara Machine & Tool Works.

majority are made in floor models.

SQUARING SHEARS. There are many kinds of squaring shears used for squaring, trimming, slitting, and cutting sheet metals into various shapes and sizes. The foot-power squaring shears has a 36-inch cutting blade.

CORNICE BRAKE. The cornice brake, Fig. 44, is a floor machine which is used for bending and folding the edges of metal. Its various operations will be described in later chapters.

PAN BRAKE. The pan brake, shown in Fig. 45 is similar to the cornice brake. It is used for bending edges in the same way as the cornice brake. The difference between the two brakes is that the pan brake has the upper blade in sections that can be easily removed. In this way the pan brake can reach in between the sides of a box or pan to bend the last side.

POWER SHEARS. The power shears are similar to the squaring shears, and are shown in Fig. 46. Power shears are motor operated and are run either by a mechanical or a hydraulic arrangement. Though power shears are available in the smaller sizes, they are generally used in larger sizes. The ten-foot power shear is a very common size.

PRESS BRAKE. This brake, Fig. 47, is another machine for bending metal.

Figure 47. Press brakes use dies to form metal and are suited to production line operations rather than a variety of different operations. Courtesy: Verson AllSteel Press Co.

This machine is quite different from the cornice or the pan brake because it bends or forms the metal by pressing it into special dies. The dies of the press brake are changed to fit the operation being done. The press brake is more of a production tool than the cornice brake. That is, it is better suited to doing a large number of the same operations rather than doing many different operations. Press brakes are available in all sizes from four-feet long up to thirty-five feet long. The most common size is the ten-foot brake. Figure 48 shows a ten-foot press brake.

Review Questions

1. Name three different types of scratch awls.
2. Name the major parts of a file.
3. Name two general cuts on files.
4. What tool is used for drawing large circles and arcs?
5. Name two types of hacksaw frames.
6. What rule instrument is used for finding the circumference of a circle?
7. What tool is used to remove particles from a file?
8. Name four shapes of files.
9. What type of shears is used in cutting pipes?
10. Name five tools used in cutting sheet metal.
11. What type of shears is used in cutting inside circles?
12. What type of shears is used in cutting outside circles and disks?
13. Describe a riveting hammer, a setting hammer, a ball peen hammer, and a raising hammer.
14. Name and describe ten different types of bench stakes.
15. Name three types of soldering irons.
16. Name and explain the use of two floor machines.
17. When and where should a mallet be used.
18. Tell the uses of the cornice brake, the bar folder, and the press brake.
19. What is the difference between the burring and turning machines?
20. Distinguish between a turning machine and a regular elbow edging machine.
21. Name as many machines used in sheet metal work as possible. (A student should be able to name at least twelve machines.)
22. What machine is used for turning small burrs on metal disks?
23. Name the machine used for turning burrs on bottoms of cans, pails, etc.
24. Describe the use of a groover and a rivet set.
25. Explain with the aid of sketches the difference between straight-blade and combination-blade snips.
26. Explain how to tell a right-hand from a left-hand snips.

3

SAFETY IN THE SHEET METAL SHOP

How important are safe work habits? How can we learn to work safely? What are the common general sheet metal shop safety rules? What are the safe practices which apply to the squaring shears, brakes, and soldering?

One of the most valuable skills you can acquire in your sheet metal work —or anything else—is the formation of a positive safety attitude. Moreover, the development of your knowledge and skills in sheet metal shop practices is not separate from your knowledge of and attitude toward safety, but is an integral part of it. The worker with such an attitude will have increased value to his employer because of a minimum of time lost due to on-the-job injury. In addition, he will carry the importance of such attitudes into his off-the-job hours as well. Furthermore, since the National Safety Council reported that, in one recent year alone, nearly seven out of ten workers' deaths and more than half of the injuries occurred off the

job, the importance and value of developing positive safety attitudes both on and off the job cannot be overemphasized. However, this chapter will deal specifically with some of the more common hazards in the sheet metal shop and will outline some of the generally accepted safe practices which are employed to avoid them.

Positive attitude

It is not difficult to be constantly aware of the importance of safety when you know how vital it is to you to cultivate a positive attitude toward safe work habits. Did you know, for example, that the time lost due to on-the-job injuries equals the loss of one full year's employment for one worker in every ten in American industry every year?

The absence of a sound attitude toward safety becomes immediately apparent to you when you consider the consequences of neglect in only one area of safe practice—that of putting on a pair of protective goggles when required, as in Fig. 1. In one State (Pennsylvania) in one year alone, industrial eye injuries have accounted for up to 4% of the total workmen's compensation cases and have proved to be the most costly and *permanent* of all disabilities. Since we all value the sight of *both eyes,* the conclusion here is obvious.

Safe practices in the sheet metal shop make good sense! Why? First, because the only right way to use a tool or machine in the shop is the safe way. Second, by engaging in unsafe practices you risk injury to yourself and/or damage to your tools and machinery. Industry has recognized the importance of safe practices by the safety programs they conduct and by the safety regulations which have been established. All safety rules should receive 100% enforcement in the sheet metal shop. Never let there be exceptions to the enforcement of safe practice for any reason.

In the field of traffic safety, evidence shows that where traffic enforcement is increased, traffic accidents decrease. The implications here for the enforcement of sheet metal shop safety rules are clear.

The following rules for safety as applied to the sheet metal shop have been established for three very good reasons: (1) to protect you and your co-workers from bodily harm, (2) to minimize damage to the facilities, machinery and tools with which you must work, and (3) to provide you with experience in safety concepts as they apply not only to sheet metal work but to all vocational fields. Remember, however, that the keystone to your personal safety and that of your co-workers rests not so much with any series of rules as with your own positive safety attitude and awareness.

Figure 1. Always wear protective goggles when grinding. Whenever possible, direct sparks toward a wall. Courtesy: Heating and Air Conditioning Contractor Magazine.

General safety

1. Keep your mind on your job!
2. The sheet metal shop is no place to play! Careless or thoughtless acts such as playing, running, tripping, or pushing may cause accidents resulting

in serious injury. Whether you are in the sheet metal school shop classroom or place of business, remember why you are there and conduct yourself accordingly.

3. Lift by crouching as close to the load as possible keeping your back muscles locked so that the back is held rigid and with your leg muscles in tension ready to do the work. If the load is not within your lifting capacity, always secure help in lifting the load. It is a sign of good judgment to ask for such help. Remember that the after effects of a back strain, arm or leg strain or hernia could plague and possibly restrict your activity for the rest of your life.

4. Report any injury immediately! Failure to do so can have serious consequences for you in unnecessary infections and resulting time lost.

5. Never carry tools in your pockets. Should you fall, sharp ends might be driven into your body or even more commonly you will gouge another worker.

6. Wear snug fitting clothing. Loose garments are easily caught in machinery. Never wear wrist watches, rings, long sleeves or neckties when working around machinery.

7. Don't use dull tools. Using dull tools means that you will either damage them permanently or wound yourself.

8. Report damaged tools and machinery. The possibility of someone being injured or the tool or machine being damaged beyond repair increases when such damage goes unreported.

9. Always use a file with a handle. See Fig. 2. Using a file without one will eventually mean a skinned hand or other wounds.

10. Avoid hand cuts by using a brush rather than your hand to remove chips from machine areas.

11. Oily rags and other material subject to spontaneous combustion should be kept in self-closing metal receptacles.

12. Never remove guards from machines!

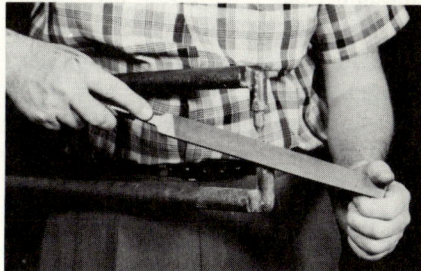

Figure 2. File tangs should always have a handle. Courtesy: Heating and Air Conditioning Contractor Magazine.

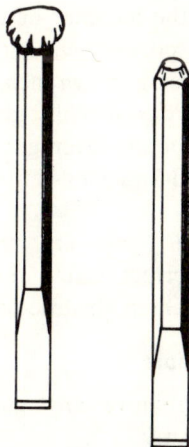

Figure 3. Grind off mushroom heads on chisels.

13. When you enter a new shop, learn immediately where the fire extinguishers and exits are located.

14. Do not hold small work in your hand when working with a screwdriver or chisel. It may slip and skin your hand.

15. Gas fumes, mist from paint spray and fine dust can cause explosions. Always report any such concentrations immediately.

16. Chisels, punches, and similar tools often burr over the top after continual pounding. These are called "mushroomed" heads. See Fig. 3. These mushroom heads will splinter off when hit and cause cuts and steel slivers in the arms and face. Grind off all mushroomed heads whenever they start to form.

17. Never use a hard hammer on machined, tempered, or hardened surfaces. Use a soft-faced hammer such as brass, lead, or rawhide. Using a hard hammer will damage the finished work. In the case of hardened work either the hammer or the work will splinter, possibly cutting you.

18. When using a wrench, always pull—never push. This gives you greater control and leverages and will avoid skinned knuckles if the wrench slips.

19. Whenever you are in doubt about the correct safety procedure, ask your foreman (instructor).

Squaring shears

1. Do not remove any guards on squaring shears.

2. Learn the capacity of the squaring shears you are using and do not try to cut metal heavier than the capacity of the shears.

3. The greatest danger with the squaring shears is cutting off the ends of the fingers. This is one of the most common of all accidents in the sheet metal shop and has happened countless times. Never put your fingers under the blades of the squaring shears. See Fig. 4.

4. Do not reach behind the shear blade to hold small pieces being cut off. The danger in this is that the tips of the fingers cannot be seen and can easily be placed under the blade.

5. Keep your fingers clear of the hold-down on the shears or they may be crushed when the metal is cut.

6. Do not try to hold small pieces of metal while they are being cut. They are liable to tip up and tip your fingers into the blades.

7. Avoid getting the foot caught under the foot treadle. Two or more persons attempting to operate a machine is an unsafe act which is often the cause of this kind of accident.

Brakes

1. Do not place your hand in the cornice brake when someone else is operating the handle.

2. Never place your hand in the dies of the press brake unless the main switch is off and locked.

3. When operating the cornice brake, see that no one else is near enough to the counterbalance balls to be hit by them. If you are working near the cornice brake, be careful to stay clear of the counterbalance balls. See Fig. 5.

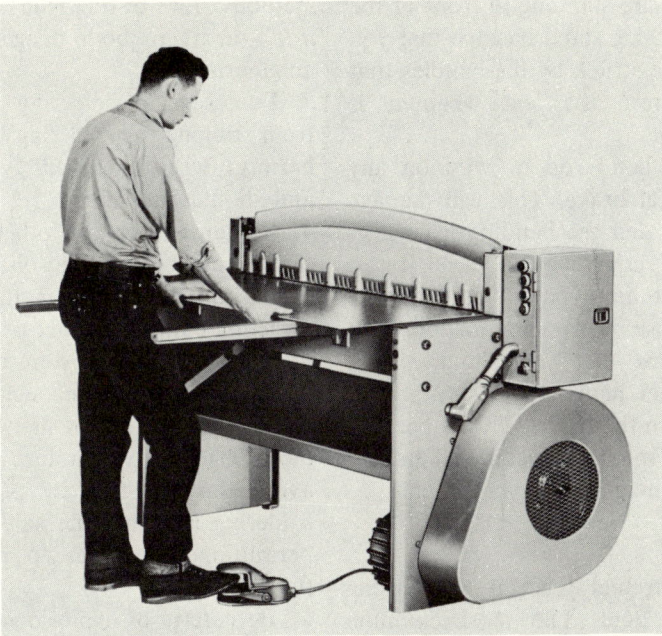

Figure 4. Care should be exercised when using the squaring shears since they can cut off fingers unless caution is used. Courtesy: O'Neil-Irwin Mfg. Co.

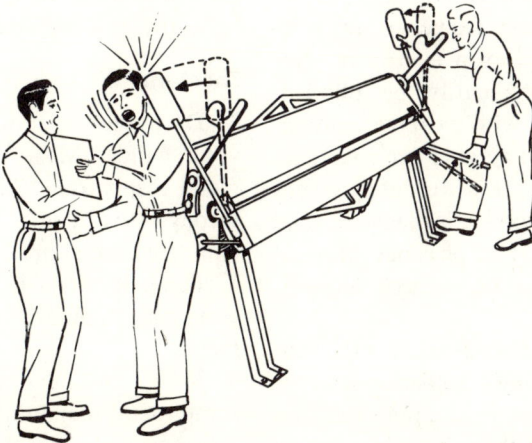

Figure 5. Be sure that no one is in a position to be injured by counterbalance balls when operating the brake.

4. If you are standing in front of the cornice brake, stand back so that you will not be struck by the handles that project from the leaf when it is swung up.

5. Never bend rod or wire on any sheet metal brake. This will damage the blade and the bending leaf.

6. Never pound on a sheet metal brake with any type of steel hammer. Always use a wooden mallet. This also means that you should never use a steel hammer on sheet metal which is in the brake. This is because you may miss the metal and hit the brake, damaging it beyond repair.

Soldering

1. Be extremely careful when using soldering acid. The most common flux for soldering in the sheet metal shop is hydrochloric acid (commonly called raw acid). This acid is not concentrated, but is still dangerous if used carelessly. It will ruin your clothes and will burn your skin. However, its greatest danger is to your eyes. If you get even a drop in your eye, you could easily be blinded. Treat the acid with extreme caution. If you do get any acid on your skin or in your eyes, it is absolutely essential to wash it off with plenty of cold water as quickly as possible. Medical aid should then be secured immediately.

2. The safest and most efficient method of testing a soldering iron for the correct heat is to apply the iron to the solder. When the solder begins to flow, the correct temperature has been achieved. Other old fashioned methods for testing the soldering iron's heat are both dangerous and amateurish.

3. Fumes from soldering flux and from tinning a soldering iron are harmful when breathed in quantity and should be avoided.

4. Molten solder (or other metals) often spatter if dropped on a cold or moist surface because molten metals sometimes trap a pocket of moisture under them. This moisture then turns to steam and, when enough pressure builds up, the molten metal may be blown back into your face. You can avoid this situation by placing the soldering iron into the acid flux and permitting the solder to run down the iron.

5. Be careful of explosions from gas firepots. Stand to one side when lighting the pot. If the gas does not ignite immediately, turn off the valves before investigating the reason for the failure. Be sure that all valves are in the off position before attempting to light any gas appliance.

Sheet metal

1. Do not let sheet metal slip through your hands. Most cuts from sheet metal result from allowing it to slide through the hands. Almost always, cuts from metal are a consequence of a slicing motion. If you avoid this, you will minimize such cuts from metal.

2. When cutting out a pattern, the scrap metal remaining often comes to a sharp point. Snip these points off to avoid later possible injury.

3. Be careful of "fish hooks" and

burrs on the edges of sheets. When the beginner cuts sheet metal with snips, he usually leaves small, needle-like, curved slivers of metal on the cut edge. Sheet metal workers call these "fish hooks" because they are curled and are as difficult as a fish hook to remove when they are run into a finger. Whenever you cut sheet metal, examine the edge and trim off any "fish hooks" that may be there to prevent possible cuts.

Review Questions

1. Why is it important to study safety rules?
2. What are the reasons for having safety rules in the sheet metal shop?
3. What are the most common causes of cuts from sheet metal?
4. What are the greatest dangers near the soldering bench? What are the proper methods of avoiding these dangers?
5. Explain what "fish hooks" are in sheet metal work.
6. What are the dangers involved in putting your fingers in the brake?
7. What are the safety hazards concerning the counterbalance balls on the brake?
8. Why must you never bend rods or wires on the brake?
9. Since you are not hitting the brake itself, why is it wrong to pound on sheet metal with a steel hammer while the sheet metal is in the brake?

4

SHEET METALS – AND THEIR CHARACTERISTICS

How is the thickness of sheet metal determined? What are the uses of the various metals? In what sizes can each of the various metals be purchased? What are other materials that the sheet metal worker commonly uses? What are the common types of sheet metal? What are the advantages of the different types of sheet metal?

Not only is it essential for the sheet metal worker to know the tools and machines of his trade and how to use them safely, but it is also important to know the materials and supplies of the trade. A finished job may be a masterpiece of fine workmanship, however, it would also be virtually useless if the wrong material were used. It is therefore extremely important to know what the correct materials are for a given job.

In this chapter you will learn about sheet metal materials—their grades, sizes and characteristics, as well as where they are used. A number of tables are provided showing the thickness of sheets in both gage numbers and decimal parts of an inch.

When you can answer the questions at the end of this chapter, you are ready to start using the tools and materials that you have been studying.

Sheet materials

A large quantity of sheet metal used is steel rolled into sheets of various thicknesses and then coated with zinc, tin or lead. Other common metals and alloys which are rolled into sheets and used by the sheet metal worker are: zinc, copper, aluminum, and stainless steel.

Before studying the applications of these various materials, it is important that you understand the difference between coated and solid sheets. Some sheets, such as copper, stainless steel, and aluminum are made of the same material throughout. Other sheets, particularly steel, have a surface coating of a different metal. The

Number of Gage	THICKNESS		WEIGHT	Number of Gage
	Approx. thickness in fractions of an inch	Approx. thickness in decimal parts of an inch	Weight per square foot in POUNDS avoirdupois	
10	9–64	.1406	5.625	10
11	1–8	.125	5.	11
12	7–64	.1094	4.375	12
13	3–32	.0938	3.75	13
14	5–64	.0781	3.125	14
15	9–128	.0703	2.8125	15
16	1–16	.0625	2.5	16
17	9–160	.0563	2.25	17
18	1–20	.05	2.	18
19	7–160	.0438	1.75	19
20	3–80	.0375	1.5	20
21	11–320	.0344	1.375	21
22	1–32	.0313	1.25	22
23	9–320	.0281	1.125	23
24	1–40	.025	1.	24
25	7–320	.0219	.875	25
26	3–160	.0188	.75	26
27	11–640	.0172	.6875	27
28	1–64	.0156	.625	28
29	9–640	.0141	.5625	29
30	1–80	.0125	.5	30

Table I. U.S. Standard Gages for sheet and plate iron and steel.

purpose of such a coating is to protect the steel from corroding and therefore make it last longer.

The important difference between coated and solid sheets is this. Solid sheets can be welded, sanded: filed or given any other process that cuts into the surface, without damaging the corrosion resistance of the sheet. On the other hand, the coated sheet must never have its surface damaged because, in doing so, the coated surface is removed and corrosion resistance is thereby destroyed.

Sheet gages

The thickness of metal sheets is designated by a series of numbers called *gages.* Each gage designates a definite thickness. While several gage systems are in use, the U.S. Standard Gage is most commonly used for iron and steel sheets. This system is shown in Table I.

As you work with sheet metal, you will learn to distinguish between the various gages of the USS Sheet and Plate Gage merely by feeling the sheet with your fingers. This, however, requires practice and experience.

As a means of remembering the approximate thickness of the various gages, remember that 16 gage is approximately $\frac{1}{16}$ of an inch and that when the gage of a metal is increased by 6 gage numbers, its thickness is decreased by approximately $\frac{1}{2}$.

For example:

16 gage is approximately $\frac{1}{16}$-inch thick

22 gage is approximately $\frac{1}{32}$-inch thick

28 gage is approximately $\frac{1}{64}$-inch thick

Metal sheets other than steel sheets are gaged by a different system than the USS Sheet and Plate Gage. Table II shows the gage system used for some common metals and also shows the relationship of the gage system

Table II. Comparative decimal and fractional thicknesses for commonly used metals and their commonly used gage systems.

MATERIAL	GAGE SYSTEM	Approx. Decimal Thickness	Approx. Fractional Thickness										
		.141	.109	.078	.063	.050	.038	.031	.025	.019	.016	.013
		9/64	7/64	5/64	1/16	1/20	3/80	1/32	1/40	3/160	1/64	1/80
		VERTICAL COLUMNS SHOW APPROXIMATE EQUIVALENTS IN EACH GAGE SYSTEM										
Galvanized Iron	US Standard Sheet & Plate	10	12	14	16	18	20	22	24	26	28	30
Black Iron	US Standard Sheet & Plate	10	12	14	16	18	20	22	24	26	28	30
Tin Plate	Tin Plate Gage								5x	3x	1x	1C
Copper	Ounces per square foot				48oz	40oz	30oz	24oz	18oz	14oz	12oz	10oz
Aluminum	Decimals of and Inch		.100	.080	.064	.050	.040	.032	.025	.020	.015	.012
Stainless Steel	US Standard Sheet & Plate	10	12	14	16	18	20	22	24	26	28	30

used for them to that of the USS Sheet and Plate Gage. Anyone who works with sheet metal should know the gage system used for each of the common metals and should have at least a general knowledge of the relationship of the various gage systems to the USS Sheet and Plate Gage.

Gage also refers to a tool used for measuring and determining the thickness of the metal when it has not been marked on the sheet. The front of the gage, as shown in Fig. 1, is marked with the U.S. Gage numbers opposite a series of slots. The thickness of each gage in decimal parts of an inch is marked on the back of the gage. The measurement is made by sliding the parallel sides of the various slots over the sheet; the slot that makes a snug fit denotes the gage of the metal.

When using a sheet metal gage, remember that coated sheets will read one gage thicker than they actually are. This is because the steel is rolled to the proper gage thickness when it is uncoated and then the coating is applied. In addition, coated sheets generally have a thicker coating near the edge than they have closer to the center. As a consequence then, a 24 gage sheet of coated steel will actually measure 23 gage.

To determine gages of metal and wire, it is important that the worker knows how to read and use the micrometer. Since the micrometer is a delicate tool, it must be handled carefully. Avoid dropping the micrometer and sliding or forcing the work to be measured between the spindle and the anvil. Open the spindle to insert the work. Learn how to tighten the spindle sufficiently to get an accurate reading. If the spindle is repeatedly tightened too much, the frame will be sprung and the micrometer made useless.

How to read the micrometer

A person does not have to be a mathematician to read the micrometer. Once he understands the divisions on the spindle and the thimble, he can easily take readings.

Fig. 2 illustrates a standard micrometer. Study the working parts, and follow the instructions below.

1. The 1″ micrometer is held in the right hand (provided the user is right-handed) across the palm and fingers. The little finger is curled around the frame. Revolve the thimble by using the thumb and the forefinger. The spindle revolves with the thimble.

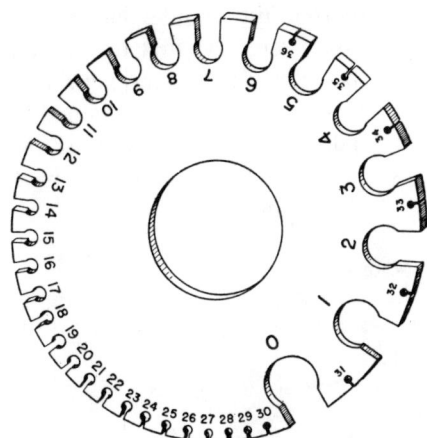

Figure 1. Sheet metal gage. Courtesy: L. S. Starrett Co.

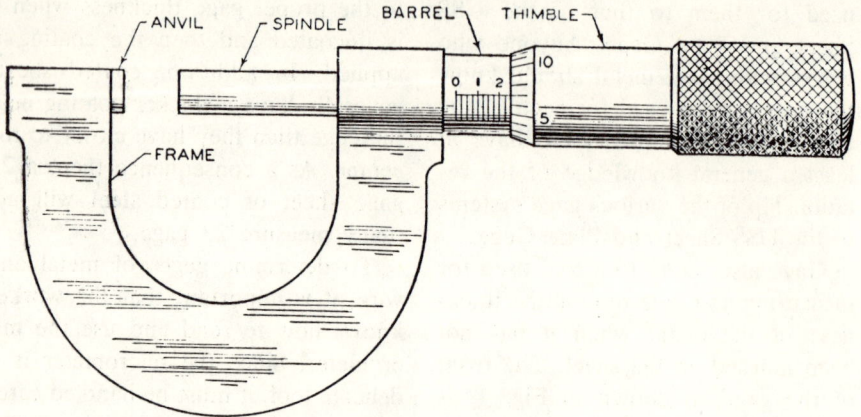

Figure 2. Micrometer parts identification.

2. Place the article to be measured between the anvil and the spindle, then carefully tighten the spindle, using only a light pressure between the thumb and forefinger.

3. The measurement of the opening between the spindle and the anvil is shown by lines and figures on the barrel and the thimble. For example: one complete turn of the thimble changes the opening between the spindle and the anvil .025″. Also, each line on the barrel represents .025″. Four complete turns of the thimble change the opening between the spindle and the anvil

.100″. Each number, therefore, represents .100″, making readings of .100″, .200″, .300″, etc. The beveled edge of the thimble is divided into twenty-five equal parts, each division representing .001″. These divisions are marked every five spaces by 0, 5, 10, 15, and 20. When 25 of these divisions have passed the horizontal line of the barrel, the spindle has moved .025″ and the first line of the barrel is visible, denoting .025″. The final reading is obtained by adding the three figures shown by the following examples in *A, B, C,* and *D* of Fig. 3:

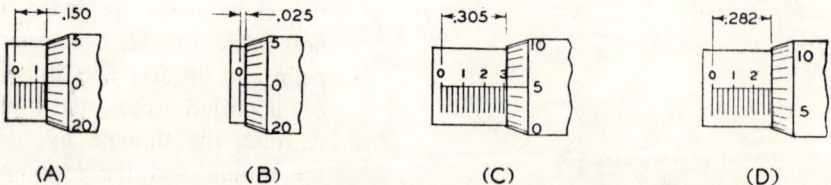

Figure 3. Changing micrometer readings to readings on the common rule instrument.

Fig. 3 *A*

Number of 10ths on barrel, last visible figure (one)	.100″
Number of .025 spaces on barrel (two)	.050″
Number of divisions on thimble (none)	.000″
Total	.150″

Fig. 3 *B*

Number of 10ths on barrel, last visible figure (none)	.000″
Number of .025 spaces on barrel (one)	.025″
Number of divisions on thimble (none)	.000″
Total	.025″

Fig. 3 *C*

Number of 10ths on barrel, last visible figure (three)	.300″
Number of .025 spaces on barrel (none)	.000″
Number of divisions on thimble (five)	.005″
Total	.305″

Fig. 3 *D*

Number of 10ths on barrel, last visible figure (two)	.200″
Number of .025 spaces on barrel (three)	.075″
Number of divisions on thimble (seven)	.007″
Total	.282″

To change the micrometer reading to fractions on the common rule, simply multiply the micrometer reading by the denominator of the fraction that is to be used, as previously outlined.

Fig. 4 illustrates a combination of four readings. Write down the readings, then refer to the answers found below:

Galvanized sheet metal

Galvanized sheet metal consists of soft steel sheets coated with zinc. Usually the steel is dipped in an acid bath for cleaning, and then is dipped in a tank of molten zinc to coat the sheet. Sometimes, however, the zinc is put on by an electroplating process and is known by such trade names as

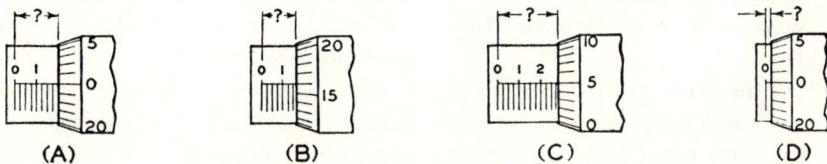

(A)   (B)   (C)   (D)

Figure 4. Problems in micrometer reading.

Readings of the problems from Fig. 4 are as follows: *A* .200″; *B* .166″; *C* .280″; *D* .025″.

Zincgrip and *Paintgrip*. The electroplating process is distinguishable from galvanized coating because electro-

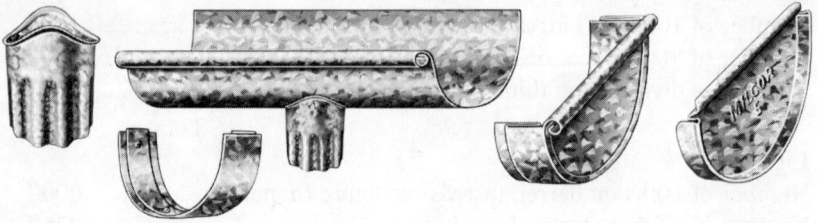

Figure 5. Galvanized sheet metal is used where corrosion resistance is necessary. Courtesy: Inland Steel Products Co.

plating gives a sheet an even, grey color and is used principally for its ability to hold a painted surface.

Galvanized sheet metal can be easily recognized by its typical spangled appearance, as shown in Fig. 5. These spangles are from the molten zinc as it cools on the sheet. Since galvanized is a coated sheet, its corrosion resistance is dependent upon the condition of the zinc coating. Zinc is highly resistant to corrosion and, as long as it remains intact on the sheet, galvanized steel will have high corrosion resistance. A good quality galvanized sheet should last from 5 to 10 years under constant contact with water. However, if the zinc is damaged through welding, grinding, or any other process, then the steel will be exposed and this portion of the sheet will rust through very quickly.

Of all the sheet metals, galvanized is one of the least expensive. Its cost is in the same general range as plain steel sheets, and steel bar. It is probably the most commonly used of all types of sheets in the general sheet metal shop. Air conditioning ductwork is made almost entirely of galvanized.

All types of roof flashing and gutters are made principally from galvanized also. In addition to this, all general sheet metal objects such as tanks, signs, and boxes are made from galvanized because of its low cost and good corrosion resistance.

Good quality galvanized can be bent and straightened out several times without the zinc peeling from the sheet. All galvanized sheets bend well, with no problems in breaking when they are bent severely. It solders well, but welding is complicated by the fact that the zinc gives off toxic fumes and a residue which makes the weld itself more difficult. In addition, welding destroys the coating on the sheet, and for this reason galvanized sheet metal is seldom used in applications requiring welded joints. Galvanized can be painted, though it is good practice to wash the sheets with a dilute solution of acid before the primer is applied. This etches the sheet which allows the primer to hold better.

Like all sheet metals, galvanized can be obtained in widths of 24", 30", 36", and 48", with 36" being the most commonly stocked size.

Sheet lengths generally are 96" or 120". However, other lengths and widths can be specially ordered.

Black iron

Black iron and steel in the form of sheets are not extensively used due to rust, corrosion, and the difficulties of soldering. The sheets are used for objects that are to be painted. They come in the same weights, gages and sizes as galvanized iron.

Tin plate

Tin plate is iron or steel sheeting coated with pure tin and is gaged by terms of the sheet metal trade such as 1C (pronounced "one c"), 1X (pronounced "one cross"), or by the weight of the sheets in a base box. A base box is the unit of measure for tin plate and contains one hundred and twelve sheets 14" x 20". A double box contains 112 sheets 20" x 28". The weight of this base box is called the base weight and varies with the thickness of the plate.

The terms *coke* and *charcoal plate* are commercial terms which refer to the thickness of the coating. Sheets with a light coating of tin up to two lbs. per box are called coke tin plate, while sheets with a heavier coating up to seven lbs. per base box are called charcoal tin plate. *Dairy plate* has a coating of tin from 7 to 14 lbs. per base box. *Terne plate* is black plate coated with a mixture of lead and tin ranging from 8 to 40 lbs. per double box.

Table II compares the fractional and decimal thicknesses of commonly used metals as well as the gage systems employed to measure them. Notice, for example, that 1X is equal to approximately the U.S. Standard 28 gage steel, and 5X is equal to approximately 24 gage steel as shown in Table I. Notice also that the 1C indicates a lighter gage than the X series.

Tin Plate was formerly used for roofing, food containers, dairy equipment, and furnace fittings. Since the development of stainless steel, tin plate is used to a very limited extent in the sheet metal trade. It is still used for "tin cans," though even in this use it is being replaced by other materials. In the sheet metal shop, dairy equipment and other food containers are almost always made of stainless steel, with tin plate only used for occasional odd jobs.

Copper

Copper is a solid sheet, easily recognized by its typical reddish color. Until the mid 1800's, copper, along with tin plate was the principal metal of the sheet metal worker. In fact, Paul Revere, immediately after the American Revolution, pioneered one of the first copper rolling mills in America.

The great advantage of copper is its high corrosion resistance. There are many examples of copper roofs on cathedrals in Europe that were installed in the Middle Ages and are still in good condition. Another desirable feature of copper is its beauty. For many types of architecture—especially to supplement brickwork—

copper adds warmth and color that cannot be duplicated by any other type of metal. Copper sheet is comparatively high in cost, running about three times the cost of galvanized iron.

In the sheet metal trade today, the greatest use for copper is in architectural sheet metal. It is used extensively for high quality roofing on public buildings. A properly installed copper roof will require no additional care for the life of the building, which makes it a cheap roofing material when compared to the maintenance costs of other roofs over a fifty year period. Gutters, downspouts, roof flashings, and hoods are some of the common applications for copper. Many restaurants use copper hoods where appearance is a factor, especially in installations against dark wood panelling where copper complements the color of the panels.

Copper sheets are available in either cold rolled or hot rolled sheets. Cold rolled sheets are sheets that have been through a final process of running through finishing rolls. This gives the metal a smooth finish and work hardens it to a half-hard condition. Cold rolled copper is still softer than galvanized iron and is bent and formed easily. Though cold rolled copper is much stiffer than the hot rolled, it will not be as rigid as steel sheets, and usually a thicker sheet of copper is used than would be used of steel under the same conditions. Cold rolled copper is the type commonly used in the sheet metal shop.

Hot rolled copper is copper that has had only the hot rolling process and has not been rolled while cold. It does not have the shiny appearance of cold rolled copper and is much softer. Hot rolled copper is used when the metal will be subjected to stretching when it is formed, since it is soft enough to take severe forming. As it is formed, the hot rolled copper work-hardens and approaches the hardness of cold rolled copper. Copper that work-hardens can be annealed (softened) by heating it up to a cherry red and then cooling either by quenching in water or allowing to cool in air.

Copper is gaged by ounces per square foot. When the gage of copper is spoken of as "16 ounce" it is meant that it is of a thickness that weighs 16 ounces per square foot. Table II shows how the copper gages compare to other sheet metal gages.

Copper solders well, even though the high heat transfer ability of copper makes it necessary to use very large soldering irons to get the copper hot enough to melt the solder. Copper is not ordinarily welded, though it is possible. Usually when copper must be connected by a stronger method than soldering, it is brazed.

Aluminum

Sheet aluminum is never pure aluminum but is an alloy, which means small quantities of other metals are added to it. The fact is that pure aluminum is very soft and is seldom used, especially in sheet form. Aluminum sheet contains copper, silicon, iron, and manganese. Other alloys of aluminum contain these elements plus magnesium, chromium, and nickel. However, all the alloys consist of at least 90% aluminum. There are about a dozen different alloys of aluminum used in industry for different applications. Each of these alloys have several grades of hardness so that over forty grades of aluminum with different properties are available.

Aluminum alloys are designated by alloy number. For instance, a common sheet aluminum used in the sheet metal shop is number 3003. Many times in the shop, this aluminum is not ordered by alloy number but by the term "commercial half-hard" since it is the standard alloy for ductwork, garage doors, panels, and awnings. After the alloy number, another letter and sometimes a number follow to designate the hardness of the sheet. The letter "O" means annealed (soft). "H" stands for work-hardened, and "T" stands for heat treated. After the H and T designations a number may follow to designate a specific hardness. For instance, the old ½H (half-hard) designation for alloy 3003 is now given as "H14."

Aluminum can easily be recognized by its whitish appearance and by its lightness. Some aluminum sheets have a shiny appearance that the beginner mistakes for stainless steel. Aluminum never has the grained appearance that stainless steel does and can be distinguished from it because of this. Aluminum is generally solid sheet. Some sheets designated as *Alclad* are coated sheets since they consist of an aluminum alloy sandwiched in between two extremely thin sheets of pure aluminum. The Alclad sheets are made to increase the corrosion resistance of the aluminum sheet.

Aluminum is gaged by its thickness in decimal parts of an inch, given to the nearest thousandths. A sheet is said to be "Oh-four-Oh" which means it is .040″ or forty thousandths of an inch thick.

The working properties of aluminum depend upon the alloy number and the degree of softness of the alloy. For some alloys, the "O" designation may work as well as galvanized iron, while the "H" hardness may be so hard that it cannot be bent without breaking. For other alloys, however, even the "O" designation is too hard to bend without breaking. For the commercial half-hard sheets in the sheet metal shop, these sheets can be bent and formed with as much ease as galvanized iron.

Aluminum can be welded. Though in former years aluminum welding was considered an unusual skill, its use has increased so much that today any skilled welder can weld it. Aluminum is still not considered solderable in ordinary sheet metal shops. Nevertheless, aluminum can be soldered with a special flux and special solder. However, it requires skill and practice since the solder must be applied at exactly the right temperature. Though aluminum is soldered in many production operations where conditions can be controlled, it is still too difficult for the average sheet metal worker. Whenever an object requires soldering, it is made from one of the more easily soldered metals.

Aluminum is often used in the sheet metal shops because of its pleasing appearance. Many large buildings use aluminum prominently because of its appearance and because of its corrosion resistance. Another reason for its use is its lightness. Since aluminum weighs about ⅓ as much as iron, its use on a large building will reduce the total building weight considerably. Aluminum has also found extensive use in thousands of mass production items such as kitchenware, trailer bodies, and thousands of small parts.

Stainless steel

Stainless steel is another sheet metal with many different types. There is no one kind of stainless steel which is always used in the sheet metal shop. Rather, there are many different types from which to choose. Stainless steel is a high grade steel to which has been added such elements such as manganese, silicon, phosphorous, chromium, nickel, and molybdenum. Of these elements, chromium and nickel are in the largest quantity. According to the particular type of stainless, it will contain from 10 to 30% chromium and from 10 to 25% nickel.

Stainless steel is classed by type number such as type 302. There are over forty types of stainless steel available. These are distributed through three series of numbers: the 200 series, the 300 series, and the 400 series. Stainless steel is classified according to the heat treating properties of the steel and also its alloy content. The number is of great importance due to the fact that handbooks list by types the characteristics of each, the recommended uses, and what chemicals will not damage it as well as what chemicals will.

The common type of stainless used in the sheet metal shop is type 302. This is the type that is used for architectural work, containers of all sorts, and for sinks and counters in restaurant work. However, for special applications such as photography labs where special chemicals are used, the sheet metal worker must look in a handbook showing the type of stainless recommended for a specific use.

Another designation is the finish number. Every type of stainless steel can be ordered in several different classes of finish from a number 1, which is unpolished, up to a number 7 which is virtually a mirror finish. The finish that is usually used on standard stainless steel jobs in the sheet metal shop is the number 3 finish.

Stainless steel has a silver-chrome appearance and generally can be easily recognized by its "grained" appearance. The grain in stainless steel is caused by the minute polishing scratches generally found on most finishes. These all run in the same direction just as the grain in wood. Just as in wood, it is easier to cut the metal with the grain than across it. Unpolished stainless has no grain and has a dull gray finish very similar in appearance to unpolished aluminum. The student may confuse these two metals; however, stainless can be easily identified by its greater weight and by its greater resistance to bending.

Stainless steel is gaged by the USS Sheet and Plate Gage in the same manner as other steel sheets. The only difference is that stainless sheets are rolled more accurately and are therefore closer to exact gage dimensions.

Though some stainless sheet is available in a hardened state, almost all of the types used in the sheet metal shop are in the unhardened state and can be bent in the brake as severely as can galvanized iron sheet. The principle difference between stainless and other sheet metals is its extreme toughness. Though it can be bent as severely as galvanized, its toughness makes it more difficult to bend. It is also more difficult to cut and requires more pressure to shear. The general rule is to add four gages to the capacity of any shear or brake when using them on stainless, since capacity ratings are based upon mild steel. This means that a shear rated for cutting 16 gage, has only a capacity of 20 gage for stainless steel.

Stainless steel is a solid sheet, not coated. This, along with its beauty and corrosion resistance, is its great advantage. It can be welded and the welded joints ground off and polished until the weld is not visible, yet its corrosion resistance is not affected.

Though stainless is tough, it can be readily worked in the sheet metal shop. Any skilled welder can weld it, and though special flux and solder are advisable it can be easily soldered.

The cost of stainless is high, running about seven times the cost of galvanized iron. However, in applications where galvanized may last only five years, stainless will last indefinitely. Because of its almost complete resistance to corrosion, the high cost of stainless does not necessarily mean it is the most expensive metal to use, since its long life often makes it the cheapest material to use in the long run. Stainless was developed in 1918, so it is one of the newest metals in common use. Its beauty and long life have made it one of the most popular of all the sheet metals. Canneries, dairies, food processing plants, restaurants, and any other industries that process foods, use stainless almost exclusively since it is not only long lasting but also easy to keep clean and always keeps its neat and clean appearance. Wherever corrosion conditions are high, as in chemical plants, stainless is necessary since it is the only metal that will last for any length of time. In addition, stainless is used extensively for architectural work—many of the largest buildings in New York City used stainless steel exclusively for their outside covering.

Lead

Another sheet metal commonly stocked in the sheet metal shop is lead. Lead is one of the oldest of sheet metals. Many medieval churches still have lead downspouts and gutters in use which were installed when the church was built. Since the development of stainless steel and the still newer plastics, lead has lost its prominence in the sheet metal field. However, it is still used in highly corrosive conditions such as a tank for acid; and it is still used in places where repairing a leak would mean extensive work in removing sections of a building. An example of this would be a lead shower pan laid under the tile floor in a second story installation.

Lead comes in rolls, since it is too soft to be handled in sheets. It is gaged in pounds per square foot, and its cost is about three times that of galvanized iron. Lead is so soft that it can be formed by hand without the use of the brake. It can be soldered, though the melting point of lead and that of solder are so close that care must be taken not to allow the lead to get hot enough to melt.

Oxides of metal

When considering the characteristics of the different sheet metals, the student should also consider the importance of the oxides of that metal. Though we speak of the characteristics of a metal, what we are actually referring to most of the time are the characteristics of the oxide of the metal.

Whenever a metal is exposed to air, the oxygen in the air unites with the metal to form a chemical film over the metal. *This chemical is called the oxide of the metal.* Iron rust is actually iron oxide. The green chemical that often forms on copper is an oxide of copper.

The importance of the oxide is that the characteristics of the oxide determine many of the characteristics of the metal. Rust (iron oxide) forms quickly and is porous and flaky. Since iron oxide is porous, it allows moisture to seep through it and form more oxide underneath. Since it is flaky, as soon as a large amount of oxide is formed it flakes off to expose more iron which will form more oxide. This action eventually eats through the iron, which is the reason why iron is a poor metal to be exposed to corrosive conditions.

Stainless steel, on the other hand, forms an oxide that is transparent, tough, and impervious to air and almost every chemical. This transparency is the reason stainless steel keeps its lasting beauty. The toughness of the oxide is the reason for the long life of stainless, since actually, nothing ever contacts the metal itself.

Copper and lead also have oxides which are impervious to air and most chemicals and this is why they are so long lasting.

Aluminum oxide is hard to dissolve with any chemical. In addition, it reforms almost instantaneously. This is the reason why aluminum is difficult to solder. To solder any metal you must remove the oxide with a flux to have the solder contact the metal and not the oxide. Aluminum oxide is difficult to dissolve with any flux and usually forms again before the solder

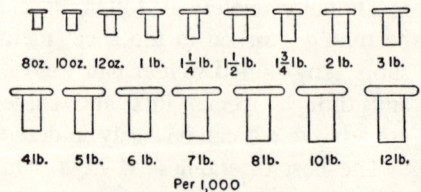

8oz.	10oz.	12oz.	1 lb.	$1\frac{1}{4}$ lb.	$1\frac{1}{2}$ lb.	$1\frac{3}{4}$ lb.	2 lb.	3 lb.

4 lb.	5 lb.	6 lb.	7 lb.	8 lb.	10 lb.	12 lb.

Per 1,000

Figure 6. Types of rivets.

can be applied. The flux must be applied at exactly the right temperature, and the solder applied at this same temperature, then the oxide will not form as quickly and the metal can be soldered.

Rivets

Black and tinned rivets from the small 8 oz. to the extra large 12 lb. (see Fig. 6) are extremely useful in a number of riveting operations that will be explained later.

Another type of rivet that is extremely useful in the sheet metal shop is the soft iron rivet with either a round or a flat head. Such rivets are available in assorted sizes.

Bolts

Every shop should have a good supply of flat and roundhead stove bolts of various sizes, as shown in Fig. 7. These are useful for fastening parts or assembling jobs that may later be

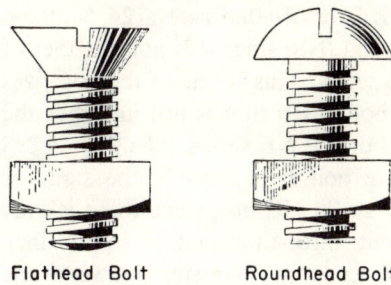

Flathead Bolt   Roundhead Bolt

Figure 7. Bolts commonly used in sheet metal work.

disassembled. A supply of washers will also be useful.

All the bolts used in the shop are the American National Thread Form. This thread form has two major series of threads, the National Fine and the National Coarse Series. Table III shows the diameters and threads per inch for the bolts in each of these series. The sheet metal shop commonly uses the ¼-20 NC bolt for much of its work. Another size commonly used is the ³⁄₁₆ stove bolt.

Size	Threads per inch National Coarse	Threads per inch National Fine	Threads per inch National Special
4	40	48	
6	32	40	
8	32	36	
10	24	32	
12	24	28	
14	..	..	20 & 24
3/16	..	..	24
1/4	20	28	
5/16	18	24	
3/8	16	24	
7/16	14	20	
1/2	13	20	
9/16	12	18	
5/8	11	18	
11/16	..	..	11 & 16
3/4	10	16	

Table III. National Fine and National Coarse bolt diameters and threads per inch.

This is designated as $\frac{3}{16}$-24 National Special (NS) since it is not in either of the series. This is one of the few sizes of bolts used that is not in either the NC or the NF series. The $\frac{3}{16}$-24 NS stove bolt is practically the same as the 10-24 NC bolt since there is only about three-thousandths of an inch difference in diameter between the two. The 10-24 NC tap is usually used to cut threads for a $\frac{3}{16}$-24 NS bolt since they are so close to the same size.

Metal screws

This type of screw is designed especially for sheet metal work and tap their own threads in the hole. The threads extend over the entire length of the screw as shown in Fig. 8, making it possible to fasten two pieces of metal together with the metal tight against the underside of the head. Screws are available in numerous kinds and sizes. Figure 8 also shows the different types of heads and points available in sheet metal screws.

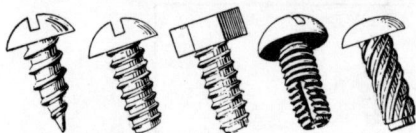

Figure 8. Common screws designed for sheet metal work.

Nails

Many types of nails such as copper, zinc coated, and tinned, are used in metal work. Copper nails are used wherever copper is used. The tinned nails are used extensively in all kinds of tin roofing, and galvanized nails

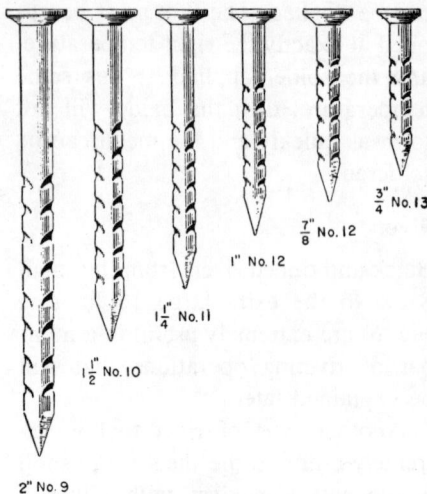

Figure 9. Types of commonly used nails.

are used in all galvanized construction. Figure 9 shows some of the commonly used nails.

Wire

Tinned, copper, or galvanized wire is available in a variety of sizes and is shipped in 100 lb. rolls. Wire is used for handles, for wiring tops of pans and boxes, and for many other uses.

Types of wire

Though the metal worker may occasionally make projects from the more expensive types of wire such as aluminum, stainless steel, or copper, the more common types of wire such as steel and iron are used for ordinary jobs. Steel wire is stronger, and should be used where strength is needed. To facilitate soldering and to prevent rust and corrosion, these types of wire are coated with zinc, tin, or copper, and are usually referred to as galvanized, tinned, or coppered wire.

Sizes of wire

Wire manufacturers recommend use of the United States Wire Gage to determine size when ordering wire. However, when making wired edges, the allowance for the edge depends upon the diameter of the wire. Therefore, to get an accurate measurement of the thickness of the wire, it is necessary to use a micrometer.

Review Questions

1. Explain the difference between coated and uncoated sheets, and what the significance of these designations are.
2. Make a chart of the sheet metals listed below, describing (1) appearance, (2) composition, (3) gage system, (4) two typical uses, (5) comparative cost, and (6) the gage that is .025" thick.
   A. Galvanized iron
   B. Tin Plate
   C. Copper
   D. Aluminum
   E. Stainless steel
3. What are the commonly used sizes for sheet metal sheets?
4. Why is tin plate used less than formerly? Name two applications of any kind of tin plate that you have personally seen.
5. What is the oxide of a metal?
6. What is the importance of an oxide?

7. What is the difference between hot rolled and cold rolled copper? Explain in terms of its processing, its characteristics, and its uses.
8. Make a chart showing the advantages and disadvantages of the following metals.
   A. Galvanized iron
   B. Tin Plate
   C. Copper
   D. Aluminum
   E. Stainless Steel
9. Make a chart comparing the sheet metals listed below for (1) bending, (2) soldering, (3) welding, (4) corrosion resistance, (5) lasting appearance, (6) expected length of service, and (7) weight.
   A. Galvanized iron
   B. Tin Plate
   C. Copper
   D. Aluminum (commercial half-hard)
   E. Stainless Steel

5

USING PATTERNS AND CUTTING METAL

What is a pattern? When are patterns used? How are patterns transferred? How are the metal cuts made after the pattern has been transferred?

In this chapter you will start using some of the tools and materials that were introduced in the previous chapters. You will learn how to square up a piece of metal, how to transfer patterns, and how to cut around the outline of the pattern after it has been transferred. Working drawings are used in designing objects of all kinds in the sheet metal field. It is equally important to be able to visualize the finished job from the working drawing or to visualize how the pattern will look by studying a picture of the object. In other words, a sheet metal craftsman should be able mentally to take an object apart and put it together again.

Using patterns and making drawings

PATTERNS. This chapter is not intended to show how patterns are developed, but to show how to use the pattern after it has been developed. Sheet metal articles are made of flat pieces of metal cut according to outlines that are drawn or traced on the sheets of metal. To obtain the correct size and shape, patterns are used. These patterns may be drawn on paper first, then transferred to the metal, or they may be laid out directly on the metal. It is better for the beginner to draw the patterns on paper first, since the paper pattern can be cut out and fitted together and any corrections made, saving valuable material. Patterns that are used repeatedly are made of metal and are called *templates* or *master patterns*. Paper patterns soon become worn and inaccurate if used repeatedly.

The term *stretchout* refers to the distance across the flat pattern or flat

56

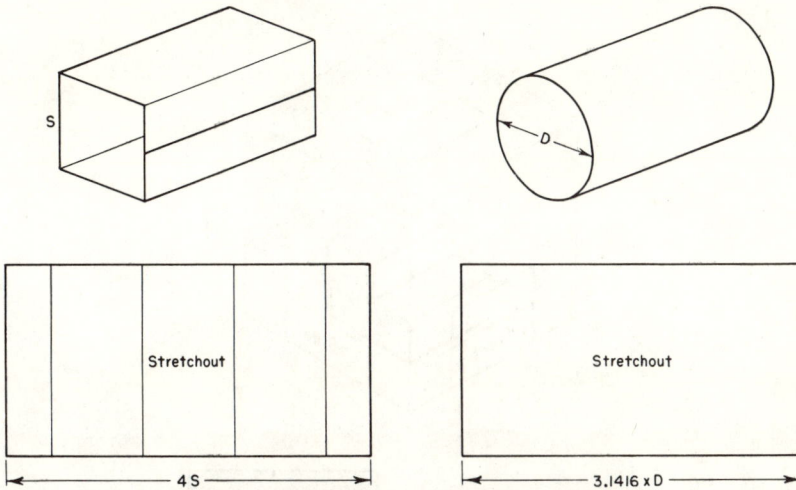

Figure 1. Stretchouts for square and cylindrical objects.

piece of metal before it is formed into shape. The illustration in Fig. 1 shows the stretchouts for square and cylindrical jobs. The stretchout is the same as the distance around the object. On a round pipe it would be the circumference of the pipe.

Layout, in general, refers to the method of developing the lines which form the pattern. The common methods of layout are: *simple pattern layout, parallel line development, radial line development,* and *triangulation.* These methods are treated in Chapters 12, 13, 14, and 15.

Pictorial drawings

Pictorial drawings show the object as it actually appears after being formed into shape. This is illustrated in Fig. 2. Such a drawing cannot serve as means of giving accurate information for the fabrication of the project because the true shape and size of the sides is not shown.

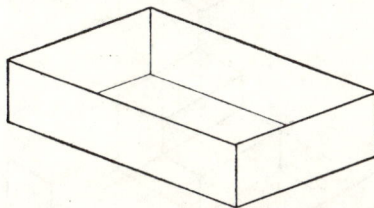

Figure 2. Pictorial drawings show the shape of objects as they appear after forming.

Mechanical drawing

A working or mechanical drawing shows the exact size and shape of each side. See Fig. 3. Notice that each view is just what you see by looking directly at the various sides as in the illustration. Since some of the views are alike—top and bottom, front and back, right and left end—it is only necessary to make the number of views required to show the size and shape of the object. In most cases this will be three—top, front, and end views.

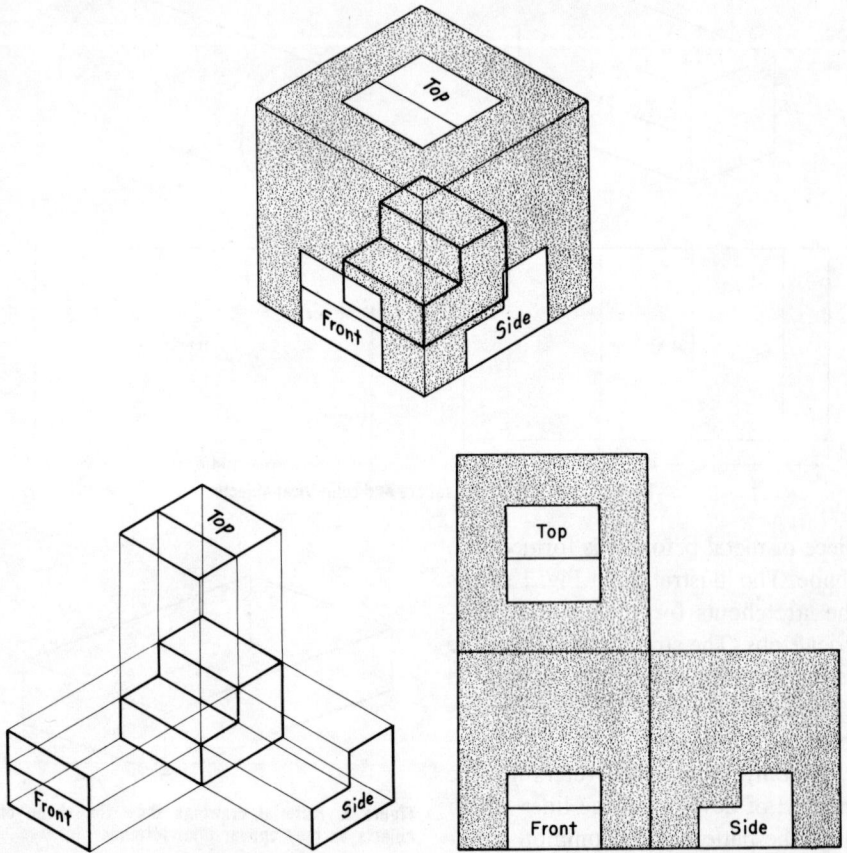

Figure 3. The white areas in the drawing at the right are mechanical or working drawings. The drawings at the left and top show the placement of various views in relation to each other.

In sheet metal work, the term *elevation* is applied to any view which shows the height of the job. Unlike conventional drafting terms such as top, front, and end views, the term *plan view* refers to the top view, *front elevation* refers to the front view, and *end elevation* refers to the end view. With this information, a pattern, such as shown in Fig. 4, is easily developed. The X symbols near the end of the lines indicate the places where

the metal is to bent or folded. These lines are called *brake lines*.

The working drawing, which may be a blueprint (blueprints are exact reproductions of working drawings and can be made quickly and inexpensively) should give all the information necessary to complete the job.

Pattern information

The master pattern should contain all of the allowances and details neces-

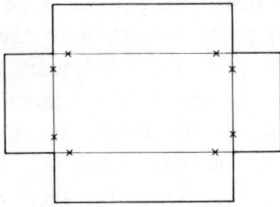

Figure 4. Pattern for a pan.

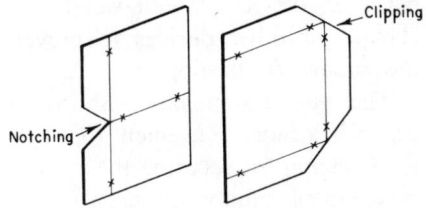

Figure 5. Notching and clipping.

sary to fabricate the job. In addition, this information is contained in the specifications, or written description, which include the following:

ALLOWANCE FOR EDGES. Different types of edges are used to stiffen the edges of the sheet metal articles, and to eliminate the sharp sheet metal edge which may cut someone. Edges are made by bending the metal in various ways, or by wrapping the metal around wire, flat bar, or angle. The amount of metal allowed for the edge depends upon the type of edge used. The advantages of each type of edge and the amount of metal to allow for each one will be discussed in Chapter 7.

ALLOWANCES FOR SEAMING. Sheet metal parts are joined by seams of various kinds. The addition of the seams makes it necessary to add material to the pattern. Allowances for each type of seam will also be given in Chapter 7.

PRICK PUNCHING BRAKE LINES. On metal patterns, the brake lines are prick punched. If the master pattern is being traced from a paper pattern, the brake lines are prick punched through the paper pattern onto the metal.

Every brake line should be prick punched because many of the brake lines must be bent from the other side of the metal. The student often tries to avoid prick marking all the lines, and this invariably means several return trips from the brake to the bench to prick mark a line that is needed. Put a prick mark near the end of each brake line as shown by the X marks in Fig. 4. These prick marks should be located about $1/4''$ from the end of the line so they can be easily covered if the job is soldered.

NOTCHING AND CLIPPING. Notching and clipping are used to cut away portions of the metal to prevent overlapping and bulging on seams and edges. The operations are different as illustrated by Fig. 5. Detailed information will be given in Chapter 12 about the allowances necessary for notching and clipping.

TRACING AROUND A METAL PATTERN. When tracing around a metal pattern, the pattern should be held in

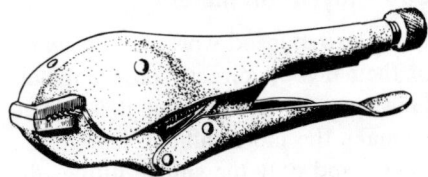

Figure 6. Clamp pliers.

place on the metal with weights, C clamps, or other devices to prevent the pattern from slipping.

The vise clamp pliers shown in Fig. 6 is a more convenient tool than the C clamp for securing the pattern. It operates simply by pressing the hand grips together. An adjustable screw on one of the handles makes it possible to regulate it for any thickness of work.

A sharp scratch awl is usually used to scribe around the outline of the metal pattern.

Transferring a paper pattern to metal

Trying to trace around a paper pattern is very difficult since the paper will wrinkle at the slightest pressure. The best method of transferring a pattern from paper to metal is not to cut out the paper pattern at all, but leave it intact on the paper. Then lay it over the metal with weights to keep it from moving, and prick mark through the paper at the ends of all lines and at intervals around curves. If possible, prick mark the center points of any arcs that must be swung. Then remove the paper and with a rule and scratch awl, draw lines connecting all prick marks in the proper manner.

Direct layout on metal

Many experienced workmen do many of their layouts directly on the metal. However, for the student it is better to make the more difficult layouts on paper, and only the simple fittings directly on the metal.

PREPARING THE METAL. One of the first steps in preparing to lay out a pattern on metal is to square the left end of the metal. Sheet metal is not usually squared before it leaves the factory. The steel square may be used for this purpose, or the sheet may be squared directly by the use of the squaring shears. The next step is to see that the sheet of metal lies perfectly flat on the bench and not on the bench plate.

The measurements for the layout on metal should be taken from the bottom of the sheet and from the squared-up line at the left end of the sheet. Patterns are always located in the lower left hand corner of the sheet. This practice minimizes the waste of metal when cutting out patterns.

MARKING IRREGULAR CURVES. When laying out a pattern on metal, a series of points along any irregular curve are located and then a smooth curve must be drawn through these points. The most common method of doing this is by means of a flexible rule instrument such as is shown in Fig. 7. These instruments are made of spring steel so they can be bent to a curve and still return to their original straightness. Though the one shown is a two-foot folding rule, flexible rules can be obtained in many lengths. In fact, most three-foot circumference rules used in the sheet metal shop are flexible rules. Fig. 8 shows how the rule can be bent through several of the points along the curve and a smooth curve drawn in with a scratch awl or a pencil.

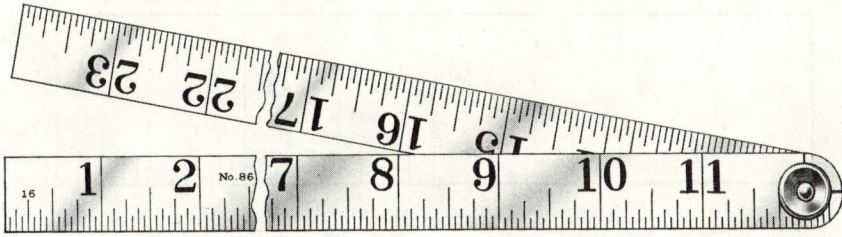

Figure 7. Example of one type of flexible rule instrument. Courtesy: Lufkin Rule Co.

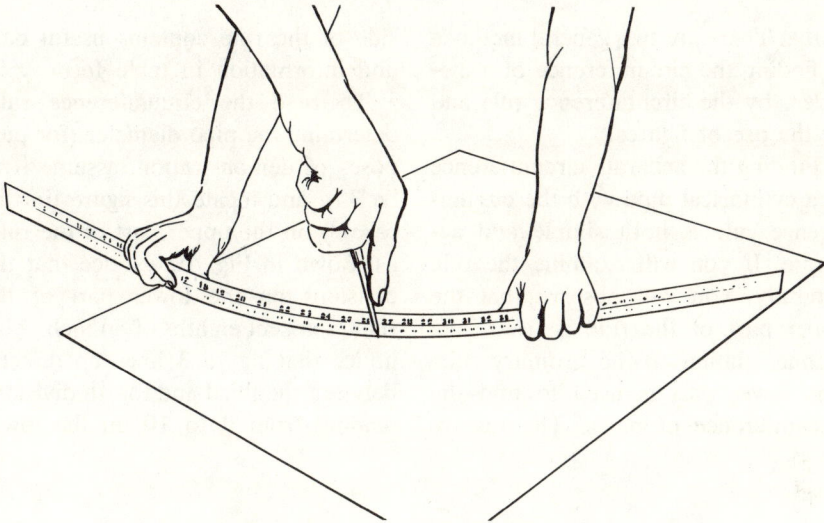

Figure 8. Locating points on a curve by using another type of flexible rule.

Taking measurements

HOW TO READ THE COMMON RULE. In denoting measurements taken with a rule, the symbol ′ is always used for feet and ″ for inches. If you will examine the section of the rule shown in Fig. 9, you will notice that the inch is divided first into two parts, each being one-half inch long. The halves are again equally divided into quarters of an inch and again into eighths and sixteenths of an inch. For very accurate measurement, some rules are divided into thirty-seconds and sixty-fourths of an inch. Practice using the rule, making lines 1¹⁄₁₆″ long, 3⅝″ long, etc., until you can take measurements quickly and accurately. Remember that a fraction is a part of a whole number, 1, and consists of a numerator and denominator as shown by the following example:

1 (numerator)
—————————
4 (denominator)

HOW TO READ THE CIRCUMFERENCE

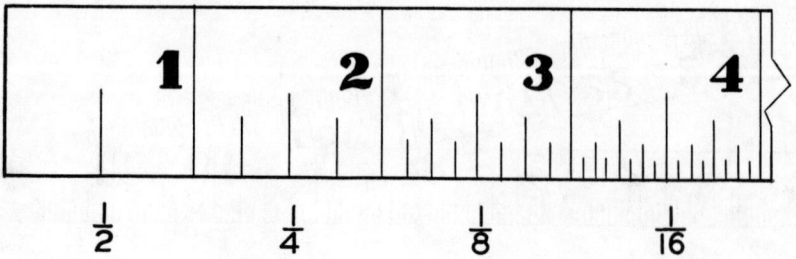

Figure 9. Fractional divisions of an inch as read on the common rule.

RULE. There are two general methods of finding the circumference of a cylinder: by the circumference rule and by the use of figures.

Finding the accurate circumference of a cylindrical pipe with the circumference rule is both simple and accurate. If you will examine the rule carefully, you will observe that the upper part of the rule is used in a manner similar to the ordinary rule. The lower part is used to find the circumference of pipes. The reverse side of the rule contains useful data and information in table form.

To read the circumference rule, determine the pipe diameter (for purposes of demonstration, assume it to be 3″), and locate this figure (in this case 3) on the upper part of the rule, as shown in Fig. 10. Notice that the divisions on the lower part of the rule represent eighths of an inch. Also notice that figure 3 lines up directly between the third and fourth divisions reading from 9 to 10 on the lower

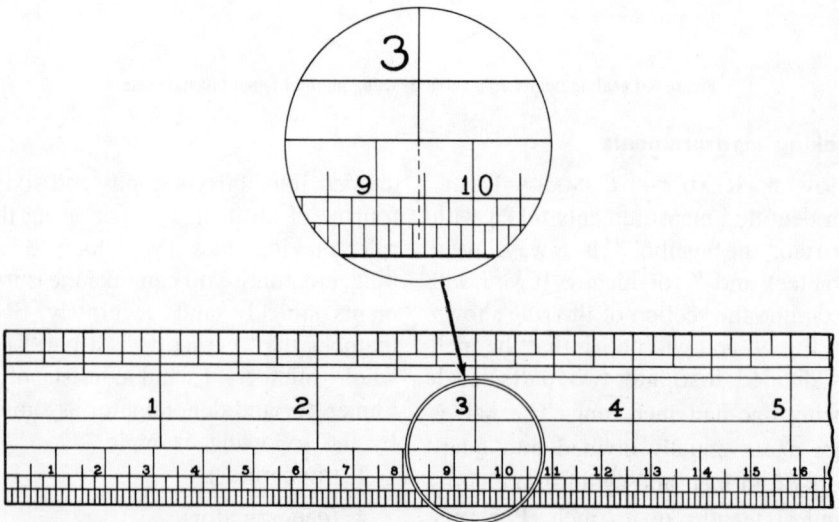

Figure 10. Circumference rule.

part of the rule. The circumference is then read as 9⁷⁄₁₆″. Usually, the eighths on the lower part of the scale can be used for the circumference reading.

FINDING CIRCUMFERENCE BY USE OF FIGURES. Occasionally the sheet metal worker desires to find the distance around a pipe without the use of a circumference rule. The method for doing this is to multiply the diameter of the pipe by 3.14 or 3⅐. The former is generally preferred. For example, suppose that a pipe 5″ in diameter is to be made. The first step would be to find the circumference in inches. This can be done in the following steps:

1. Multiply 3.14 by the diameter, 5″.

$$\begin{array}{r} 3.1416 \\ \times 5'' \\ \hline 15.7080'' \end{array}$$ circumference of pipe

2. Change the decimal .7080 to a fraction that can be read on the common rule. To do this, multiply the decimal .7080 by the denominator of the fraction that is to be used, such as 8, 16, 32, etc., depending upon the accuracy required. In this problem, use 16 thus:

$$\begin{array}{r} .7080 \\ \times 16 \\ \hline 42480 \\ 7080 \\ \hline 11.3280 \end{array}$$ or ¹¹⁄₁₆

3. The decimal .7080 can now be read as the fraction ¹¹⁄₁₆. This makes 15.7080″ = 15¹¹⁄₁₆″, which can be read directly from the common rule.

Hence, we see that multiplying the decimal by the denominator of any of the fractional inch graduations on the rule will give the numerator of the desired fraction as shown by the preceding example.

Cutting metal

CUTTING STRAIGHT AND CURVED LINES. Though there are many specialized snips used for special occasions, the sheet metal worker generally uses four different snips for all his cutting. 1. The bulldog snips are used for general cutting in heavy metal—about 24 gage or thicker. 2. The combination snips are also used for general cutting from 24 gage and thinner. Since a great deal of the sheet metal used is 24 gage or lighter, the combination snips are probably the most commonly used snips in the sheet metal worker's box. 3 and 4. Airplane snips—both right-hand and left-hand—complete the sheet metal worker's usual set of snips. The airplane snips are used for both heavy and light sheet metal. They can cut up to 16 gage with comparative ease. The advantage of airplane snips is that they can cut very small and complex curves that would be difficult or impossible to cut with bulldogs or combination snips. They are also the best snips to cut inside circles and inside corners as shown in Fig. 11.

There is more to using snips than merely working the handles. Both practice and knowledge are necessary to be able to make a clean cut on sheet metal in all sorts of circumstances. Too often the student of

CURLED SCRAP METAL

HOLE

RIGHT HAND AIRPLANE SNIPS

CIRCLE DRAWN ON METAL

LEFT HAND SNIPS
CUTTING INTO CORNER

HOLE CUT IN METAL

LINE ON METAL

RIGHT HAND SNIPS
CUTTING INTO CORNER

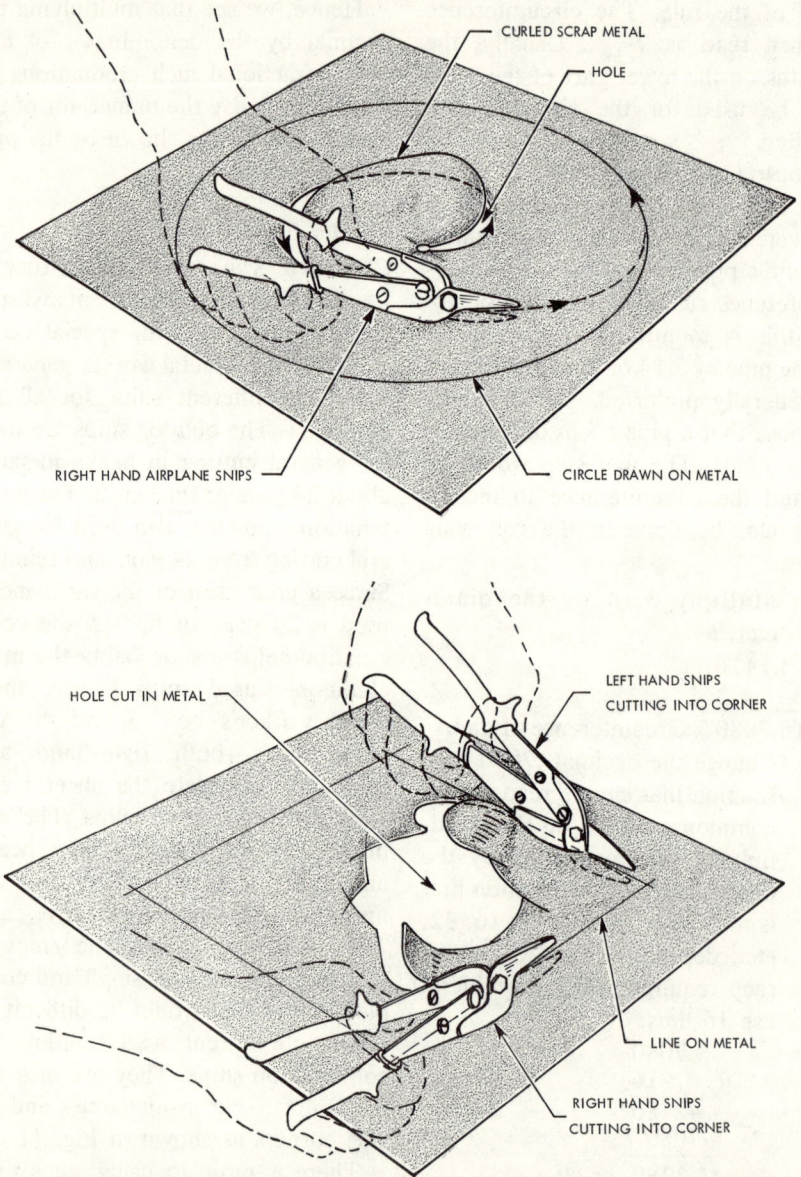

Figure 11. Airplane snips are used to make small or complex cuts in sheet metal.

sheet metal work will at first cut very jagged and rough edges on the metal. Since these edges reflect upon the entire job and in many ways affect the quality of the finished job, it is essential that the student master the snips.

It is impossible to do a workmanlike job in sheet metal until you first learn how to cut sheet metal skillfully. As much as any other trade, successful sheet metal work depends upon accurate accomplishment of each individual operation for a complete, skilled job. If any given operation is done sloppily, the result will be evident throughout the rest of the operations. Like any skill, the operation of snips depends upon practice. However, much of the mastery of snips also depends upon knowledge. If you study the following rules to learn the proper use and care of snips and practice these guides, then you will find that mastery of the actual hand processes is relatively simple.

1. *Keep the small piece of metal over the bottom blade of the snips.* In using snips, the greatest problem is not in making the actual cut, but in getting the snips into the end of the cut. This is because one piece of metal must slide over the bottom blade of the snips and up over the snips handle. If the metal sheet is large, it resists the bending necessary to accomplish that operation and makes it difficult to get the snips into the end of the cut. This in turn makes it difficult to control the snips after they are in the cut. However, if the piece of metal is narrow, it will naturally curl during the cutting operation itself and will curl up over the snips blade with no trouble. Even if the piece is too large to curl naturally, when it is the smaller of the two pieces it will still be easier to lift it up out of the way.

2. *Trim off excess metal before making the cut on the line.* The reason for this is. the same as discussed previously. If the excess metal is trimmed to within a ¼″ of the line, then when the final cut is made the scrap will curl up out of the way and the cut can be made easily.

3. *Whenever possible, rest the blade and handle of the snips on the workbench.* This rule does not apply to airplane snips, since they are too small to use in this manner. However, all other snips should be rested on the bench rather than held in the air. Doing this allows you to use your arm muscles instead of your wrist muscles for the cutting operation, therefore giving more power and control over the cut. In addition, using your arm muscles means that your arm will not tire as quickly.

4. *When notching, keep the end of the snips blades at the point where the notch will end.* It is common for students to put the blades beyond the end of the notch. This results in having to make a very slow and careful cut to avoid cutting past the notch. And even with care, the cut will very often go slightly past the notch. Since bends are generally made to the corner of notches, this results in the metal breaking at the corners when the bend is made.

5. *Keep oil from the blades of snips.* A drop of oil should occasionally be put on the swivel bolt of snips to keep them moving freely. However, do not allow it to run onto the blades, since this will cause the metal to slip out of the blades.

6. *Cut only sheet metal with snips.* The clearance on snips blades is for sheet metal thicknesses only. If you use them to cut wire, no matter how soft the metal, you are almost sure to nick the blades.

7. *Don't force snips.* Extending the snips handles, placing all your weight on the handles, or pounding on the backs of the blades puts more pressure on the snips blades than they are designed for and will spring the blades making them useless. If snips blades are "sprung" there is too much clearance between the blades which means that when small edges of sheet metal are trimmed, the blades will bend the edge rather than cut it. Another common result of "sprung" blades is that the tips of the blades no longer meet, which means that notches cannot be made with the tip of the blade.

CUTTING INSIDE CIRCLES. Many times a hole must be cut in sheet metal. This operation employs the same methods as cutting any type of sheet metal and some additional ones as well. If a large sheet metal punch is handy, the hole can be started by punching a large hole. Many times a punch is not available and the hole is started by making a slit with the peen of the tinner's hammer or with a hammer and chisel. Once the slit is made, then the blade of the airplane snips is inserted and a spiral cut is made gradually increasing the diameter until about ½" away from the line. Trim out all the excess metal from the hole, leaving about ½" from the line. Then the second cut on the line is made without interference from the excess metal in the hole and an accurate cut can be made.

If a square hole must be made instead of a round one, the same procedure is followed except that both the right-hand and left-hand airplane snips are used to cut into the square corners, as shown in Fig. 11.

Using the compound-lever shears

The compound-lever shears, because of the arrangement of levers, has a mechanical advantage sufficient to allow the cutting of metal up to 12 gage steel. The lower handle is bent to

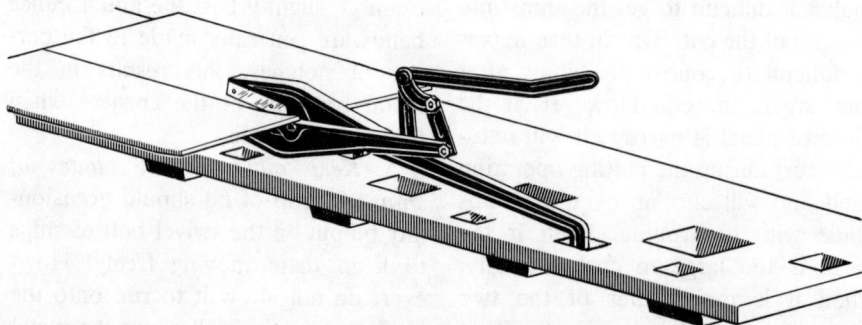

Figure 12. Using compound shears.

allow the shears to be placed in the bench plate. Fig. 12 shows how the metal is placed in the shears when cutting.

Bench lever shears

A shears which is used in almost every sheet metal shop is shown in Fig. 13. This is a heavy duty shears —models are available to cut $\frac{3}{16}''$ thick metal with ease. The operating principle of these shears is the same as snips except that they are built stronger and have a compound leverage system for greater power. The blades are designed to cut curves and circles as well as straight lines. When using this type of shears, keep the good piece of metal over the lower blade and run the scrap piece under

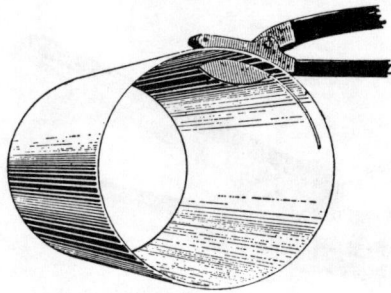

Figure 14. Double cutting shears used in cutting pipe.

the upper blade since the piece that goes under the upper blade will be curled and distorted by the cutting action.

Cutting pipe

Cutting pipe requires different methods for pipes of different gages. The double-cutting shears are indispensable to the sheet metal worker when cutting apart light gage pipe. When in good condition, they will not leave burrs or ragged edges. These shears have a center cutting blade that operates between the double jaw when cutting. The center blade is pointed and can be easily inserted in light gage metal to start the cut, as shown in Fig. 14. When cutting 24 gage metal pipe, use a sharp cold chisel to make the opening for the blade.

Another important feature of some double-cutting shears is an attachment which is designed for crimping the small ends of pipes after they are cut. Fig. 15 illustrates a separate crimper.

Cutting pipes of 22 gage or heavier requires another method, inas-

Figure 13. Bench lever shears. Courtesy: Beverly Shear Mfg. Co.

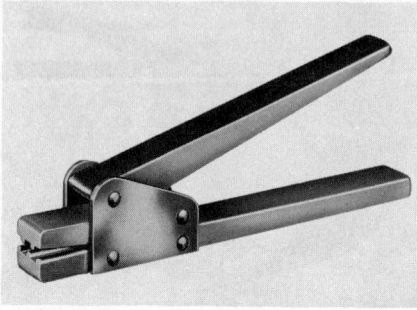

Figure 15. Pipe crimper. Courtesy: Warner Oberly Mfg. Co.

much as double-cutting shears are designed only to cut light gage metal. The most common method of cutting heavy gage pipe is to place a lead cake over a stake and cut around the scribed outline of the pipe, using a sharp cold chisel and a heavy hammer.

Motor-driven hand shears

Many modern sheet metal shops have stepped up production through the use of one or more models of hand power shears. These shears are designed to cut straight and irregular curved lines. With a little practice, anyone can use hand power to cut out templates with hairline accuracy, without burrs, and without distortion of

Figure 16. Unishear. Courtesy: Stanley Tools.

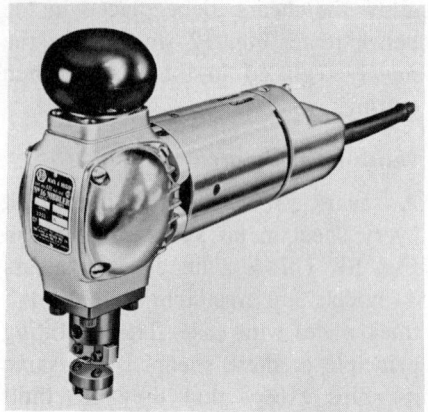

Figure 17. Nibbler. Courtesy: Black & Decker Mfg. Co.

the metal. The shears shown in Fig. 16 have sufficient capacity to cut 18 gage metal. Others are made to cut 16 or 12 gage metal. A great advantage of these portable shears is that they can be taken right to the job and plugged into any electric outlet or light socket.

Nibbler

Another common cutting machine in the sheet metal shop is the nibbler, shown in Fig. 17. The nibbler is actually a fast acting punch that "nibbles" a small hole out of the metal at every stroke. The strokes on a nibbler are very fast—faster than the eye can follow. The advantages of the nibbler are that it can cut very heavy metal in any intricate form and also that the piece of metal being cut is not distorted since both pieces remain perfectly flat during the cutting action.

Band saw

Another tool used in the modern

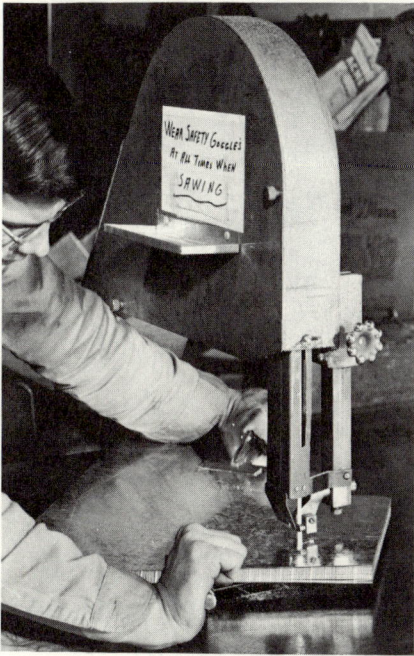

Figure 18. Band saw.

sheet metal shop is the metal cutting band saw. The band saw is used principally for cutting large numbers of the same pieces. Fig. 18 shows how the proper number of pieces of the correct size are clamped together with one pattern on the top. Note the deep throat on this saw, which was especially designed for sheet metal cutting. Then all the pieces are cut in one operation instead of singly. The sheet metal worker never uses the band saw as a substitute for snips to cut a single piece of metal, since using snips is faster and more economical on single pieces.

The squaring shears

The principal parts of the squaring shears shown in Fig. 19 are as follows:

The bed is the horizontal, rigid, cross-ribbed channel section. The top of the bed has two transverse T slots for the front and bevel gages. It also has graduations for setting the front gage and a large depression in the center of the bed to give clearance for grasping the metal.

The crosshead is the horizontal beam connecting the housings for supporting the upper cutting blade and the hold-down clamp.

The housings are the two vertical standards supporting the crosshead and are of truss construction.

The foot treadle is used to force the cutting blades together when cutting metal.

The hold-down acts as a clamp for holding the metal in place and also serves as a safety guard.

The extension arms or front brackets are for supporting the front gage.

The two graduated scales for setting gages are located conveniently on the top of the bed.

The front gage can be fastened in the T slot on the bed or front brackets for the purpose of making straight or angular cuts.

The side gage is located on each side of the bed and is used for squaring the corners of the sheet metal.

The bevel gage is attached to the bed of the shears for making angular cuts.

The back gage (not shown) is mounted on the rear of the shears and used to cut large metal pieces.

Fig. 20, shows the 36″ foot-oper-

Figure 19. Squaring shears. Courtesy: Peck, Stow & Wilcox Co.

ated squaring shear used in every sheet metal shop.

When using the squaring shears, remember the danger of cutting off your fingers. Be sure never to put your fingers under the blades. Remember also, that another common accident to be avoided is putting one's foot under the foot treadle with the result that one's foot is stamped.

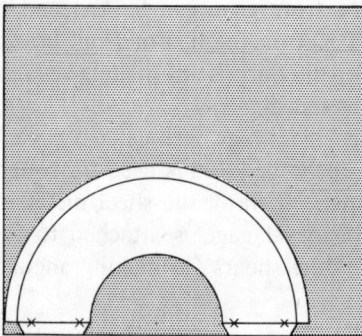

PROPER POSITION
(A)

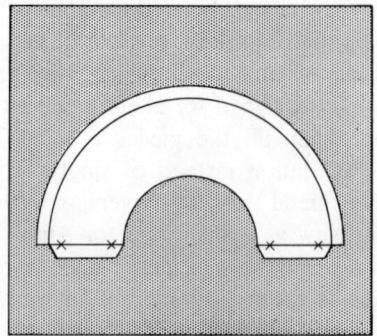

IMPROPER POSITION
(B)

Figure 20. Proper and improper position of pattern on material.

Review Questions

1. Describe a master pattern.
2. Name five tools used for cutting metal.
3. What tool scribes metal patterns?
4. What is the difference between a pictorial drawing and a mechanical drawing?
5. What type of shears is used for cutting a pipe into two sections?
6. Explain how to avoid wasting metal when cutting out patterns.
7. With the circumference rule, find the circumference of the following sizes (diameters) of pipe: 3″, 5″, 7½″, 11″.
8. What cutting tool is used to cut an inside circle?
9. Why should a piece of metal be squared before using?
10. Without looking at the list of tools in Chapter 2, see how many you can remember. Explain their uses.
11. Give two ways by which patterns are transferred onto metal.
12. What is the difference between a paper pattern and a template?
13. Name two tools used for cutting circles in metal.
14. What shears are used to cut a metal disk?
15. Describe ten of the principal mechanical parts of the squaring shears.
16. What is meant by a stretchout?

Projects

Project 5-1. Transferring paper and metal patterns onto metal

AIM. To develop the ability to transfer paper and metal patterns to metal.
OPERATIONS. (transferring a paper pattern onto metal using a pencil)

1. Cut around the outline of the paper pattern with a pair of scissors (use any pattern). Stay at least 1″ outside the outline.
2. Place the sheet of metal to be used on the wood part of the bench. If the metal rests on the bench plate, the point of the prick punch will become dull if punched on the iron surface.
3. Place the paper pattern on the metal in the proper position to avoid waste. See Fig. 20.

4. Place metal weights on the paper pattern to keep it from creeping, as shown in Fig. 21. "C" clamps should not be used with a paper pattern.
5. Make slight indentations with a sharp prick punch on all bend lines and on the outline lines as described in this chapter.
6. Remove the weights and cut out the pattern using the proper snips.

OPERATIONS (transferring a metal or master pattern onto metal)

1. Place the metal on the bench in the same manner as in previous operations.
2. Place the metal pattern on the metal in the proper position.
3. Secure the pattern with weights

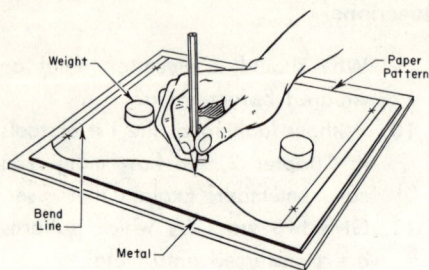

Figure 21. Transferring paper pattern to metal.

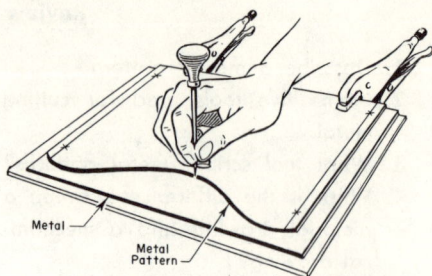

Figure 22. Transferring metal pattern to metal.

or vise-clamp wrench to keep it from creeping.

4. Scribe on the metal the outline of the pattern with a sharp scratch awl, as shown in Fig. 22.

5. Make slight indentations with a sharp prick punch on all bend lines.

6. Remove the weights or vise-clamp wrench and cut out the outline using the proper hand snips.

7. Check the pattern before forming to shape.

Project 5-2. Squaring a piece of metal

AIM. To develop skill in squaring metal with the squaring shears and to develop an understanding of the operation of the machine.

SPECIFICATIONS. Square the four sides of a piece of metal to any convenient size.

OPERATIONS

1. Place the sheet to be squared between the cutting blades with one side against the right-side gage.

2. Extend the edge to be trimmed about ¼″ beyond the lower

cutting blade. This distance should never be less than the thickness of the sheet.

3. Pull the hold-down handle to clamp the sheet in place.

4. Keeping both hands on the metal, step on the foot treadle to cut the piece of metal. Be sure the fingers are free of the cutting blades.

5. Release the foot treadle gradually, keeping the foot on the treadle until it is back in place.

6. Release the hold-down handle and remove the metal.

7. Place the edge that has just been trimmed against the right-side gage, again extending the sheet about ¼″ beyond the lower cutting blade, and repeat the cutting operation.

8. Set the front gage to required size.

9. Place the squared edges of the metal against the front and right gage.

10. Hold the metal in place with your hands and repeat the cutting operation.

11. Reset the gage to the size desired.

12. Cut the remaining edge.

Project 5-3. Cutting a piece of metal to any desired size using the front gage

AIM. To develop skill in squaring metal and cutting to any desired length.

SPECIFICATIONS. Cut a piece of metal 4″ × 10″ with the corners squared.

OPERATIONS

1. Place the sheet to be squared between the cutting blades with one side against the right-side gage.
2. Square a corner (two edges) of the piece of metal.
3. Set the front gage to 10″.
4. Place a squared edge against the front gage.
5. Clamp metal into place using the hold-down handle.
6. Press down on the foot treadle to cut the metal. Keep the foot on the treadle until the treadle is back in place.
7. Reset the gage to 4″, the desired width, and complete the operation.

Project 5-4. Drawing the stretchout for a rectangular pipe

AIM. To learn how to use the stretchout of a pipe in laying out a pattern on paper.

SPECIFICATIONS. Draw the stretchout for a square pipe 4″ × 4″ and 6″ long.

OPERATIONS

1. Obtain paper and drawing instruments.

2. Draw a line equal to the stretchout of the pipe.
3. Draw another line parallel to and 6″ away from the first.
4. Square up one end and mark off 4″ intervals for the corner lines.
5. Turn the drawing in to the instructor for checking.

Project 5-5. Drawing the stretchout for a round pipe

AIM. To practice determining the stretchout for round pipe.

SPECIFICATIONS. Draw the stretchout for a round pipe 6″ long and 4″ in diameter.

OPERATIONS

1. Obtain paper at least 8½″ × 14″ and drawing materials.
2. Determine the stretchout by the method shown in Chapter 5.
3. Draw out the pattern according to this stretchout and length and have it checked by the instructor.

Project 5-6. Cutting metal with snips

AIM. To develop skill in cutting metal with snips.

SPECIFICATIONS. Using thin scrap sheet metal, lay out the shapes shown in Figs. 23, and 24 and then cut them out.

OPERATIONS

1. Using dividers, lay out the circles shown in Fig. 23.
2. Use the squaring shears to trim the excess metal. Leave about ½″ from the line to trim off with snips.

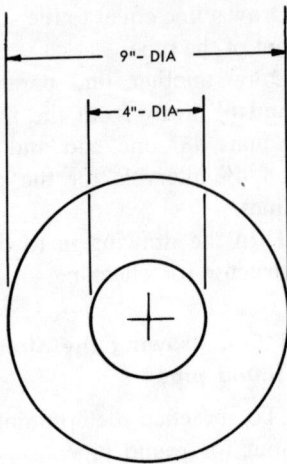

Figure 23. Cutting circular shapes on sheet metal.   Figure 24. Cutting notched shapes on sheet metal.

3. Use combination blade snips or airplane snips to cut the outside circle.

4. Punch a large hole inside the inner circle, or make a slit with a hammer and chisel.

5. Using airplane snips, cut out the excess metal from the inside. Stay about ½″ away from the line.

6. Trim off the metal to the inside circle, using airplane snips. Turn the circle in to the instructor.

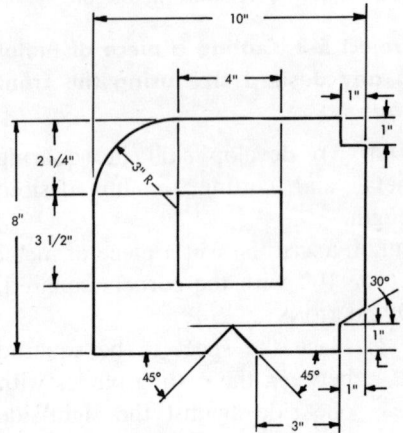

7. Lay out the shape shown in Fig. 24.

8. Trim off excess with the squaring shears.

9. Following the rules for using snips given in Chapter 5, cut the outside shape and the notches. Do not overcut on the corners of the notches.

10. Make a hole inside the center square and use airplane snips to trim off excess metal and then trim to the line.

6

PUNCHING, DRILLING, AND RIVETING

When are rivets used in fabricating sheet metal? How is the proper size rivet selected? What is the proper distance between rivets? How are rivets removed?

Whenever sheet metal is fabricated, holes must often be drilled or punched in it for bolts, rivets, or attachments of some type.

Though not as commonly used as formerly, the riveted seam is still used quite often in the shop. Its applications are where spot welding is not practical, and the metal is too heavy for seaming. In such cases, rivets are the best means of making the seam. Making the holes in the proper size and spacing for the riveted seam determines to a large extent the strength and the appearance of the riveted seam.

This chapter will give general rules to follow in hole forming and riveting. However, it is only through practice that you will gain the proficiency needed.

Making holes

A successful riveting operation depends upon the accuracy and size of the rivet holes and upon the correct size and spacing of the rivets. The holes for the rivets may be punched or drilled, depending upon the thickness of the metal. Light sheet metal is usually punched, while the heavier metal is drilled. Drilling is more accurate and distorts the metal less.

SIZE OF HOLES. The size of the hole depends upon the size of the rivet, which in turn depends upon the thickness of the metal. A good job of riveting is controlled to a great extent by the size of the hole, as shown in Fig. 1. If the hole is too large for the rivet, as shown by *A*, the head will not be properly formed and will pull out eas-

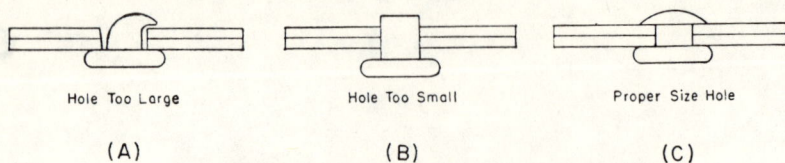

Hole Too Large   Hole Too Small   Proper Size Hole

(A)   (B)   (C)

Figure 1. Proper and improper rivet hole sizes.

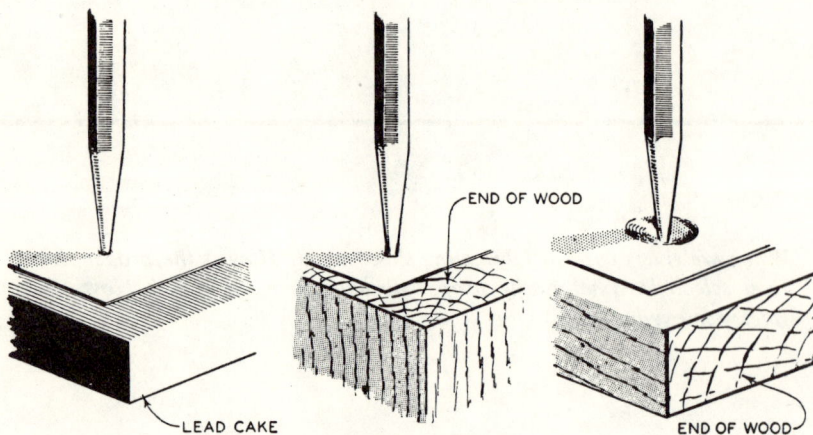

END OF WOOD

LEAD CAKE   END OF WOOD

Figure 2. Using a solid punch.

ily. If the hole is smaller than the rivet, the rivet is not inserted entirely through the metal, resulting in insufficient material for forming the head. This is shown at *B*. The best clearance is one that will allow the rivet to be inserted easily and quickly with sufficient material protruding to form the proper head, as shown at *C*.

USING THE SOLID PUNCH. Though solid punches such as the ones shown in Fig. 2 may be used against a block of wood to make a hole in sheet metal, this method is used only when others are not available. Solid punches are slow and inefficient compared to other methods and should therefore be avoided when possible. Modern sheet metal shops generally have a turret punch such as the one shown in Fig. 3. These punches are of different capacities and sizes. The size most used is for holes from $\frac{1}{8}''$ up to $2''$ in diameter. Small punches are capable of punching $\frac{1}{8}''$ thick metal (11 gage) and the largest size capable of punching metal $\frac{1}{20}''$ thick (18 gage) or lighter. These punches are designed so the upper punch and the lower die are mounted on two revolving tables or turrets. The turrets can be released and turned instantly to allow for immediate setting for the hole desired. They have an advantage over hand lever punches in that they have a deeper reach (generally $18''$),

Figure 3. Turret punch. Courtesy: Rotex Punch Co., Inc.

and they have an immediate setting, while the lever punches require several minutes to change and involve the hazard of misplacing the loose punches and dies. In using a turret punch, the student should check and double check that he has the same size punch and die aligned. If a large punch is aligned with a small die, the result will be either a broken punch or a damaged machine.

USING THE HAND LEVER PUNCH. The hand lever punch is used by the metal worker for general fabrication work including button punching. In button punching, the die is set so that the punch makes indentations but does not punch through the metal. Button punching is used in duct and similar work where but little strength is re-

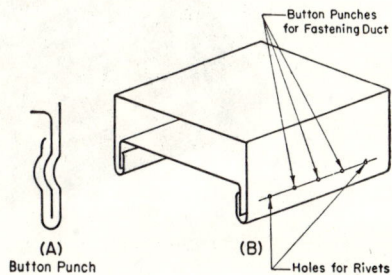

Figure 4. Button punching.

quired. The ends of the duct are fastened with bolts or rivets and the space in between is button punched. This keeps the seam from opening. The illustration in *A* of Fig. 4 shows how the material is button punched,

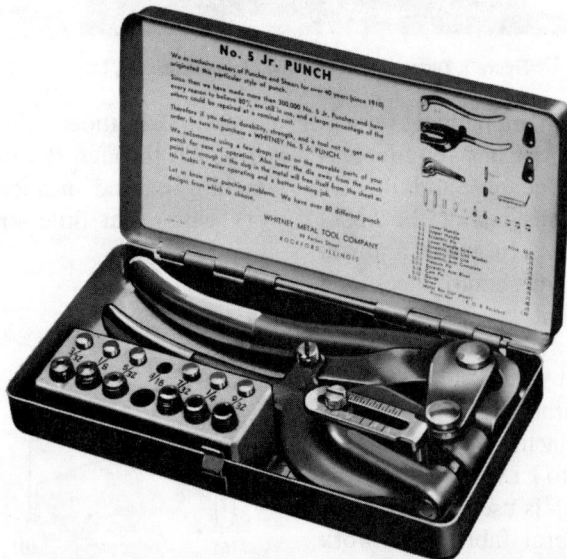

Figure 5. Hand lever punches and punch & die kit. Courtesy: Whitney Metal Tool Co.

and in *B* the method of button punching a duct.

The general operations of all hand lever punches of the type shown in Fig. 5 are the same but the methods of changing the punches and dies are different. In general, the punches and dies are changed in the following steps:

1. *Remove the die with a screw driver or key for the purpose.*
2. *Open the punch.*
3. *Remove the threaded collar.*
4. *Remove punch from collar.*
5. *Replace the correct size punch in collar.*
6. *Replace the threaded collar.*
7. *Return the levers to normal position.*
8. *Replace the correct size die.*
9. *Adjust the die with a screw driver until the punch just barely punches a clean hole.*

While the gage can be used to punch holes a uniform distance from the edge of the metal, it is better to lay out centers and then punch the holes. The centers are marked with a prick punch. In punching the hole, the centering point of the punch is placed in the prick point on the work. The hole is then completed by pressing down the upper lever.

Drilling holes

Sheet metal workers sometimes find it necessary to drill holes when working with heavy material. The holes can be drilled by hand or by machine. When drilling by hand, the electric hand drill is used. Twist drills are used as the cutting tool when drilling holes. The size of the drill is marked

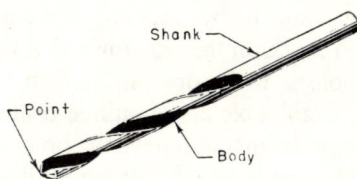

Figure 6. Principal parts of straight shank drill.

on the shank of the drill. The principal parts of a twist drill are *body, shank,* and *point,* as shown in Fig. 6. The size may be designated by one of four systems—fraction, number, letter.

Though there are other types of shanks, the most common is the straight shank twist drill. The chuck capacity of the hand operated drill is from $\frac{1}{64}''$ to $\frac{1}{4}''$ diameter in a straight shank twist drill, while the portable electric hand drill capacity can be obtained with chuck capacities of $\frac{1}{4}''$, $\frac{3}{8}''$, or $\frac{1}{2}''$.

In drilling a hole by hand, make sure that the work is securely clamped If possible, back up the work with a piece of wood. This will stiffen the sheet metal and will prevent damage to the work, the table, or the drill. Select the proper size drill by checking the size on the shank. Be sure the drill is straight and sharp. Insert the drill in the chuck and rotate the drill to see if it runs true. Enlarge the prick punch in the work by center punching it. Place the point of the drill in the center punch mark and rotate drill briefly, then check to see that the drill is properly centered in the hole. (If the drill is not properly centered, it may be drawn over with the center punch by making a center punch mark on the side toward which the hole is to be drawn.) Return the drill to the hole and continue drilling through the metal, relieve the pressure slightly and continue drilling until the hole is completed. Remove the drill and return the hand drill and twist drill to their proper places.

When using the electric drill press, see Fig. 7, remember the following rules:

1. *Make sure the holes are properly located and center punched.*
2. *Check the drill size. If the number is not clear, use a drill gage (device with holes corresponding to drill sizes).*
3. *Use high speed drills when using a drill with a high speed motor, as such drills are designed for high speeds.*
4. *Know what type of material is being drilled.*
5. *Be sure the drill is properly centered in the chuck by turning on the power for an instant.*
6. *Be sure the work is mounted properly in a holding device such as a vise or C clamp.*
7. *Adjust the table so that the point of the drill is slightly above the work, using the adjustable stop to secure the proper depth of the hole to be drilled. Be sure the drill does not bore into the table.*
8. *To reduce friction, use lubricants such as lard, or soluble oil and water for low carbon steels.*
9. *Check the centering of the drill*

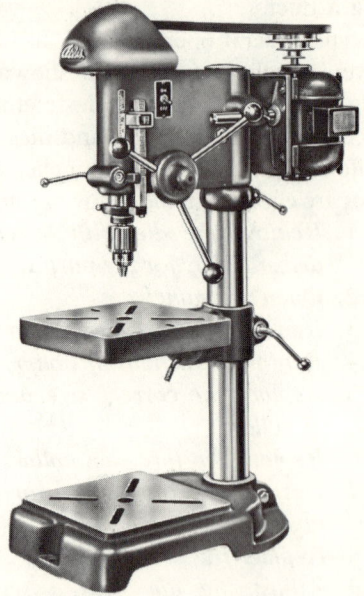

Figure 7. Electric drill press. (Courtesy: Atlas Press Co.)

after the point has just started in the metal; relocate the hole with a center punch if necessary.
10. *Feed the drill with a light, even pressure to prevent bending the drill.*
11. *Remove and return the drill to its proper place when finished.*
12. *If the drill does not produce a chip, it is dull. Stop immediately and have it sharpened.*

Riveting

Riveting may be done by hand or by machine. When the job is performed by hand, as is usually the case in sheet metal work, it is done with a hammer and rivet set.

TYPES OF RIVETS. There are many

types of rivets used in sheet metal work. The four most common types are the tinners', flathead, roundhead, and countersunk head as shown in Fig. 8. Tinners' and flathead rivets are used in most jobs of fabrication. The countersunk head is used when a flush surface is desired, and the roundhead when exceptional strength is required. Setting of these rivets is explained in following pages.

PARTS OF A RIVET. Each rivet consists of a head and a cylindrical body or shank. These are shown in Fig. 9. The end of the rivet which is upset is referred to as the formed or upset head. The length and diameter are measured as shown in the illustration immediately above.

RIVET SIZES. The size of tinners' rivets is determined by the weight of 1,000 rivets. For example 1 lb. rivets weigh 1 lb. per thousand, 2 lb. rivets 2 lb. per thousand. The length and diameter are shown in Table I.

Flathead rivets vary in diameter from $\frac{3}{32}''$ to $\frac{7}{16}''$ in $\frac{1}{32}''$ steps. Other rivets vary in diameter from $\frac{3}{8}''$ up to $1''$ in $\frac{1}{16}''$ steps.

Flathead, roundhead, and countersunk rivets may be purchased in various lengths depending upon the thickness of the sheets being joined. SELECTING PROPER RIVET SIZES. There are no definite rules to follow in selecting the size of a rivet. In general, the length should be sufficient to protrude through the pieces being joined from one, to one and one-half times the diameter of the rivet, as shown in Table II. This allows ample material for forming the upset head. FORMING RIVET HEADS. The shallow, cup-shaped hole shown by the cross-

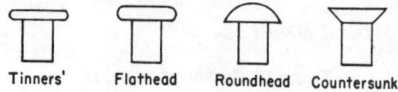

Figure 8. Types of rivets.

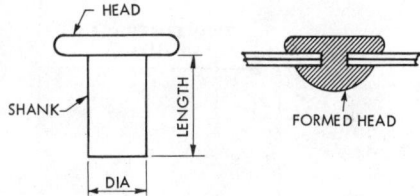

Figure 9. Parts of a rivet.

Table I. Tinners' Rivets.

Size	Diameter in Inches	Length in Inches	Size	Diameter in Inches	Length in Inches
4 oz.	.070	$\frac{1}{8}$	3½ lb.	.165	$2\frac{1}{64}$
6 oz.	.080	$\frac{9}{64}$	4 lb.	.175	$1\frac{1}{32}$
8 oz.	.089	$\frac{5}{32}$	5 lb.	.185	$\frac{3}{8}$
10 oz.	.095	$1\frac{11}{64}$	6 lb.	.203	$2\frac{5}{64}$
12 oz.	.105	$\frac{3}{16}$	7 lb.	.220	$1\frac{3}{32}$
14 oz.	.109	$1\frac{3}{64}$	8 lb.	.225	$\frac{7}{16}$
1 lb.	.112	$\frac{7}{32}$	9 lb.	.238	$2\frac{9}{64}$
1¼ lb.	.120	$1\frac{5}{64}$	10 lb.	.241	$1\frac{5}{32}$
1¾ lb.	.135	$\frac{1}{4}$	12 lb.	.253	$\frac{1}{2}$
2 lb.	.140	$1\frac{7}{64}$	14 lb.	.275	$3\frac{3}{64}$
2½ lb.	.148	$\frac{9}{32}$	16 lb.	.295	$1\frac{7}{32}$
3 lb.	.160	$\frac{5}{16}$			

Table II. Recommended Sizes for Tinners' Rivets.

Gage of Metal To Be Seamed	Size of Rivet Suggested
30	12 oz.
28	14 oz.
26	1 lb.
24	1½ lb.
22	2 lb.
20	3 lb.
18	4 lb.

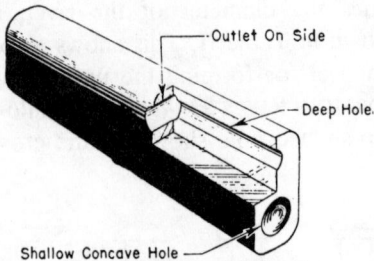

Figure 10. Section of a rivet set.

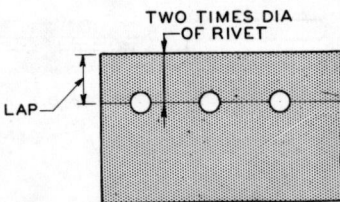

Figure 11. Lap required for riveting.

section view of a rivet set, Fig. 10, is used to form the head on the rivet. The deep hole is used to draw the sheets and the rivet together, and also to draw the rivets directly through thin metal without previously punching a hole. The outlet on the side allows the sheet metal slugs to drop out. The rivet set selected should have a hole slightly larger than the diameter of the rivet.

A good job of riveting can be done with not more than six normal blows of the hammer, and after a little practice this number can be cut in half. A skilled mechanic will perform the operation in sequence, as shown in Fig. 12, by striking one blow on the rivet set to draw the sheets together around the rivet; one blow to flatten the rivet down and another blow on the rivet set to complete the formed head of the rivet.

SPACING RIVET HOLES. Rivet holes should be spaced according to the specifications of the job. *The space from the edge of the metal to the center of the rivet line should be at least twice the diameter of the rivet,* as shown in Fig. 11, to prevent the rivets from tearing out. The minimum distance between rivets should be sufficient to allow the rivets to be drawn without interference, or about three times the rivet diameter. The maximum distance between rivets should never be such that the material is allowed to buckle between rivets.

The method of spacing rivet holes for longitudinal seams in pipe is somewhat different from the manner in which the rivet holes are spaced for cross seams. See Fig. 13.

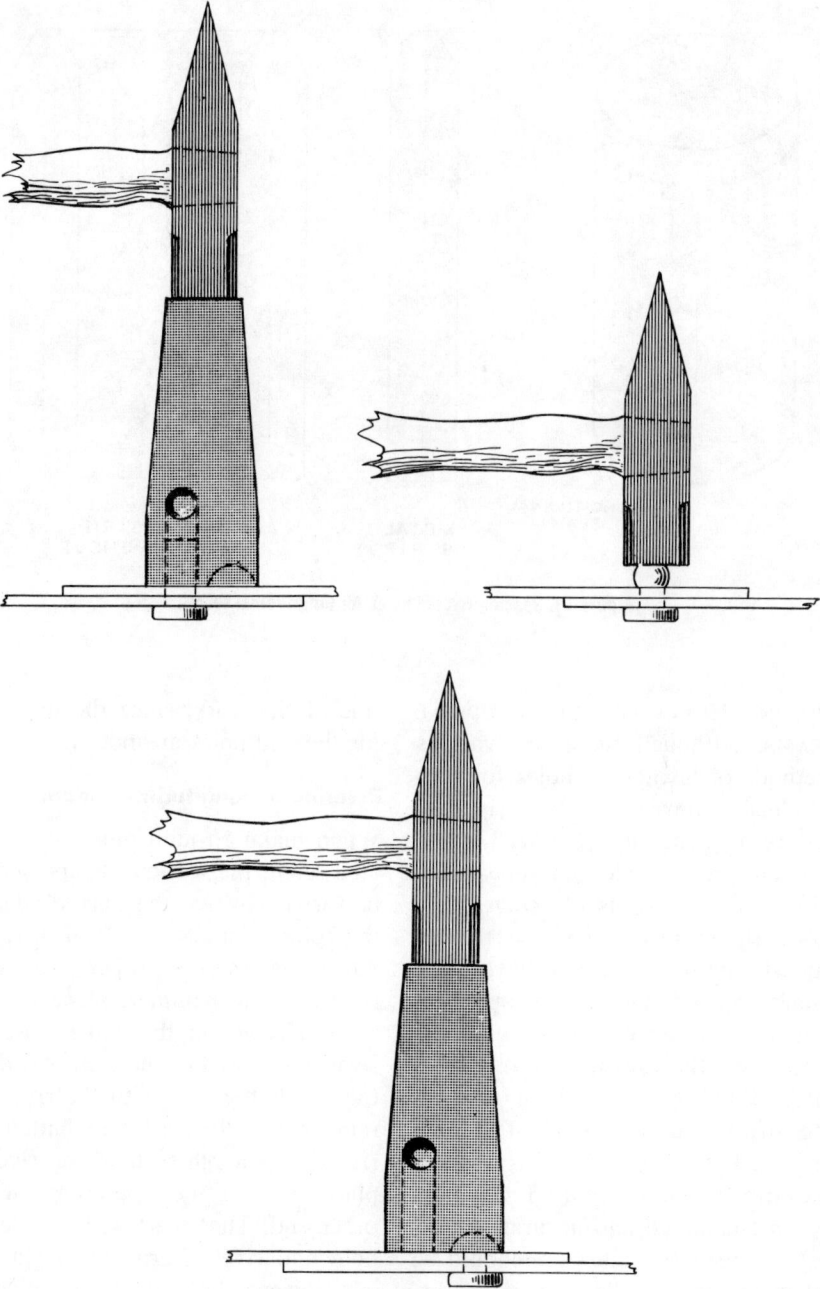

Figure 12. Steps in forming rivet head.

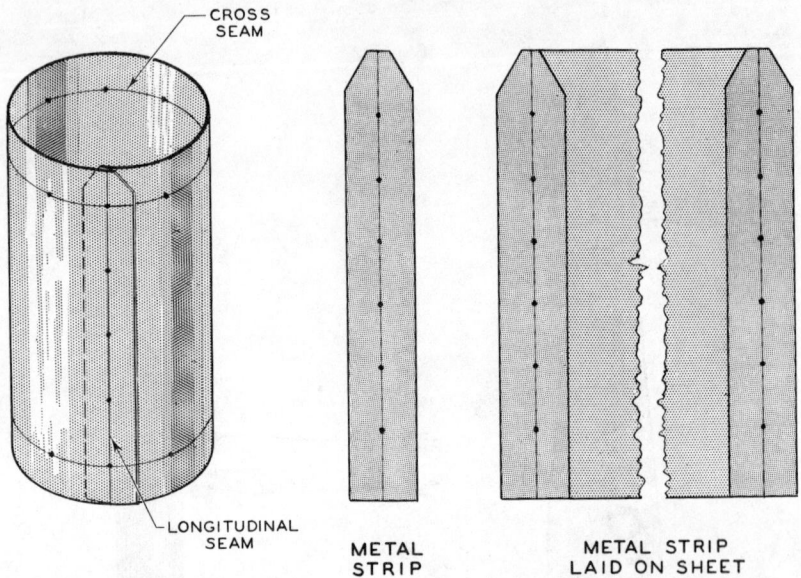

Figure 13. Spacing riveted holes for longitudinal seams.

SPACING HOLES FOR LONGITUDINAL SEAMS. Although there are various methods of laying out holes for longitudinal seams, the metal strip procedure is generally preferred when the same job is laid out repeatedly. This method consists of using a narrow strip of metal in which the required number of holes have been evenly spaced and center punched. The strip is laid on the edge of the metal and the location of the holes marked by prick punching through the strip onto the metal. The only drawback to this method is that as the strip is continually used, the holes become enlarged and accurate marking becomes difficult. Care should be taken to see that the strip is not reversed when switching to the opposite side of the work, since the distances for the end holes are not alike.

Riveting a longitudinal seam

When making round pipe with a riveted seam, the section of pipe should be formed so that the burred edge of the holes is on the outside of the pipe. After selecting the proper size rivets, rivet set, and hammer, place the job to be riveted on the stake. Insert a rivet in one end of the cylinder, draw the sheets together with the rivet set, remove the rivet set and flatten the rivet just enough to hold the rivet in place. Repeat the operation on the other end. Then start with the center hole and rivet alternately, right and left, toward the ends of the pipe. It may be that a bulge between the two

Figure 14. Feathering a riveted seam.

pieces will develop due to slight mis-alignment of the holes. If this happens, working from the center out will allow the bulge to be worked to the end of the pipe. The end rivet can still be removed and the bulge eliminated.

FINISHING A RIVETED SEAM. The seam is placed over the stake and the edges are flattened together, or *feathered*, with a mallet as shown in Fig. 14.

Removing rivets

There are occasions when it is necessary to remove a rivet. One method used for heavy gage material is to place the head of the rivet into a common nut a little larger than the head of the rivet and then punch the stem out through the formed head as shown in Fig. 15, and as described by the following steps.

1. *Place the rivet on a solid stake with the formed head upward (A).*
2. *With a ball peen hammer, flatten the head as much as possible without distorting metal (B).*
3. *Center punch the center of the head (C).*
4. *Place the head of the rivet into a nut a little larger than the head of the rivet. With a solid punch slightly smaller than the size of the rivet shank, punch the shank out of the head (D).*

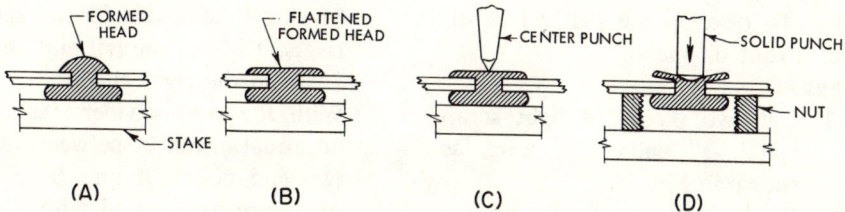

FORMED HEAD   FLATTENED FORMED HEAD   CENTER PUNCH   SOLID PUNCH

STAKE   NUT

(A)   (B)   (C)   (D)

Figure 15. Sequence of steps in removing a rivet.

On light gage sheet metal, the most satisfactory method of removing a rivet is by drilling. In this method the following steps are used.

1. *Flatten and center punch the exact center of the formed head.*
2. *Select a twist drill slightly smaller than the shank of the rivet.*
3. *Drill into the head of the rivet just up to the surface of the metal.*
4. *Remove the rivet head with a cold chisel.*
5. *Remove the sheared rivet with a solid punch as previously described.*

Still another method is to cut off the formed head using a sharp cold chisel, the remainder of the rivet being removed with a solid punch. In any method it is important to keep from distorting the metal or elongating the rivet hole.

Review Questions

1. For what is a solid punch used?
2. What is the advantage of a turret punch?
3. What is meant by the term button punching?
4. What is the purpose of the centering point on the end of the hand lever punch?
5. Sketch four types of rivet heads.
6. What is the total weight of 500, four pound rivets?
7. What is the recommended rivet size for seaming 26 gage?
8. What is the purpose of the hole in the side of the rivet set?
9. How is the width of the lap on a riveted seam determined?
10. Why is there an indentation in the rivet set?
11. When making a riveted seam, why is it necessary to rivet the ends first?
12. What is a metal strip used for when making a riveted seam?
13. What is meant by the term feather-edging a seam?
14. Give two ways to remove a rivet.

Projects

Project 6-1. Laying out the pattern for a riveted seam

AIM. To develop the method of direct layout on metal.

OPERATIONS

1. Cut two pieces of light scrap metal, 3″ wide, 18″ long, as shown in Fig. 16.
2. On both sheets, scribe a rivet line parallel to the edge and in from it a distance equal to twice the rivet diameter. (The rivet size will be 1 lb.)
3. Mark off the spaces for the end rivets, 1″ from the left end and 2″ from the right end.
4. With the steel dividers, space off equal distances between the two end points *A* and *B*. (Six rivets are to be used with five 3″ spaces between.)

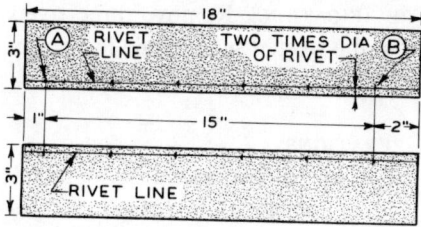

Figure 16. Method of laying out pattern for riveted seam.

5. Place the piece of metal on a flat wood surface and make the indentation marks using a prick punch and hammer.
6. With a lever punch or a turret punch of the proper size, punch holes through the indentation marks.

Project 6-2. Making a riveted seam

AIM. To develop the method of making a riveted seam and skill in the use of the rivet set.

OPERATIONS

1. Place together the two pieces of metal cut for Project 6-1 with the burrs of the holes turned up and the lap on the under side as shown in Fig. 17.
2. Using 1 lb. rivets, insert the rivet in the end hole; place the deep hole of the rivet set over the rivet, and strike the set a sharp blow with a riveting hammer. Keep the rivet head on a solid foundation.
3. Remove the rivet set and strike the rivet one or two blows with the riveting hammer, flattening the rivet sufficiently to make it fit tightly in the hole.
4. Place the indentation of the rivet set over the partly flattened rivet, and form the head. If the rivet head has been flattened too much in step 3, the rivet set will touch the sheet metal and leave scars when the rivet head is formed.
5. Insert the rivet in the hole at the opposite end and rivet as just described.

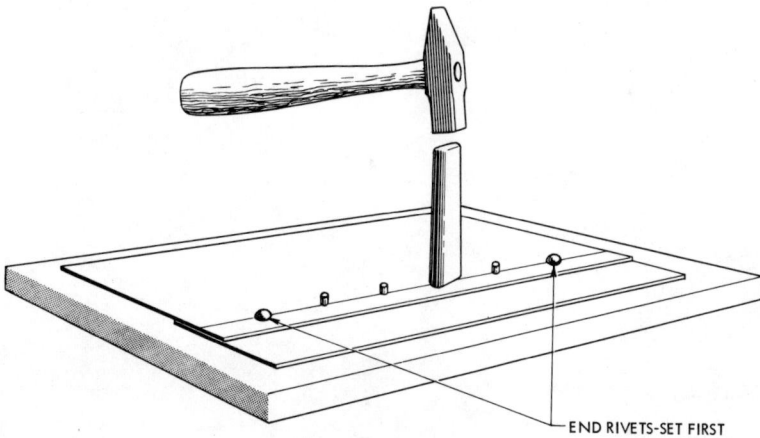

END RIVETS-SET FIRST

Figure 17. Riveting a seam.

6. Beginning with the nearest center hole, rivet alternately in each direction.

7. Turn in the finished seam to the instructor.

Project 6-3. Removing rivets from a seam

AIM. To give practice in removing rivets from a seam.

SPECIFICATIONS. Remove three rivets from the riveted seam made in Project 6-2.

OPERATIONS

1 Using a nut and a solid punch as explained in Chapter 6, remove every other rivet from the riveted seam completed in Project 6-2.

FOLDING EDGES AND MAKING SEAMS

How is the bar folder used and adjusted? How is the cornice brake used and adjusted? What are the common edges used in sheet metal work? How are they made? What are the common seams used in sheet metal work? How are they made?

Folding sheet metal to form edges and seams of various kinds is one of the most important operations in sheet metal work. The edges and seams have several purposes. They are used to improve the appearance of finished projects, to strengthen, and to fasten pieces of metal together. The equipment on hand and the amount of strain involved play an important part in selecting the kind of seam used.

Folding machines

Two types of machines are commonly used in bending or folding metal to form edges or locks for seams: 1. folders and 2. brakes. The two function differently in that the width of the bend is limited in the folding machine, while in the brake, any width of fold may be made. Each machine will be discussed to acquaint the student with their operations.

BAR FOLDER. This machine is adapted for bending edges of 22 gage metal or lighter. The bar folder shown in Fig. 1 consists of the following parts:

1. *Wing.* The wing forms the edges of the metal over the blade.
2. *Folding Blade.* The folding blade has a sharp beveled edge for forming sharp angles.
3. *Handle.* The handle turns the wing for making bends at various angles.
4. *Setscrews.* One setscrew is located in the shoe at each end of

89

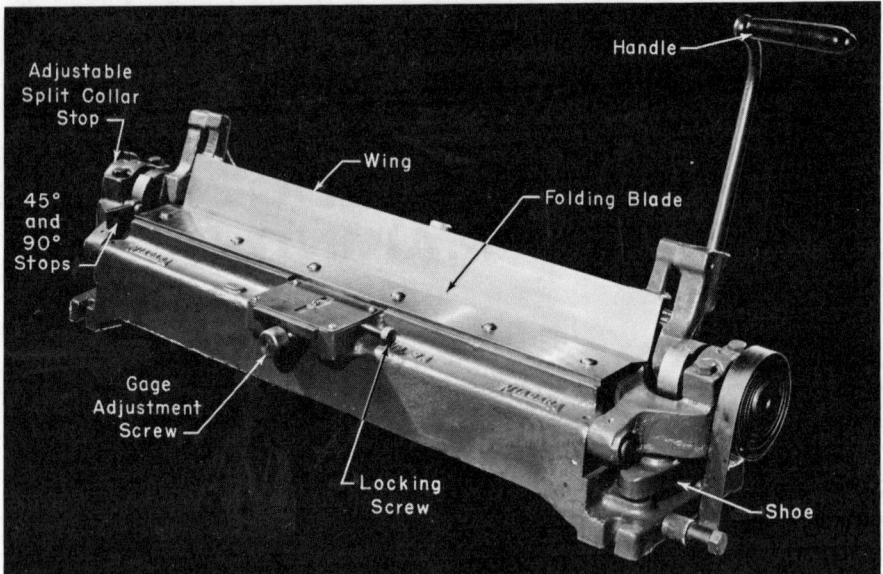

Figure 1. Bar Folder showing working parts. Courtesy: Niagara Machine and Tool Works.

the machine for the purpose of making adjustments for clearance when edging heavy metal or forming double locks.

5. *Gage adjustment screw.* This screw controls the gage for any desired width of edge by setting the dial correctly on the graduated scale.

6. *Graduated scale.* This scale is marked from $\frac{3}{32}''$ to $1''$ in sixteenth inch divisions.

7. *Locking screw.* This screw is for locking the gage adjustment to keep it from moving.

8. *Wedge adjusting screw.* This screw is located at the rear of the machine and is used for lowering or raising the wing. ·

9. *Wedge lock nut.* This is used for clamping the wedge adjusting screw firmly in place.

10. *Forty-five-degree stop.* This stop controls the handle making for a 45° bend.

11. *Adjustable collar.* This is used for setting for bends at any angle.

12. *Ninety-degree stop.* This stop controls the handle for a 90° angle.

13. *Frame.* The frame varies in length from 21″ to 36″ with a 22 gage capacity for mild steel.

Before the student actually begins to operate the bar folder, he should study the various adjustments and operations of the machine. There are six important steps that must be remembered when using the bar folder, namely:

1. *Allowance for the thickness of the metal.*
2. *Sharpness of the folded edge.*

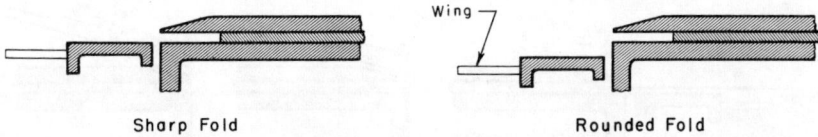

Figure 2. Cross-section view showing bar folder adjusted for sharp fold and for rounded fold.

3. *Width of the lock or edge.*
4. *Adjustment for the thickness of metal.*
5. *Angle of the fold.*
6. *Kind of metal.*

Each step should be carefully thought out before forming the edges because after the lock is turned, it is almost impossible to flatten the fold and turn it in the opposite direction without cracking or spoiling the appearance of the metal.

ALLOWANCE FOR METAL THICKNESS. When making various types of seams from metal of 26 gage or lighter, allowance for the thickness of the metal is not necessary. However, when heavier materials are to be used and accuracy is required, the actual amount of material taken up by the bend or fold must be considered. The amount necessary depends upon the thickness of the metal and the type of the seam or joint. The amount of material to be allowed for the various types of seams will be found under the topic "Seaming" later in this chapter.

SHARPNESS OF FOLDED EDGE. The sharpness of the folded edge is controlled by lowering or raising the wing. The cross-section view of the bar folder illustrated in Fig. 2 shows the wing raised for a sharp fold and then lowered for a thick, heavy edge. The wing is regulated simply by turn-

ing the wedge adjustment screw to the right for a sharp fold and to the left for a round fold. The wedge lock nut holds the wing in place when it is tightened with a key wrench.

WIDTH OF FOLDED EDGE. The illustration in Fig. 3 shows the working parts of the folder that control the width of the folded edge. The gage fingers are regulated by the adjusting screw on the graduated scale found on the front of the machine. The gage adjustment screw moves the fingers forward or backward to the required width of the lock, and the lock screw keeps the gage from creeping. The machine has a range for turning edges up to a width of one inch.

ADJUSTMENT FOR METAL THICKNESS. The clearance between the jaw and the folding blade determines the thickness of the metal that is to be bent. The setscrews in the shoes on each end of the folder will raise or lower the jaw for more or less clearance. After making the adjustment,

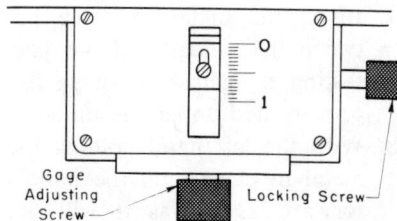

Figure 3. Gage for determining width of folded edge.

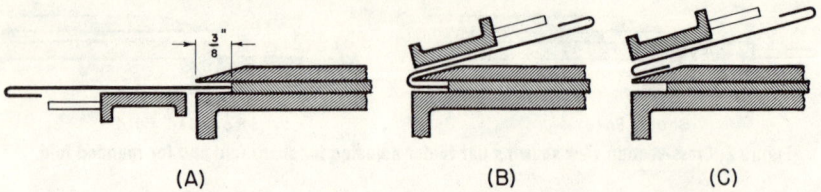

Figure 4. Cross-section view of bar folder showing how to form hemmed edge.

the lock nuts should be fastened to keep the screws from turning.

OPERATION OF THE BAR FOLDER. The procedure for making a single hem is illustrated in Fig. 4.

1. Set the gage by means of the gage adjusting screw to the width desired, in this case, ⅜ inch. See *A* of Fig. 4.
2. Tighten the lock screw to keep the gage from slipping.
3. Loosen the wedge lock nut in the rear of the machine.
4. Adjust the wedge screw to get the desired fold. For this particular operation, the fold should be sharp. Tighten the wedge lock nut.
5. Set the stop of the adjustable collar to the maximum angle.
6. Adjust the screw in the shoe on each side of the folder for the thickness of the metal. Be sure both sides of the machine are set identically.
7. Insert the metal in place between the blades and the jaw, resting it against the gage fingers located under the blade.
8. With the left hand holding the metal in place, pull the handle forward as far as it will go, making the bend, as shown in *B* of Fig. 4.

9. Return the handle to its former position and remove the sheet of metal. (Do not allow the handle to slam back.)
10. Place the sheet of metal back on the beveled part of the blade and as close to the wing as possible in the position shown in *C* of Fig. 4.
11. Hold the metal with the left hand and pull the operating handle briskly with the right hand, flattening the seam.

Brakes

There are many types of bending brakes used by sheet metal workers. The most widely used machine is the cornice brake. Before learning the operation of the cornice brake, it is well to make a careful study of the different parts of the brake. The worker should know the name of each part and where it is located. It is always well to keep in mind that skill in the operation of any machine depends on the operator's knowledge of its parts and adjustments.

PARTS OF THE BRAKE. The three basic parts of the brake are: the bed, top leaf, and bending leaf as shown in Fig. 5. In addition the parts indicated by number in the front, rear, and right side views of Fig. 5 show the parts nec-

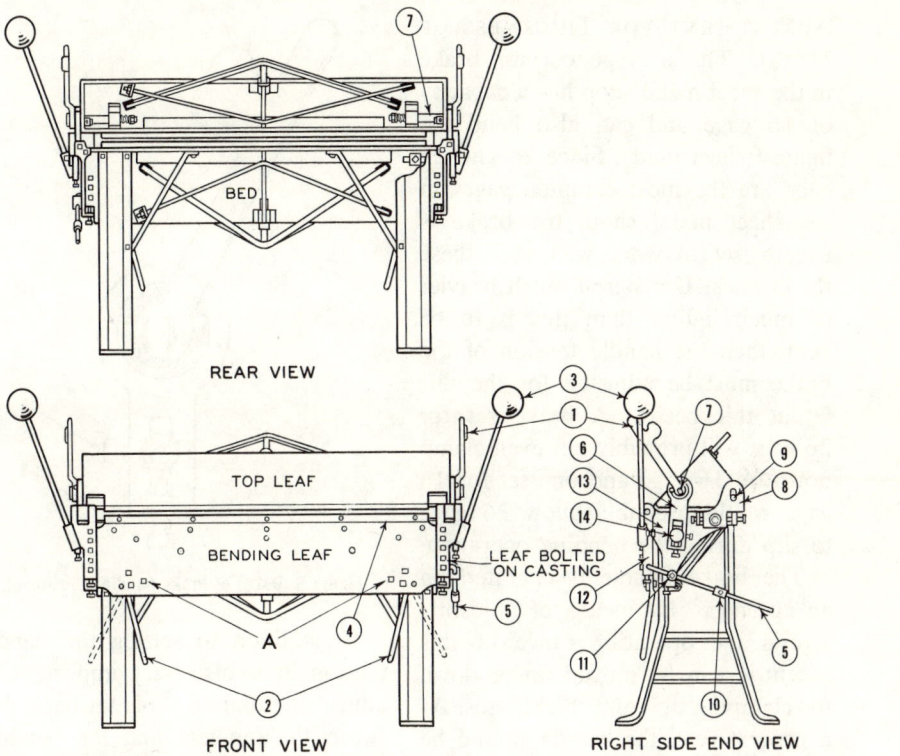

Figure 5. Cornice brake showing rear, front and right side views. Parts numbered 1-14 are those necessary for operation of brake.

essary for intelligent operation of the brake. These parts are:

1. Clamping handle on each side for holding the sheet in position.
2. Two-position handle on each side, for operating bending leaf.
3. Balance weights, adjustable to make bending operations easier.
4. Upper bending leaf bar, removable when bending small locks.
5. Adjustable stop gage, used to form any desired angle.
6. Clamping link which operates the top shaft.
7. Top shaft.
8. Slot casting for adjusting the

bending bar for various gages of metal.
9. Slot-casting pin.
10. Adjusting-stop slide on the stop gage for bending locks at various angles.
11. Stop-gage casting.
12. Bending-leaf casting.
13. Bed-end casting.
14. Link-adjusting block.

To regulate the angle of a bend when duplicate work is to be done, the adjusting stop is regulated to allow the bending bar to be raised to the desired angle for making the required number of bends.

ADJUSTMENT FOR THICKNESS OF METAL. The average cornice brake in the sheet metal shop has a capacity of 16 gage and can also bend the lightest sheet made. Since 24 and 26 gage are the most common gages in the sheet metal shop, the brake is usually set to work well with these thicknesses. If material much heavier or much lighter than this is to be bent, then the handle tension of the brake must be adjusted for the different thicknesses. A brake set for 26 gage will probably not even clamp down on 16 gage and one set for 16 gage would probably allow 26 gage to slip during the bending operation.

The brake handle is operated on an eccentric. By means of adjusting screws the operating range of this eccentric can be moved up or down for clamping different thicknesses. As a general rule, the handle should be adjusted so that about a ten-pound pull will set it. Fig. 6 shows the detail of the handle mechanism as shown by numbers 6 and 14 in Fig. 5. In Fig. 6, screw *A* is the set screw that locks the adjustment. To adjust the tension, first loosen this screw. Then turn screw *B* in to tighten the handle tension and out to loosen it. By adjusting screw *B* and testing the handle while a sample of metal is in the brake, the proper tension can be reached. Then tighten screw *A* to again lock the handle adjustment. The handle adjustment should be made on both ends of the brake. Too much difference in handle adjustment will result in uneven bending by the brake.

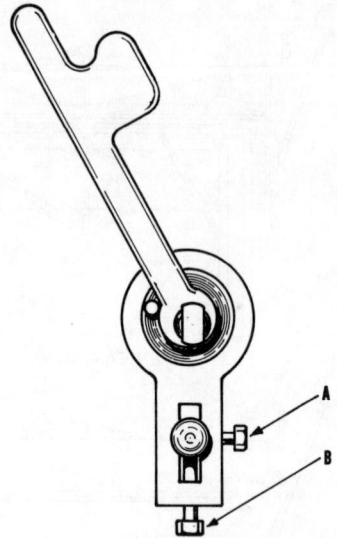

Figure 6. Detail of brake handle adjustment.

In addition to setting the handle tension, it is also very important to adjust the amount of set-back between the top leaf and the bending leaf. Fig. 7 shows the importance of this. If there were no allowance for the metal between the top leaf and the bending leaf, then the metal between the top leaf and bending leaf would crack or distort, or parts of the brake would be damaged. The general rule for set-back is to allow 1½ times the thickness of the metal for 22 gage or lighter. For everything thicker than 22 gage, allow 2 times the thickness of the metal. Exceptions for special cases may be made, of course. If for some reason a very sharp corner on the bend is necessary, the set-back could be brought up to the thickness of the metal, but never smaller than this. For very brittle metal which would break when bent,

SET-BACK MUST EQUAL 1 1/2 TO 2 TIMES THICKNESS OF METAL

TOP LEAF

BED

BENDING LEAF

(A)

WITH SET-BACK THERE IS SPACE FOR THE FORMED METAL

BENDING LEAF

TOP LEAF

BED

(B)

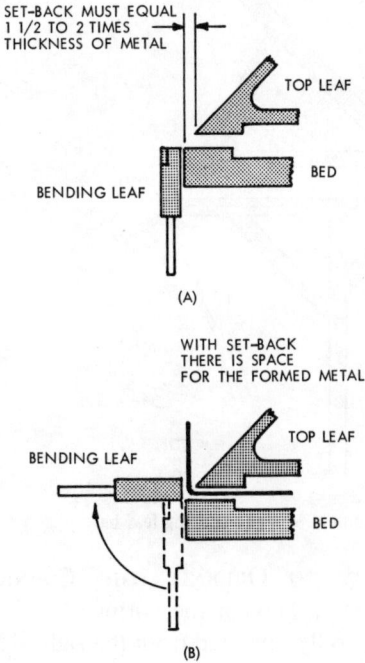

Figure 7. Adjusting set-back between brake top leaf and bending leaf.

the set-back can be very large to make a radius in the bend. In making a radius bend, a piece of sheet metal is often slipped over the nose of the top leaf to eliminate the sharp edge and further increase the bend radius.

The adjusting mechanism for making the set-back is shown in detail in Fig. 8. It is also shown as numbers 8 and 9 in Fig. 5. There is a duplicate mechanism in the other end of the brake, and both ends must be adjusted exactly the same or the brake will bend the metal more on one end than on the other.

To make the set-back adjustment, first loosen the set screw E in Fig. 8.

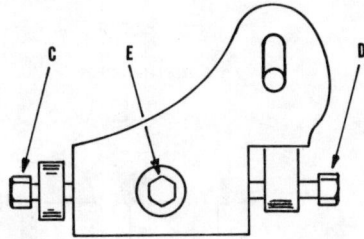

C   E   D

Figure 8. Brake set-back adjusting mechanism.

Then the two adjusting screws C and D are moved to obtain the proper set-back screw C moves the top leaf back, while screw D moves the top leaf forward. When the proper adjustment is made, both adjusting screws and the set screw must be tightened. Otherwise the top leaf will creep when it is clamped on the metal.

OTHER ADJUSTMENTS ON THE BRAKE. There are other adjustments on the cornice brake which are major ones and therefore should only be made by a qualified person.

However, an adjustment the sheet metal worker may be called upon to make is the one shown in A of Fig. 5. This is a bolt and nut through the double wall of the bending leaf. Sometimes, when bending long pieces, the bending leaf will bend to a different angle on the ends than it does in the center. Tightening or loosening these two bolts will equalize the amount bent over the entire length of the brake.

FORMING MOLDS. The formers or forming molds shown in Fig. 9 are attached to the bending leaf of the brake by friction clamps or dogs. Different types of molds are used when forming curved shapes such as cor-

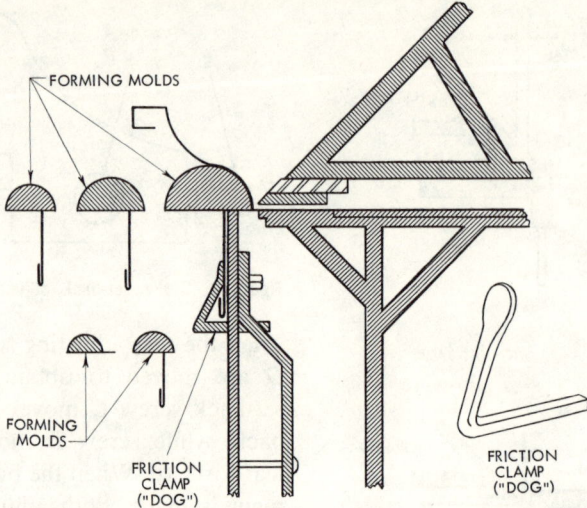

Figure 9. Forming molds and means of attachment to brake bending leaf bar.

nices, skylight bars, and many other articles having rounded and reversed bends, as shown in Fig. 10.

HOW TO OPERATE THE CORNICE BRAKE. Though the cornice brake is generally operated from the right side,

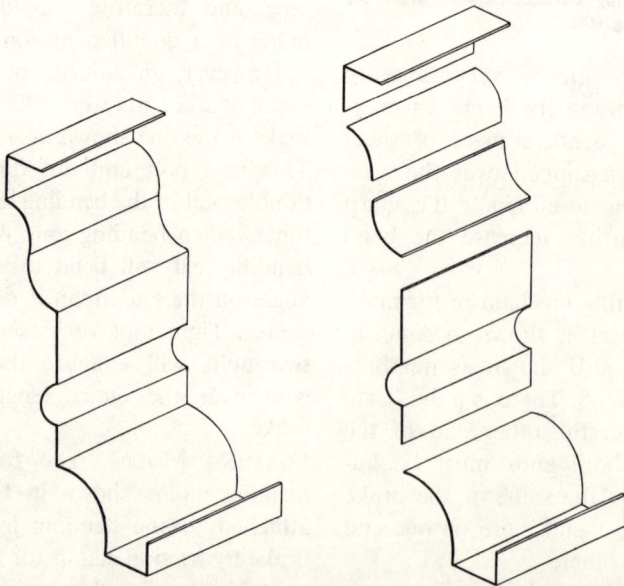

Figure 10. Rounded and reversed bends made on brake by use of forming molds.

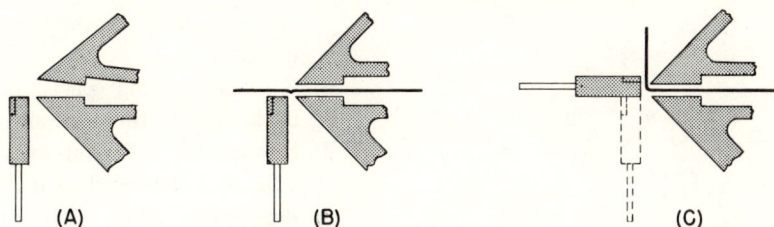

Figure 11. Making sharp right-angle bend in cornice brake.

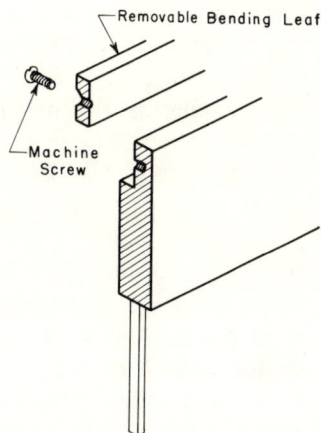

Figure 12. Removing the outer bending leaf to make narrow bends.

it is designed so that it may be operated from either side.

When making a sharp, right angle bend, the clamping bar is opened as shown in *A* of Fig. 11, by pushing back the clamping handle. The sheet of metal is placed with the prick-punch marks flush with the edge of the top leaf shown at *B*. The sheet is held in place with the left hand, and the top leaf is pulled down with the right hand to clamp the sheet to keep it from creeping. The desired bend is made by raising the bending-leaf handle to the proper position, as in *C*.

When making narrow or reverse bends of ¼″ or smaller, the ¼″

bending leaf is removed, as in Fig. 12, which enables the smaller bend to be made. This is done by removing the machine screws. Since removing this bar reduces the bending capacity of the brake, it should be replaced after making narrow bends.

When bending heavy gage metal, a reinforcing bar or angle iron is attached to the bending leaf to give it added support, as shown in Fig. 13. The bar is attached to the bending leaf by inserting friction clamps in the holes of the bending leaf.

The method of squeezing a turned edge or closing a seam is shown in Fig. 14. The seam is inserted between the clamping blades and the clamping handle is pulled forward as far as possible, closing the seam.

When forming heavy gage metal, the bending leaf is adjusted for the thickness of the metal by loosening

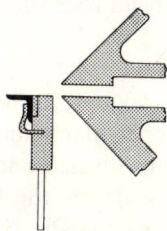

Figure 13. Attaching reinforcing bar to form heavy gage metal.

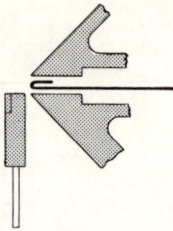

Figure 14. How to close a seam or squeeze a turned edge.

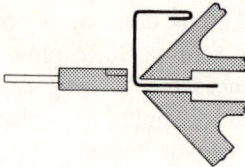

Figure 15. How to form a square duct with the cornice brake.

the cap screw and adjusting the set-screws until the bending has the proper amount of clearance.

The method of forming a square duct is shown in Fig. 15. Notice that the inside lock is turned before the duct is formed to shape.

CARE AND SAFETY IN USING THE CORNICE BRAKE. It is important that the sheet metal worker know the safe way of operating the cornice brake. Remember that the only correct way of operating a cornice brake is the safe way.

1. Never bend rods or wires in the brake.
2. Pound on metal in the brake with a wooden mallet only.
3. For proper functioning, a brake should be leveled and bolted to the floor. If the top leaf creeps when the handle is clamped down, wedge up one leg on that end until the creeping is eliminated.
4. Oil all moving parts of the brake every three months.
5. Beware of the counterbalance balls and the bending leaf handles when you are near the brake.
6. The capacity of the brake is given on a plate on the end of the brake by a double set of numbers such as "16-8." The first number is the maximum gage of metal that can be bent and the second number is the length of the brake. The capacity is for mild or "low carbon" steel, for the length of the brake when the reinforcing bar is in place. Mild steel is both ductile and malleable but has a lower tensile strength and elastic limit than "high carbon" or hard steels. Thus, 16-8 means that 16 gage metal 8 feet long can be bent when the reinforcing bar is in place. Without the reinforcing bar, the capacity of the brake is four gages lighter. Metal thicker than the gage capacity given can be bent on the brake so long as it is not for the full length. For example, on a 16-8 brake, 14 gage can be bent for a length of two or three feet, so long as the reinforcing bar is in place. When metal exceeds the thickness of the gage capacity, it depends on judgment and experience of the sheet metal worker as to whether it is beyond capacity.

7. When bending heavy metal for seams and similar operations, remember that you can gain considerable mechanical advantage through the leverage principle by clamping down the handle nearest the work first and leaving the handle farthest from the work for last.

8. Never use any pipe extensions on the brake handles to clamp down the work. You are over-straining the machine by so doing.

9. Remember that the gap in the top leaf of the brake at each end is a considerable aid in forming objects since it allows bent edges to fit in the gap without smashing them down. Often a part may be bent on one end of the brake without smashing edges; whereas it would be impossible to do on the other end.

Edges

Whenever a sheet metal object is made, some type of edge must also be formed. It is seldom that any object is made without some sort of edge to give the product a finished appearance. In addition to providing a finish, an edge eliminates the raw edge of the metal that is likely to cut someone and provides additional strength for the edge. Some edges provide only a small amount of strength, while other edges give maximum rigidity. Figure 16 shows some of the sheet metal edges commonly used.

SINGLE HEM. The *single hem* is a folded edge on the metal made in order to increase its strength and to make a smooth finished edge. It is one of the most common of all edges since it is the simplest to form. The hem is folded over in the brake and then inserted in the brake and smashed flat. The allowance for the hem is generally ¼". However, on metal heavier than 22 gage, it is common practice to increase the hem to $\frac{5}{16}$" or ⅜", since the larger edge is easier to bend. A hem is seldom over ½" wide because large hems tend to wrinkle at the edges giving a poor appearance.

DOUBLE HEM. The *double hem* is simply a single hem done twice. Again, it is an easy edge to make, but it provides much greater strength than the single hem. The allowance for a double hem is twice the hem size less $\frac{1}{16}$". The inside allowance, shown in *A* of Fig. 17 is made to the hem size—generally $\frac{5}{16}$" or ⅜". The outside allowance is made $\frac{1}{16}$" less than the hem size. This is because the outside line is bent first and it must be short so that it does not cover up the second bend line.

Wired edges

For a greater amount of strength than that provided by the double hem, the *wired edge* is used. This is done by wrapping the sheet metal around a piece of wire. In manufactured products, wired edges are often formed without any wire and are simply hollow circles of metal. In the sheet metal shop, however, the wire is always used in the edge. The wired

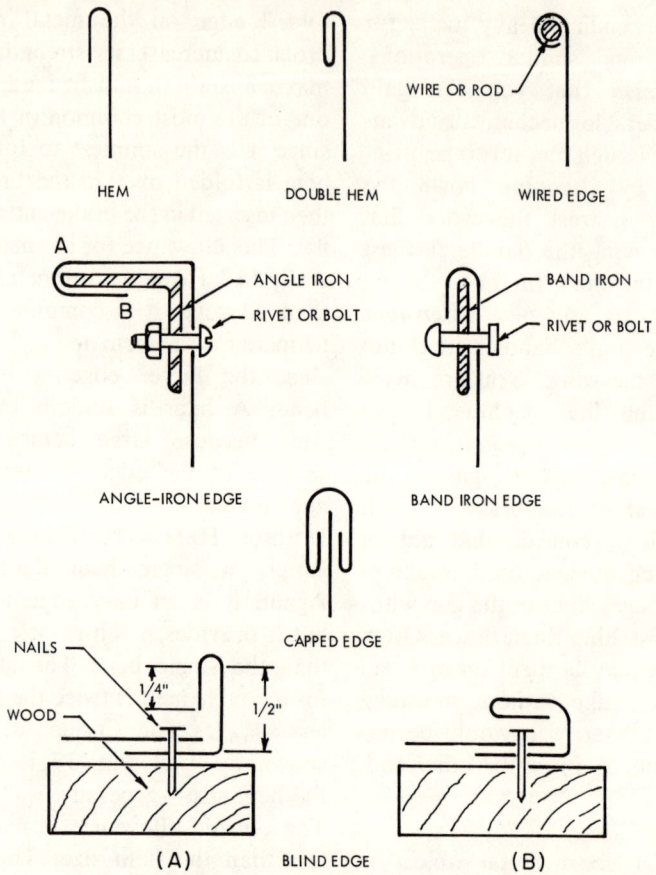

Figure 16. Some of the commonly used sheet metal edges.

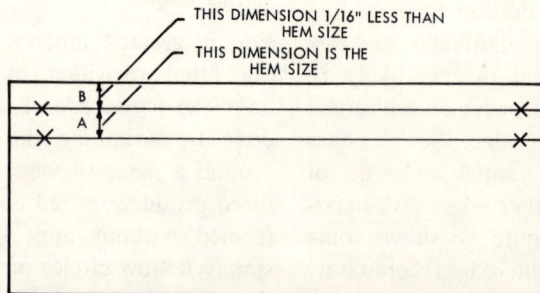

Figure 17. Inside and outside allowances for double hem.

edge is not used as often as it once was because of the time and skill involved in producing it. However, every student who studies the sheet metal trade should know how to make a wired edge.

ALLOWANCE FOR A WIRED EDGE. The allowance added to the pattern for a wired edge depends upon the diameter of the wire. For 26 gage and lighter, 2½ times the diameter of the wire is added to the pattern. For example, if ¼″ diameter wire is to be used, allowance for the wired edge = ¼″ × 2½ or ⅝″.

For 24 gage metal and heavier, allowances must be made for the thickness of the metal in addition to the diameter of the wire, which varies from 2 to 2½ times the thickness of the metal.

The allowance for a wired edge may also be found by folding a narrow strip of metal around the wire, then straightening it out and measuring it. This gives the exact amount required for the edge.

PREPARING A WIRED EDGE. There are a number of methods by which the edges of sheet metal may be prepared for wiring. The method selected depends largely upon the shape of the article. Cylindrically shaped articles, whenever possible, are wired before they are formed to shape. Tapering articles are wired after they have been formed. The following review of information should be studied carefully before starting wiring projects:

1. Wired edges for cylindrical articles should, whenever possible, be wired while the metal is flat.

2. The cutting pliers or cutting nippers should be used to cut wire.

3. Bolt cutters can be used to cut heavy wire and rod.

4. The bar folding machine should be used whenever possible in making a wired edge.

5. A cornice brake is used to turn the edges of extra long metal.

6. A properly turned edge in the bar folding machine makes it unnecessary to use a mallet to form the metal over the wire.

7. When using the cornice brake, it is necessary to use a mallet to form the metal over the wire.

ANGLE IRON AND BAND IRON EDGES. For maximum strength, the band iron edge or the angle iron edge is often used. The band iron edge provides as much strength as a wired edge and is easier to form. The angle iron edge provides more strength than any other edge and is equally easy to form. These two edges are really the same except that they employ different shapes of stock around which the metal wraps. Depending upon the conditions of the job, the band iron may be most suitable or the angle iron may be best. The amount of metal to allow to wrap around the edges is the thickness of the angle or bar plus ⅜″. Thus, if ⅛″ band or angle is used, the distance from *A* to *B* in Fig. 16 would be ⅛ + ⅜ = ½″. Generally, 1″ × ⅛″ band iron or 1″ × ⅛″ angle iron is used for the stock. However, any size could be used.

CAPPED EDGE. The capped edge

shown in Fig. 16 is generally an emergency edge used when the ordinary edge was forgotten or, more often, when a sheet metal object is cut down and a raw edge is exposed that must be covered. The width of the cap is generally about ½″ on each side, though it will vary with job conditions. It is simply a strip of metal bent as shown and slipped over the raw edge of the metal. Generally, the cap is held in place by tack soldering, though it is sometimes riveted or bolted.

BLIND EDGE. The blind edge shown in Fig. 16 has many names such as "false edge" and "Dutchman." It is used to cover nail heads and the raw edges of sheet metal when sheets must be nailed to a wooden surface, such as in covering a door with metal. A formed strip of metal is slipped under the sheet and nails are driven through both pieces of metal, close to the edge as shown in *A*. After the nails are all driven in to secure the sheet, the upright edge is carefully pounded down with a mallet so that the nail heads are covered and the edge of the metal has the appearance of a double hem. This same edge can be used in the same way to finish a joint where two sheets of metal must be joined over wood.

Seaming

In sheet metal construction, there are a variety of methods for joining the edges of sheet metal. These methods, however, may be generally classified as either *mechanical* or *welded*. The choice of the seam is determined primarily by the thickness of the metal, the kind of metal, the cost of fabrication, and the equipment available for making the seam. However, it is obvious that the mechanical seam is used when joining light and medium gage metal and that, when joining heavier metal, a riveted or welded seam is necessary.

In planning the fabrication of sheet metal articles, the worker should be able to visualize the type of seam that is best fitted for the specific job. It is for this reason that the various types of mechanical seams are diagrammatically shown in Fig. 18.

Types of seams

GROOVED SEAM. One of the most common types of seams used in joining the edges of light or medium gage sheet metal is called a grooved seam. This seam consists of two folded edges called "locks" as shown in *A*, Fig. 19. The two edges are hooked together as in *B*, and locked together at *C* with a grooving tool called a hand groover or with a grooving machine. The width of the lock is shown by *W*.

When making a grooved seam, it is necessary to make allowance for the amount of material that is to be added for the lock. The amount depends largely upon the width of the lock and the thickness of the metal.

The formula for finding the amount of material for a grooved seam is as follows:

24 gage or lighter = 3 × width of lock.

22 gage or heavier = 3 × width

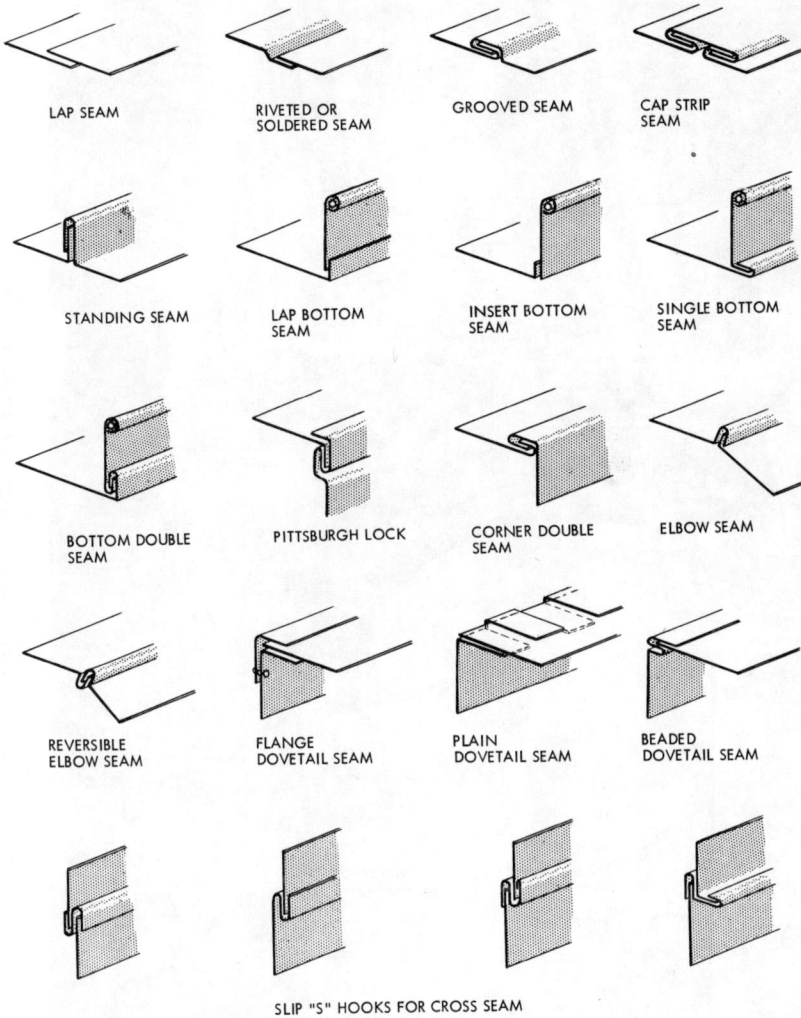

LAP SEAM	RIVETED OR SOLDERED SEAM	GROOVED SEAM	CAP STRIP SEAM
STANDING SEAM	LAP BOTTOM SEAM	INSERT BOTTOM SEAM	SINGLE BOTTOM SEAM
BOTTOM DOUBLE SEAM	PITTSBURGH LOCK	CORNER DOUBLE SEAM	ELBOW SEAM
REVERSIBLE ELBOW SEAM	FLANGE DOVETAIL SEAM	PLAIN DOVETAIL SEAM	BEADED DOVETAIL SEAM

SLIP "S" HOOKS FOR CROSS SEAM

Figure 18. Common seams used in sheet metal work.

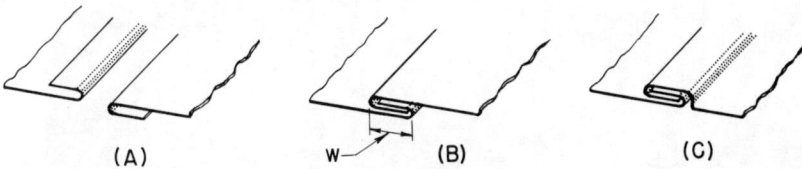

(A)   W →| (B)   (C)

Figure 19. Grooved seam formed by two "locks" shown at (A), hooked together (B), and locked together (C).

Figure 20. Pittsburgh seams are used to join corners of ducts such as these. Courtesy: Heating and Air Conditioning Magazine.

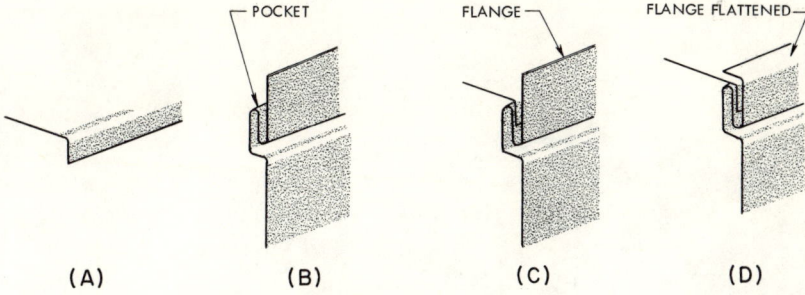

Figure 21. How to form a Pittsburgh seam.

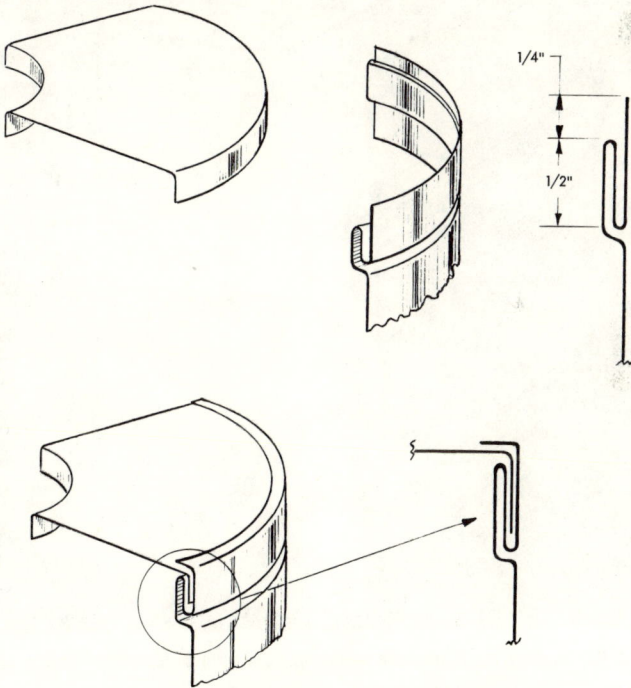

Figure 22. Pittsburgh seams can be turned on curves.

of lock plus 5 × thickness of metal.

Half of the above allowances are to be added to each side of the pat-

tern. Grooved seams are rarely used in metal heavier than 20 gage.

The most accurate method of find-

Figure 23. Roll-forming machines such as this one are used to form Pittsburgh seams.

ing the amount of material for a grooved seam is to take a 1″ strip of metal 6″ long and cut it into two parts at right angles to the length. Turn the required lock at one end of each piece and groove together. Measure the length of the strip. The difference between this dimension and the original length of the strip will be the exact amount which must be added for the seam.

PITTSBURGH SEAM. This seam is

sometimes called a hammer lock or hobo lock. It is used as a longitudinal corner seam for variously shaped pipes such as the duct shown in Fig. 20. The seam consists of two parts, the single lock as in *A* of Fig. 21, and the pocket lock at *B*. The single lock is placed in the pocket lock *C* and the flange is hammered over, *D*.

One of the advantages of the Pittsburgh seam is that the single lock can be turned on a curve and the pocket lock can be formed on a flat sheet and then rolled to fit the curve as shown in Fig. 22.

The Pittsburgh seam is the most commonly used of any seam in the sheet metal shop. It is so common that special machines called roll-forming machines, such as the one shown in Fig. 23 are in every general sheet metal shop. With these machines, the metal is inserted in one end and runs through a series of rolls so that it emerges from the other end with the pocket lock completely formed. In shops where there is no roll-forming machine, the Pittsburgh seam is formed on the brake in the steps shown in Fig. 24. The allowance for the Pittsburgh seam when formed in the brake is 1¼″, as shown in *A* of Fig. 24. Then the Pittsburgh seam is formed in the following manner:

Step 1—Bend 90° on the 1¼″ line.

Step 2—Remove metal and insert 1¼″ edge into the brake with the large part of the metal pressed tightly against the leaf of the brake. This makes a second bend ½″ from the first.

Step 3—With metal in position of Step 2, bend it as far as the brake will bend.

Step 4—Remove metal and replace in the brake as in position of Step 1. Then bend 1¼″ line (which was bent to 90° in Step 1).

Step 5—Metal will be in position shown by dotted line. With wooden mallet, beat metal down to position shown by solid lines in Step 5.

Step 6—Slide metal in brake and flatten with upper leaf.

Step 7—Remove metal and turn it over so edge of upper leaf clamps just back of the point indicated by *A*. This position is determined by holding the point indicated by *B* just past the outside edge of the bending leaf. Since the bending leaf is ½″ wide and the distance from *B* to *A* is also ½″, this means the metal is in position. After metal is clamped, bend it slightly (approximately 15° angle) as shown by dotted lines. Then pound it down with wooden mallet to position shown by solid lines.

DRIVE-CLIP SEAM. This seam is generally used in connection with S clips for connecting cross seams on ducts. However, it is sometimes used for joining other sheet metal objects.

The seam is made by turning edges as shown in *A* of Fig. 25 on the two pieces to be joined. These edges will vary with job conditions, however, the common width is ½″. The actual drive clip is formed as shown in *B* of Fig. 25. Often the clip will have to be driven on with a hammer, which is the reason for its name.

S-CLIP SEAM. The S clip is an S

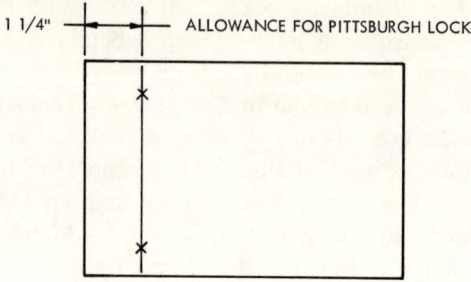

1 1/4" ◄——————► ALLOWANCE FOR PITTSBURGH LOCK

(A)

1 1/4"

BENDING
LEAF

STEP 1

1 1/4"

1/2"

STEP 2

1/2"

3/4"

STEP 3

3/4"

1/2"

STEP 4

STEP 5

STEP 6

B

A

STEP 7

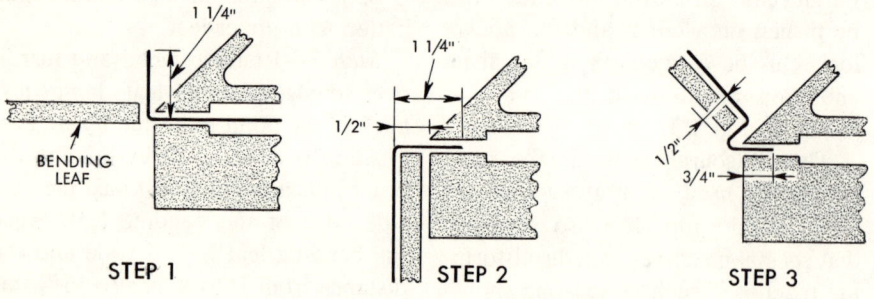

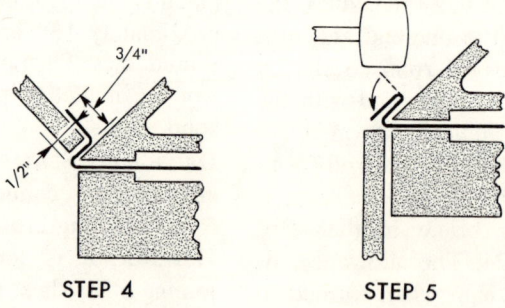

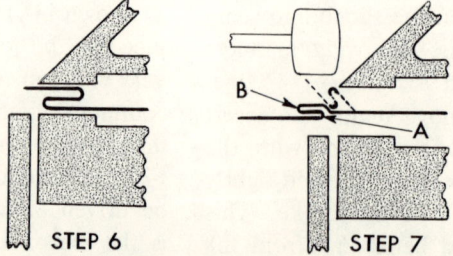

Figure 24. Pittsburgh seams may be formed on the brake by the steps shown.

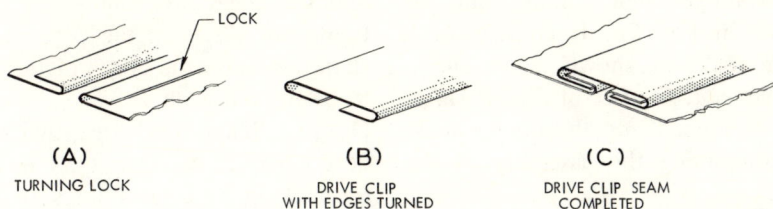

(A)
TURNING LOCK

(B)
DRIVE CLIP
WITH EDGES TURNED

(C)
DRIVE CLIP SEAM
COMPLETED

Figure 25. Drive-clip seams are made by turning edges (A), forming drive clip (B) and attaching (C).

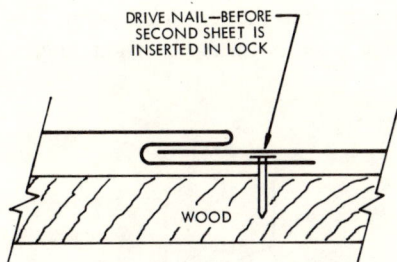

Figure 26. S clips are used to join ducts or to join sheet metal pieces covering a wall.

shaped piece of metal that forms two pocket locks for the joining metal to slip in as shown in Fig. 18. As with the drive clip, the most common application of the S clip is in joining sections of duct. However, it is also often used wherever two joining sections of metal need to be held in a flat seam and where there is no need for strength in holding the two pieces together. Often in covering a wall with sheet metal, the S clip is bent on the edge of the sheet and is used as shown in Fig. 26.

Fig. 27 shows how the S and drive clips are used to join sections of duct. SLIP-JOINT SEAM. This seam is used

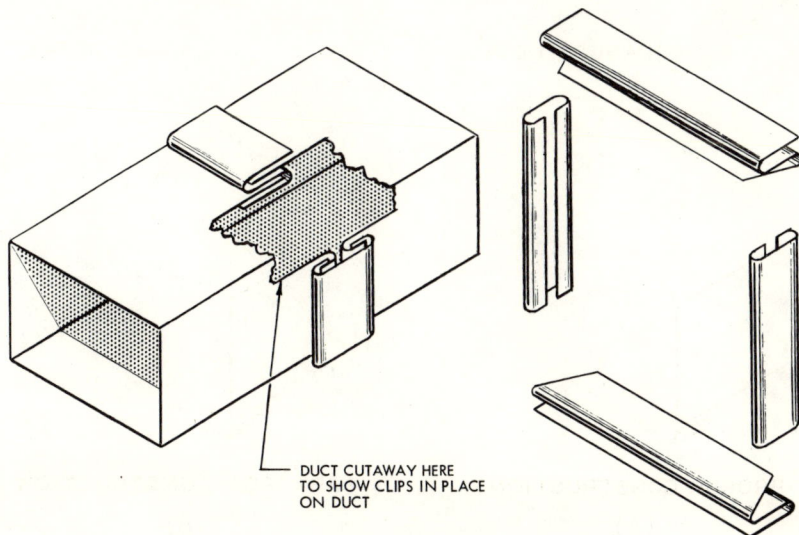

Figure 27. S and drive clips used to join duct sections.

for a longitudinal corner seam, as shown in Fig. 28. It consists of a single lock, as shown at *A* and a double lock, pictured at *B*. The single lock is slipped into the double lock, *C*, completing the assembly of the seam.

When making pipes with a slip-joint seam, as shown at *A*, in Fig. 29, great care should be taken to see that the corners of the metal are squared and the edges are trimmed. Failure to do so will twist the pipe out of shape or cause the edges of the pipe to be uneven as at *B*.

DOUBLE SEAM. There are two types of double seams. One type is used for making irregular fittings such as square elbows, offsets, boxes, etc. The double seam is made somewhat differently than the slip-joint seam. The single edge is turned at right angles,

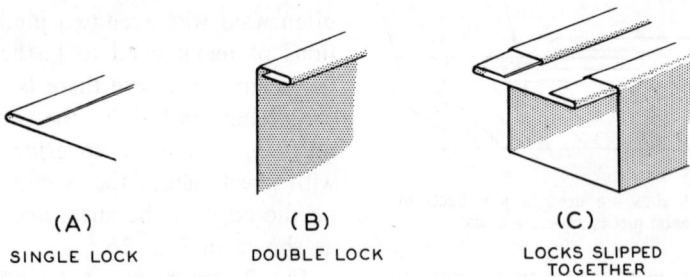

(A)
SINGLE LOCK

(B)
DOUBLE LOCK

(C)
LOCKS SLIPPED
TOGETHER

Figure 28. Slip joint seam.

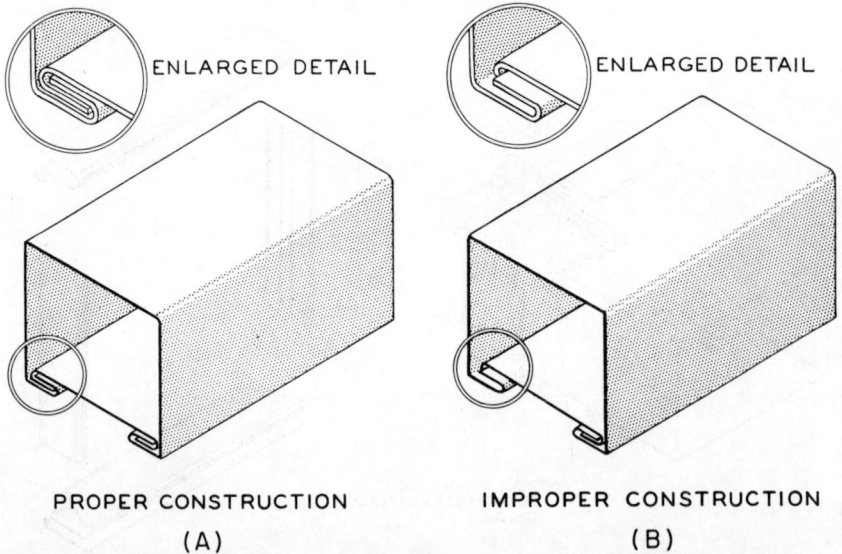

ENLARGED DETAIL

ENLARGED DETAIL

PROPER CONSTRUCTION

IMPROPER CONSTRUCTION

(A)

(B)

Figure 29. Proper and improper joining of slip joint seams in pipe construction.

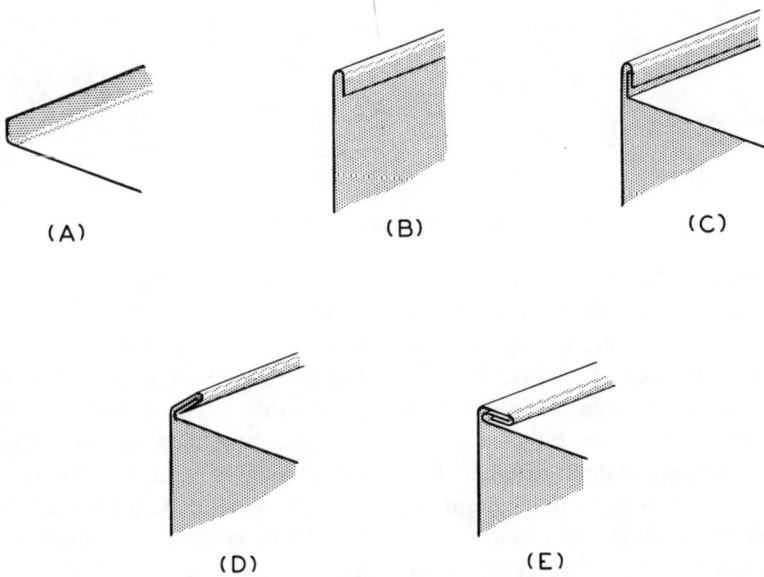

Figure 30. Making a double seam.

as shown at *A* in Fig. 30. The double edge is formed as at *B*. It is placed over the single edge as at *C*, and is double seamed over a stake, as shown at *D*. The completed seam is shown at *E*.

BOTTOM DOUBLE SEAM. This seam is used to fasten bottoms to cylindrically shaped articles such as pails, tanks, etc. The operations for making this type of seam are as follows: The single edge shown at *A*, Fig. 31, is turned on the body of the cylinder by means of a turning machine. The burr is turned on the bottom, *B*, using a burring machine. The bottom is snapped on the body, *C*, and is peened down as at *D*; the seam is completed by using a mallet as at *E*.

HANDY SEAM. A typical longitudinal seam is shown in Fig. 32. Though similar to a grooved seam, it does not require a grooving tool. The seam consists of a double edge turned at

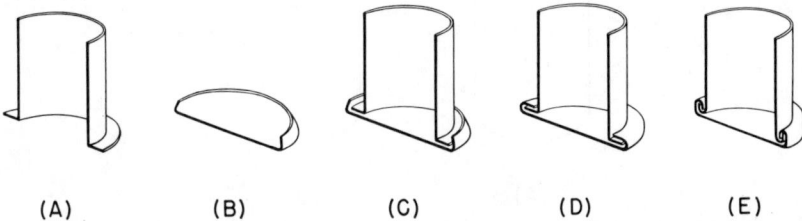

Figure 31. Making a bottom double seam to fasten cylindrically shaped objects.

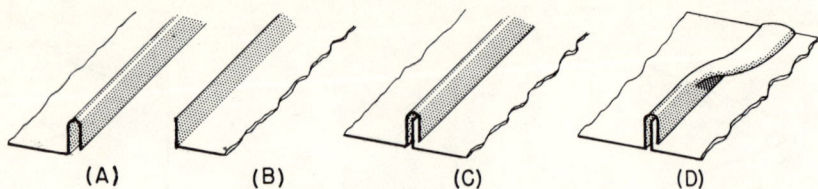

Figure 32. How to form a handy seam.

right angles, shown at *A*, and a single edge, *B.* The double edge is placed over the single edge, *C*, and is hammered over with a mallet, *D*. The handy seam prevents the edges from buckling when two full sheets of metal are being seamed together. It is generally used in large ducts requiring two or more sheets of metal.

DOVETAIL SEAM. This seam is an easy and convenient method of joining collars to flanges. There are three types of dovetails: the plain dovetail, the beaded dovetail, and the flange dovetail. The dovetail seam is principally used on round or elliptical pipe, and seldom on rectangular duct.

PLAIN DOVETAIL SEAM. This seam is used when joining a collar to a flange without the use of solder, screws, or rivets. It is made by slitting the end of the collar and bending every other tab as shown at *A* of Fig. 33. The bent tabs act as stops and the remaining straight tabs are bent over the part to be joined, as shown in *B*. This seam may be made watertight by soldering around the joint.

BEADED DOVETAIL SEAM. This seam has a bead formed around one end of the cylinder by means of a beading machine. This bead acts as a stop for the flange to rest upon and the tabs are bent over to hold the flange in place. The procedure is similar to the plain dovetail seam.

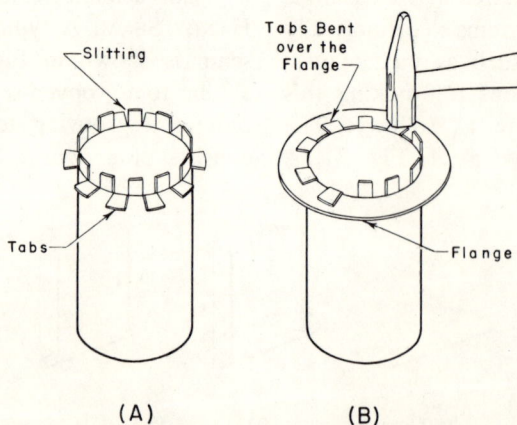

Figure 33. How to form a dovetail seam.

FLANGE DOVETAIL SEAM. Fig. 34 shows the assembly of the flange-type dovetail seam for cylindrically shaped pipes. It is used where strength and appearance are needed. The flange A is turned on the collar by means of a turning machine. The sleeve B is riveted on the inside of the collar C, and the tabs are hammered over the material to which the pipe and sleeve are fastened, D.

Standing seam

Standing seams on cross seams of large ducts, or any large sheets of metal, eliminate the need for angle iron reinforcement. This lock is easily made and provides greater convenience in fabrication. The seam is shown in the open and closed position in Fig. 35.

Another seam used very often for making cross seams for connecting two sections of duct is the *government clip*, sometimes called a pocket lock. The government clip is used in the same manner as the S and Drive clips. The difference is that the finished government clip is not flush with the duct but projects out about 1″ as shown in Fig. 36, much in the same manner as a standing seam. The government clip is formed as shown in the section view A in Fig. 36.

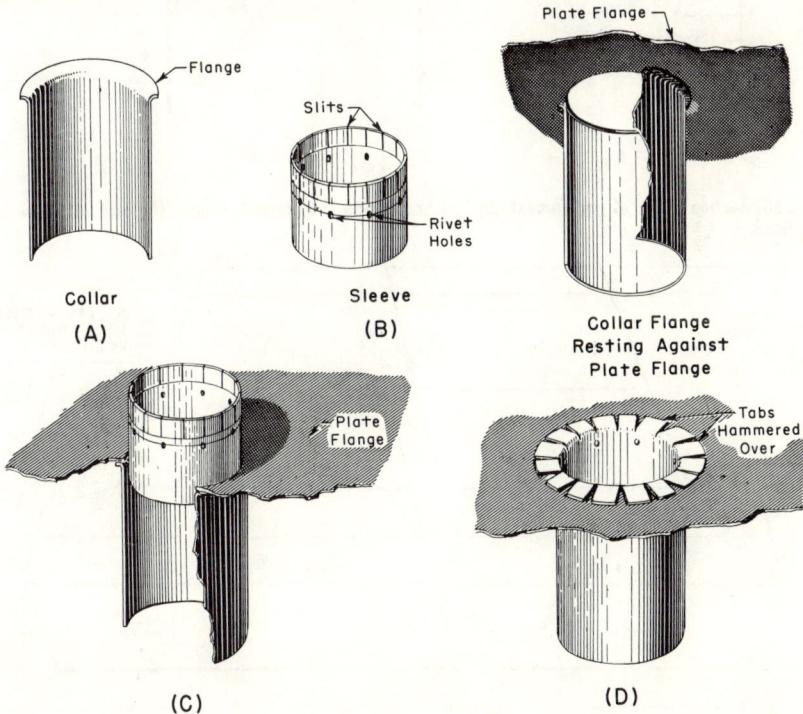

Figure 34. Flange dovetail seams are used where strength and appearance are needed.

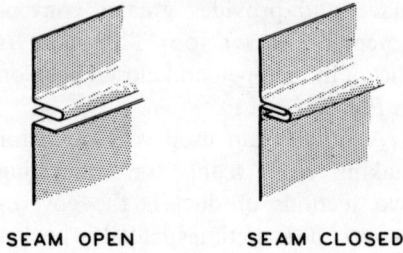

SEAM OPEN   SEAM CLOSED

Figure 35. Standing seam eliminates need for angle iron reinforcement.

Views *B* and *C* show how it is used to join the duct.

Many general sheet metal shops use so many government clips that they have special machines to cut them out. These are called clip punches or clip dies. The metal is cut into 4½″ wide strips and then cut to the proper length in the clip die. Clip dies are usually foot-operated

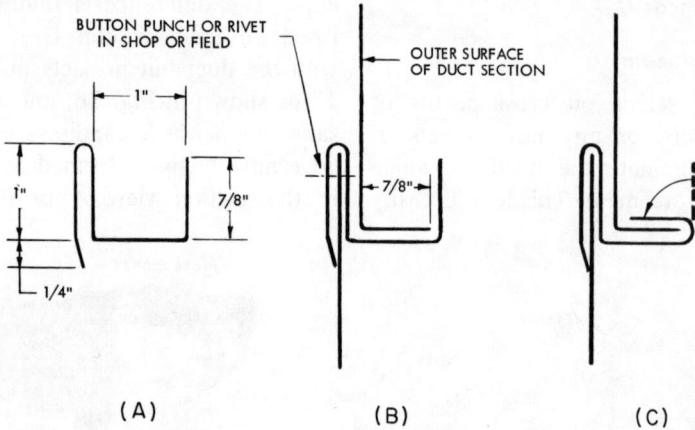

(A)   (B)   (C)

Figure 36. Section views of government clip (A) shows how it is formed. Views (B) and (C) show how it is joined.

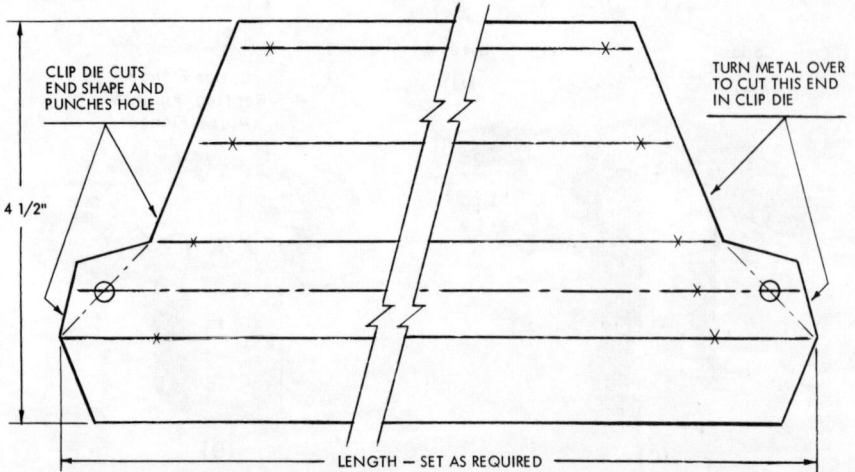

Figure 37. Government clips may be formed by clip dies as shown.

and are shaped so that one stroke of the die punches the rivet hole and cuts the end of the strip to the proper shape as shown in Fig. 37. Then the other end of the clip is turned over and cut in the same manner to give the clip blank as also shown in Fig. 37.

After the clips are cut, they are bent to the proper shape, usually in a small brake set up with special gages for quick bending of clips. When they are formed, the clips are riveted into frames such as the one shown in Fig. 38. These frames are then inserted on the end of the duct and punched or riveted securely.

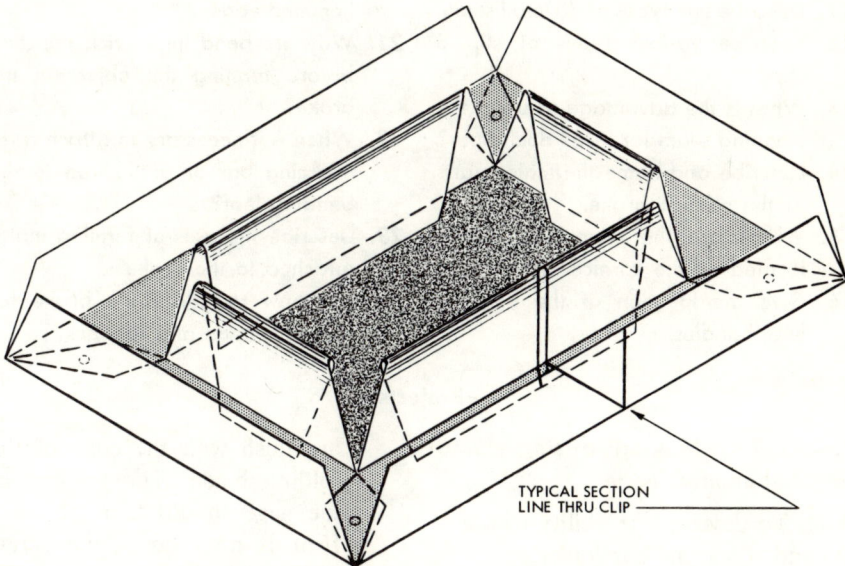

TYPICAL SECTION
LINE THRU CLIP

Figure 38. Government clips are assembled as shown here and then attached to the end of ducts.

Review Questions

1. What type of seam is used in joining light sheet metal together?
2. Describe the procedure for grooving by hand. Describe the procedure for grooving by machine.
3. What is the formula for finding the proper amount of material for a groove seam regardless of the thickness of the metal?
4. Describe the parts of a Pittsburgh lock. Use sectional drawings if desirable.
5. What types of lock are generally used for assembling cross seams of ducts?
6. Describe the slip joint. Use sectional drawings if desirable.
7. What causes the side of a square or rectangular pipe to twist out of shape?

8. What is the difference between a double-seam joint and a slip joint?

9. Describe the method of making a double seam on the bottom of a cylindrically shaped article. Use sectional drawings if desirable.

10. Why may the handy seam be used to good advantage when joining two or more sheets of metal?

11. Describe two types of dovetail seam.

12. Describe various types of slip S clips.

13. What is the advantage of using the standing seam for large duct pipes?

14. Describe and name the major parts of the cornice brake.

15. Where are the clamping handles located on the cornice brake?

16. Give the location of the bending leaf handles.

17. Why are the counter-balance weights on the brake adjusted?

18. What is the name of the bar which is removed when bending small locks?

19. Describe the method of adjusting the clamping bar for various thicknesses of metal on the brake.

20. Describe the method of smashing a hemmed edge.

21. Why are bend lines prick punched before forming the object in the brake?

22. When is it necessary to attach a reinforcing bar or angle iron to the bending leaf?

23. Describe the uses of forming molds attached to the brake.

24. Tell how to adjust the brake for handle tension and set-back.

Projects

Project 7-1. Making a single and double-hemmed edge

AIM. To develop the ability to operate and adjust the bar folder.

MATERIAL. Galvanized iron 3″ × 10″, 26 gage or lighter.

SPECIFICATIONS. Make a ⅜″ double hem on one side of a strip of metal and a ¼″ single hem on the other side.

OPERATIONS FOR SINGLE HEM

1. Cut a strip of metal to the required size.

2. Set the gage of the bar folder for a ⅜″ hem, as explained previously. (Before setting the gage, the gage adjustment should be checked by turning the gage adjusting screw until the fingers are flush with the edge of the folding blade. The reading of the gage should then be zero. If it is not, loosen the screw and set the plate.)

3. Insert the edge of the metal to be folded between the folding blade and the jaw, as shown in *A*, Fig. 39.

4. Pull the handle forward as far as possible, as demonstrated by *B*.

5. Insert the hem between the folding wing and the blade, with the folded edge facing upward.

6. Pull the handle forward as far as possible, *C*, completing the single hem.

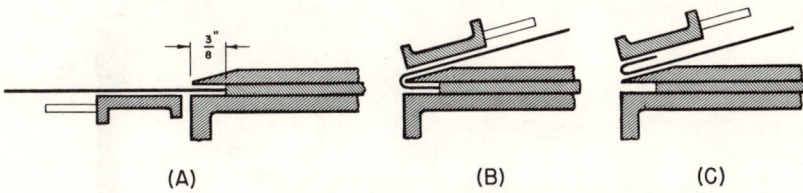

Figure 39. Method of folding single hem in bar folder.

7. Reset the gage for a ¼" width hem and repeat the operations, completing the single hem.

OPERATIONS FOR DOUBLE HEM

1. Reset the gage of the bar folder for a ⅜" width edge. (For light metal, both hems may be turned with the same gage setting, it being possible thereby to complete the double-hemmed edge before resetting the gage.)
2. Insert the ⅜" hem, with the folded edge upward, between the folding bar and jaw, as shown at *A*, Fig. 40.
3. Pull the handle forward as far as it will go, as pictured at *B*.
4. Release the metal by returning the handle to its former position.
5. Turn the metal over and insert the double hem between the folding bar and the blade, then pull the handle forward as far as possible, *C*, completing the double hem.

Project 7-2. Making a grooved seam by hand

AIM. To develop the ability to make a grooved seam by hand.

MATERIAL. Two pieces 3" × 12" 28-gage iron.

SPECIFICATIONS. Make a ¼" grooved seam by hand, using scrap metal.

OPERATIONS

1. Cut two pieces of metal to the required size.
2. Set the gage of the folder for a ¼" lock.
3. Turn the lock on each piece of metal as shown at *A*, Fig. 41.
4. Hook the two pieces together, *B*.
5. Place the metal to be grooved on a flat stake and flatten the seam slightly with a mallet. Be sure to keep the two pieces tightly hooked.
6. Select the proper size of hand groover, choosing one having a

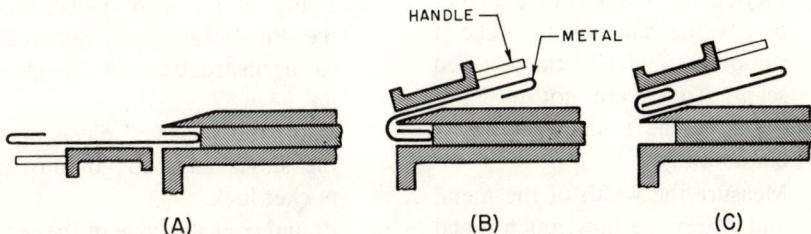

Figure 40. Method of folding double hem in bar folder.

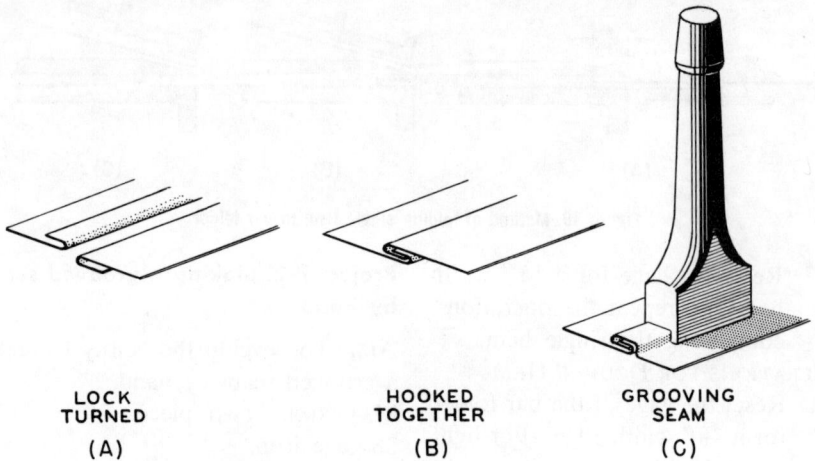

LOCK
TURNED

(A)

HOOKED
TOGETHER

(B)

GROOVING
SEAM

(C)

Figure 41. Method of making grooved seam.

slot about $\frac{1}{16}''$ wider than the width of the lock.

7. Place the groover over the seam at one end and strike lightly but firmly with a hammer, making a short groove.

8. Repeat the process and groove the other end.

9. Groove the balance of the seam by moving the groover along the seam, as shown at *C*. Keep the groover moving along the seam. Do not finish the seam in one pass. It will be a neater job to groove the seam gradually in two or three passes.

10. Flatten the seam with a mallet or riveting hammer to make it smooth, completing the grooved seam. Take care not to leave dents in the seam by careless hammering.

11. Measure the width of the metal and determine how much metal was used to form the seam.

Project 7-3. Making a Pittsburgh lock

AIM. To develop the understanding and skill necessary to make a Pittsburgh lock.

MATERIAL. One piece 28-gage galvanized iron 6″ × 6″, one piece 3″ × 6″.

SPECIFICATIONS. Make a ⅜″ Pittsburgh lock with scrap metal.

OPERATIONS

1. Cut out the two pieces of metal to the specified size.

2. Lay out the lines on the two pieces according to the drawing in Fig. 42.

3. Using the 6″ × 6″ piece, form the Pittsburgh seam according to the instructions in this chapter.

4. Using the 3″ × 6″ piece, make the single edge to go into the pocket lock.

5. Pound over the edge of the seam and turn in to the instructor.

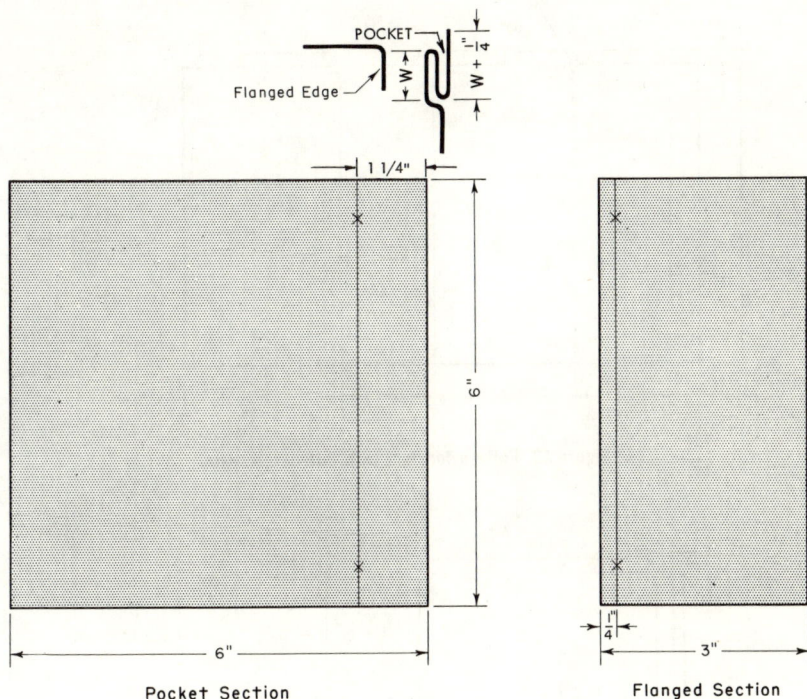

Figure 42. Pattern for Pittsburgh lock.

Project 7-4. Making a duct with a Pittsburgh seam

AIM. To learn how the Pittsburgh seam is used in making duct work.

SPECIFICATIONS. Make 6″ × 4″ duct, 12″ long, with a Pittsburgh seam on one corner.

OPERATIONS

1. On a piece of 26 gage galvanized iron lay out the pattern shown in Fig. 43.
2. Form the pocket lock for the Pittsburgh seam.
3. Bend the single edge.
4. Starting with the side nearest the single edge, bend the corners of the duct.

5. Finish the seam and turn in to the instructor.

Project 7-5. Making a duct with a double seam corner

AIM. To gain practice in using the double seam.

SPECIFICATIONS. Make a duct 6″ × 4″ long, with a double seam on one corner.

OPERATIONS

1. Lay out the pattern for the duct, as shown in Fig. 44. Prick punch all bend lines. Notice the $\frac{1}{16}$″ allowance to prevent binding when the lock is hammered over. The allowance for a double

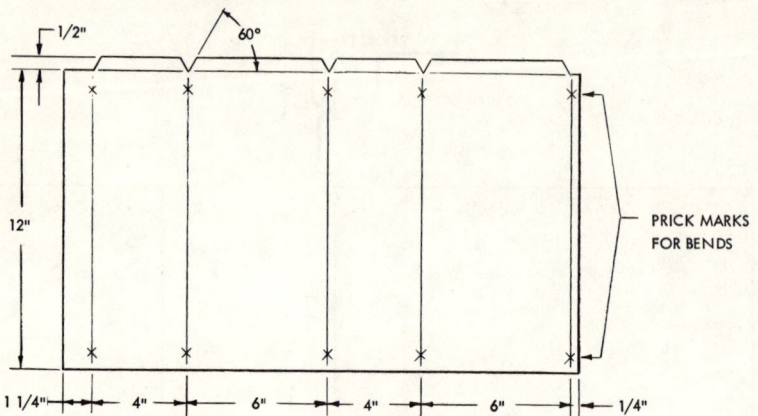

Figure 43. Pattern for duct with Pittsburgh seam.

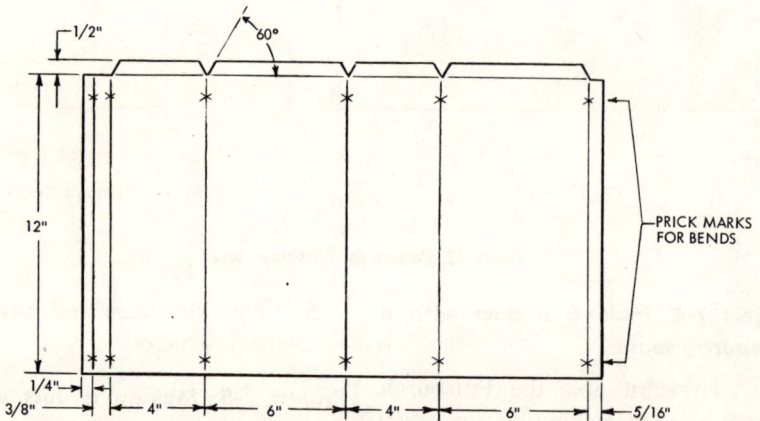

Figure 44. Pattern for duct with double seam corner.

seam is equal to three times the width of the seam, with the measurements distributed as shown.

2. Cut out the pattern.

3. Bend the $\frac{5}{16}''$ edge (right edge in Fig. 44) at a right angle, as shown at *A*, in Fig. 45.

4. Make the folded lock on the opposite end for the double seam, as shown at *B*.

5. Form the remaining bend lines to shape, *C*.

6. Place the duct with the corner to be double seamed on a stake.

7. Squeeze the lock together with a pair of tongs.

8. Hammer the lock over, using a mallet, *D*.

9. Dress (square up the corner of the seam) with a mallet or hammer. Hold a square head stake

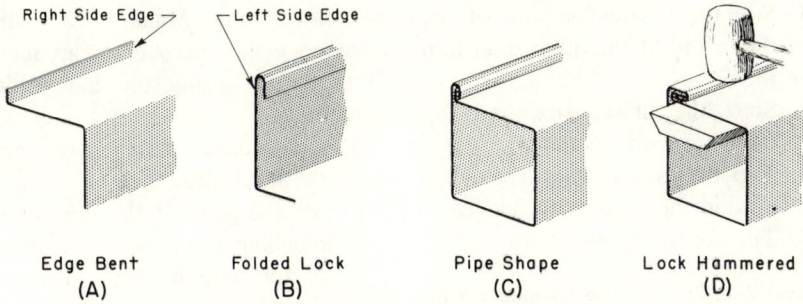

Right Side Edge   Left Side Edge

| Edge Bent | Folded Lock | Pipe Shape | Lock Hammered |
| (A) | (B) | (C) | (D) |

Figure 45. Method of making double seam corner on square pipe.

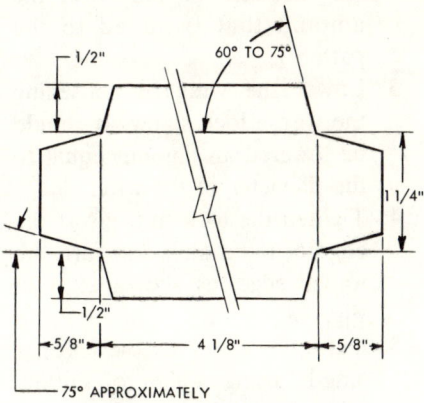

Figure 46. Pattern for Drive clip.

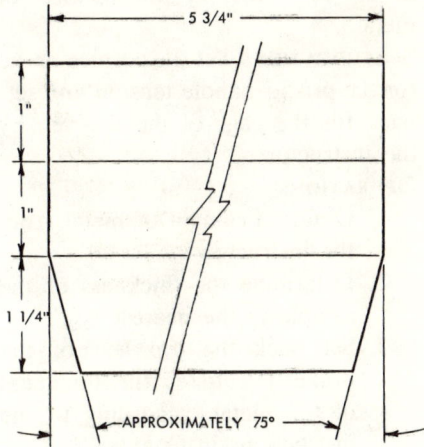

Figure 47. Pattern for S-clip.

on the inside edge of the seam to back it up while dressing the corner.

Project 7-6. Using S and drive clips to join duct

AIM. To show how to use S and drive clips and to give practice in their use.

SPECIFICATIONS. Make S and drive clips and connect the two ducts made in Projects 7-4 and 7-5.

OPERATIONS

1. Lay out and cut two pieces of metal as shown in Fig. 46 for drive clips. Bend them as described in Chapter 7.

2. Lay out and cut two pieces as shown in Fig. 47 for S clips. Bend them as described in Chapter 7.

3. On the two ducts from Projects 7-4 and 7-5, use tongs to bend the ½" edge back for taking the drive clip, as described in this chapter. *Bend the edges on 4" sides only.* The 6" sides will remain straight to receive the S clips.

4. Slip the S clips on one of the ducts and fit the other duct into them.
5. Start the drive clips and tap them on with a hammer.
6. Tap the tabs of the drive clips around the corners to finish.
7. Turn in to the instructor.

Project 7-7. Setting the cornice brake

AIM. To give practice in setting the brake for different thicknesses of metal.

SPECIFICATIONS. Set the cornice brake for the proper handle tension and set-back for the gage of metal given by the instructor.

OPERATIONS

1. Obtain a sample of metal from the instructor.
2. Determine the thickness of the sample to the nearest $\frac{1}{32}''$.
3. Set back the top leaf of the brake $1\frac{1}{2}$ times the thickness of the metal, according to the instructions in Chapter 7.
4. Set back both ends of the brake equally.
5. Put the sample in the brake and set both ends of the brake to the proper handle tension.
6. Have the instructor inspect the brake after it is completely set.

Project 7-8. Making a wired edge while the metal is still flat

AIM. To develop the ability to make a wired edge by the use of the bar folding machine, the cornice brake, and wiring machine.

MATERIAL. Lightweight scrap metal, $\frac{1}{8}''$ wire.

SPECIFICATIONS. Make a $\frac{1}{8}''$ wired edge on a flat piece of scrap metal.

OPERATIONS (using the bar folding machine)

1. Cut a piece of light gage metal to the desired size.
2. Set the gage of the bar folding machine $1\frac{1}{2}$ times the diameter of the wire or $\frac{3}{16}''$ ($1\frac{1}{2}$ plus the wire diameter which is used in the bends equals $2\frac{1}{2}$ times the diameter of the wire, the amount that is added to the pattern).
3. Lower the wing by loosening the wedge lock screw. It should be lowered an amount equal to the diameter of the wire.
4. Tighten the lock nut, insert the edge of the metal, and turn the folded edge, as shown at A in Fig. 48.
5. Cut the wire to the proper length, using a pair of cutting pliers or cutting nippers.
6. Straighten the wire on a smooth surface, using a mallet.
7. With the wire in the folded edge as at B, place the end of the wired edge between the rolls of the wiring machine, as shown at C in Fig. 48. Note that the edge of the upper roll is set just inside the edge of the metal.
8. Lower the upper roll by turning down the crank screw just enough to start turning the edge.
9. While holding the work in a horizontal position, run the wired edge through the rolls.
10. Tilt the work upward, lower the upper roll, and repeat the op-

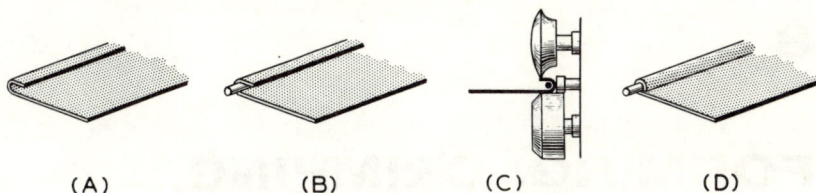

Figure 48. Wired edge construction using bar folder and wiring machine.

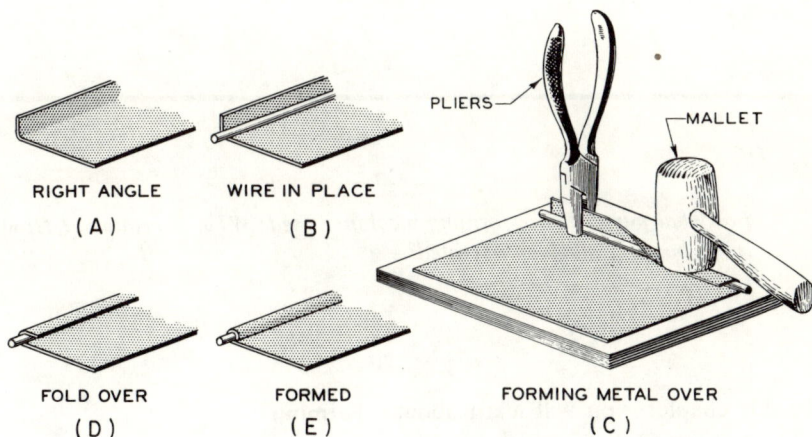

Figure 49. Operations in making wired edge using the cornice brake.

eration until the metal is fitted closely around the wire as at *D* in Fig. 48, completing the wired edge. It may be necessary to readjust the machine gage to keep the rolls on the edge of the metal.

Project 7-9. Making a wired edge

OPERATIONS

1. Cut a piece of metal to the required size.
2. Measure along the side of the metal 2½ times the diameter of the wire.
3. Place the metal on the cornice brake with the bend lines flush

with the jaws, then bend the edge at right angles as in *A* of Fig. 49.
4. Cut the wire to the proper length, using a pair of cutting pliers.
5. Straighten the wire over a smooth surface, using a mallet.
6. Place the wire in the folded edge. See *B* of Fig. 49 and hold in place with vise clamp pliers.
7. Form the metal over the wire, using a mallet or riveting hammer. The steps are shown in *C*, and *D* of Fig. 49.
8. Complete the wired edge in the wiring machine.

8

FORMING, CRIMPING, BEADING AND GROOVING

For what purposes are forming machines used? What is crimping? How is the beading machine operated?

In this chapter, you will learn about four machines, all of which play an important part in forming pipes and other cylindrically shaped objects. These four machines are: *1. the plain forming machine, 2. slip-roll forming machine, 3. crimping machine and 4. beading machine.*

There are many "tricks of the trade" which save valuable time and can be used by the student as well as the more experienced worker. These short cuts and time-savers have been used and proved to be sound, workable solutions to problems that are encountered daily. Students will readily recognize the need for such short cuts in their daily work, but it is equally important to know the uses for and operation of the machines of the trade.

Forming

SLIP-ROLL FORMING MACHINE. All forming machines have the same general function; namely that of forming sheet metal into cylindrical shapes of various diameters. While the operation of both the plain forming machine and the slip-roll forming machine is much the same, there is one important construction feature in the slip-roll forming machine which gives it an advantage over the plain forming machine. The difference is that, in the construction of the frames of the two machines, the plain forming machine has a solid housing. Note in Fig. 1 that the formed material may be readily slipped off the *end* of the front upper roll in the slip-roll forming machine. In the plain forming machine, the finished work must be slipped

Figure 1. Slip-roll forming machine. Courtesy: Peck, Stow and Wilcox Co.

over the front upper roll. That this can sometimes result in misshapen work is clear.

Otherwise, both forming machines consist of a base, three rolls and the housing. The operating handle turns the two front rolls by means of gears enclosed in the housing.

The two front rolls act as feeding or gripping rolls, while the rear roll gives the proper curvature to the work. The front rolls are adjusted by the two front adjusting screws located at each end of the machine. The rear roll is adjusted by the two screws located at the rear of each housing. The grooves in the front and rear rolls are used for forming objects with wired edges. The

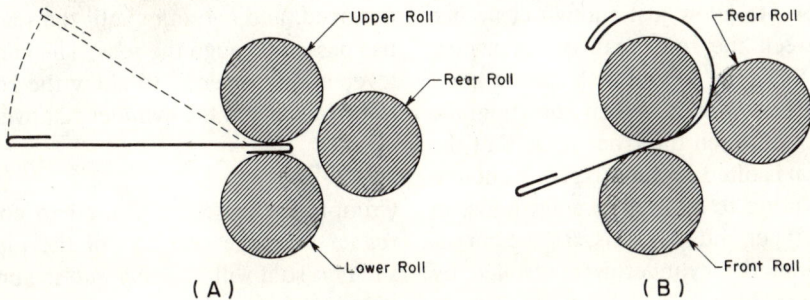

Figure 2. Starting and forming cylindrical shapes.

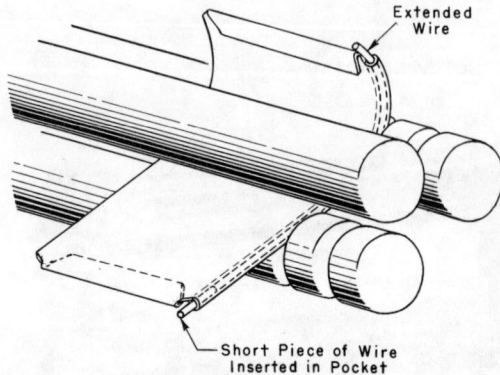

Figure 3. Forming a cylinder with a wired edge.

release allows the work to be removed by opening the upper roll.

PLAIN FORMING MACHINE. As stated previously, the functions and operation of the plain forming machine are similar to that of the slip-roll forming machine. The difference is that the rolls of the plain forming machine are mounted directly in two *solid* housings. Therefore, the upper roll cannot be released as in the slip-roll type.

FORMING CYLINDERS. Cylindrical shapes are formed by inserting the work between the two front rolls. See *A* in Fig. 2. The front rolls are adjusted by turning the front knurled screws to allow just enough clearance between the rolls to avoid smashing the locks flat so that they cannot hook together. Notice, when inserting the work between the front rolls, that the metal is tilted upward to give it enough curvature to allow it to enter between the upper and rear rolls, *B*. The curvature of the cylinder is controlled by raising the rear roll for a smaller radius or lowering it for a larger radius.

FORMING CYLINDERS WITH WIRED EDGES. When forming pails, cans, and other round articles with wired edges, the wire should extend past the metal slightly at one end. This is the end that should be inserted between the rolls as shown in Fig. 3. The wire at the other end should be slightly shorter than the metal to form a pocket to receive the wire from the other end. A short piece of wire should be inserted to prevent the pocket from being smashed. Continue to form the cylinder to the curvature desired until the ends meet. Insert the end of the wire into the pocket of the wired edge where the short piece of wire has been removed, and continue until the seam has passed through the rolls. The hand lever is then opened to allow the roll to be raised and the cylinder removed.

Crimping

Crimping is the method used to corrugate or make one end of the pipe smaller, so it will fit easily into the end of another pipe of the same dimension. This method eliminates the need of

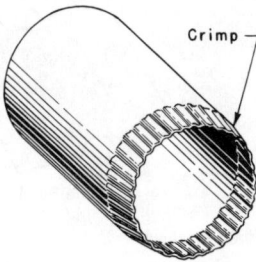

Figure 4. Crimped edge.

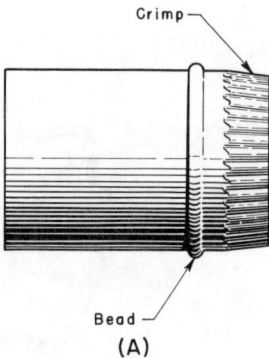

(A)

(B)

Figure 5. Combination crimper and beader (A) used to make the crimp and bead (B).

bination crimper and beader shown in *B*. The width of the crimp can be regulated by the gage. The crimping rolls may be tipped, allowing for a deep or shallow crimp by adjusting the screw on the top of the machine.

The rolls of the crimping-bead-ing machine are interchangeable. The plain rolls can be used without the bead, or they may be used as a combination of beading and crimping. The beading rolls alone can be used by replacing the crimping rolls with plain rolls.

making one end of the pattern for the pipe smaller than the other. However, crimping can be used on light gage metal only. Crimping can also be used when turning large flanges on collars since it aids in stretching the metal.

Use of the crimping machine

Very little information is necessary in the use of the crimping machine. However, the student should know its operation. Fig. 4 illustrates a crimping operation which has been performed with the plain crimpers.

Crimper and beader

The crimp and bead shown in *A* of Fig. 5 is made by means of the com-

Beading machine

The beading or swedging machine is used to make depressions in metal such as would be found in pipes, machine guards, or wherever reinforcing is necessary. The shape of the beads varies. The standard beads are the single bead, the ogee bead, and the triple bead. These are shown in Fig. 6.

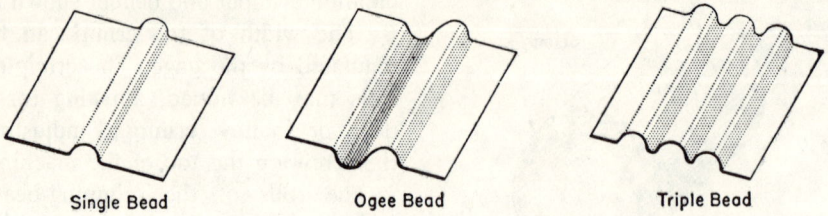

Single Bead   Ogee Bead   Triple Bead

Figure 6. Types of beads made in beading machine.

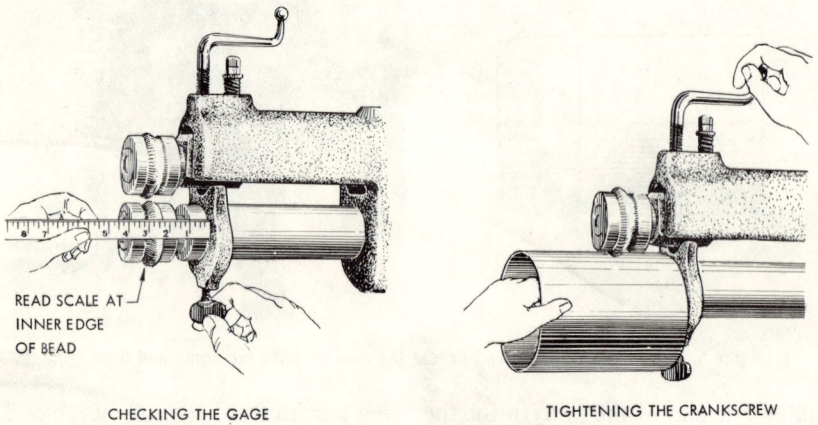

READ SCALE AT
INNER EDGE
OF BEAD

CHECKING THE GAGE   TIGHTENING THE CRANKSCREW

Figure 7. Steps in operating the beading machine.

When operating the beading machine, there are two important steps shown in Fig. 7. First, see that the gage is set properly and the thumb screw is tightened so that it cannot slip while making the bead and, second, see that the crank screw is not too tight inasmuch as this would cause the rolls to cut through the bead, spoiling with work.

Review Questions

1. What is the difference between a plain former and a slip-roll former?
2. Why is the work inserted between the rolls after they are closed?
3. Describe the method for forming cylinders with wired edges.
4. Give the procedure for forming a length of round pipe.
5. Why is it necessary to crimp one end of a length of pipe?
6. Why is a bead put on the end of a length of pipe?
7. What is meant by a combination crimping and beading machine?

Projects

Project 8-1. Making a round pipe with a grooved seam

AIM. To learn how to make the pattern for a round pipe and to form the groove seam.

SPECIFICATIONS. Lay out the pattern and make a round pipe 5″ in diameter, 7″ long, with a ¼″ groove seam.

OPERATIONS

1. Lay out the pattern shown in Fig. 8 and cut it out.
2. Bend the ¼″ edges for the groove seam on the bar folder.
3. Roll up the pipe.
4. Finish the groove seam. (See Chapter 7.)
5. Turn in the pipe to the instructor for and save for Project 8-2.

Project 8-2. Making a dovetail seam

AIM. To learn how to use a dovetail seam to connect a round pipe to a flat plate.

OPERATIONS

1. Use the round pipe made in Project 8-1.

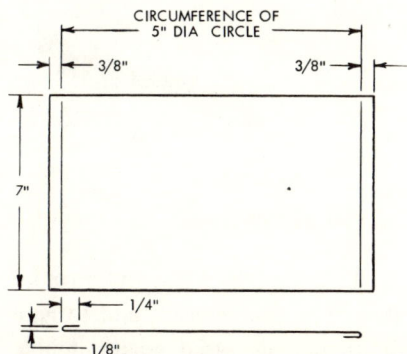

Figure 8. Pattern for 5″ round pipe, 7″ long with ¼″ groove seam.

2. With a pair of dividers, mark a line ⅜″ from the end of the pipe, as shown in *B* Fig. 9.
3. Clip the edge about every ⅝″, as shown in *B*.
4. Bend out every other tab at right angles, beginning with the tab at the seam, *C*.
5. Cut an opening in the flange the size of the collar.
6. Place the collar with the notched end in the opening and bend the remaining tabs over the flange, using a hammer, as in *C*.

A marking gage (see Fig. 10) may also be used to mark off allowances for seams. It is cut out of scrap sheet metal. The notch made is the required width of the allowance to be marked.

Project 8-3. Crimping, beading, and connecting round pipe

AIM. To illustrate the method of joining round pipe by crimping and beading.

SPECIFICATIONS. Crimp and bead the round pipe from Project 8-2 and join it to another round pipe with sheet metal screws.

OPERATIONS

1. Take the pipe used in Projects 8-1 and 8-2. Crimp it and bead one end so that it will lap 1½″ into another pipe. Read the instructions in this chapter for crimping and beading.
2. Make a second pipe according to the layout shown in Fig. 8.
3. Join the two pipes and secure with three sheet metal screws.

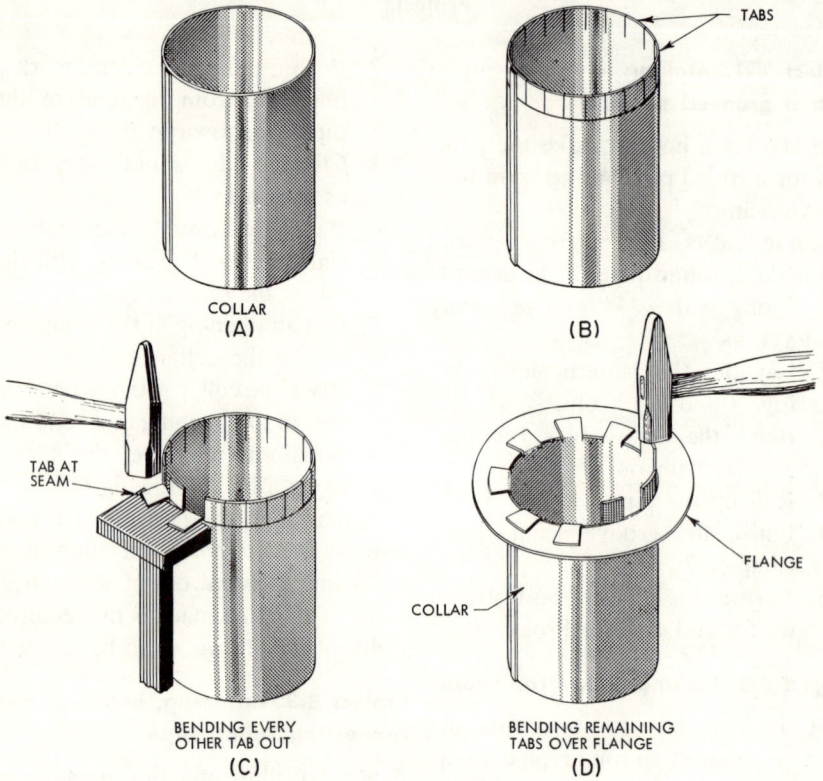

Figure 9. Making a dovetail seam.

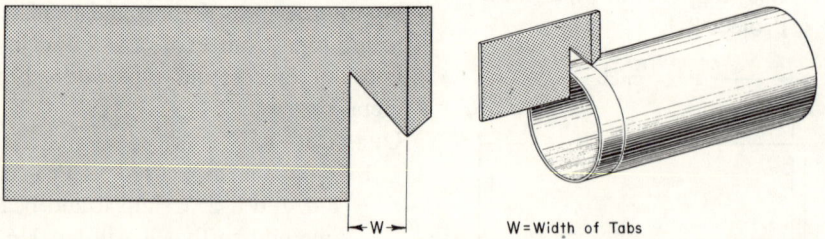

W = Width of Tabs

Figure 10. Making a marking gage to mark off seam allowances.

Make sure the pipes are straight and the seams are aligned before inserting the screws.

4. Turn in to the instructor.

Project 8-4. Making a round tank

AIM. To learn how to lay out a round tank with a double seam and to gain skill in making wired edges, double seams and groove seams.

SPECIFICATIONS. Lay out and make a

5/32" DIA WIRED EDGE

7" DIA

4"

1/4" GROOVE SEAM

1/4" DOUBLE SEAM

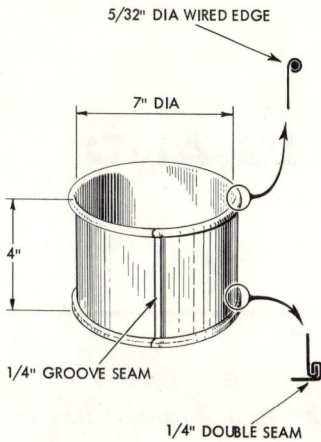

Figure 11. Making a round tank with a wired edge and double seam.

7" round tank, 4" high with a ¼" wired edge, a ¼" groove seam, and ¼" double seam.

OPERATIONS

1. Lay out the patterns for the tank shown in Fig. 11. Extreme accuracy is essential for the patterns on this project. Allow for all seams and edges. Check with the instructor before cutting the patterns.
2. Form and complete the wired edge according to the instructions in Chapter 7.
3. Bend the edges for the ¼" groove seam.
4. Roll the tank and the wired edge according to the instructions given in Chapter 8 under "Forming Cylinders with Wired Edges."
5. Complete the groove seam.
6. Turn the edge on the bottom with the burring machine.
7. On the bottom piece turn up the outside edge with the burring machine.
8. Connect the bottom to the main part.
9. Set down the seam and finish it.
10. Turn in to the instructor and then save the tank for soldering later.

9

TURNING, BURRING AND RAISING

How are edges turned with a turning machine? What is burring? How is metal raised?

Turning machines are used to form narrow edges or flanges on circular objects, for double seaming, wiring, and for stiffening edges. It is extremely important in turning edges to know how much allowance is necessary to make a neat edge. Improper turning of the edge results in an uneven and wavy edge that gives the whole job a poor appearance.

The burring machine is also used to form narrow edges on circular and irregular pieces.

Then what differences are there between the two machines? First, turning machines are well adapted for turning edges on *heavier* materials. Also, the bend made by the turning machine is a *radius* rather than a sharp bend. This makes it ideal for turning the edges for wired edges. In addition, the combination of the radius at the bend and the heavier metal makes it possible to turn wider edges with the turning machine than would

be possible on the burring machine. On the other hand, burring machines are designed for *lighter* sheet metals. Second, the edges made by the burring machine have a *sharp bend* of the corner rather than a radius.

All edges bent on a circular or curved object require that the metal must either shrink or stretch. This means that the sharp corner from the burring machine and the light metals used require that the edges bent be generally narrower than those on the turning machine. Usually a ¼" edge is the widest edge bent on the burring machine.

Also, because of the sharp corner, edges from the burring machine are best for double-seam edges such as in a bucket bottom. This is because the sharp bend makes it easier to make a neat straight edge when the edge must be pounded farther over with a hammer or mallet.

"Bumping" or raising metal in-

132

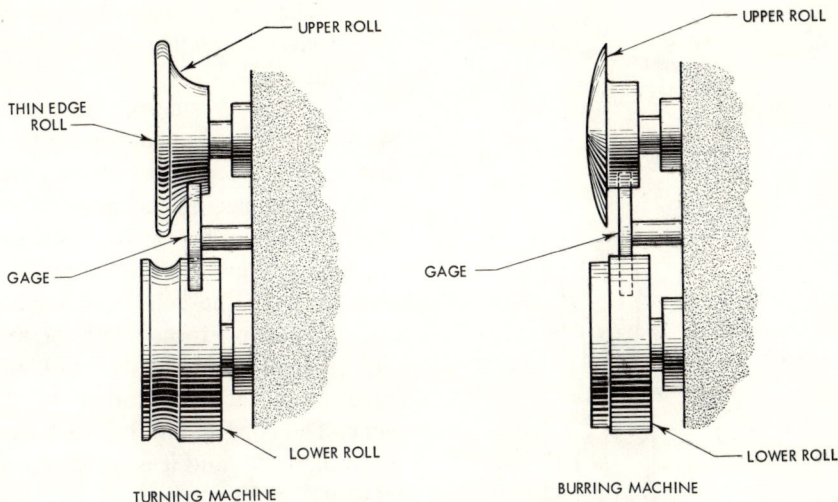

Figure 1. Front view of rolls in turning and burring machine.

volves shaping flat sheet into forms for various purposes such as covers and ornaments. While raising involves considerable skill, it can be done reasonably well by the student provided that correct procedures are followed.

Burring and turning machines

Though burring and turning machines are similar in design, the shape of rolls and location of gages are different in each. This is primarily due to the different purposes for which each one is intended.

The illustration of the front views of the rolls in Fig. 1 shows the location of the gages and the shape of the rolls. Compare views and you will note that the gage of the turning machine is located in *front* of the rolls and the gage of the burring machine is located to the *rear* of the rolls.

The turning machine is made in two sizes and is furnished with thin and thick rolls. These rolls are easily changed by placing the prongs of the spanner wrench, shown in Fig. 2 in the holes located in front of the rolls and turning the wrench counterclockwise. The upper roll of the burring machine shown in the illustration has a sharp beveled edge and is generally used for turning burrs, single edges, etc.

Preparing edges

PREPARING EDGES WITH THE TURNING MACHINE. For a wired edge, the distance must be equal to 2½ times the diameter of the wire. This measurement is taken from the face of the gage to the center of the upper roll, as shown in Fig. 3. The gage is adjusted by turning the knurled nut at the side of the machine. Care must be taken so that the rolls are not tightened too much on the first revolution. Otherwise a deep groove will

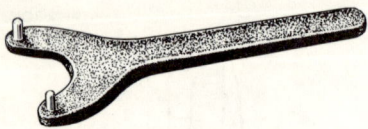

Figure 2. Spanner wrench.

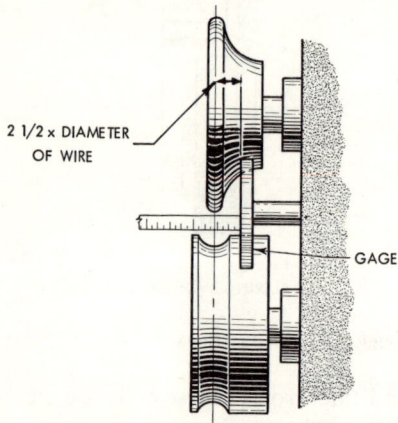

2 1/2 x DIAMETER OF WIRE

GAGE

Figure 3. Adjusting the gage.

run in the metal stretching the metal and making the turned edge too long for the wired edge. The proper procedure for turning an edge for wiring is as follows:

1. Set the gage to 2½ times the diameter of the wire.
2. Tighten the crank screw just enough to pull the work through the rolls, but not enough to run a groove in the metal.
3. Make one complete revolution of the work.
4. Tilt the work upward, tighten the crank screw enough to keep pulling the work through and make a second pass through the machine.
5. Tilt the work as far as possible, tighten the crank screw, and

make the last pass through the rolls, completing the edge for the wire.

PREPARING AN EDGE FOR A DOUBLE-SEAM BOTTOM. The edge is made by first setting the gage to the required width, then placing the edge of the object between the rolls, tightening the crank screw enough to pull the work through the rolls, and making one revolution. Proceed with the second revolution, tilting the work upward after each revolution of the work. The edge should not be turned more than 90° and it is preferable to leave it at a 75° angle.

PREPARING EDGES FOR ELBOWS. Though the regular turning rolls can be used for preparing edges which join sections of round elbows having tight seams, the V shaped edging rolls, as in Fig. 4, are generally used for making loose elbow locks.

Using the combination machine

The combination machine, shown in

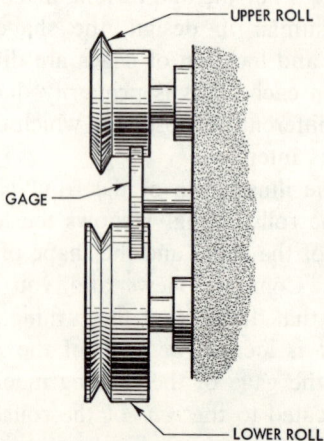

UPPER ROLL

GAGE

LOWER ROLL

Figure 4. V shaped elbow edging rolls.

Fig. 5, has a two-in-one reversible gage that can be applied to the front of the machine for turning operations and to the rear of the machine for burring operations. This machine, with its variety of interchangeable rolls, takes care of turning, burring, wiring, elbow edging, and flanging operations. The only difficulty with this type of machine is the need to change rolls and gages for various operations.

PREPARING EDGES WITH THE BURRING MACHINE. The burring machine is generally used to turn small burrs on circular disks for pail covers, bottoms, etc. The operation of the machine, which is shown in Fig. 6, requires considerable practice to produce neat edges quickly and consistently. It is therefore advisable for the student to cut a number of small disks about 6″ in diameter and practice until he is able to turn a good edge.

It is often said that turning an edge on the burring machine is difficult without an actual demonstration. However, if the student will follow the instructions given here, he will produce very good results with practice.

1. Hold the left elbow tightly against the body.
2. Hold the disk tightly between the thumb and the side of the index finger, as shown in A of Fig. 6.
3. Note the U shaped piece of metal as a hand guard against cuts.
4. Hold the arm rigid throughout the entire operation.
5. Tighten the crank screw just

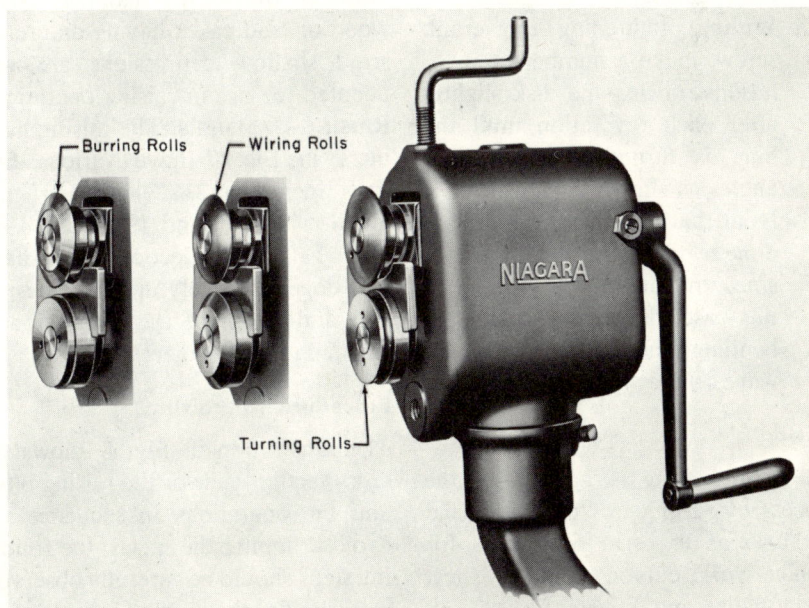

Figure 5. Combination bench machine with rolls. Courtesy: Niagara Machine and Tool Works.

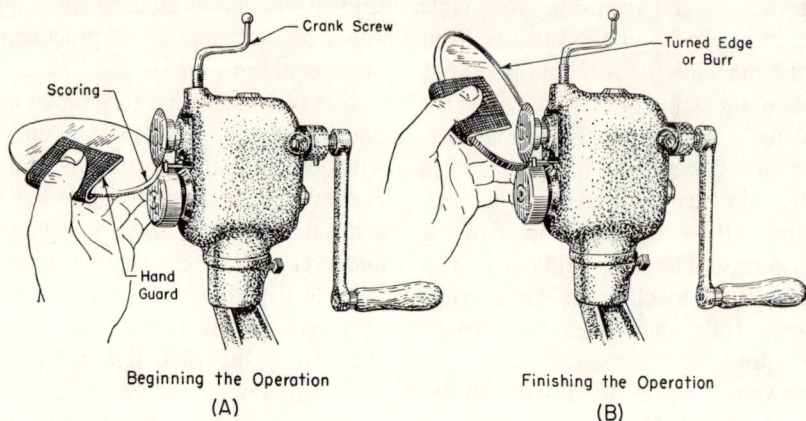

Figure 6. How to operate a burring machine.

enough to pull the metal through the rolls. The tightness of the rolls has little effect on the actual bending.

6. Make one revolution, scoring the edge slightly.

7. Without tightening the crank screw, make a number of revolutions, raising the disk slightly after each revolution until the burr is turned to the proper angles as shown in *B* of Fig. 6. Note that the actual bending is done by tilting the metal up, and, since the metal is shrinking in this case, the more gradual the bending, the less wrinkles and waves there will be in the edge.

Raising

The term *raising* is applied to the process of raising or "bumping" flat metal so as to form ornaments for cornice work, curved moldings, sheet metal balls, and covers for various objects. This operation is performed by a raising hammer and a raising block, such as shown in Fig. 7.

RAISING BLOCK. The raising block is made of various materials which are capable of giving resistance to the blows of the raising hammer. Hardwood or lead cakes having differently sized shallow depressions are well adapted for use in raising operations.

RAISING HAMMERS. The raising hammers in Fig. 7 have various face sizes including 2⅛″ and 1¾″; 2″ and 1½″; 1⅝″ and 1⅜″; and 1⅜″ and 1⅛″. The selection of the hammer depends largely upon the desired size and depth of the depression to be made in the object.

Procedure for raising

The illustration in Fig. 8 shows the cross section view of the raising block and the operations in sequence. To avoid crimping the metal, the following steps should be carefully observed:

1. Begin the raising operation at the outer edge of the disk, *A*.

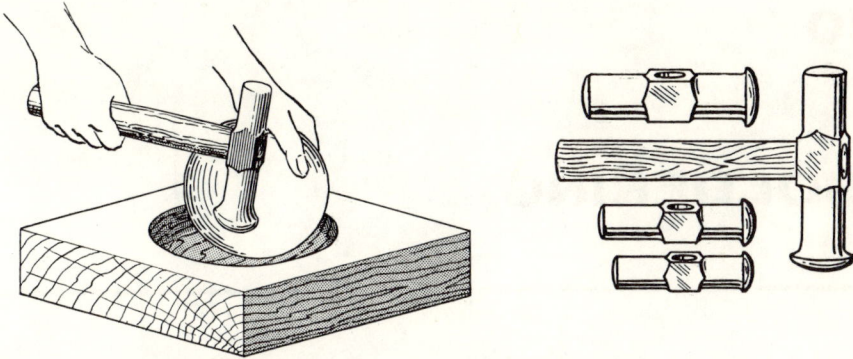

Figure 7. Using the raising block (left); raising hammers (right).

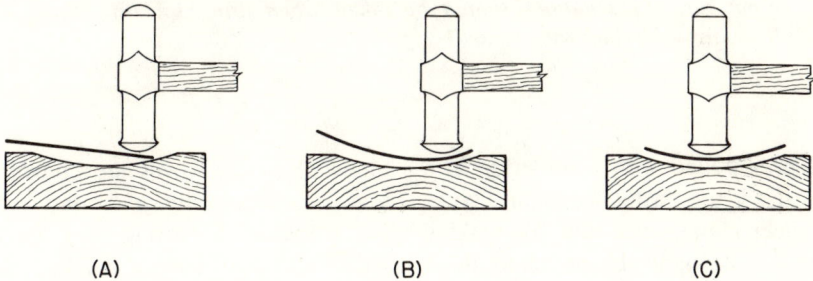

(A)　　　　　　　　　　　(B)　　　　　　　　　　　(C)

Figure 8. Begin raising operation at outer edge (A), turning with each blow (B) until disk has desired depression (C).

2. Work inward toward the center, gradually turning the metal as each blow is struck, shown in *B*.

3. Continue working toward the center, gradually raising the disk until the desired depression is completed. This is shown at *C* of Fig. 8.

4. Place the inside of the raised disk over the rounded head of the teakettle stake. Using a mallet, strike light blows to smooth out all wrinkles.

Review Questions

1. What machine turns burrs on disks?
2. What are the differences between the turning and burring machines?
3. What is meant by the term "raising" metal?
4. Draw the upper and lower turning rolls.
5. Draw the upper and lower burring rolls.
6. Draw the upper and lower elbow edging rolls.
7. Give examples of objects you could make using: (a) turning rolls, (b) burring rolls, and (c) elbow edging rolls.

10

SOLDERING

How is a soldering iron tinned? What is the purpose of a soldering flux? What safety precautions should be taken when using soldering flux? How are soldering irons heated?

Solders applied with a soldering iron are used for fastening many types of sheet metal work and for making seams watertight. In order to do a good job of soldering, the student must know the kind of material being soldered, the kind of solder and flux which are most suitable, and the proper soldering iron for the specific job.

The material in this chapter is presented so as to give the student not only the proper procedures for soldering, but also the reasons for performing each step. For example, students sometimes make the mistake of using too much solder. What then results is a job whose appearance and quality is poor.

Soft solders

The term "soldering" is a broad one but it generally refers to the *joining or uniting of two or more pieces of* *metal by means of an alloy having a lower melting point than the pieces being joined*. Soldering may be divided into two general classes, *hard soldering* and *soft soldering*. Hard solders are those having a melting point over 750° F and include such processes as silver soldering and brazing. However, it is soft soldering that is most frequently and generally used by the sheet metal worker and it is therefore with this process that we shall be concerned in this chapter.

PROPERTIES OF SOFT SOLDER. Soft solder is composed of tin and lead and its melting point depends largely upon the proportions of these two elements. For example, solder composed of half tin and half lead, commonly called "half-and-half", melts at about 365° F, while solder consisting of 10% tin and 90% lead has a melting point of about 563° F.

Soft solders are classed by the

proportion of each element, by weight. Therefore, "50-50" means that the solder consists of 50% tin and 50% lead by weight. It is important to note that the percentage of tin is always given first. Thus, "60-40" contains 60% tin and 40% lead, while "40-60" contains 40% tin and 60% lead. In the sheet metal shop, the preferred solder proportion is 50-50 since this gives a low melting point without too much expensive tin. Other trades have found that different proportions of tin to lead are better suited to their particular needs. Generally, increasing the tin content lowers the melting point of the solder. However, this is *only* true up to about 87% tin content. After that point, as the tin content increases the solder's melting point rises.

It is well to remember that the strength or bonding quality of a soldered seam depends on more than the melting point of the solder used. For example, a poorly tinned soldering iron may be heated to a temperature of 700° and still distribute the solder in the seam a satisfactory way.

Bar and wire solder

Solder in bar or wire form is generally used in the sheet metal trade. Although solder can be obtained from manufacturers in bars from ½ to 1½ pounds, as shown in Fig. 1, some sheet metal shops prefer to prepare their own solders by melting the the correct proportions of tin and lead into molds that cast their shop name on the bars.

In addition to the bar form, solder is available in triangular or round

Figure 1. Standard bar of solder.

bars about the size of a lead pencil and about 18″ long. It is also available in ⅛″ or 1/16″ diameter wire. This can be either solid or hollow wire either with an acid or rosin flux in its center. This is called "acid core" or "rosin core" solder. Manufacturers of solder will pour the solder in any size or shape that the contractor specifies.

Soldering fluxes

Flux is used to remove the oxide film that is always present on metal. If no flux were used, this oxide film would increase as the metal's temperature increased to the melting point of the solder thereby making adherence of the solder to the metal difficult if not impossible. Rather than bonding to the metal, the solder would only lie loosely over the oxide film.

There are two general classes of soldering flux: corrosive and non-corrosive. Acids are corrosive and should therefore be washed off immediately after the soldering operation is completed. Rosin is a non-corrosive flux. It may be in the form of a lump, powder, paste, or liquid.

Hydrochloric acid

Hydrochloric acid is often known by the commercial name of "muriatic acid." It is used for making zinc chloride and for cleaning off dirty parts of the metal before they are soldered. In the sheet metal shop, hydrochloric acid is usually called *"raw acid."*

Though the terms hydrochloric acid and muriatic acid are often used interchangeably, there is one difference of which the student should be aware. Muriatic acid is the *commercial* term and comes in one strength only—a medium strength acid. Hydrochloric acid is the *chemical* name and can be in any strength from a very mild dilute to concentrated and dangerous acid.

Raw hydrochloric acid can be identified by its yellow color when it is clean. It also has a sharp and pungent odor. However, the surest identification of raw acid is to put a small amount on a piece of galvanized metal. If the liquid bubbles and smokes and turns the zinc coating black, it is raw acid.

Zinc chloride

Zinc chloride is often called cut, cured, or killed acid. It is unequaled as a flux when soldering galvanized metals, zinc, brass, copper, and lead. It is also used for soldering tin which has become tarnished by being exposed to the weather.

Cut acid is colorless and odorless. However, it is as corrosive and dangerous as raw acid and therefore should be treated with care. One method of distinguishing cut acid from raw acid is by putting a small amount on a piece of galvanized metal. If the reaction discussed previously occurs, the acid is raw. If no reaction occurs, then the liquid is cut acid.

SAFETY. With both raw and cut acid, it is extremely important to remember that these acids are highly dangerous and to treat them with the utmost caution. They will eat holes into clothing and may cause painful skin burns. Their greatest danger is that they can cause blindness if gotten into the eyes. If any acid is gotten into or around the eyes, they should be washed immediately with plenty of cold water. *A doctor should be consulted at once regardless of whether or not there is a burning sensation.* Often the reaction of the acid in the eye is delayed and may not occur for several hours. See Chapter 3 for additional soldering safety precautions.

PREPARATION OF ZINC CHLORIDE. Zinc chloride is prepared by pouring

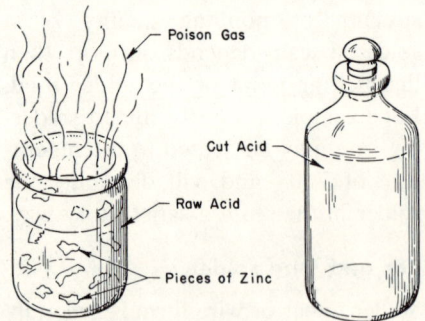

Figure 2. Preparing zinc chloride (cut acid) flux.

hydrochloric acid into a jar having a large opening at the top. This allows the acid to boil without running over. Place the jar near an open window or out of doors where the fumes can escape. Put a small quantity of zinc cut into small pieces into the acid as shown in Fig. 2. As the boiling action slows down, continue adding zinc until the acid will no longer boil. The cut acid should be filtered through a very fine copper screen or cloth to remove all dirt left by the dissolving of the zinc before putting it in tight glass containers for storage.

Rosin

Rosin is the by-product of oil of turpentine and is a common, non-corrosive type of flux for soldering metals such as bright tin plate and terne plate. Rosin may be applied as a powder, melted on the metal with a warm soldering iron, or made into a paste by adding enough benzine to make it a semi-solid. Palm oil mixed with rosin also makes a satisfactory soldering paste.

Rosin is a non-corrosive flux and, though it does not work well on dirty metals, it is essential for electrical or radio connections. Acid fluxes used on these connections will eventually cause corrosion and poor connections. Rosin flux will not.

Types of soldering irons and handles

Soldering irons are made of solid pieces of copper and vary in shape and weight. The body of the soldering iron, called the "head", is usually octagonal in shape. The pointed end is referred to as the "point" or "tip" and is forged into various shapes for different kinds of work. Soldering irons are classified according to their shapes and sizes.

Sizes of soldering irons

Soldering irons are designated by weight *per pair*. For example, an iron

marked with a "3" indicates that it and its mate will weigh three pounds. One 3 pound iron will weigh 1½ pounds *without the handle and shank*.

The standard sizes of soldering irons per pair are 1, 1½, 2, 3, 4, 5, 6, 8, 12, and 16 pounds. The 12 and 16 pound irons are used for roofing and other heavy soldering operations.

Handles

Soldering iron handles are made of wood or fiber. The cheaper handle is made with small grooves around the ferrule, on which a piece of wire is wound to keep it from splitting. The better grade of handle has a metal ferrule at the end where the rod is inserted. This keeps the handle from burning when the iron is heated. A special handle for heavy irons has a large flange to keep the heat away from the hand. All three types of handles are shown in Fig. 3.

New wooden handles are put on as follows: heat the point of the rod until it becomes red hot, then push

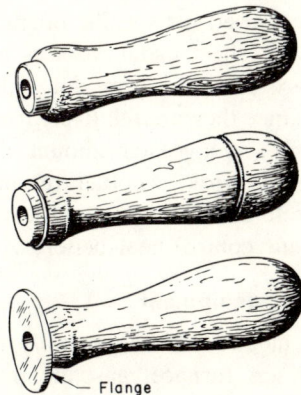

— Flange

Figure 3. Soldering iron handles.

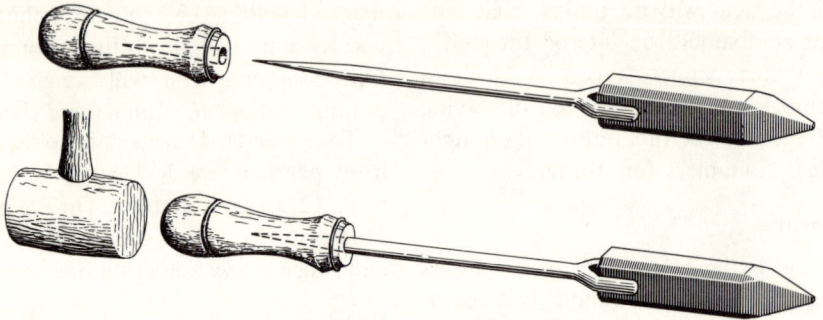

Figure 4. How a soldering iron handle is replaced.

it into the handle about two or three inches. Remove the rod and allow it to cool. Replace the handle over the rod and force them together by striking the end of the handle with a mallet, as shown in Fig. 4. Care should be taken not to split the handle.

The most common type of modern handle manufactured cuts a thread on the stem of the soldering iron rod as it is screwed on. This handle is well protected from burning or charring.

Electric soldering irons

The electric soldering iron shown in Fig. 5 is used for specific operations. However, sheet metal workers prefer standard soldering irons for ordinary work since they are relatively trouble-free and give a greater amount of heat for heavy work. Another reason for this preference is that standard soldering irons control heat better.

Heating equipment

Sheet metal workers generally use a bench gas furnace, gasoline pot, or a tinners' charcoal pot for heating soldering irons.

Gas furnace

The bench type of gas furnace, shown in Fig. 6 is especially designed to heat soldering irons. For heating six pound irons or less, a furnace with one Bunsen burner is sufficient. For larger irons, a furnace equipped with two burners should be used.

The gas furnace is equipped with shutoff valves and a pilot light. The base and the cover of the furnace are lined with asbestos. A steel shelf is located in the rear to protect the tinned points of the iron.

LIGHTING THE GAS FURNACE. For safety, every furnace should be in a well ventilated area. It is preferable that a fume hood and exhaust system be installed over the furnace. When lighting the furnace, observe the following safety precautions:

1. Check the shutoff valve to see that it is closed.
2. Remove any dirt from inside the furnace.
3. Light a small piece of crumpled paper and place it in the mouth of the furnace. At the same time, turn the handle located on

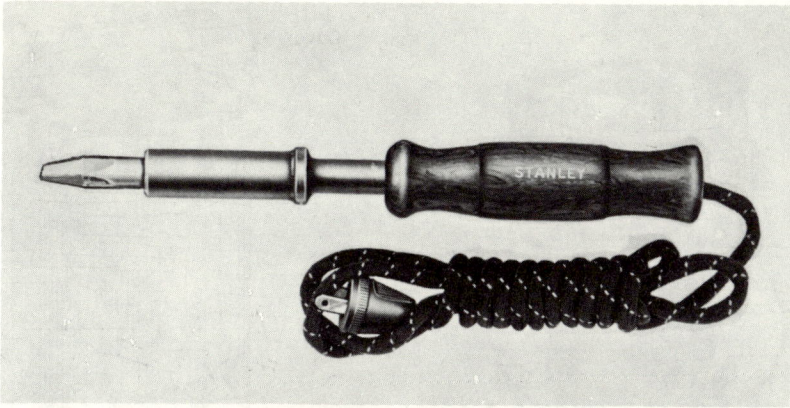

Figure 5. Electric soldering iron.

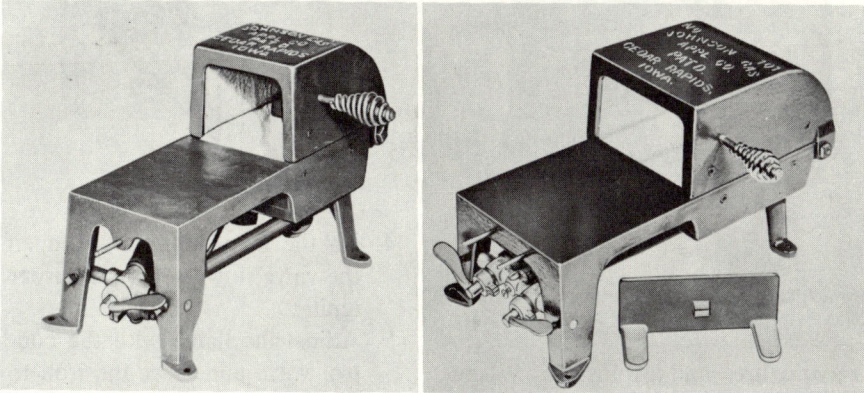

Figure 6. Gas bench furnaces: single burner (left) and double burner (right). Courtesy: Johnson Gas Appliances Co.

the front of the furnace. After the furnace is properly lighted, control the burners by working the valve handle. The small pilot light near each burner will relight the gas when the valve handle is turned to the "on" position. Always stand to one side when lighting the furnace. This will avoid burns in case the fire does flash out when it catches.

When not in use, the furnace shut-off valve should be turned off, leaving only the pilot light burning. At the close of the day the main line valve and the branch line valve should be turned off.

Gasoline fire pot

The gasoline fire pot shown in Fig. 7 is useful for heating soldering irons since it is portable. Since these pots use gasoline as fuel, use *extreme caution*

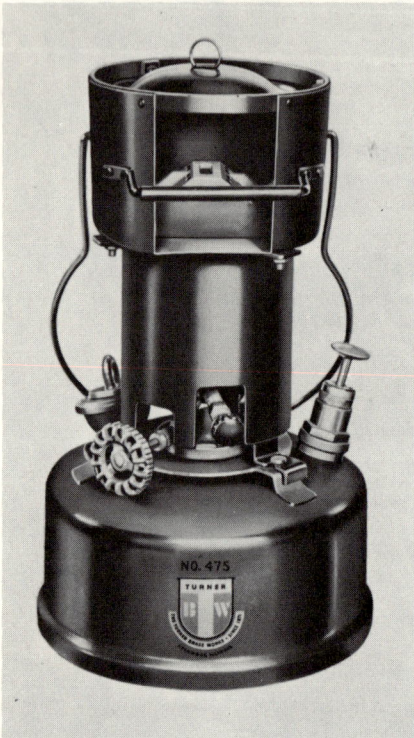

Figure 7. Gasoline fire pot. Courtesy: Turner Brass Works.

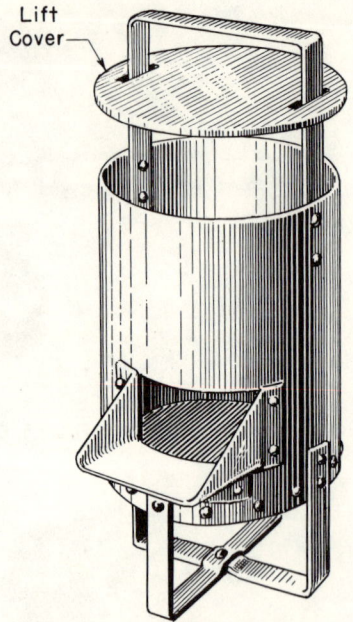

Figure 8. Tinners' charcoal pot.

to avoid fires and explosions. When lighting a gasoline fire pot, proceed as follows:

1. Force a limited amount of air (usually five or six strokes is sufficient) into the tank with the attached pump.
2. Fill the cup with gasoline by turning the control valve slightly. Turn the valve off when the cup is full. If any gasoline spills from the cup, wipe it off completely allowing it to dry before lighting the cup.
3. With a lighted match, ignite the gasoline in the cup.

4. As the flame dies down, open the valve slowly until the burner ignites.
5. Adjust the flame with the control valve and place the iron to be heated into the flame.

Tinners' charcoal pot

The charcoal pot shown in Fig. 8 is preferred by many mechanics for jobs such as roofing, when clean, uniform heat is required. The charcoal pot is lighted in the following manner:

1. Place a small amount of crumpled paper in the bottom of the pot.
2. Partly fill the pot with medium-sized charcoal and light the paper with a match.
3. After the charcoal has begun to

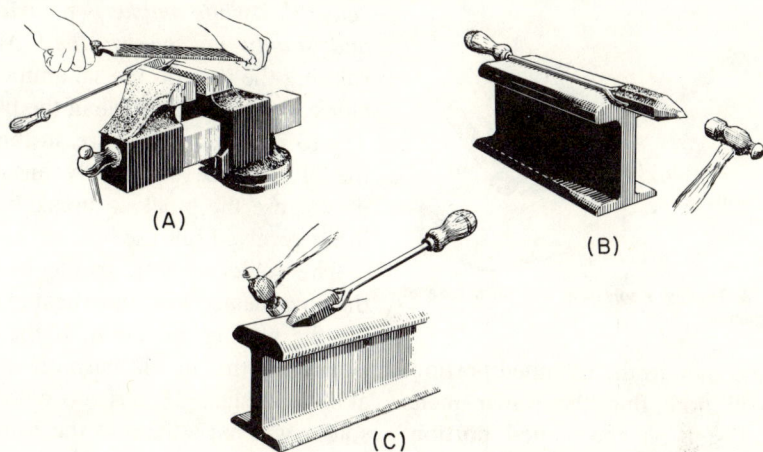

Figure 9. Steps in forging a soldering iron.

burn, fill the pot with charcoal.

4. Partly close the cover, putting the iron to be heated into the fire.

Preparing for soldering

FORGING THE SOLDERING IRON. Sometimes soldering irons become so misshapen that filing the point will not form it properly. In this case soldering irons are forged to the desired shape as follows:

1. Heat the iron to a cherry red.
2. Place the iron in the vise and file the part to be forged with a coarse file to remove all scales. This is shown in *A* of Fig. 9.
3. Place the shank end of the iron against the anvil as shown in *B* of Fig. 9. With a heavy hammer, force the misshapen point back into the body of the iron.
4. Reheat the iron and place it on the anvil, striking solid blows with a heavy hammer, as shown in *C* of Fig. 9.

5. Repeat the forging operat' when necessary.

Filing and tinning the soldering iron

Tinning a soldering iron means *covering the point with solder*. A well tinned iron is absolutely necessary to a good soldering job and one of the most common mistakes made is to try to solder with a poorly tinned iron. Unless the soldering iron is properly tinned, a good soldering job is impossible.

There are several important reasons for tinning a soldering iron. First, tinning keeps scale and corrosion from forming on the soldering iron point and it therefore acts as insulation. This scale and corrosion acts as an insulation and does not permit the heat to transfer from the iron to the solder. Tinning prevents the formation of the scale and therefore allows more heat to flow from the iron at the tinned area. Second, if you touch some solder first to the tinned portion of a hot soldering

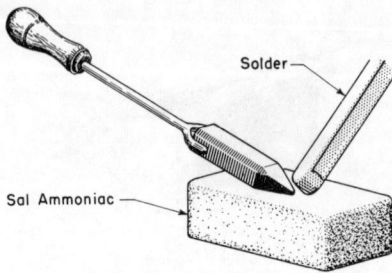

Figure 10. Tinning a soldering iron on a cake of sal ammoniac.

iron and then to the untinned portion, you will note that the solder melts much faster on the tinned portion. This is due to the fact that tinning permits proper heat escape from the iron. Finally, tinning allows the solder to flow properly from the point to the metal. Since tinning keeps the soldering iron point clean, it therefore keeps dirt and scale out of both the solder and the seam.

The first step in preparing for tinning is to heat the iron as for soldering. The body of the iron is then clamped in a vise and filed, the point is filed using a coarse file. This filing removes the pits and old tinning. Then a fine file is used to smooth off the rough edges of the corners of the point.

After the filing operation is completed, reheat the iron enough to melt the solder. When a small portion of solder has been applied, rub the tip lightly back and forth on a block of sal ammoniac, as shown in Fig. 10.

If the solder will not ahere to the point, it is because the soldering iron is not hot enough. The iron should be hot enough to cause white smoke to rise from the sal ammoniac. *However, care should be taken here be-*

cause this white smoke is a toxic gas and should not be breathed. When rubbing the iron on the sal ammoniac block, do not wear a hole in the block. Try to rub over the entire surface of the block since using only one spot may cause the block to break before it has received full use.

The soldering iron should be neither overheated nor underheated during the tinning operation. If the iron is too hot, the tin will burn off as fast as it is applied. If it is too cold, the solder will not adhere to the iron.

It is important to keep in mind that the tinned surface will be ruined if the iron is overheated no matter how well the iron has been tinned. Therefore, when the iron is not in use for a few moments, it should be pulled slightly out of the fire or the flame should be lowered. An indication that the tinning is being burned off the iron is a brilliant green flame in the firepot at the tip of the iron. This color is due to chemical reactions which mean that the tinning is being oxidized by the flame.

Applying the soldering flux

Applying the flux is important and carelessness in its application has ruined many soldering jobs. Liquid fluxes are applied with a small brush, sometimes called a swab. Care should be exercised to avoid dropping flux anywhere except where the soldering is to be done. Dip the brush in the flux and spread it lightly on the place to be soldered, as shown in Fig. 11. Powdered flux, such as rosin may either be sprinkled on the place to be

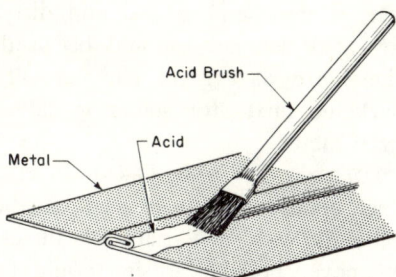

Figure 11. Apply soldering flux by dipping brush in flux and spreading it lightly over the place to be soldered.

soldered, or it can be melted on the metal with a hot soldering iron.

Avoid flipping or dropping an acid brush. As noted previously, serious burns and eye injury can be sustained through such carelessness.

Using dipping solution

In the process of heating the soldering iron, the tinned part of the point becomes discolored and should be cleaned off before beginning the soldering operation. This is done by plunging the point of the soldering iron into a solution composed of ½ ounce of powdered sal ammoniac and one quart of clean water immediately after removing it from the fire. This operation is shown in Fig. 12.

Another method, though not as good as the dip, is to wipe the iron lightly and quickly with a rag. However, never use woolens since this will spoil the tin coating on the soldering iron.

The dip is also a handy method of determining whether the iron is hot enough to use for soldering. With practice and observation, the sound of the iron in the dip will tell you

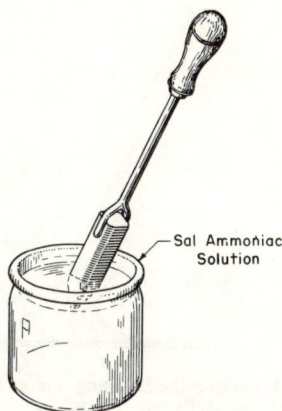

Figure 12. Cleaning tinned soldering iron in sal ammoniac solution.

whether the temperature is correct. A dull, slow bubbling sound is characteristic of a cold iron. A sharp, fast sizzling sound indicates that the iron is hot enough to do a good job.

Tinning for various jobs

The number of sides of the iron which it is necessary to tin depend on the type and position of the work. For example, when soldering vertical or upright seams, the iron should not be tinned on more than two sides. Most craftsmen prefer only one side, since a soldering iron tinned on all sides will not retain the solder. This is because solder will flow around the tinned sides of the point dropping off at the tip. If the iron is tinned on only one or two sides, this will not happen.

Position of the soldering iron

The position of the soldering iron is important because the iron does two things as it is applied to the parent metal:

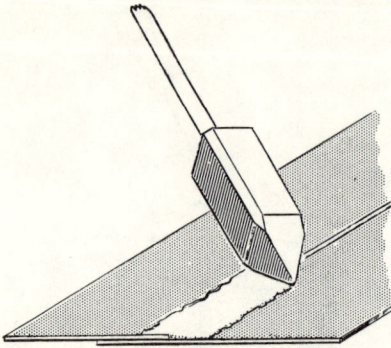

Figure 13. Position the soldering iron so that the solder will flow uniformly.

1. It heats the metal to the melting point of the solder.
2. It melts the solder and keeps it in a liquid state while soldering.

To do the former, it is important that as much of the point of the iron is resting on the metal as possible to allow maximum heat transfer from the iron to the metal. See Fig. 13. It should be remembered that the greater part of the heat is in the body and the base of the point — not in the tip. However, special work sometimes requires soldering with only the tip of the iron.

Since melted solders will flow to the hottest point on the metal, the soldering iron should be held as shown in Fig. 13 so that the solder will be pulled into the seam.

Soldering metals of various types

SOLDERING GALVANIZED METAL. In soldering galvanized metal, the principal question concerns whether one should use raw acid or zinc chloride as the flux. If the galvanized is bright and clear, zinc chloride can be used to make a well-bonded joint. However, if the metal is dull and dirty, raw acid definitely should be used. There are also good commercially marketed fluxes for soldering galvanized metal.

SOLDERING TIN AND TERNE PLATE. Steel, coated with tin or lead, can be soldered with a variety of fluxes. Whenever possible, rosin should be used because of its non-corrosive action upon metal. If the metal is dull, as would be true of used or old tin plate, zinc chloride can be used satisfactorily. Always wipe or wash the flux from the metal immediately after completing the soldering.

SOLDERING COPPER AND BRASS. If the surface of the sheet copper or brass is free of oxide, it can be easily soldered by using zinc chloride as the flux. If the copper or brass is dull, it can be cleaned by applying raw acid directly to the metal with an acid brush. The raw acid should be washed off with a damp rag before applying the zinc chloride for soldering. All flux should be washed off of the metal after soldering.

SOLDERING STAINLESS STEEL. Stainless steels can be soldered easily with prepared soldering fluxes designed especially for that purpose. If these special fluxes are not available, prepare the surface of the metal in the same way as the surface of tarnished copper is prepared. Scratch the surface with sandpaper and, with a small brush, apply raw acid to the parts to be soldered. After the acid has been left on the metal for the required time (which varies with the type of stainless steel and the strength of the acid), it should be wiped clean with a damp rag. The metal is then soldered in the same manner as copper, using regular half-and-half solder with zinc chloride as the flux. The flux should be thoroughly cleaned from the metal surface after soldering.

SOLDERING LEAD. Rosin flux is considered best for soldering lead. However, with lead, the surface must be scraped with a tinner's scraper immediately after cleaning, since this metal quickly oxides. The soldering iron must be well tinned and not too hot. There should be some solder between the hot iron and the lead at all times to keep the lead from melting.

Soldering seams

SOLDERING FLAT SEAMS. The illustrations in Fig. 14 show the proper and improper methods of soldering a flat seam. The seam at *A* shows how it looks when it is properly "sweated" together with a well-tinned and properly heated soldering iron. The seam at *B* shows the same seam when soldered with an iron which is too small, improperly tinned, and not sufficiently heated. Notice the blocked tunnel or opening at the joint of the seam which does not permit the solder to fuse the seam properly.

The two seams illustrate the difference between "sweating" and "skimming." Generally, soldered sheet metal seams are sweated. *Sweating* means holding the soldering iron in the proper manner, at the correct temperature, and in the proper position so that the solder flows completely through the seam. Sometimes joints are *pre-tinned and sweated*. This means that the pieces of metal are covered with a thin coat of solder before they are joined. Then the joint is sweated in the usual manner. A pre-tinned joint will show little solder on the surface but will have a completely sweated joint.

Skimming, as shown in *B* of Fig. 14 is generally an improper method of soldering. It only skims over the surface of the seam and therefore is weak and likely to leak.

Another term commonly used is *tacking.* This refers to the process of

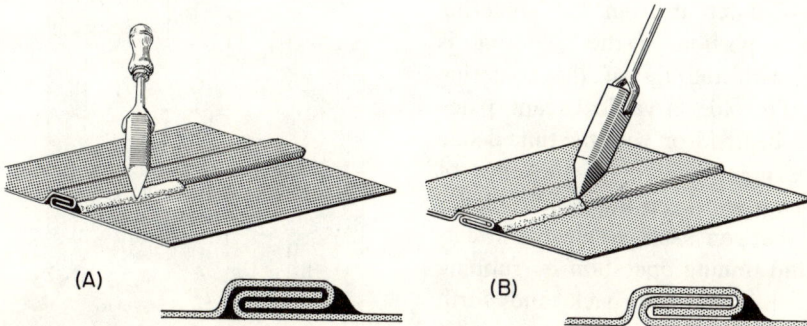

(A)   (B)

Figure 14. Proper method of soldering flat seams (A) permits solder to flow consistently in and around seam; improper method (B) does not.

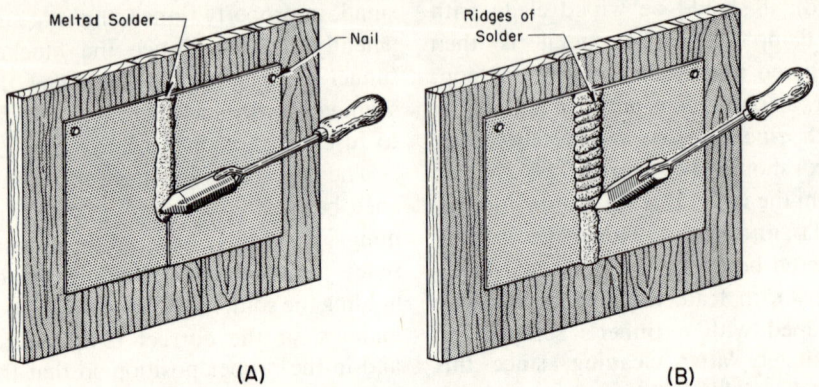

Figure 15. Begin soldering vertical seams by rubbing the iron back and forth as it is moved down the seam (A); then make ridges of solder with a left to right motion across the seam (B).

melting small drops of solder at intervals along a seam for the purpose of holding it in place until it is properly soldered.

SOLDERING COPPER SEAMS. When soldering copper seams, the same condition will be found as is shown in *B* of Fig. 14 if the parts to be soldered are not properly tinned. There is another important fact to be remembered when soldering copper. *Never use raw acid for soldering copper.*

SOLDERING UPRIGHT SEAMS. "Pointing up" is the term used to describe soldering vertical seams. This operation is different from flat soldering since a portion of the soldering is done with the tip of the soldering iron. To solder a vertical seam, place a well-heated iron with the tinned side of the point toward the top edge of the seam and keep the handle higher than the iron itself. Begin the sweating and tinning operation by rubbing the soldering iron back and forth across the seam. This is shown in *A* of Fig. 15. When the tinning opera-

tion has been completed, a reheated iron is again placed at the top of the seam with the tip of the iron touching the seam and with the handle elevated above the body of the iron. Apply a small portion of the solder. Move the iron back and forth across the seam, making small ridges as shown in *B* of Fig. 15. Continue until this seam is completed.

The illustration in Fig. 16 shows the soldering iron held in the wrong position. Note that the solder is dropping off the soldering iron. The illus-

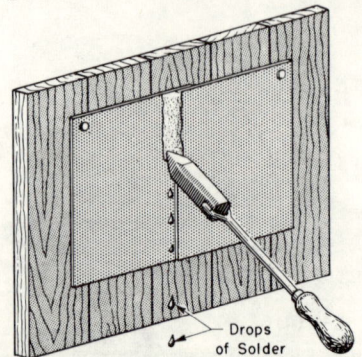

Figure 16. NEVER hold the soldering iron in this position to solder a vertical seam.

tration shows that it is impossible to solder a vertical seam correctly with the soldering iron handle lower than the iron.

Requirements for successful soldering

The successful application of soldering depends upon several elements including: properly tinned iron, application and type of flux, properly blended solder, type of soldering iron, correctly heated iron, properly prepared surface, oxidation of metal, the mechanical ability of the individual doing the soldering, etc.

When the student learns the requirements of successful soldering technique, he has made a good beginning. Thereafter, soldering skill will increase with application and with practice as the student continues training.

The illustrations in Fig. 17 demonstrate some things to avoid when soldering. They are presented as an aid to forming proper soldering technique and show such pitfalls to good soldering as:

1. *Poorly forged and tinned iron.* It is impossible to solder with a poorly forged or tinned iron.
2. *Overheated iron.* The temperature of the soldering iron should never be so hot that it will not hold a proper tinned coating.
3. *Broken handle.* Obviously, it is impossible to control the iron effectively when the handle is broken.
4. *Using raw acid on tin.* Solder will not correctly adhere to tin with raw acid as flux.
5. *Dirty solder.* It is impossible to solder with dirty or greasy solder.
6. *Bar too small.* A stub or small piece of solder is too short to hold in the hand.
7. *Soldering with the tip of the*

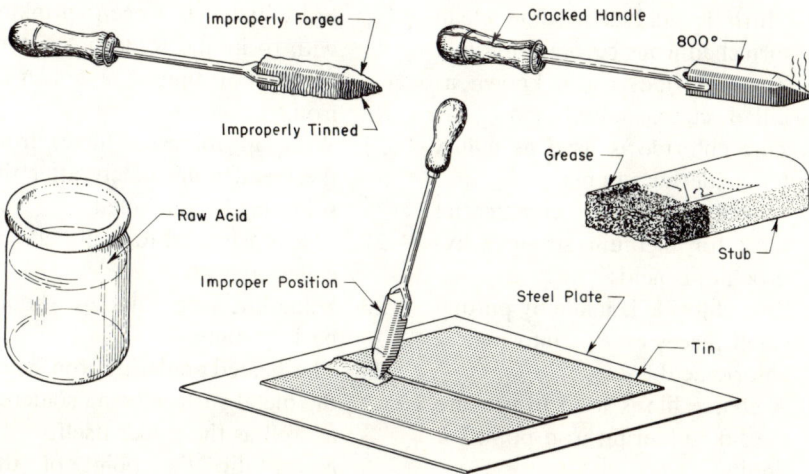

Figure 17. Examples of poor soldering procedures.

iron. It is impossible to get the proper flow using only the tip of the soldering iron.

8. *Soldering over a piece of steel.* A steel plate under the metal being soldered absorbs heat thus chilling the solder as it is applied. This makes for a poorly soldered joint.

9. *Cold iron.* The soldering iron must be hot enough to make the solder flow smoothly over the metal.

The following review should be studied before proceeding to the projects at the end of this chapter.

1. Solder used in the sheet metal shop is generally a 50-50 composition of lead and tin.

2. Tacking means melting drops of solder along a lap seam to hold it in place.

3. The two general classes of soldering are soft and hard.

4. A soldering iron must be tinned in order to do proper soldering.

5. Muriatic acid is used to clean tarnished irons before soldering.

6. Zinc chloride is also known as killed, cut, or cured acid.

7. Zinc chloride is used as a flux for soldering copper.

8. Muriatic acid is a commercial term for medium strength hydrochloric acid.

9. Zinc chloride is made by putting small pieces of zinc into hydrochloric acid.

10. A coarse file is used to prepare the hot soldering iron point for tinning.

11. A fine file is used to prepare corners of the soldering iron before tinning.

12. The three most commonly used soldering irons are: pointed, bottom, and roofing.

13. When soldering vertical seams, the soldering iron should not be tinned on more than two sides.

14 "Pointing up" is a term used to indicate soldering vertical seams.

15. The melting point of soft solder depends upon the proportions of tin and lead in the solder.

16. The term "sweating" means soldering surfaces so as to make the solder to run between the two surfaces completely filling the joint.

17. Sheet copper should be tinned before soldering it.

18. Gas furnaces should always be turned off when not in use.

19. Red-hot soldering irons cannot be tinned.

20. Rubbing a soldering iron on a brick which has been sprinkled with rosin and solder is another method of tinning a soldering iron.

21. Wipe all corrosive fluxes from the metal immediately after the soldering is completed.

22. The brush used to apply acid is called a swab.

23. Soldering iron handles should be kept tight.

24. The heated soldering iron heats the metal surface being soldered as well as the solder itself.

25. Never dip the point of the soldering iron into the flux.

26. Keep soldering flux free of dirt.
27. Always apply a lighted match before turning on the gas furnace.
28. Never stand directly in front of the gas furnace when lighting it.
29. When making zinc chloride, avoid inhaling fumes.
30. Sal ammoniac is used in the soldering dip solution.
31. Short stubs of solder may be attached to a new bar by melting the ends together.

Review Questions

1. What is meant by the term sweating?
2. What type of flux is used to solder sheet copper?
3. What type of flux is used to solder tin plate?
4. What type of flux is used to solder galvanized metal?
5. What is meant by a dip?
6. What are the two general types of soldering?
7. Describe how a soldering iron is tinned.
8. Describe how a soldering iron is forged.
9. What is the common tin to lead ratio in soft solder used in sheet metal shops?
10. Name four types of soldering irons.
11. Describe the procedure for making zinc chloride.
12. What is meant by the term tacking?
13. What is the commercial name for hydrochloric acid?
14. What is the difference between hard and soft soldering?
15. Why should a soldering iron be filed before forging?
16. Why should corrosive fluxes be washed off of the metal after soldering?
17. Describe the procedure for soldering upright or vertical seams.
18. What are the principal corrosive fluxes?
19. What are the principal non-corrosive fluxes?
20. When making zinc chloride, why should the jar in which it is being made be placed in ventilation?
21. Name several characteristics of a poor soldering job.

Projects

Project 10-1. Forging and tinning a soldering iron

AIM. To teach the proper method of preparing a soldering iron for soldering.

OPERATION A. Forging the soldering iron.

1. Select, if possible, a badly worn, blunt, soldering iron for practicing purposes.
2. Heat it almost red in the gas furnace.
3. Place the soldering iron in the vise and file it with coarse file until the scales are removed.

4. Replace the iron in the furnace and heat to a cherry red.
5. With the handle of the soldering iron in the left hand and a heavy hammer in the right hand, place the end of the body of the iron against the anvil. Strike the point or tip of the iron, forcing it back into the body as previously explained in the chapter.
6. Reheat the soldering iron and place it on the rail at the required angle and forge into shape, turning the iron around as it is being forged.
7. Reheat the iron and repeat this operation until the iron is smooth and drawn to the required shape. The soldering iron is now ready for tinning.

OPERATION B. Tinning a soldering iron.
1. Heat the soldering iron body.
2. Place the heat of the iron in the vise at a slight angle.
3. File the point on the sides to be tinned with a coarse file.
4. File the corners and tip smooth with a fine file, removing all burred or rough edges.
5. Reheat the iron. Rub the point on a block of sal ammoniac and apply some solder at the same time.

OPERATION C. Alternate method of tinning a soldering iron.
1. Heat, file, and reheat the soldering iron, as in previous operations.
2. With a pinch of rosin on a rough brick, rub the point of the iron, applying a little solder as it is being tinned. Do not overheat the soldering iron or it will not tin properly. A well finished soldering iron can be spoiled by too much heat before it is tinned and such an iron becomes pitted by being burned too many times. Therefore, care should be exercised to control heat distribution.

Project 10-2. Soldering a flat seam on various types of metals

AIM. To teach the method of flat soldering.

OPERATION A. Soldering galvanized metal.
1. Make a groove seam 8″ long with two pieces of galvanized metal.
2. Place the seam to be soldered in the proper position.
3. Apply some raw acid on the seam with a swab.
4. Dip the point of the soldering iron in the dipping solution or wipe with a damp cloth. Apply beads of solder to the opening of the seam.
5. Hold the soldering iron in the right hand, placing the iron on the metal with the side of the point on the seam.
6. Draw the iron along the seam, adding more solder whenever necessary. Always begin at the end of the seam and draw the iron forward.
7. Reheat the soldering iron from time to time so the sweating effect will be uniform throughout the seam.

8. Wash the acid from the metal.

OPERATION B. Soldering sheet copper.

1. Make an 8″ grooved seam with two pieces of copper.
2. With an acid brush, apply raw acid to the seam. Let it stand a few minutes and then wipe it off with a clean damp rag.
3. Heat and tin the soldering iron.
4. Apply the soldering flux, in this case zinc chloride.
5. Begin the soldering with a hot soldering iron starting at the end and drawing the soldering iron forward.
6. Reheat the soldering iron often to keep it hot during the entire soldering operation.
7. Wash the flux free of the metal. When soldering sheet copper, the parts to be soldered may be tinned before making the groove seam.

OPERATION C. Tinning sheet copper for soldering.

1. Clean the parts to be soldered by applying clean, raw acid.
2. Wash off the acid with a slightly damp cloth.
3. Melt some solder on the metal with a hot soldering iron, holding the iron on the metal until the solder begins to flow.
4. Draw the soldering iron along and at the same time add solder to tin the copper with a thin coating of solder.
5. Reheat the soldering iron whenever necessary.
6. The used flux should be removed and new flux applied before the soldering is completed.

Project 10-3. Soldering an upright seam

Soldering vertical or upright seams requires practice and patience. The student should study the illustrations in Fig. 15 of this chapter. Notice that the seam is tinned with the flat side of the pointed soldering iron. At the same time, the solder is sweated into the seam. This is important, since it makes the process of pointing or leading the seam easier to perform and it strengthens the soldered seam.

AIM. To teach the method of soldering a vertical seam, using tin, copper, and galvanized metal. Tools and equipment required include an acid brush, soldering iron, furnace, necessary tools for making a flat seam (grooved, lap, or folded), pieces of scrap metal, 50-50 solder, and fluxes.

OPERATION

1. Make the flat seam, using scraps of tin, copper, and galvanized metal. Hammer the seams smooth.
2. Nail the metal to the wall.
3. Apply the soldering flux.
4. Begin at the top and sweat the seal with a correctly prepared soldering iron, using the flat side of the pointed iron.
5. Apply a little flux.
6. With the soldering iron reheated, begin at the top and move the tips of the iron back and forth across the seam. Apply a little solder as the soldering iron is moved down the seam.
7. Apply the solder as needed.
8. Solder the remaining seams.

11

DRAWING FOR PATTERN DRAFTING

What instruments are used in pattern drafting? What geometric figures are used in making patterns. How are these figures drawn? How are the principles of geometric construction applied to pattern drafting?

Pattern drafting plays a vital part in the development of many sheet metal projects. Therefore, this chapter is a general review of the drafting equipment necessary to produce such patterns as well as the geometric constructions which are frequently employed in layout work. Much of the pattern layout work done by the sheet metal worker applies the principles of geometric constructions such as found in describing perpendiculars, bisecting angles, and dividing lines into equal segments. It is also important to be familiar with the lines and angles used to produce such constructions since obviously all patterns are composed of such lines and angles.

One of the most important aspects of pattern development is the ability to visualize the finished job from the flat pattern. Once this ability has been developed, it is much easier to con-struct patterns even for complicated projects. All pattern drafting should be done with accuracy so that the finished projects do not have to be bent or twisted into the intended shape.

Fundamentals of pattern drafting

Professional sheet metal craftsmen must not only be able to perform mechanical operations both by hand and by machine, but must often be able to design and develop their own patterns. With this in mind, information is presented here which the student will apply in subsequent chapters dealing with specific methods of developing patterns.

Methods of developing patterns

A *pattern* is a flat outline of the object that is to be made. When this outline is cut and formed into its final shape, it becomes the desired object. When

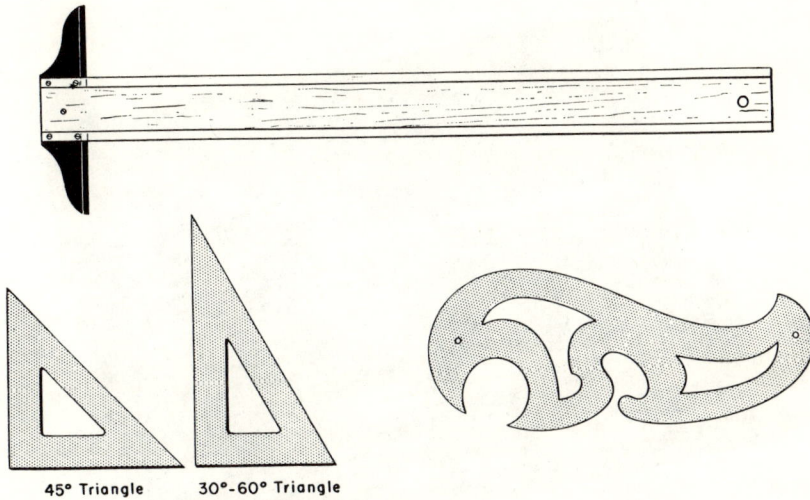

45° Triangle   30°-60° Triangle

Figure 1. T squares, triangles, and French curves are used to draw horizontal, vertical and slanted lines and curves.

patterns are used repeatedly, they are generally made of metal and patterns of this kind are termed *templates* or master patterns.

The commonly used methods by which such patterns are developed for sheet metal objects are: *parallel line development, radial line development,* and *triangulation.* Each of these methods will be discussed in subsequent chapters.

Drafting equipment

The student should provide himself with a complete set of drafting tools such as is shown in Fig. 1. This equipment includes:

DRAFTING BOARD. The purpose of the drafting board is to hold the paper in place when a development is being drawn. The sides of the board act as a guide for the T square. Conventional drafting boards are usually 18″

× 24″, but larger boards for other purposes are available.

T SQUARE. The purpose of the T square is to aid in drawing horizontal lines and to act as a guide for triangles. Swivel head T squares are employed to draw a series of lines at a specified angle.

TRIANGLES. Two triangles are necessary—the 45° and the 30°-60°.

IRREGULAR CURVES. Irregular (or French) curves are used to connect points not in a straight line and to draw irregular curves. However, the student is urged to practice freehand drawing for this purpose whenever convenient, since it will be found useful in making larger developments.

DRAFTING INSTRUMENTS. Some of the more important of such instruments are shown in Fig. 2. A drawing set should include: a large pencil compass for large arcs and circles, a

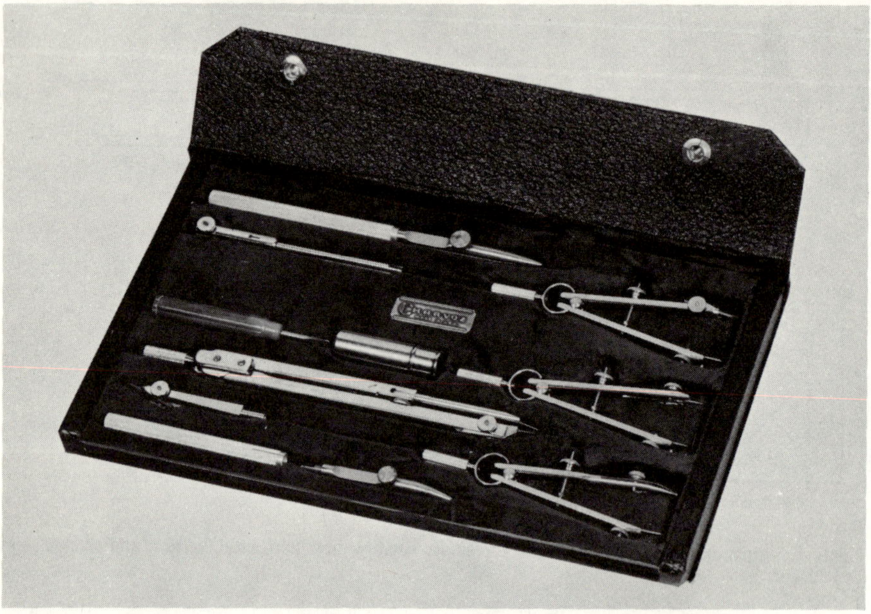

Figure 2. This standard drawing set contains the instruments used to make most drawings. Courtesy: The Charvos Company.

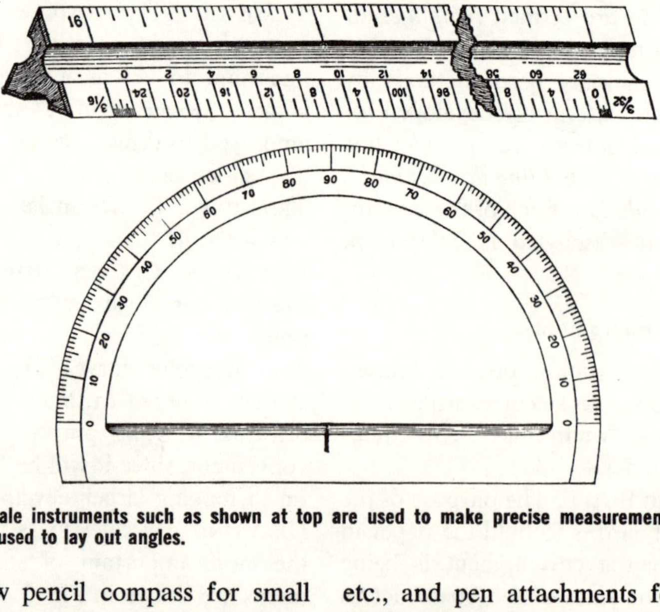

Figure 3. Scale instruments such as shown at top are used to make precise measurements and protractors are used to lay out angles.

small bow pencil compass for small arcs and circles, large and small dividers for spacing profiles, circles, etc., and pen attachments for ruling ink drawings.

SCALES. The triangular scale, shown

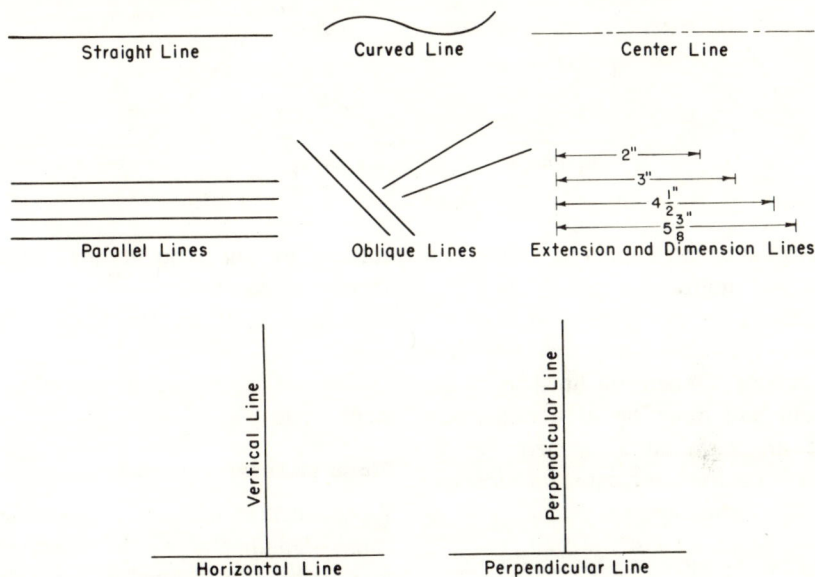

Figure 4. Some of the important lines used in developing sheet metal patterns.

in Fig. 3, may be used for making measurements. However, a common rule which is graduated in $\frac{1}{16}$″, $\frac{1}{8}$″, etc., can also be used for this purpose.

PROTRACTORS. Protractors, also shown in Fig. 3 are used to draw angles of various sizes.

PENCILS. Pencils used for pattern drafting should have both strength and smoothness. Grades of such pencils vary from H to 9H—the "H" indicating the hardness. For most drafting work a 2H pencil will be found to be satisfactory.

Lines

A variety of lines are used in the design and development of sheet metal patterns. The more important of such lines are shown in Fig. 4.

The following information concerning lines should be studied carefully.

A line is a measurement of length. It is produced by the motion of a point and may be straight or curved.

A straight line is one having the same direction throughout. It is the shortest distance between two points.

A curved line is one whose direction is continually changing.

Parallel lines are lines having the same course which do not meet. They are equally distant from each other.

Horizontal lines are parallel to the horizon.

Vertical lines are at right angles or perpendicular to the horizontal line.

Oblique lines may be drawn at any angle *between* the vertical and horizontal positions.

Perpendicular lines are referred to as upright lines. They may be at right angles to a given line.

Center lines are used to show the

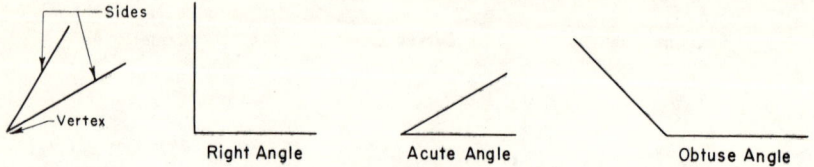

Figure 5. Angles.

axes of symmetrical parts, circles, and paths of motion.

Dimension and *extension lines* are used with figures to show the sizes of objects. Dimension lines show the extent and direction of a dimension and are terminated by arrowheads. Extension lines indicate the termination of a dimension.

Angles

An angle is formed by the meeting of two straight lines as shown in Fig. 5. The lines are called the *sides* of the angle and the point of intersection is called the *vertex*. Angles are drawn by use of the protractor or triangle.

Right angles are angles of 90°,

formed by one straight line perpendicular to another.

Acute angles are less than a right angle.

Obtuse angles are greater than a right angle.

Plane surfaces

Plane surfaces have only two dimensions—length and width. A polygon may be broadly defined as any figure made up of plane surfaces and having many sides. The illustration in Fig. 6 shows only those polygons related to pattern development. In addition, the following definitions of some of the more familiar polygons will be helpful.

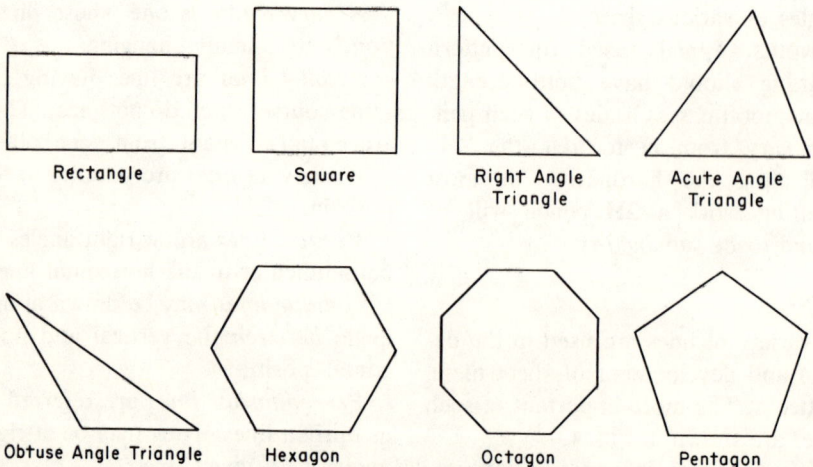

Figure 6. Types of polygons.

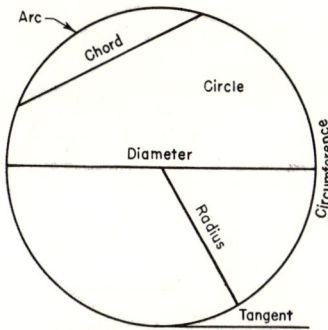

Figure 7. Parts of a circle.

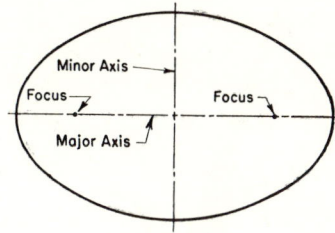

Figure 8. Ellipse.

A *rectangle* is a four-sided figure whose angles are right angles.

A *triangle* is a figure bounded by three straight lines and having three angles.

A *right-angle triangle* is a triangle with one of its sides at a right angle.

An *acute-angle triangle* has all acute angles.

An *obtuse-angle triangle* has one obtuse angle.

A *pentagon* has five equal sides.

A *hexagon* has six equal sides.

An *octagon* has eight equal sides.

CIRCLES. A circle is a plane figure bounded by a curved line called the *circumference,* every part of which is equally distant from the center. The illustration in Fig. 7 shows the following parts of a circle.

An *arc* is any part of the circumference of a circle.

A *chord* is a straight line joining the extremities of an arc.

The *diameter* of a circle is a straight line drawn through its center to opposite points on the circumference.

The *radius* of a circle is a straight line drawn from the center of the circle to any part of the circumference.

A *tangent* is a straight line of unlimited length which touches the circumference of the circle at only one point.

ELLIPSE. An ellipse is a plane figure bounded by a curved line described about two points in such a manner that the sum of the distances from every point in the curve to the two fixed points is always the same. The two points are called *foci,* the two lines are the major and minor axes. See Fig. 8.

Solid geometric figures

The following solid geometric figures are often found in sheet metal pattern drafting. Solids have three dimensions —length, breadth, and thickness.

A *cone* is a solid having a circular base and a curved surface joining at a point called the *apex,* as shown in Fig. 9.

A *right cone* is a cone having the apex centered above the center of the base. The axis is perpendicular to the base.

The *oblique cone* is a cone having the apex off center to the base.

The *frustum* of a cone is that por-

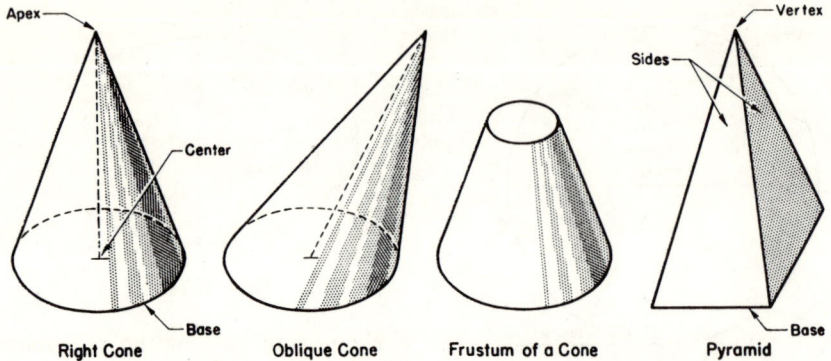

Figure 9. Types of cones and pyramids and terms used to describe their parts.

tion of a cone included between the base and a plane parallel to the base.

A *pyramid* is a figure whose base is a polygon and whose lateral faces are triangles which meet at a point called the *vertex*.

Geometric constructions

Many of the situations which arise in pattern drafting layout work can be solved by employing the following geometric constructions.

BISECTING A STRAIGHT LINE. See *A* of Fig. 10. Let *ST* be the line which is to be divided into two equal parts. From the ends of *ST,* with any radius greater than half but less than the length of *ST,* scribe the intersecting arcs *UV* and *WX*. A line drawn through the intersecting points will bisect the line at *Y*.

DIVIDING A LINE INTO EQUAL PARTS. See *B* of Fig. 10. Let *ST* be the line to be divided. Bisect *ST* at *U*. Bisect lines *SU* and *UT* at *V* and *W*. Continue bisecting until the required number of parts (2, 4, 8, 16, etc.) are found.

A method, shown in *C* of Fig. 10, of dividing a line into any number of equal parts is as follows: draw line *ST* to the required length; draw a slant line *SU* to any angle and to a length that can be conveniently divided with a rule into the required number of spaces. Connect point *V* (last division) with the end of the line *ST* at *T* to give the line *TV*. Lines drawn parallel to *TV* through the numbered points will give the required number of equal divisions.

STEPPING-OFF EQUAL DIVISIONS. In pattern drafting, one of the more common operations is dividing a circle into equal parts and dividing the stretchout of the circumference of this circle into the same number of parts. The methods discussed in the preceding section can be used to accomplish this. Most sheet metal men, however, use a system called "stepping-off."

Whenever a circle must be divided into equal parts, the usual number chosen is six to the half-circle since this is the most convenient. The drawing in *D* of Fig. 10 shows how to divide a half-circle into six equal spaces. After

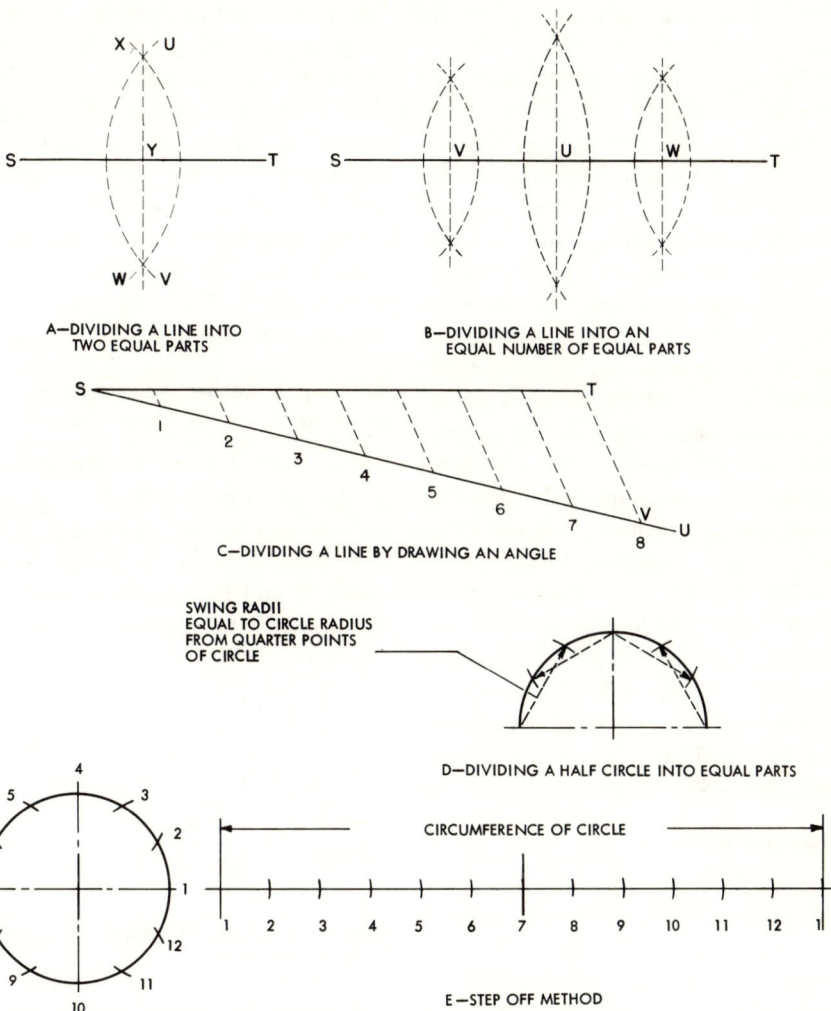

A—DIVIDING A LINE INTO
TWO EQUAL PARTS

B—DIVIDING A LINE INTO AN
EQUAL NUMBER OF EQUAL PARTS

C—DIVIDING A LINE BY DRAWING AN ANGLE

SWING RADII
EQUAL TO CIRCLE RADIUS
FROM QUARTER POINTS
OF CIRCLE

D—DIVIDING A HALF CIRCLE INTO EQUAL PARTS

CIRCUMFERENCE OF CIRCLE

E—STEP OFF METHOD

Figure 10. Dividing lines by geometric construction methods.

the half-circle is drawn, leave the dividers set equal to the radius of the circle. Swing this radius from the quarter points of the circle to divide each quarter-circle into three equal parts.

After the circle is divided into equal parts, as shown in *E* of Fig. 10, determine the circumference of the circle from the circumference rule and draw a line equal to this circumference. Next measure the mid-point on the circumference line. This can be done by bisecting the line as shown in the preceding section. By dividing the circumference in half, the first stepping-off can be done on half of the circumference to save time.

To step off the equal spaces, set the dividers to one of the spaces on the circle. This will not be precisely the space for the circumference line since the dividers are measuring across a chord rather than around the arc. Step the distance off on one half of the circumference line. In six steps the dividers will probably be short of the half-way mark on the circumference line. Adjust the dividers to approximately one-sixth of this error and step off again. When the total number of spaces equals the half-way mark exactly, then step off the other half of the circumference to divide the line into the same spacing as the circle. With a little practice, you will be able to set and step off the correct distance in the second or third attempt and you will find that this is the most practical method after you gain experience.

Bisecting angles

The method of bisecting angles is shown in Fig. 11. To bisect a right

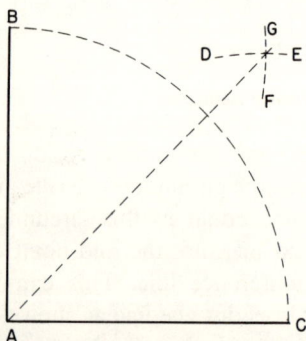

Figure 11. Bisecting an angle using geometric construction.

angle, proceed as follows: draw the right angle *BAC* to any desired size. With *A* as center and any convenient radius, describe the arc *BC*. With *B* and *C* as centers and a radius great enough to interest, scribe arcs *DE* and *FG*. Draw a straight line from *A* through the intersecting point of arcs *DE* and *FG*. This line will be the bisecting line. The same procedure is followed for bisecting other angles.

Erecting a perpendicular to a straight line at a given point

See Fig. 12. Let *AB* be the line and *C* the given point. With *C* as center and any radius, draw semi-circle *AD*. With *A* and *D* as centers, strike arcs *GH* and *EF*. A line drawn from the point of intersection of the arcs

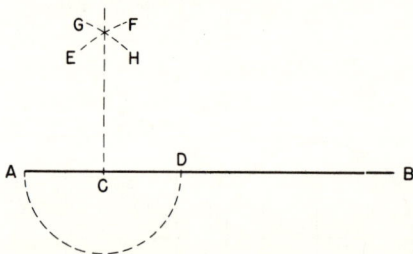

Figure 12. Erecting a perpendicular to a straight line at a given point.

to point *C* will be the perpendicular line.

Constructing polygons

The construction of regular polygons is shown in Fig. 13. The steps for each figure should be followed carefully since understanding the procedure will help the student in shortening his pattern development work time.

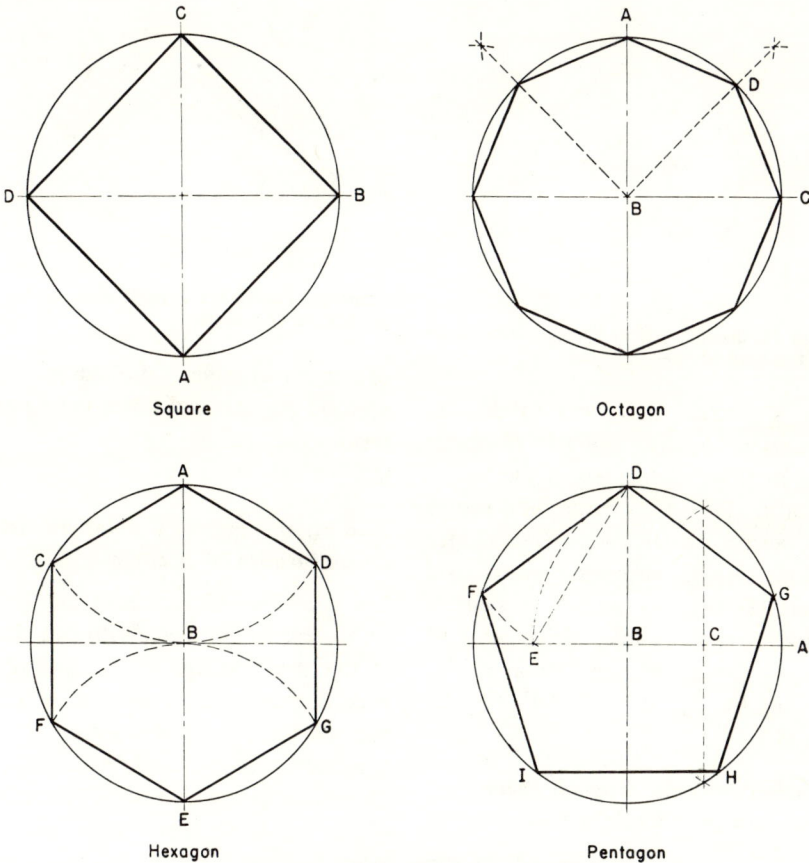

Figure 13. Constructing regular polygons.

CONSTRUCTING A SQUARE WITHIN A CIRCLE. See Fig. 13. Draw the circle, dividing it into quarters by drawing two diameters at right angles to each other. Connect points *A, B, C,* and *D,* completing the square.

CONSTRUCTING A HEXAGON. A hexagon, as shown in Fig. 13, may be constructed as follows: Draw the circle to the required size. Draw two diameters at right angles. With a compass set to equal the radius of the circle and with *A* and *E* as centers, scribe

the arcs *CD* and *FG* as shown. Connect points *A, D, G, E, F,* and *C* with straight lines, completing the hexagon as shown.

CONSTRUCTING AN OCTAGON. Draw the circle in Fig. 13 to the required size, dividing it into quarters. Bisect the angle *ABC* at *D.* Thus, *AD* and *DC* equal two sides of the octagon. Repeat this procedure for the remaining three quarters to complete the construction of the octagon.

CONSTRUCTING A PENTAGON. As in

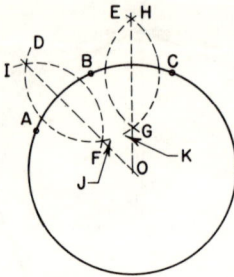

Figure 14. Drawing a circle through three points not in a straight line.

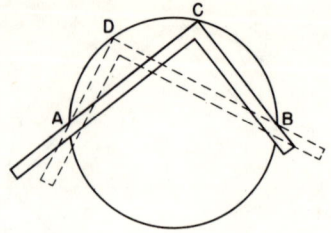

Figure 15. Finding the opposite point on the circumference of a circle.

Fig. 13, scribe the circle to the desired size, drawing the two diameter lines at right angles. Bisect the radius *AB* at *C*. With *C* as center and radius *CD,* scribe arc *DE.* With *D* as center and radius *DE,* scribe the arc *EF* and point, *G.* With *G* and *F* as centers and the same radius, strike arcs *H* and *I.* Complete the pentagon by drawing the chords, *GD, DF, FI, IH,* and *HG.*

Drawing a circle through three points not in a straight line

Let *A, B,* and *C* in Fig. 14 be the given points. With *B* as center, scribe the arcs *EK* and *DJ.* With *A* and *C* as centers, scribe arcs *IF* and *HG.* Draw the two perpendicular bisectors until they meet at *Q.* This gives the

center to complete the circle. This method may be used when finding centers for metal disks, completing circles, etc.

Finding the opposite point on the circumference of a circle

Let *A* in Fig. 15 represent one point on the circumference. With the blade of the steel square on the circumference of the circle at point *A,* and the heel of the square touching the circumference of the circle at any other convenient point, as *D* or *C,* the point where the blade touches the circumference of the circle, *B,* will be a point opposite *A* on the circumference of the circle. This method is used for locating holes for pipe dampers, placing ears on pails, etc. No measurements are necessary in this procedure.

Review Questions

1. What are the purposes of dimension and extension lines?
2. What is meant by a polygon?
3. Name four kinds of polygons.
4. Name three common geometric angles used in pattern drafting.
5. What are the parts of a circle?

6. What is an ellipse?
7. Describe the frustum of a cone.
8. Describe a right cone.
9. Describe an oblique cone.
10. What are the principle drafting instruments used in pattern drafting?
11. What are three principle methods

by which patterns are developed?

12. What are the purposes of the drafting board?

13. Describe a hexagon.

14. Name several objects which are hexagonal in shape.

Projects

Project 11-1. Drawing a line parallel to a given line

AIM. To apply the principles of geometric construction to pattern layout work.

OPERATIONS

1. Draw a straight line of any length.
2. From points *A* and *B*, erect perpendiculars as shown in Fig. 16.

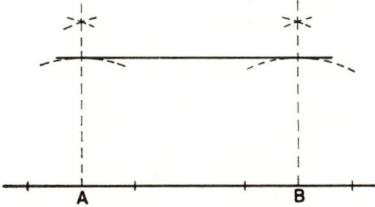

Figure 17. Drawing a 90° corner arc using a compass.

Figure 16. Drawing a line parallel to a given line.

3. With points *A* and *B* as centers and any given radius, strike arcs cutting the perpendiculars as shown.
4. Draw a line through the points of intersection of the arcs and the perpendiculars. This line will be parallel to line *AB*.

Project 11-2. Connecting 90° lines with a 90° arc of a given radius

AIM. To learn how to make radius corners as required in pattern drafting.

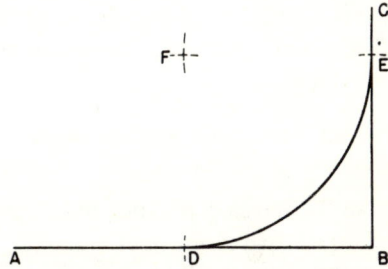

OPERATIONS

1. Draw a right angle of any size, such as *ABC* in Fig. 17.
2. Set the compass to the radius required for the 90° arc.
3. With *B* as center, scribe arcs cutting the lines at *D* and *E* as shown.
4. With points *E* and *D* as centers, and with the same radius, scribe intersecting arcs as at *F*.
5. With *F* as center and the same radius, scribe *DE,* which is the required 90° arc.

Project 11-3. Drawing polygons

AIM. To learn the various shapes of polygons.

OPERATIONS

Draw the following to full size: 1. hexagon inscribed in a 3″ diameter circle, 2. pentagon inscribed within a 3″ diameter circle, 3. right angle triangle with 2″ sides, and 4. acute triangle of any size.

Project 11-4. Drawing the parts of a circle

AIM. To give practice in learning the parts of a circle.

OPERATIONS

Draw a circle with the diameter, radius, chord, tangent, and circumference labeled.

Project 11-5. Stepping-off equal divisions on a line

AIM. To develop practice in stepping off equal spaces on lines.

SPECIFICATIONS. Draw three lines and step them off into twelve equal spaces.

OPERATIONS

1. Draw a straight line 7″ long and step it off into twelve equal spaces according to the instructions in this chapter.

2. Repeat this process with a line 9½″ long, and with a line 8¼″ long.

Project 11-6. Dividing a half-circle into six equal spaces

AIM. To give practice in dividing a circle into six equal spaces.

SPECIFICATIONS. Draw a half-circle with a 2″ radius and step it off into six equal parts.

OPERATIONS

1. Draw a half-circle with a 2″ radius.

2. Divide the half-circle into quarter-circles.

3. Following the directions in this chapter, divide the half-circle into six equal parts.

4. Turn in to the instructor for checking.

12

MAKING AND NOTCHING SIMPLE PATTERNS

What are the steps involved in laying out simple patterns on metal? What are the basic methods of notching? How should the patterns appear for a simple box, rectangular duct, rectangular duct elbow, and round pipe?

In the first 10 chapters, you were primarily concerned with the tools, machines, and materials which are used in the sheet metal trade. Chapter 11 presented you with the instruments and the commonly used geometric constructions which are employed in order to produce sheet metal patterns. However, in order to be able to usefully apply the information in Chapter 11, it is clearly necessary to develop the ability to be able to actually lay out such patterns on metal.

Many of the layouts in sheet metal work are known as *simple patterns*. These patterns are so called because no advanced drafting knowledge is required in order to execute them; but only a basic understanding of how to measure, draw, and apply the principles of straight lines, arcs, circles, and the other geometric constructions with which you were presented in the preceding chapter.

Steps in laying out a simple pattern directly on sheet metal

Though many of the patterns the sheet metal worker lays out may vary to some degree, the steps by which such patterns are laid out remain the same. By applying the following steps in the process of laying out a pattern, you will avoid both errors and waste.

1. *Check the sheet metal on which your pattern will be made.* Often the bottom of a sheet will have a slight bow in it from the rolling process. Check the bottom edge of the sheet with a straightedge since any such bowing or warping in the metal will necessarily affect accuracy.

2. *Square up the left-hand end of the sheet.* The ends of the sheet are seldom perfectly square at the edges. Therefore, it is necessary on any layout to square to the left-hand end of the sheet to the bottom edge. The usual method is to use a two-foot or three-foot square and draw a line about ¼″ from the end so as to be square with the bottom edge.

3. *Always make your layout in the lower left-hand corner of the sheet.* One of the chief characteristics of the true craftsman in any trade is the ability to do a job with the least amount of waste material. When the pattern is laid out as close to the lower left-hand corner as possible, the metal above and to the

right of the pattern will then be usable for other patterns.

4. *Measurements should be from the bottom and left-hand square line.* In Fig. 1, the line measurements shown would be taken from left to right, and from the bottom up. Never try to cut your metal exactly to size and measure in from all four edges to make the layout. This increases the chance of error since it is then much more possible to miscalculate the size or get the metal slightly out of alignment. If the sheet is left uncut and measured from left to right and from the bottom up, the entire width and length of the sheet is available on which to work.

5. *Make measurements at both*

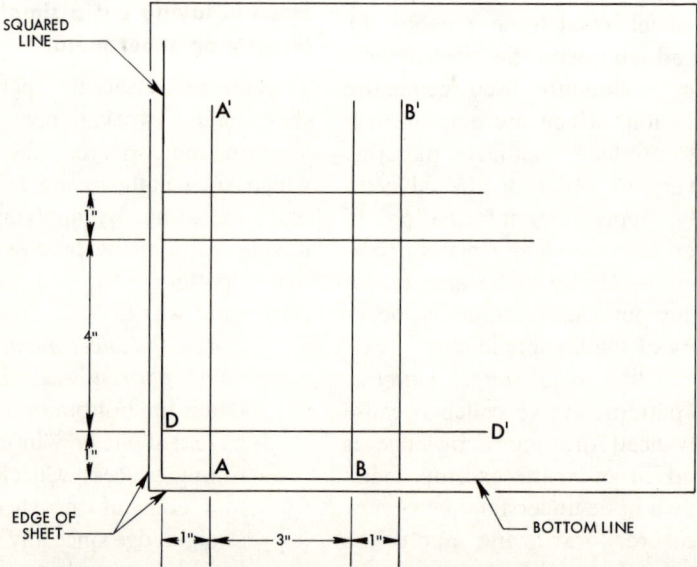

Figure 1. Layout measurements should be taken from left to right and from the bottom up.

*ends of each line and draw a
line through the two points.* Ordinarily, one line at the left-
hand end of the sheet is squared
only. Do not try to square other
lines from the edges as would
be done in mechanical drafting.
In Fig. 1, if line *AA'* is to be
1″ from the squared line, the
proper method is to measure 1″
at *A* and 1″ at *A'* and then
draw a line through these two
points. Line *BB'* is 3″ away
from *AA'*, so 3″ from *A'* and *A*
should be marked and a line
drawn through these two points.
The horizontal lines, such as
DD' are handled in the same
way. One inch from the bottom
line is measured at *D* and *D'*
and the line is drawn through
these two points.

6. *Draw in all the vertical lines and
horizontal lines.* Then add lines
for miters, notches, seams,
edges, and laps. If all vertical
and then all horizontal lines are
drawn, the basic pattern is generally complete. It is therefore
important to be sure that all
lines are drawn *before* starting
to cut out and form the metal.

7. *Prick mark all bend lines.* Before starting to form the pattern, prick mark all bend lines
about ¼″ from the end of the
line. In addition to making
bends from the unmarked side
of the metal, you may want to
mark some other patterns from
the first pattern. In that case,
prick marks will show the bend

lines. Do not depend upon the
corners of notches for bend locations.

8. *Study the shape of basic patterns.* Box patterns, for example, may be in a variety of sizes
and may use different seams
and edges. However, they will
always be in the same basic
shape. As was mentioned in
Chapter 11, one of the most important considerations in developing a pattern is the ability
to visualize the finished job
from the flat pattern.

9. *After you have made the layout, check overall dimensions
on each side of the pattern.* This
is particularly important on patterns drawn with parallel lines.
When, as in Fig. 1, parallel
lines are employed, the width
of the pattern at the top and
bottom should obviously be the
same. If they vary more than
$\frac{1}{16}$″, this indicates an error in
measurement.

Notching and clipping

Notching and clipping are used to cut
away portions of the metal to prevent
overlapping and bulging on seams and
edges. Both are separate operations.
SQUARE NOTCH. The square notch, as
illustrated in Fig. 2, is used on pans
and boxes to enable the corners to
fit together. The size of the notch is
determined by the bend lines as shown
in the illustration.
45° NOTCH. The 45° notch made in
the form of a V is used when double-
seaming the ends of projects such as

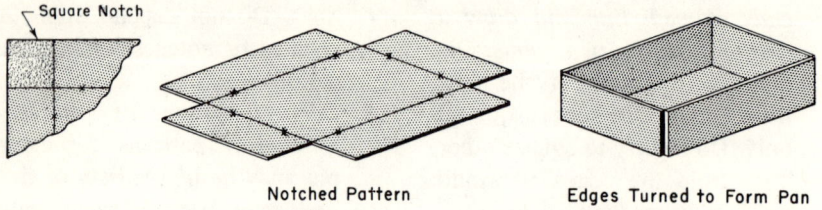

Square Notch

Notched Pattern   Edges Turned to Form Pan

Figure 2. Square notches are used on pans and boxes.

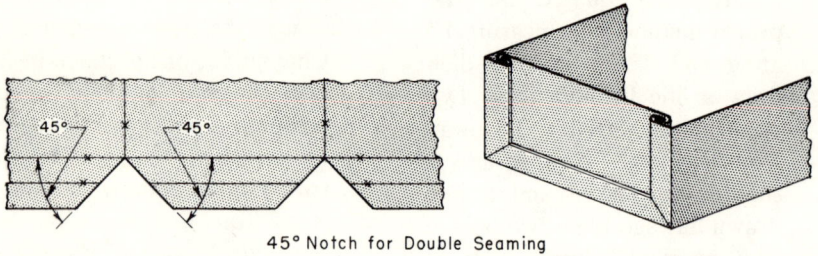

45°   45°

45° Notch for Double Seaming

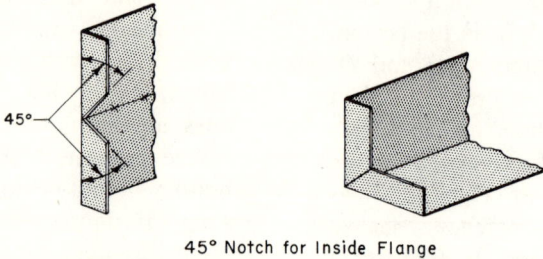

45°

45° Notch for Inside Flange

Figure 3. 45° notches are used in inside flanges or when double seaming the ends of pans.

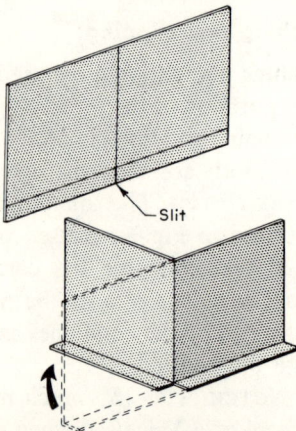

Slit

Figure 4. Straight notch.

pans, or when making a 90° bend on any job with an inside flange, as illustrated in Fig. 3. When the bend of an inside flange meets at an angle other than 90°, the notch must be marked to the necessary angle.

STRAIGHT NOTCH. Fig. 4 shows how to make a straight notch or slit edge.

NOTCHES FOR WIRED EDGES. In places where wired edges cross seams, the pattern is notched to prevent the material from overlapping. The angle of the notch is usually 30°, and the distance from which the notch is started is 3½ times the diameter of the wire, as is shown in Fig. 5.

CLIPPING. When a single hem meets at right angles, the pattern is clipped at a 45° angle as shown in Fig. 6. Angles other than 45° may be used depending upon the shape of the pattern. On some patterns, a combination of these processes may be necessary in order to obtain a proper fit.

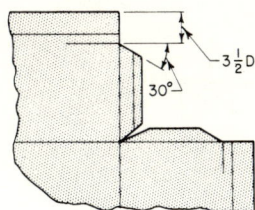

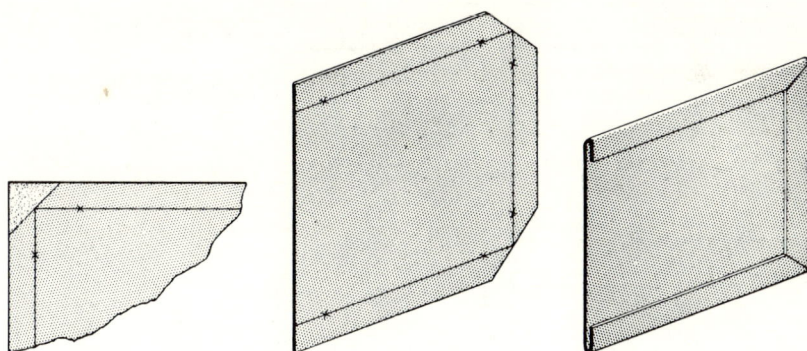

Figure 5. Notches where wired edges cross seams prevent the material from overlapping.

Figure 6. Clipping for single hem.

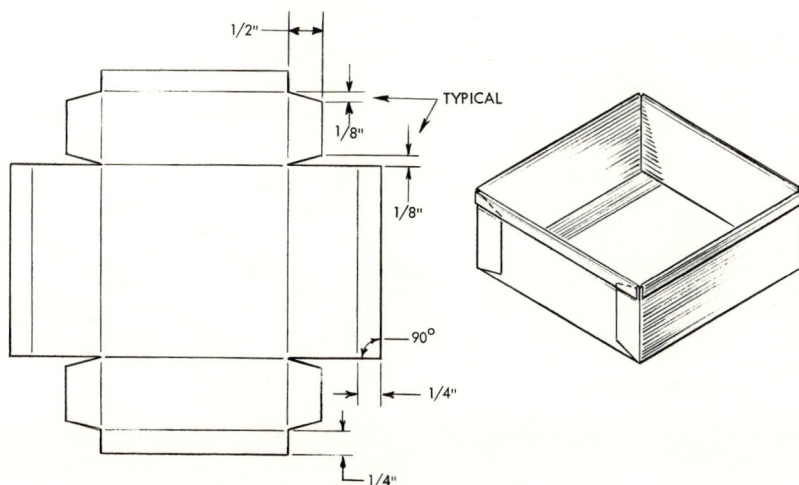

Figure 7. Pattern for one-piece box with ½″ lapped corners and ¼″ single hem.

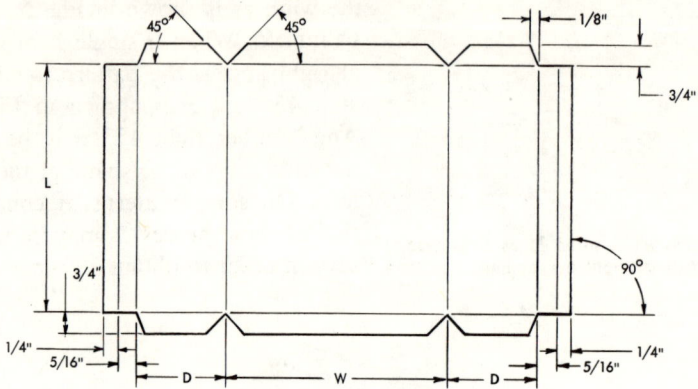

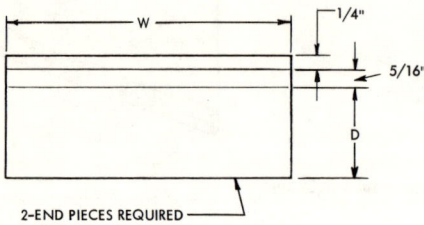

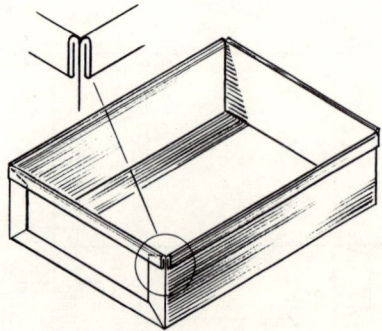

Figure 8. Pattern for three-piece box with ¾″ laps and 5/16″ double hem. Laps may be spot welded, riveted, or soldered.

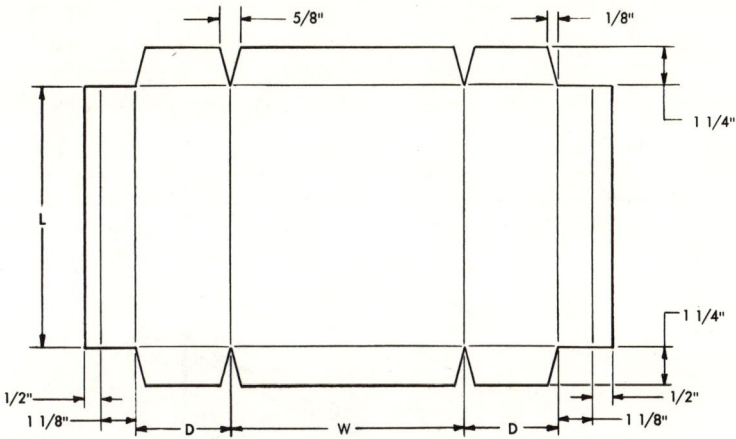

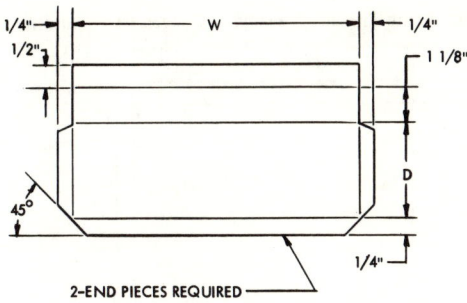

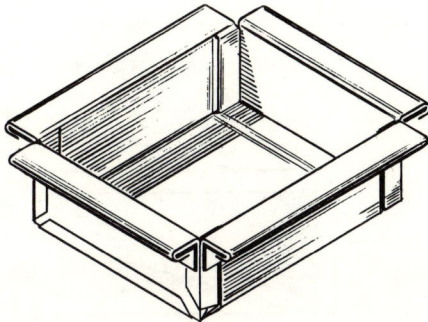

Figure 9. Pattern for box with 1″ × 1″ × ⅛″ angle iron edge with end set in with Pittsburgh seam.

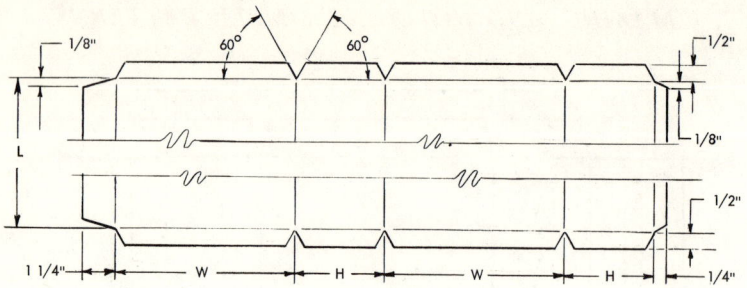

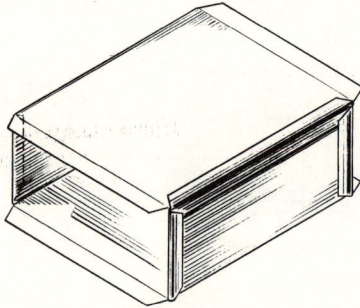

Figure 10. Pattern for one-piece duct with Pittsburgh seams and edges for S and drive clips.

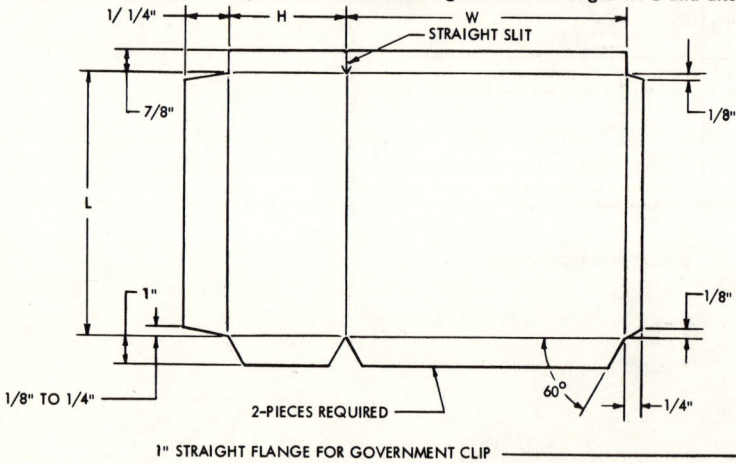

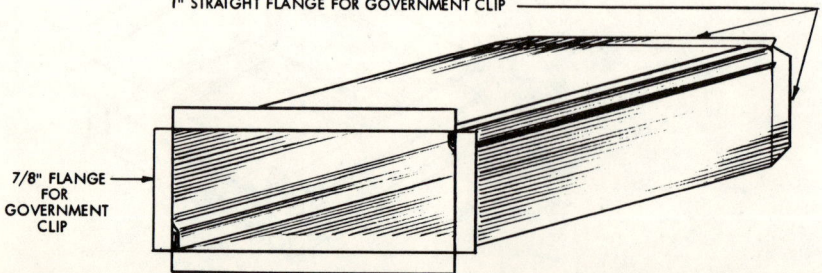

Figure 11. Pattern for two-piece duct with Pittsburgh seams and edges for government clips.

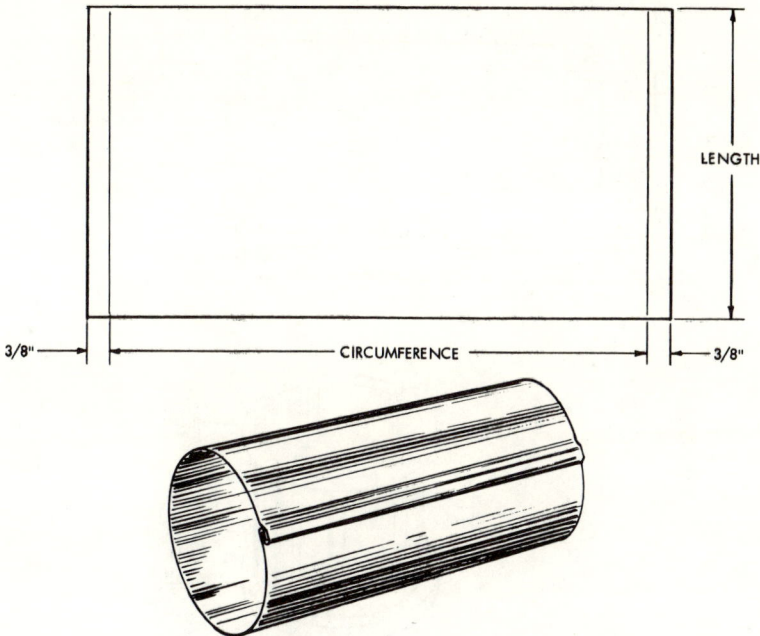

LENGTH

3/8"   CIRCUMFERENCE   3/8"

Figure 12. Pattern for round pipe with ¼" groove seams.

Basic patterns

While many of the patterns used by the sheet metal worker may differ in size or in the various operations used, many patterns follow the same basic forms. The basic pattern forms shown in Figs. 7 through 14 represent the commonly used patterns and notches. The student should study these patterns for their general shapes as well as for the allowances for seams and edges and for the method of notching.

Review Questions

1. What is meant by notching a pattern?
2. What is meant by clipping a pattern?
3. Why should the bottom of a sheet be checked for straightness?
4. Which end of a sheet should be squared?
5. In what part of a sheet of metal should a pattern be laid out?
6. Why is it poor practice to try to cut a piece of metal exactly to size before the pattern is laid out?
7. Make a drawing to ½ scale with all dimensions of a box with ½" laps on the corners and a 5/16" double hem around the top. Make the box 6" × 8" and 3" deep. Draw in the notches with a colored pencil.
8. Make a pictorial sketch of a box. Make it to any convenient dimensions and any edge other than a double

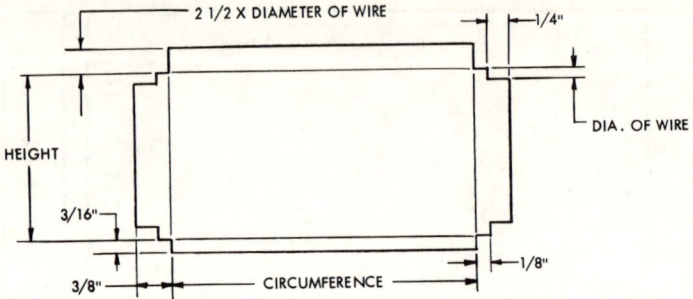

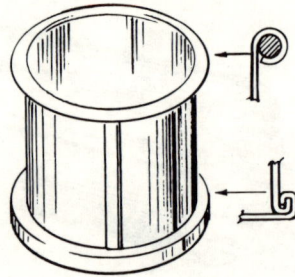

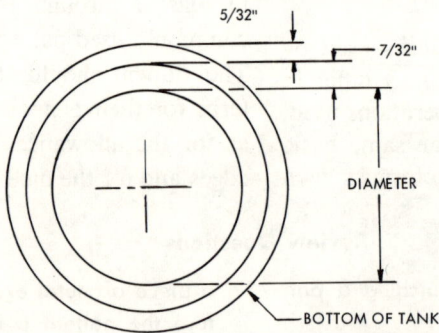

Figure 13. Pattern for tank with wired edge.

hem. Sketch the patterns for the box roughly to scale making it in three pieces with Pittsburgh seams on corners. Insert all dimensions on the sketch and patterns and indicate the notches with colored pencil.

9. Sketch the pattern for a rectangular duct in two pieces. Make it 10" × 8" and 18" long with corners joined by Pittsburgh seams and allowances for S and drive clips on the ends. Make the pattern to scale, but not necessarily to full scale. Draw in the notches with colored pencil.

Projects

Project 12-1. Making the pattern for a one-piece box

AIM. To develop skill in laying out patterns for pans and boxes.

SPECIFICATIONS. Lay out and make a one-piece box 6″ × 4″ and 1″ high, with ½″ laps and spot welds on the corners and ¼″ hems around the top.

OPERATIONS

1. Lay out the pattern for the box shown in Fig. 15. Use 26 gage galvanized metal. Allow for all seams and edges. Check your layout with the instructor before cutting it out.

2. Bend the hems to the outside of the box.

3. If a pan brake is available, bend

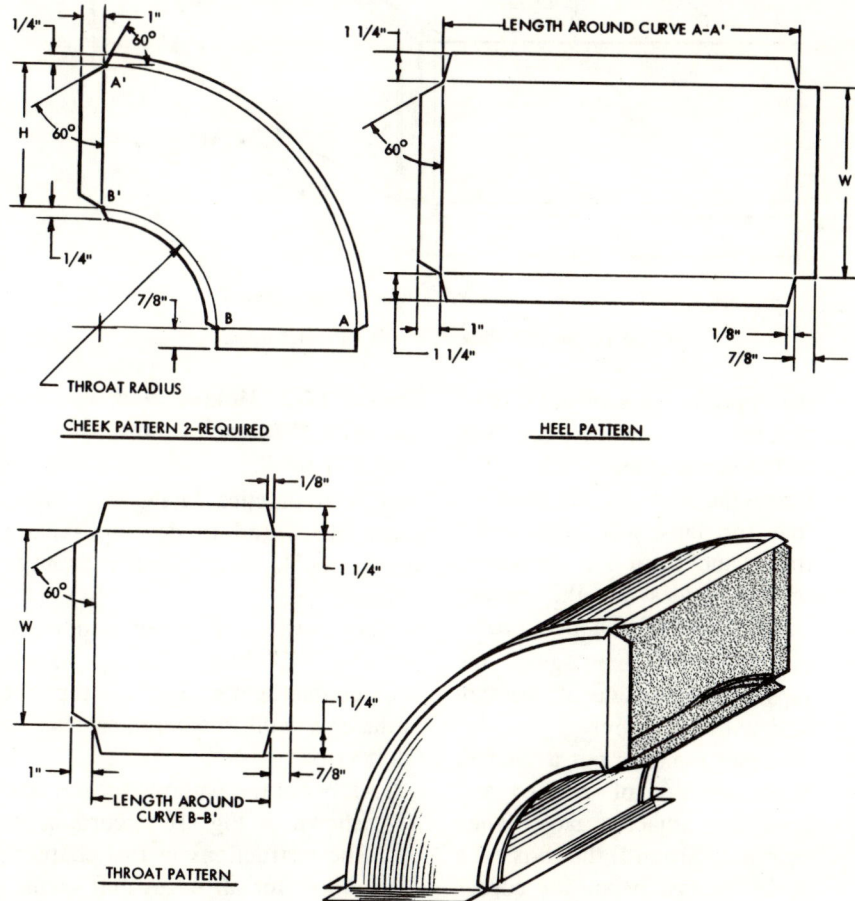

CHEEK PATTERN 2-REQUIRED

HEEL PATTERN

THROAT PATTERN

Figure 14. Pattern for rectangular duct elbow.

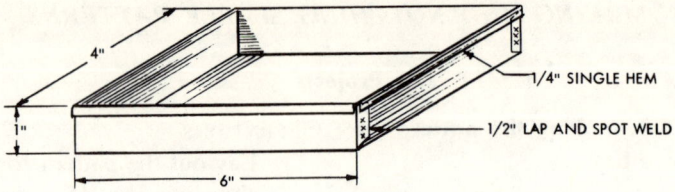

Figure 15. Box with ½″ corner lap and ¼″ hem.

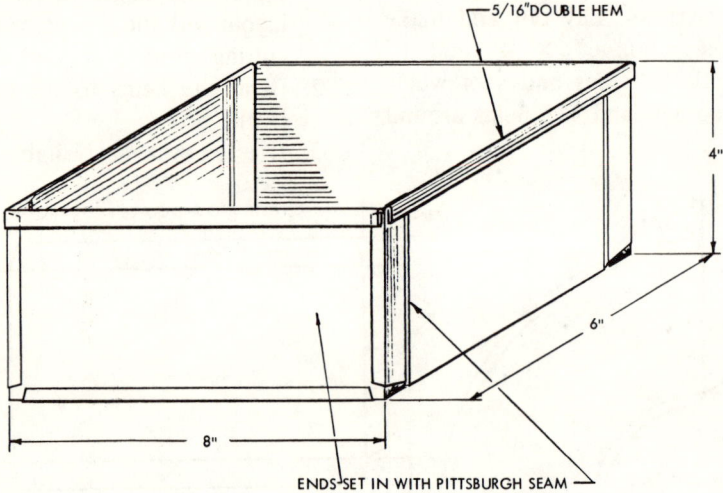

Figure 16. Box with ends set in with Pittsburgh seam.

the opposite sides of the box so that the lap allowances are bent at the same time.

4. Open the ends of the hem so that the laps will tuck under them, and bend the remaining opposite sides on the proper width finger of the pan brake. As the side is bent, guide the laps to the outside of the pan and under the hems.

5. If a pan brake is not available, bend one side of the box and then the adjacent side. Then continue around the box. To make the last bend, one corner of the box will have to be flattened out.

Project 12-2. Making a three-piece box with Pittsburgh seams

AIM. To practice laying out three-piece boxes and to develop skill in using double hems and Pittsburgh seams.

SPECIFICATIONS. Lay out and make an 8″ × 6″ box, 4″ deep with a $\frac{5}{16}$″ double hem around the top. Set in the ends with Pittsburgh seams.

OPERATIONS

1. Lay out the patterns for the box shown in Fig. 16 according to the instructions in this chapter. Allow for all edges and seams. Check with the instructor before cutting out.

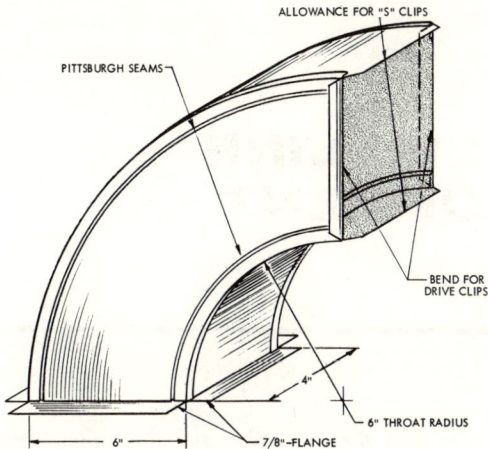

Figure 17. Duct with Pittsburgh seam.

2. On the large piece, form the Pittsburgh seam first.
3. Next form the double hems to the outside.
4. Next bend the corners to form the sides.
5. On the end pieces, first form the double hem to the outside. Next bend the single edge for the Pittsburgh seam to the inside.
6. Set the ends into the pocket lock and tap over the seam to finish the box.
7. Turn in to the instructor and then save for soldering practice.

Project 12-3. Making a duct elbow

AIM. To learn how to lay out and make duct fittings, and to learn how to use a Pittsburgh seam on a curved section.

SPECIFICATIONS. Make a 90° duct elbow, 6″ × 4″ with a 6″ throat radius.

OPERATIONS

1. Lay out the patterns for the duct elbow shown in Fig. 17 according to the instructions given in this chapter. Allow for all seams and edges and have the instructor check the patterns before cutting them.
2. Cut out the cheek patterns and notch them.
3. Turn the single edges on the curves with the burring machine.
4. On the heel and throat patterns, make the bends for the Pittsburgh seams.
5. Roll the heel and throat to fit the curves of the cheek.
6. Open up the Pittsburgh seams with a screw driver, if needed, to assemble the elbow.
7. Turn in to the instructor.

13

PARALLEL LINE DEVELOPMENT

On what surfaces may the principles of parallel line development be applied? What is the purpose of a profile and how is it used? How are measuring lines used in parallel line development? How are patterns developed for round pipe elbows? How are patterns developed for round pipe intersections?

All sheet metal patterns are developed by one of three methods—parallel line development, triangulation, or radial line development. In *parallel line developments,* the sides run parallel to one another as in patterns for ducts, elbows, and tee joints. In *radial line developments,* all the sides meet at a common center as with cones and pyramids. In sheet metal work, many irregularly formed shapes cannot be developed by either of these two methods. Such shapes are so formed that, although straight lines can be drawn through them, the lines would not run parallel to one another, nor would they all slant at the same angle to meet at a common center. Examples of such shapes may be found in Fig. 1, Chapter 14. Such surfaces can develop through measurement of the surface, part by part, and adding one part to another until the entire surface is developed. This is the essential procedure in the third method of pattern development called *triangulation.*

Developing the patterns for straight rectangular duct

In Chapter 12, you learned how to lay out simple patterns. These were basically parallel line layouts since they involved primarily rectangular shapes with straight sides. Fig. 1 shows the patterns for a straight rectangular duct. This is a simple pattern but it involves basic principles which the student should understand. Therefore, the procedure used in constructing this pattern should be studied so that you will understand how they apply to more advanced operations.

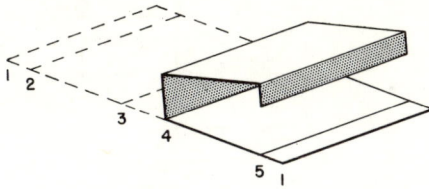

PATTERN BEING FORMED INTO SHAPE

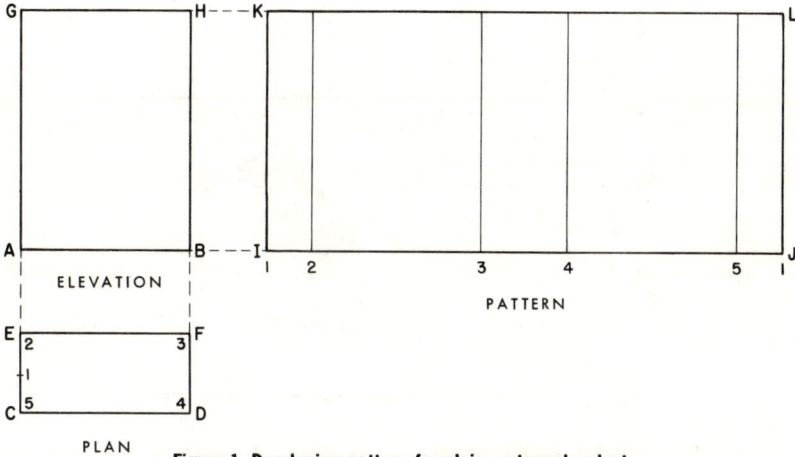

ELEVATION

PATTERN

PLAN

Figure 1. Developing pattern for plain rectangular duct.

In all parallel line developments, the first step is to draw an elevation or side view. After this view is drawn, measuring lines are drawn from it and measured and projected to the pattern. *For plain rectangular duct, the measuring lines on the elevation view are the corner lines of the duct.* After measuring lines are located on the elevation view, then the stretchout of the pattern is drawn and the measuring lines are located on the pattern stretchout in the same relative location as they are on the pattern. In the pattern in Fig. 1, measuring lines 2, 3, 4, and 5 are the corner lines, while line 1 is the seam line.

After the measuring lines are lo-cated on the pattern stretchout, the lengths of the lines are taken from the elevation or side view and transferred to the same lines on the pattern. In the pattern in Fig. 1, all of the lines are the same length and while this step could be eliminated in this particular problem in subsequent illustrations, you will see its importance.

Thus, in laying out this simple duct, you will have used many of the basic principles which parallel line development employ. In developing any pattern by parallel line developments:

1. Draw a side or elevation view of the pattern.
2. Locate the measuring lines on the side view.

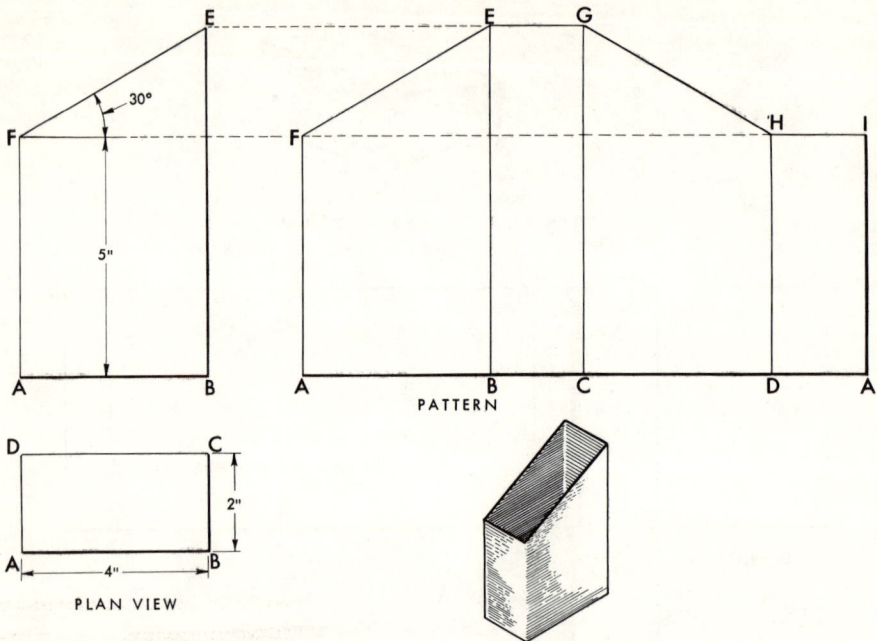

Figure 2. Laying out pattern for rectangular duct with a miter at one end.

3. Draw the stretchout of the pattern. (See Chapter 5 for the definition of "stretchout".)
4. Locate the measuring lines from the side or elevation view on the pattern stretchout. These lines must be the proper distance apart and in the proper relation to each other as dictated by their location on the side view.
5. Transfer the lengths of the measuring lines from the side or elevation view to the same lines on the pattern.
6. Connect the points located on the measuring lines.

Developing the pattern for rectangular duct cut at a miter

Mastering pattern drafting consists of two steps: 1. learning the basic principles, 2. learning to apply these principles to typical problems. The principles explained earlier in this chapter and illustrated by Fig. 1 apply in the same way to a rectangular duct with an end cut at an angle. This section will explain how they apply.

Fig. 2 shows a rectangular duct with one end cut at an angle. This is a common problem whose solution has many applications.

Step 1 in laying out this pattern by parallel lines is to draw the side (or elevation) view of the duct. This is best done by *first* drawing the plan view and then projecting the lines up to draw the side view, as shown in Fig. 2.

Step 2 is to locate the measuring lines on the side view. Since this is a rectangular duct with a plain miter, the corner lines are the only measuring lines needed. Therefore, all of the measuring lines on the side view are already located.

Step 3 is to draw the stretchout of the pattern. Since this is a 2″ × 4″ duct, the total stretchout without seam allowance is 12″.

Step 4 is to locate the measuring lines. Since the corner lines are the measuring lines in this case, the corner lines are drawn on the stretchout at intervals of 4″, 2″, 4″, and 2″.

Step 5 is to transfer the lengths of the measuring lines from the side view to the pattern. The dotted lines in Fig. 2 show how these points can be projected over to the pattern. Note that line *AF* on the pattern is made to the exact length of *AF* on the side view and line *BE* on the pattern is made the same length as *BE* on the side view. After points, *F, E, G, H,* and *I* are located, lines are drawn to connect them and complete the pattern.

Developing the patterns for a rectangular duct with a double angle

The previously explained procedures showed how the steps in parallel line layout applied to an actual problem. Here we shall see how the same principles apply to a slightly more complicated operation. Note that the principles used are still exactly the same and only the method of application varies.

Fig. 3 shows a rectangular duct

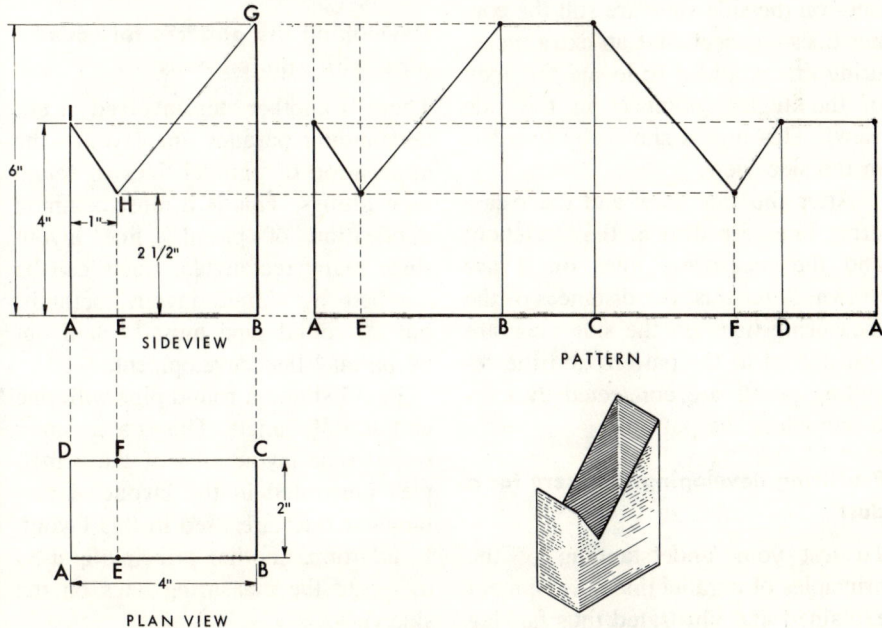

Figure 3. Pattern for rectangular duct with a double angle cut at one end.

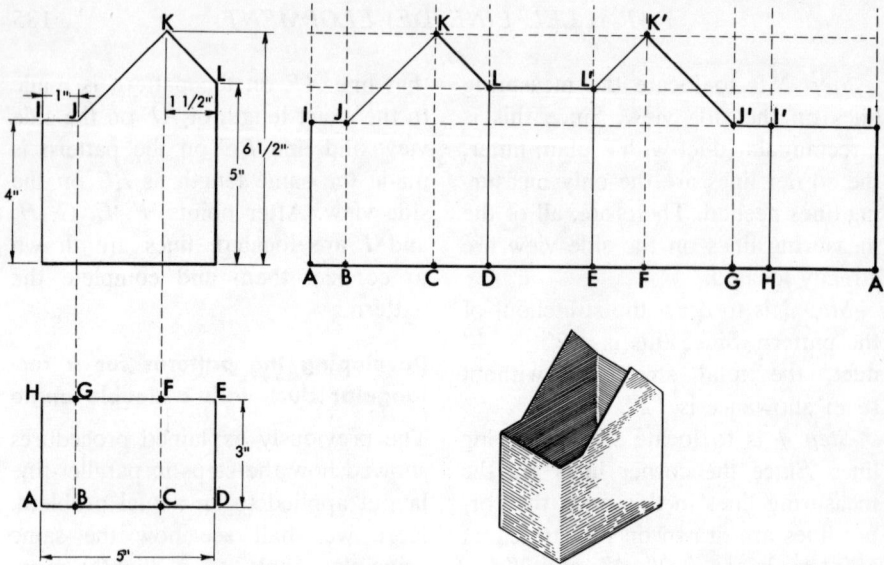

Figure 4. Pattern for a rectangular duct with irregular angles on one end.

with a double angle cut in one end. The steps in laying out this pattern are still the same. First, draw the plan and side views. The measuring lines on the side view are still the corner lines—except that an extra measuring line is added to locate the apex of the angles (point *H* in the side view). This line is shown by line *HE* in the side view.

After the side view and the measuring lines are drawn, the stretchout and the measuring lines on it are drawn. After this, the distances of the measuring lines on the side view are transferred to the pattern and the resulting points are connected by lines to complete the pattern.

Practicing developing a pattern for a duct

To test your understanding of the principles of parallel line development explained and illustrated thus far, lay out the pattern for the duct shown in Fig. 4. No explanation is given for this layout, but based on information previously presented, the pattern should not prove difficult.

Developing the patterns for round pipe with mitered ends

There is another step involved in understanding parallel line layout—the application of parallel lines to round pipe fittings. This is a most common application of parallel line layout since many rectangular ducts can be handled by simple layout methods, but *all* round pipe must be laid out by parallel line development.

Fig. 5 shows a round pipe with one end at a 30° angle. This is a common round pipe layout. All of the principles illustrated in the layout of rectangular duct are used in this layout. In addition, another principle is used to locate the measuring lines on the side view.

Since there are no convenient cor-

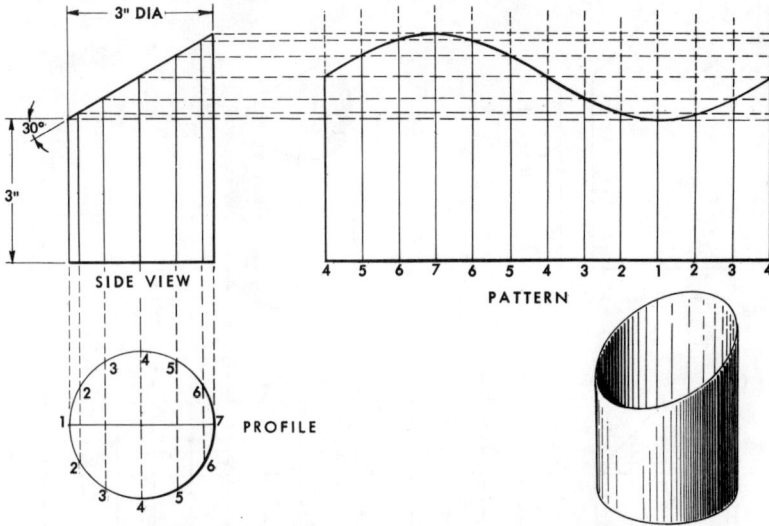

Figure 5. Pattern for a round pipe with a miter at one end.

ners to use as measuring lines, they must be located on the side view in a manner that makes them easy to locate on the pattern. If the plan view is divided into 12 equal spaces on the circumference by the method explained previously, then the lines are located in equal spaces on the pattern stretchout. Notice that the lines are projected up from the plan view to locate them on the side view. Though they do not appear to be equally spaced on the side view, they in fact are. The side view is a view of the pipe surface curving away from the view and does not show the distance around the surface in its true length.

This method of dividing the plan view into equal spaces and projecting them up to the side view is a common procedure and is used every time a pipe with a curved surface is laid out. When the plan view is used in this manner, it is called a *profile.*

A profile is the shape of the fitting at that particular point. The general practice is to draw only half of the plan view when it is used as a profile, since the other half is a duplicate. Fig. 6 illustrates this.

After the side view is drawn and the measuring lines are located, the stretchout of the pattern is drawn and is divided into the same number of equal spaces as are on the plan view.

Refer to Chapter 11 for methods of dividing a line into equal spaces.

After the side view and the pattern stretchout are marked with the measuring lines, then the next step is to transfer the lengths of the measuring lines to the pattern. This may be done by projecting the lines as shown, or it may be done by setting dividers to the lengths on the side view and marking this length on the corresponding line on the pattern. After all of the points are located, the curve of the miter is

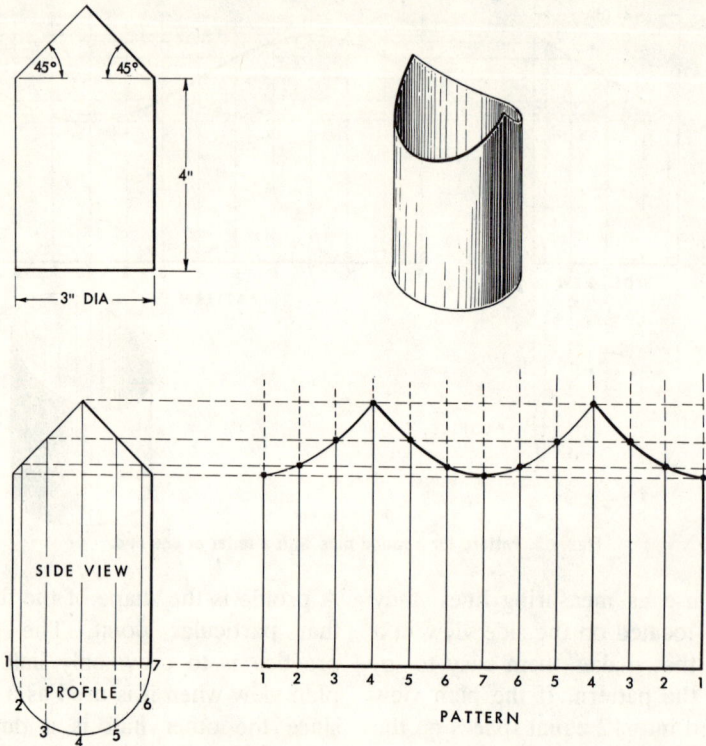

Figure 6. Developing the pattern for a round pipe with double angle at one end.

drawn through these points The curve may be drawn freehand, with a drawing curve, or by bending a flexible rule through these points and marking around the rule with a pencil or scratch awl.

Practicing developing a pattern for a round pipe

To test your knowledge of parallel line development as applied to round pipe fittings, lay out the pattern for the fitting shown in Fig. 6.

Developing the patterns for intersecting pipes

A common group of round pipe fit-

tings laid out by parallel line developments are intersecting pipes, commonly called *tees*. These are laid out as any problem in parallel lines. However, there is one new principle to learn when laying out intersecting pipes. The principle is the development of the intersection line of the two pipes. This line is called the *miter line*.

Fig. 7 shows a typical development using a miter line between intersecting pipes. Since this is a common situation, it should be thoroughly understood and studied.

The patterns for this tee cannot be laid out until the miter line is devel-

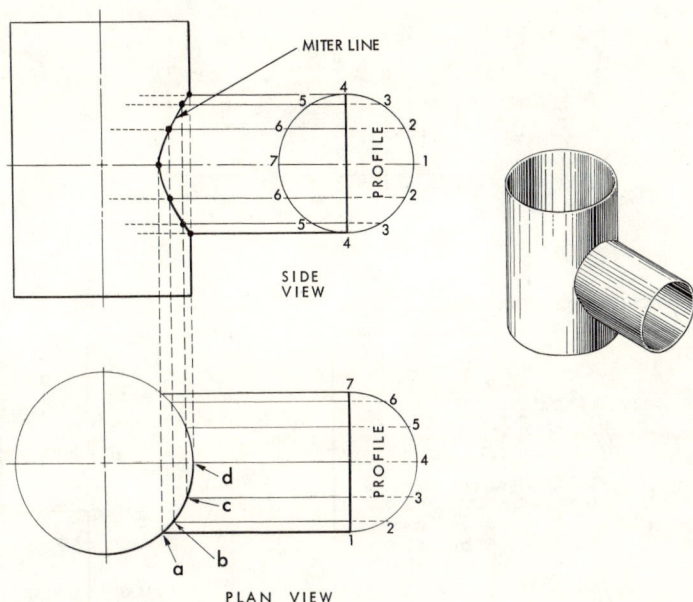

Figure 7. Developing the miter line for intersecting pipes of different diameters.

oped. This, therefore, is the first step in laying out such a pattern.

The side view and the plan view are first drawn. Then profiles are drawn for the intersecting pipe on both the side view and the plan view. The profiles are divided into equal spaces—generally six to the half-circle. Lines are then projected from these spaces. On the side view the lines are projected indefinitely for later intersection of lines from the plan view. On the plan view, the lines are projected until they touch the curve of the circle of the main pipe as at *a*, *b*, *c*, and *d*, Fig. 7. From these points, lines are projected through the side view to intersect the lines from the side view profile.

Since the profile on the side view and the profile on the plan view lo-

cate the same measuring lines, when point *a* on the plan view is projected to the intersect line on the side view, this gives the exact spot where line *1* intersects the curve of the main pipe and it therefore is a point on the miter line. When all of the points are found by the intersection of corresponding lines, the miter line is drawn in and then the patterns for both pipes can be laid out by parallel lines. The completed patterns are shown in Fig. 8.

There are several short cuts used on the layout. Notice that the plan view is attached to the side view and that only half of the plan is drawn. This eliminates many unnecessary lines. Notice also that the pattern for the tee is not developed by projecting the lines from the side view. Instead, the distances on the side view

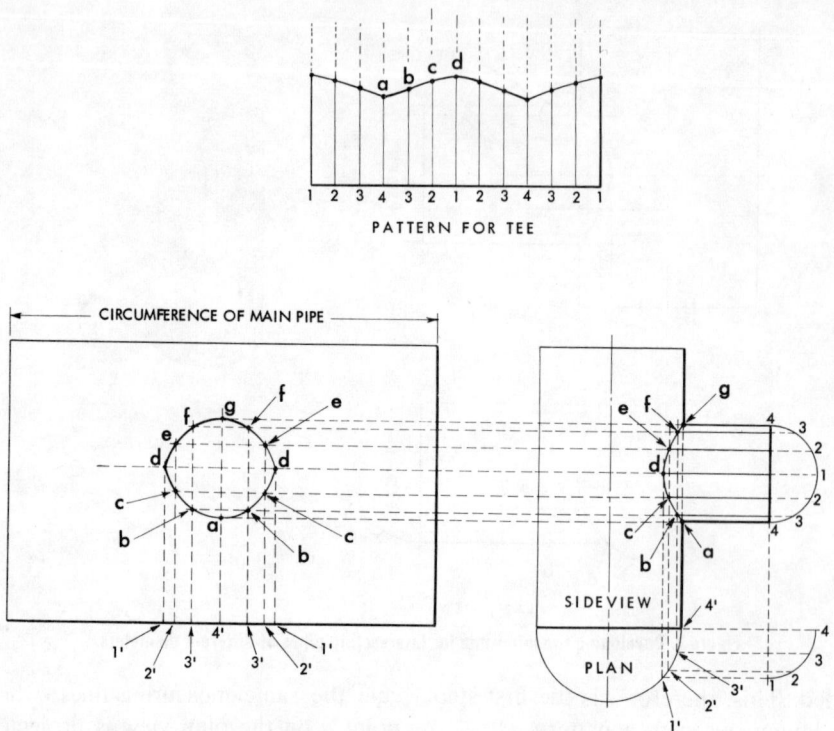

Figure 8. Developing patterns for a round tee.

are stepped off by dividers and transferred to the proper lines on the pattern. The distances are taken from line *4-4* to the miter line. For example, for line *2*, the distance on the side view from line *4-4* to point *c* is taken and transferred to line *2* of the pattern to locate point *c*.

The layout of the hole pattern is also done by parallel lines. Notice that the spacing of the vertical measuring lines on the pattern is different. Since the lines of the stretchout must be the exact duplicate of the lines on the side and plan views, the line spacing is taken from the plan view since this gives the spacing of these lines.

In this case, they are not equally spaced, but as long as they are taken in the proper order and the correct spacing, this does not matter.

Practicing developing a pattern for a tee intersecting at an angle

Fig. 9 shows the layout for the patterns for a tee intersecting at an angle. This will give you an opportunity to apply the methods of tee layout to a different type of problem. Though the operation appears more difficult than the previous one, the solution is the same. Thus, you can see how understanding and applying basic principles will help you to handle many varieties

5" DIA

3" DIA
AT 45° ANGLE

7"

2"

7 6 5 4 3 2 1 2 3 4 5 6 7

PATTERN FOR TEE

7 6 5 4
PROFILE
3
2
1

SIDE
VIEW

7'-1'
6'-2'

PLAN
VIEW

7-1
6-2
5-3
4

5'-3'

4'

4'   4'
5'-3' 5'-3'
6'-2' 7'-1' 6'-2'

PIPE PATTERN WITH HOLE

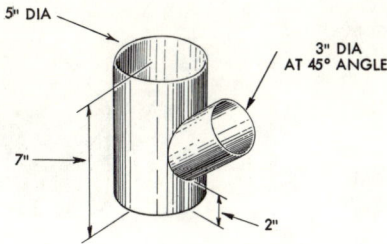

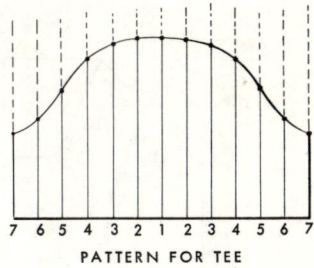

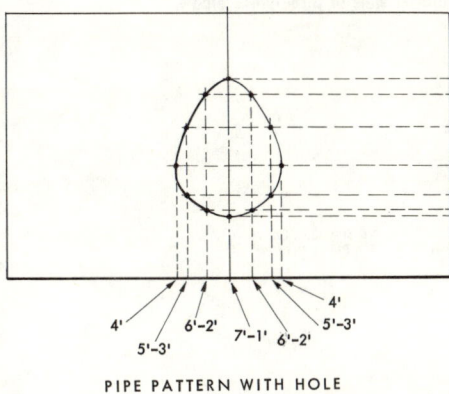

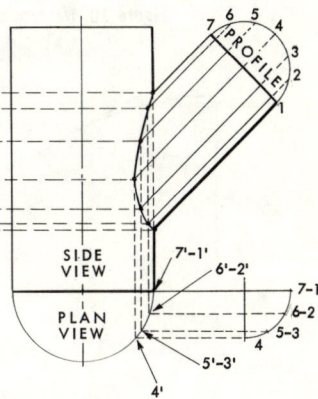

Figure 9. Patterns for a tee intersecting at an angle.

of problems. Lay out the patterns for Fig. 9 to check your understanding of this phase of parallel line layout.

Developing the patterns for a round elbow

Another important application of parallel line layout is laying out the patterns for round elbows. This again is the application of basic principles of layout with one new principle involved. This principle is the location of the miter lines on the elbow.

Before studying the layout of the round elbow, study Fig. 10 to learn the parts and nomenclature of the elbow. Just as in tees, *the intersection of two pipes is called a miter*. Note also that the inside radius is called the *throat* and the outside radius is called the *heel*. The throat radius is indicated by *r* and the heel radius by *R*. The sections of the elbow are called *gores*.

Just as in any parallel line layout, the first step is to draw the side view and develop the miter lines. For the round elbow, the miter lines are straight lines with no need for developing. However, the method of spacing these lines is important. The purpose of the spacing is to make angle *a* and *b* equal so that the pattern for the end gore can also be used for the

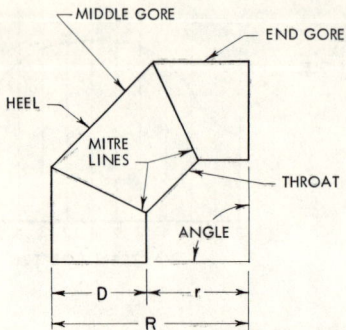

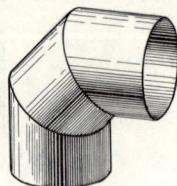

Figure 10. Nomenclature and pictorial view of three-piece elbow.

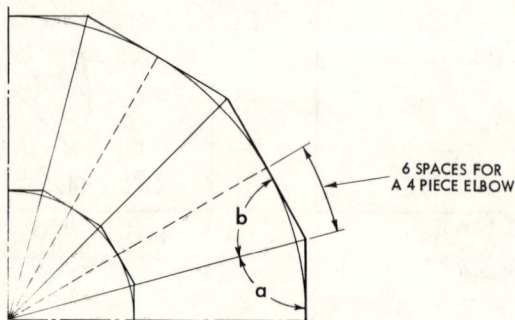

NUMBER OF SPACES = 2 TIMES NUMBER OF PIECES, MINUS 2

S = (2 X N) – 2

FOR A 4 PIECE ELBOW:
NUMBER OF SPACES = (4 x 2) – 2
SPACES = 6

Figure 11. How to space miter lines for round elbow.

pattern of the middle gore. If these two angles are different, then two different patterns must be laid out. If one space is used for each of the end gores, and two spaces are used for each of the middle gores, then all the angles will be equal. To obtain this spacing, multiply the number of gores in the elbow by two and subtract two from this result. The answer is the number of spaces in which to divide

the heel curve of the elbow. After the spaces are stepped off around the curve, then the miter lines are drawn in as shown by the solid lines in Fig. 11.

After the miter lines are located, the pattern for the first gore of the elbow is laid out as shown in Fig. 12. Other than the special method of obtaining the miter lines, the layout is a typical parallel line development. First

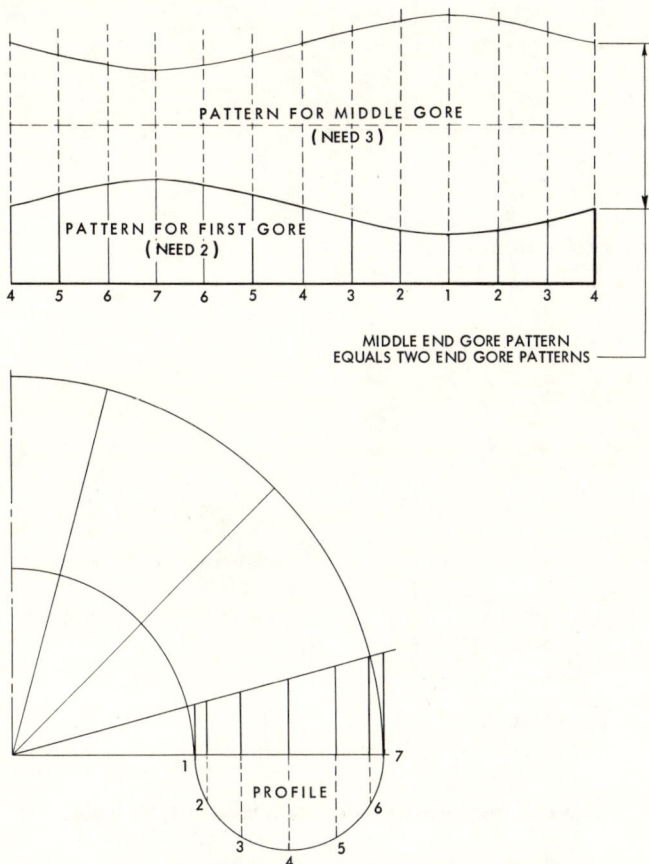

PATTERN FOR MIDDLE GORE
(NEED 3)

PATTERN FOR FIRST GORE
(NEED 2)

4   5   6   7   6   5   4   3   2   1   2   3   4

MIDDLE END GORE PATTERN
EQUALS TWO END GORE PATTERNS

PROFILE

1   7
2   6
3   5
4

Figure 12. Laying out pattern for first gore of elbow.

draw the profile and space it equally. Project these spaces up into the side view to locate the equally spaced measuring lines. Then transfer these lines to the pattern in their proper spacing and length.

The first gore pattern is the only pattern developed. This pattern is cut out of sheet metal and the middle gore patterns are marked from it, since the middle gores are exact duplicates of the end gore except that they are equal to two end gores.

Note that the numbering of the measuring lines of the pattern is arranged so that the seam line of the pattern is on the side of the elbow rather than the heel or throat. It is standard practice to keep the seams on the side and staggered — that is the seams alternate to opposite sides of the elbow at each gore. The method of numbering and measuring lines need not be the same as shown so long as it is a method which enables you to identify the lines easily.

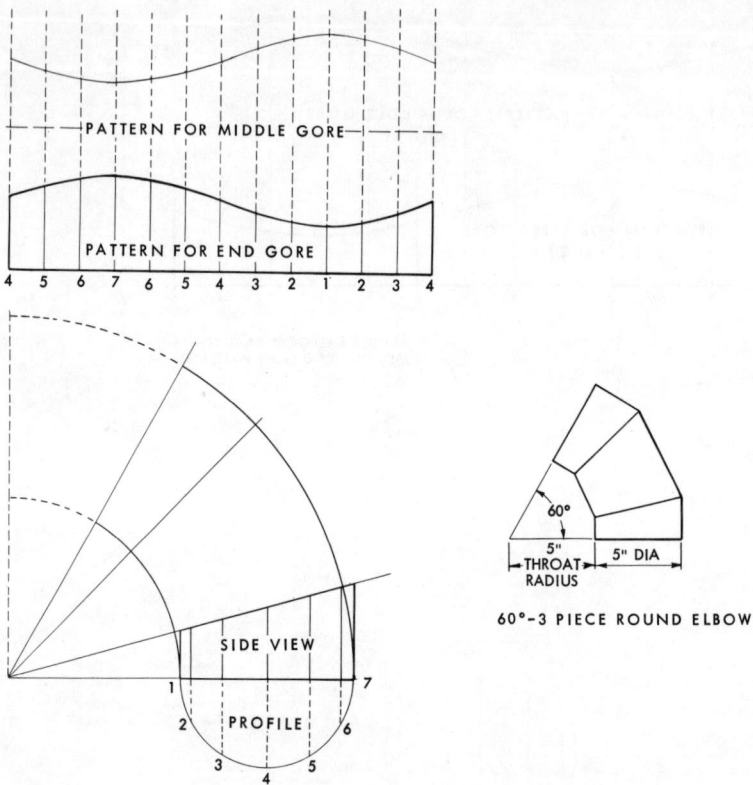

Figure 13. Developing the patterns for a three-piece, 60° elbow.

Practicing developing an elbow gore pattern

Fig. 13 gives the layout of a typical elbow pattern. Test your knowledge of parallel line development in this application by laying out the first gore pattern as shown.

Review Questions

1. Describe the layouts in which parallel line developments are used.
2. Why is it important to learn basic principles in pattern drafting rather than memorizing steps?
3. List the steps involved in laying out a parallel line development.
4. Explain what a profile is and what its purpose is.
5. Why is the profile divided into equal spaces and projected up to the side view rather than dividing the side view into equal spaces?
6. What is a miter line?
7. Give the number of spaces into which to divide the heel of a round elbow for: (a) four gores, (b) six gores, (c) eight gores.

14

TRIANGULATION

What is triangulation? On what kind of surface is triangulation used? What are true lengths? How are true lengths identified on a drawing? How is the true length of a line found? How do you triangulate from two known points to find a third point? How do you apply the basic principles of triangulation to the development of patterns for sheet metal objects?

Chapter 13 discussed parallel line development. In this chapter, you will learn how to apply triangulation, another of the three basic methods of layout. As stated in Chapter 13, triangulation is the method of developing the surfaces of objects whose sides slant at different angles. Broadly speaking, what triangulation involves is working from two known points to locate a third point. Surfaces are measured and laid out one point at a time until the entire surface is developed.

Fig. 1 shows some typical objects which might be laid out by the triangulation method.

As you did with parallel line development, concentrate on learning the basic principles of triangulation rather than memorizing of the steps involved in the specific examples presented in this chapter. Mastery of triangulation depends first on understanding these principles and then how to apply them. Do not leave any section of the chapter or any of the practice examples until you thoroughly understand them. An understanding of each section of this chapter depends upon an understanding of the preceding sections.

The triangulation method of layout

As stated previously, triangulation is the method used for objects whose sides are not parallel (objects *with* parallel sides are laid out by parallel

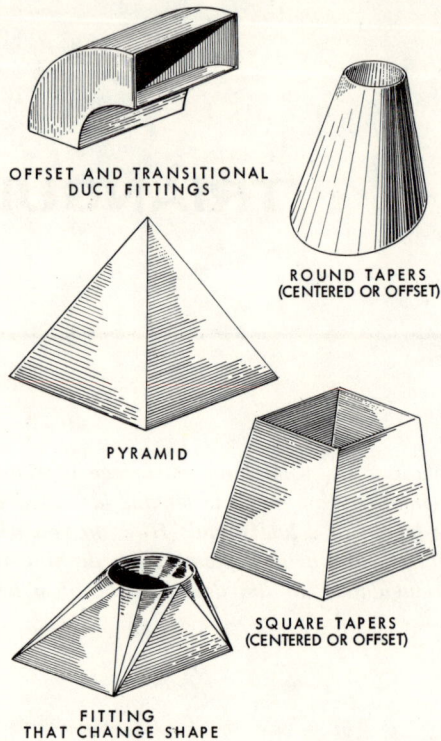

OFFSET AND TRANSITIONAL
DUCT FITTINGS

ROUND TAPERS
(CENTERED OR OFFSET)

PYRAMID

SQUARE TAPERS
(CENTERED OR OFFSET)

FITTING
THAT CHANGE SHAPE

Figure 1. Some typical fittings and shapes which may be laid out by triangulation.

line development), sides which do not incline toward a common center (such objects are laid out by radial line developments), and for some conical objects not readily handled by radial line development. The triangulation method is basically:

1. Dividing the surface into triangles.
2. Finding the true lengths of the slant sides.
3. Drawing the triangles one at a time.

There are three steps involved in the triangulation method:

1. The construction of the plan and elevation view.
2. The development of the true lengths.
3. The layout of the pattern.

Plane surfaces

To understand triangulation, it is first important that you understand what a plane surface is. Once you understand this, it will be much easier to interpret lines on the elevation and plan views.

A plane surface is a surface having two dimensions — length and width. For example, a desk top is a plane surface as is the surface of a piece of flat sheet metal. Plane surfaces may be at any angle. Thus, a *horizontal plane*

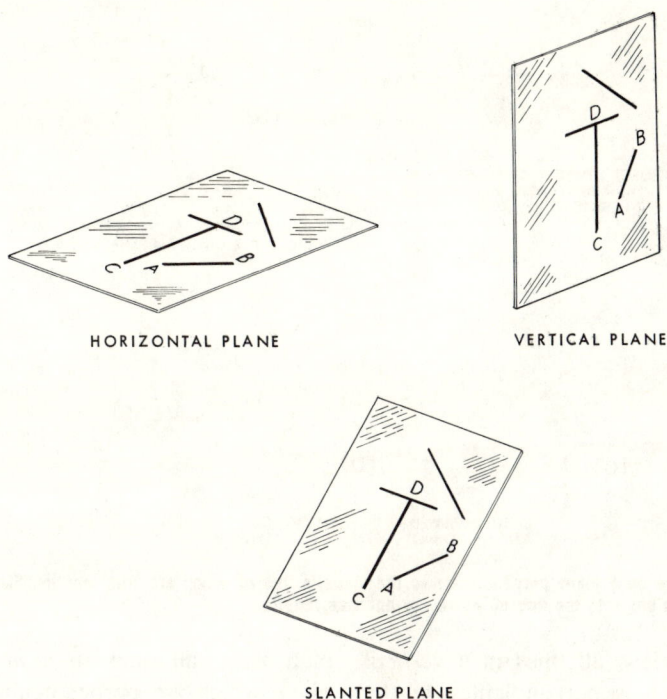

HORIZONTAL PLANE

VERTICAL PLANE

SLANTED PLANE

Figure 2. Plane surfaces may be at a horizontal, vertical, or slanted angle.

has its surface level with the horizon; a *vertical plane* has its surface at right angles or perpendicular to the horizontal plane; a *slanted or oblique plane* has its surface at any angle between the vertical and horizontal planes.

A straight line—by its definition—must lie on a plane surface. Fig. 2 shows the three plane surfaces with lines drawn on them to illustrate this. Note that lines may be drawn at any angle on the plane surface. For example, on the horizontal plane in Fig. 2, lines *AB* and *CD* are at different angles but are on the same plane. This fact will be applied when you work with true lengths.

Identifying true lengths

On an elevation or plan view, some lines are true lengths, while others are not. Before these true lengths can be found, it is necessary to first be able to distinguish between the lines on the drawing which are true lengths and the lines which are not true lengths. When they are not, the true lengths of the line must be found and it is here that the concepts regarding plane surfaces are necessary.

On any drawing, *lines which are perpendicular to the viewer's line of vision are true lengths*. Lines which are slanted or at an angle to the line of vision are *not* true lengths. This is illustrated by Fig. 3. Therefore, on an

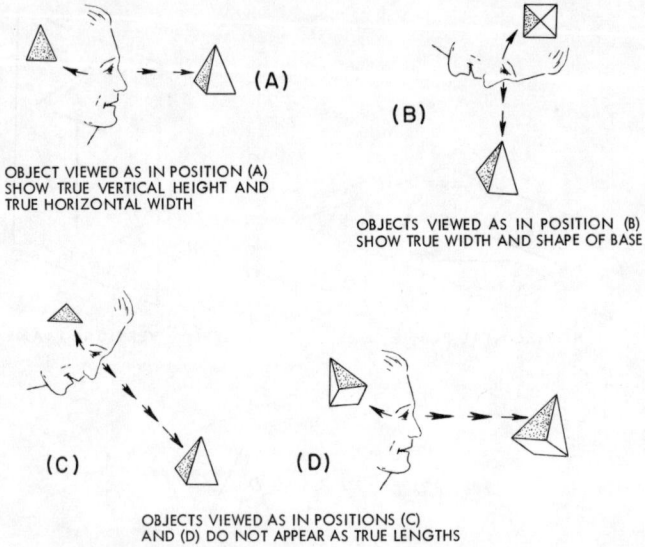

OBJECT VIEWED AS IN POSITION (A)
SHOW TRUE VERTICAL HEIGHT AND
TRUE HORIZONTAL WIDTH

OBJECTS VIEWED AS IN POSITION (B)
SHOW TRUE WIDTH AND SHAPE OF BASE

OBJECTS VIEWED AS IN POSITIONS (C)
AND (D) DO NOT APPEAR AS TRUE LENGTHS

Figure 3. Lines on a plane perpendicular to the viewer's line of vision are true lengths. Slanted lines or lines on an angle to the line of vision are not true lengths.

elevation view, all lines in a *vertical plane* which is perpendicular to the line of vision are true lengths. In the

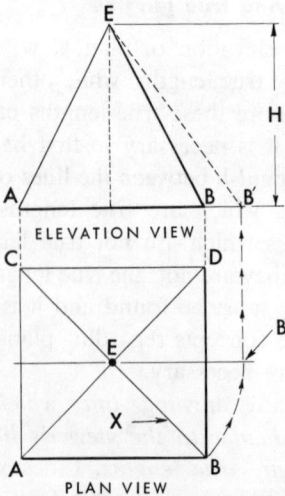

ELEVATION VIEW

PLAN VIEW

Figure 4. In this pyramid with a square base, lines AB, BC, CD, and DA in the plan view and line AB in the elevation view are true lengths.

plan view, all lines in a *horizontal plane* which are perpendicular to the line of vision are true lengths. *All others are not!*

As an example of this, Fig. 4 shows the elevation and plan views of a pyramid with a square base. On the plan view, base lines *AB, BD, CD,* and *CA* are on a horizontal plane and therefore are true lengths. Lines *EA, EB, EC,* and *ED* are on slanted plane and are not true lengths.

Likewise, in the elevation view, line *AB* is in a vertical plane perpendicular to the line of vision and is therefore a true length. Here too, lines *EA* and *EB* are on planes slanted to the line of vision and therefore are not true lengths.

Practicing identifying true lengths

To test your ability to identify true

ELEVATION VIEW

PLAN VIEW

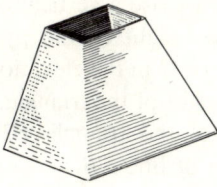

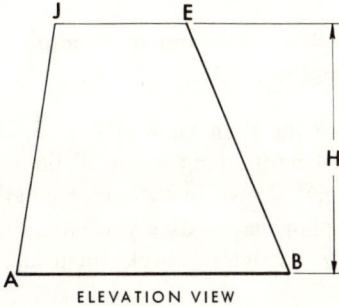

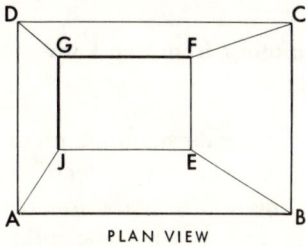

Figure 5. Identifying true lengths.

TOP

FRONT

PICTORIAL VIEW

SIDE

Figure 6. Finding the true length of the hypotenuse of a sheet metal triangle.

lengths, list the true length lines on the plan view of Fig. 5. You should have listed lines *AB, BC, CD, DA, JE, EF, FG,* and *GJ*. These are the true length lines on the drawing.

Finding true lengths

Once you have learned how to identify a true length, you must next be able to find true lengths yourself. There are several methods by which true lengths may be found. However, the method used by sheet metal workers is to draw the line in a true view and then measure it.

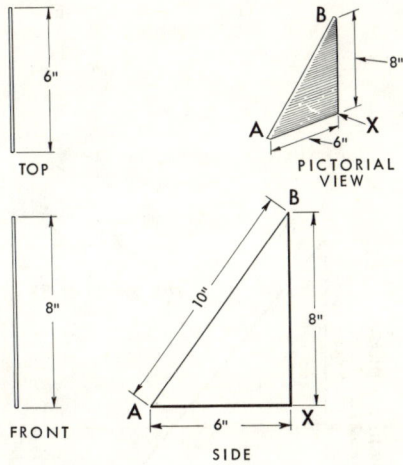

One method is illustrated by Fig. 6. Here we have a piece of sheet metal cut to a triangle as is shown in the pictorial view. We know that the base of the triangle is 6″ and the height is 8″. What we wish to know is the length of the hypotenuse (the side of a right-angled triangle that is opposite the right angle) *AB*. A top view shows only the 6″ base and a front view shows only the 8″ height. In both of these views, side *AB* is slanted to the line of vision and therefore not shown in its true length. However, if a side view is drawn, line *AB* is on a perpendicular plane to the line of vision and is shown in its true length which is 10″.

Now let's apply this procedure to the pyramid shown in Fig. 4. As stated previously, we know that line *EB* is not shown in its true length in the plan view. To find the true length

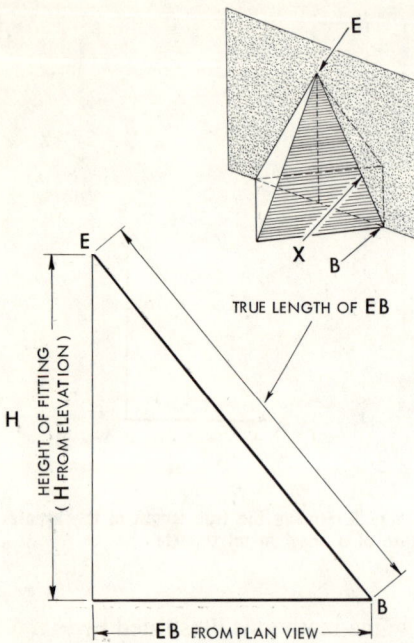

TRUE LENGTH OF **EB**

H — HEIGHT OF FITTING (H FROM ELEVATION)

EB FROM PLAN VIEW

Figure 7. To find the true length of a line you must rotate your point of vision to a point where the line is perpendicular to your line of vision.

BE must rise a vertical distance equal to the height of the pyramid. Thus, distance *H* in the elevation view shows the height of the triangle. The hypotenuse of the triangle *EB* is the true length of line *EB*.

Practicing drawing true length triangles

From the plan view of Fig. 5, draw true length triangles for all lines that are not shown in their true length in the plan view. After you have drawn these triangles, check them against Fig. 8.

Triangulating from two known points

If you have understood the preceding sections on how to identify *true lengths* and *how to find a true length,* there is one other basic principle needed for an understanding of triangulation. This is *how to locate a new point by measuring from two known points.* If you thoroughly understand these three basic principles, then you will be able to quickly grasp the layout of any triangulation problem because these three principles form the basis of every layout problem employing triangulation.

of *EB* you must change your point of vision to point *X* which is perpendicular to the plane of *EB*. If an elevation view from this point of vision is then drawn, the true length of line *EB* is shown. Fig. 7 shows this view. Notice that the triangle in Fig. 7 is similar to the sheet metal triangle in Fig. 6. If you think of line *EB* in the plan view of Fig. 4 as the plan view of a sheet metal triangle, then you can see that *EB* must be the horizontal distance the line travels. Thus, *EB* is the base of the triangle shown in Fig. 7. Since the line *BE* runs from the bottom to the top of the pyramid, line

Figure 9 shows a pyramid with a rectangular base similar to the one in Fig. 4. The difference is that the apex in Fig. 9 is off-center. We shall lay out the pattern for Fig. 9 to illustrate the principle of locating a new point by measuring from two known points.

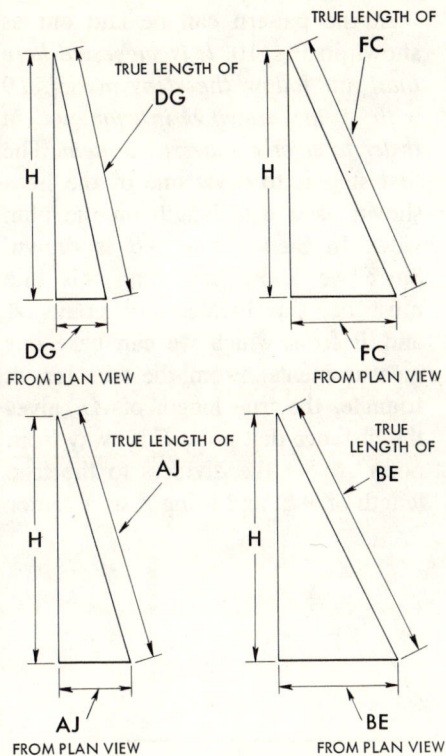

Figure 8. True lengths of lines (Figure 5) not shown in true length.

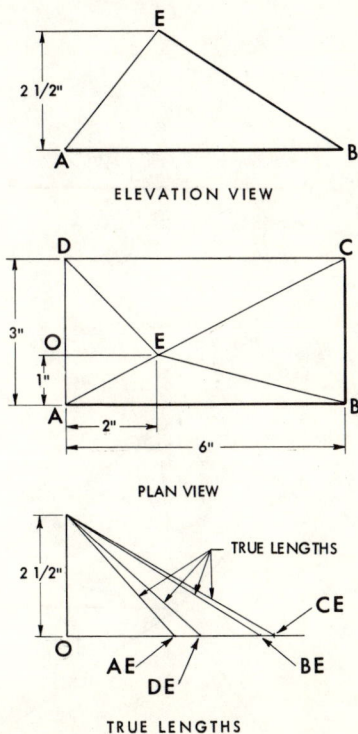

Figure 9. Pyramid with off-center vertex and rectangular base.

The first process in laying out this pattern is to find the true lengths for the lines that are not true lengths on the drawing. This is shown in Fig. 9 also. Notice that in finding the true lengths, separate triangles were not drawn for each line. Since each triangle has the same vertical height, time can be saved by drawing all the lines on one triangle as shown. Each of the lines is taken from the plan view and measured out from point 0 on the true length triangles. This is the way true lengths are commonly found in the sheet metal shop layout.

After the true lengths are found, then the pattern can be laid out as shown in Fig. 10. *It is suggested here that you follow the steps in Fig. 10 with your drawing instruments in order to clearly understand them.* The first step is to draw one of the lines shown as a true length on the plan view. In Step 1 line *AB* is drawn. Since we know how long this line must be, this locates two points *A* and *B* from which we can base our measurements. From the true length triangle, the true length of *AE* gives the distance that point *E* is away from point *A*. Set the dividers to the true length of *AE,* and using *A* as a center

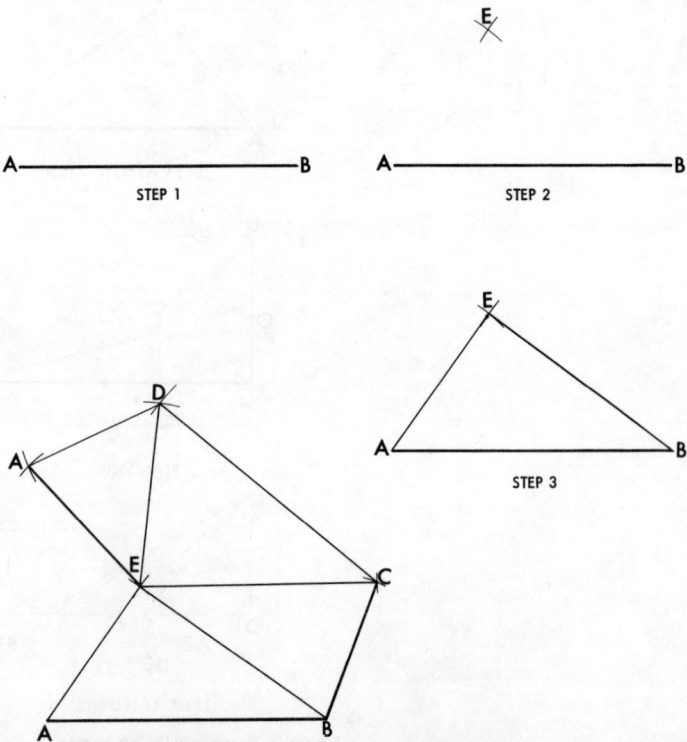

Figure 10. Locating a new point from two known points by triangulation.

describe an arc as shown in Step 2. To be the proper distance from *A*, point *E* must be on this arc. However, there is only one place on the arc where *E* will also be the proper distance from *B*. To locate the proper distance from *B*, set the dividers to the true length of *BE* and swing it from *B* as shown in Step 2. The intersection of these two arcs gives the location of point *E* at the correct distance away from points *A* and *B*. Connect the points as shown in Step 3 and the first side of the pyramid will be formed. Note that it forms a triangle. Breaking down the surface of an object into triangles and forming these individual triangles on the pattern is the basis of development of the process called triangulation.

After the first side is formed, the same process of measuring from two known points is repeated to form the second side. In this case, point *C* on the pattern must next be located. This is done by measuring from points *B* and *E*. The distance from *B* to *C* is a true length on the plan view. Therefore *BC* can be taken directly from the plan view and swung from point *B* on the pattern. The true length from *E* to *C* is taken from the true length triangle and swung from *E*. The intersection of these two arcs gives point *C* and the second side can be drawn in.

The other sides of the pyramid are found in the same manner. After point *C* is located, then point *D* is found by measuring from *E* and *C*. After *D* is found, then *A* is located by measuring from *E* and *D*.

Practicing laying out a rectangular transition by triangulation

To test your knowledge of triangulation methods, lay out the pattern for the rectangular transition shown in Fig. 11. In the plan view, the dotted lines are measuring lines drawn on the surface of the fitting to form the triangles necessary for triangulation. This fitting actually amounts to a duplication of the layout of the pyramid except that eight triangles are formed on the pattern instead of four as may be seen in the illustration.

The pattern is started by first finding all the true lengths necessary for the lines on the plan view. After all the true lengths are found and labeled, then start the pattern by drawing line *AB* which can be taken directly from the plan. Next swing the true length of *AF* from *A* and swing your dividers the true length of *BF* from *B* to locate point *F*. After *F* is found, locate point *E* next by locating the distance *FE* from *F* (this is a true length on the plan) and by locating the true length of *AE* from *A*. This completes the first side of the pattern.

The next point to locate is *G*. This is done by measuring from points *F* and *B*. Line *FG* can be taken directly from the plan view, while line *BG* must be taken from the true length triangle.

After point *G* is located, then point *C* is found by measuring in the same manner as before from points *G* and *B*. The rest of the layout is repetition, finding points *H, D, E,* and *A* in that order.

ELEVATION VIEW

PLAN VIEW

TRUE LENGTHS

PATTERN

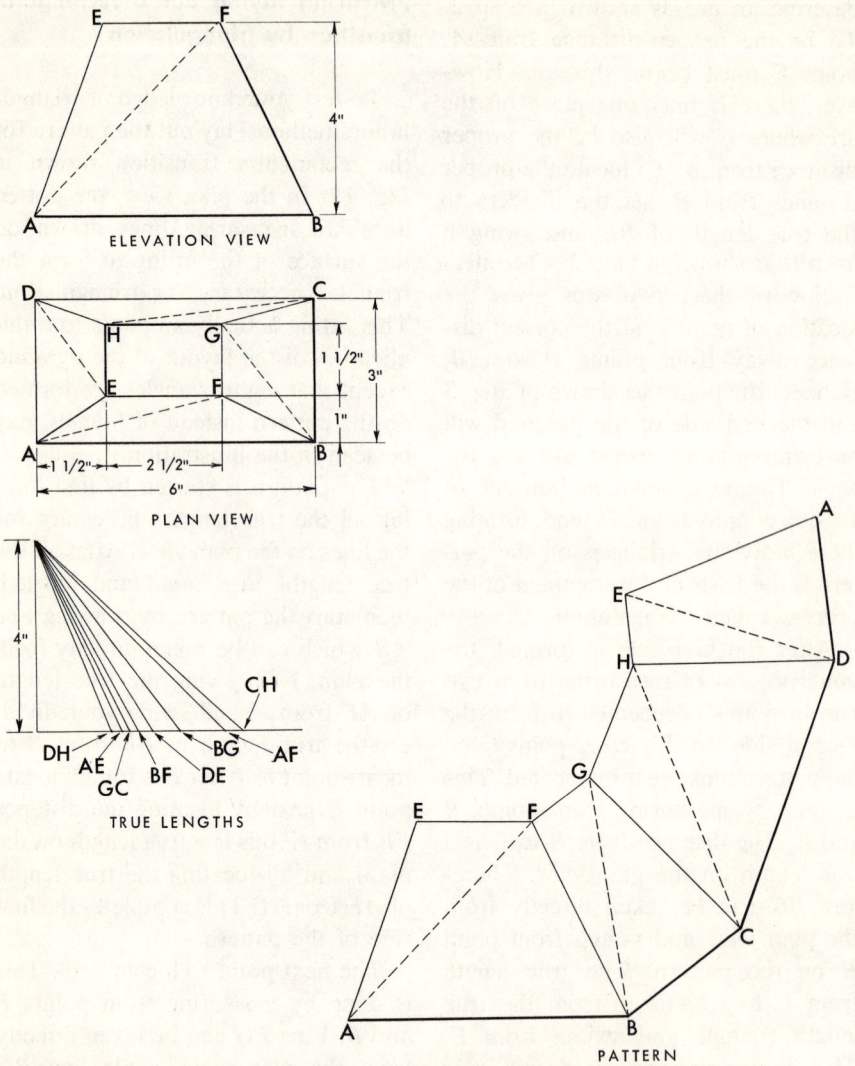

Figure 11. Laying out rectangular transition by triangulation.

Triangulating a round taper

You should now have an understanding of the basic principles of triangulation. To fully master this method of layout you should now learn how to apply it to various typical operations. One very common situation is triangulating a round taper. Though this problem illustrates a round taper, the same methods would apply if the taper were elliptical or any other circular shape.

Figure 12 shows the plan and elevation of a round taper that is offset. The first step in the layout of this problem is to establish the measuring lines on the plan view. This is done by dividing both circles into 12 equal parts. Notice that this is quite similar to one of the procedures in parallel lines. After the circles are divided into equal parts then the measuring lines are drawn in as shown. This layout is again the same as the pyramid and the rectangular transition in that triangles are formed on the plan view and on the pattern.

For example, the first triangle is formed by *8-9-1*. The dotted line shown in the plan view from *8* to *9* is only to illustrate the triangles formed and are never in on the plan view.

After the plan view is drawn, the measuring lines located and the true lengths found, the pattern can be started. This is done by drawing a line and marking the true length of line *8-1* on it. This gives two known points from which to measure. Next locate point *9* by taking the distance *8-9* from the plan view and swinging it from point *8*. Next take the true

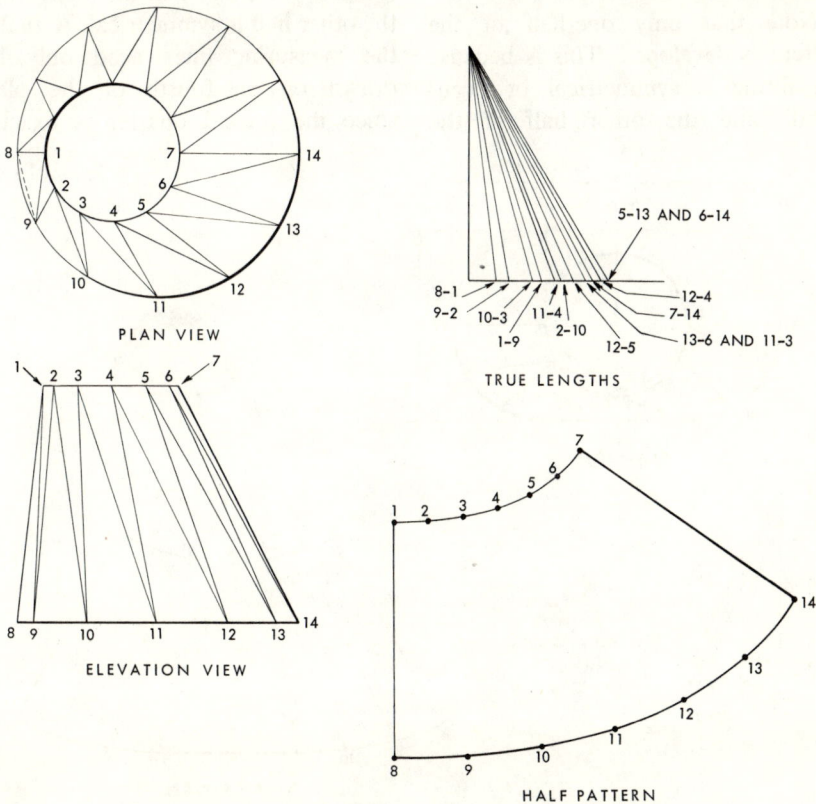

PLAN VIEW

TRUE LENGTHS

5-13 AND 6-14

8-1
9-2
10-3
11-4
1-9
2-10
12-5
12-4
7-14
13-6 AND 11-3

ELEVATION VIEW

HALF PATTERN

Figure 12. Laying out pattern for round taper that is offset.

length of line *1-9* from the true length triangle. Then swing it from *1*. The intersection of these two arcs gives point *9*.

Point *2* is located next by measuring from points *1* and *9*. After *2* is found then *10* is next located by measuring from *2* and *9*. After *10* is found, then *3* is next located by measuring from points *2* and *10*. Points *11, 4, 12, 5, 13, 14,* and *7* are found in the same manner and in the order given. If you will think of the plan view as a road map and follow the measuring lines, you will have little trouble in finishing the pattern.

Note that only one-half of the pattern is developed. This is because the fitting is symmetrical or "centered" and the other half of the

fitting is exactly the same. Therefore it saves time to work on only half of the plan which is general shop practice in any case when objects are symmetrical.

Practicing laying out an oval-to-round fitting by triangulation

Figure 13 shows an oval-to-round fitting. Test your knowledge of triangulation by laying out the pattern. This is an illustration of how the basic principles of triangulation apply to many different shapes.

On this pattern the measuring lines are drawn on only half the plan, since the other half is symmetrical. Actually the measuring lines need only be drawn on one-fourth of the plan since the second quarter is exactly

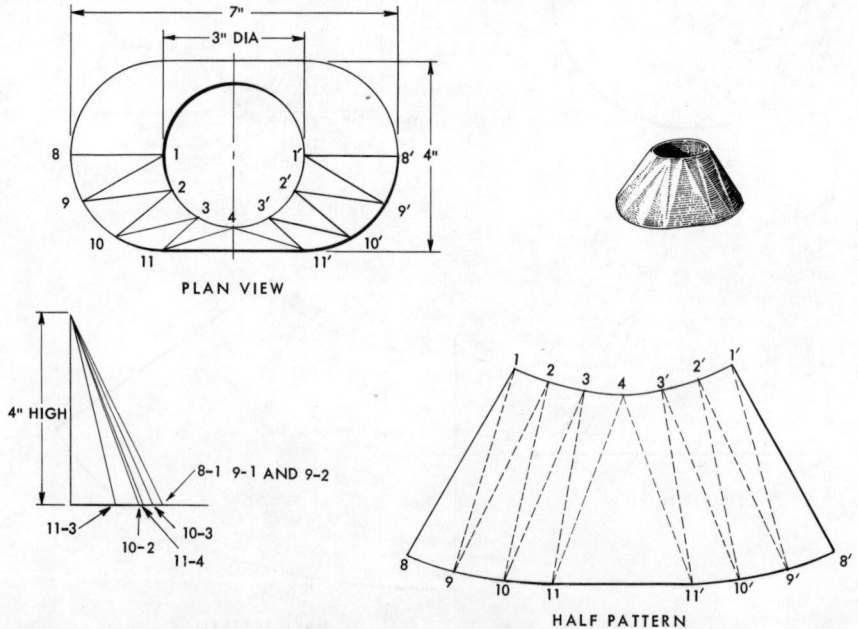

PLAN VIEW

HALF PATTERN

Figure 13. Developing an oval to round fitting by triangulation.

the same as the first quarter, the true length lines will also be exactly the same and there is no need to find them again.

This problem is almost a repetition of the round taper. The only difference is that a straight section is added into the bottom circle to make it an oval. The triangle formed by *11-11'-4* is a flat surface while the rest of the fitting is curved.

This fitting could be started just as with the round taper. However, it is more convenient to start with line *11-11'* and from these two points locate point *4*. Then, since the quarter patterns are duplicates, work from the center toward both ends at the same time. In other words, when the arc for *11-3* is swung, at the same time swing *11'-3'* since this is the same length. This cuts down time involved in setting the dividers by half.

Triangulating a square-to-round

Figure 14 illustrates the triangula-

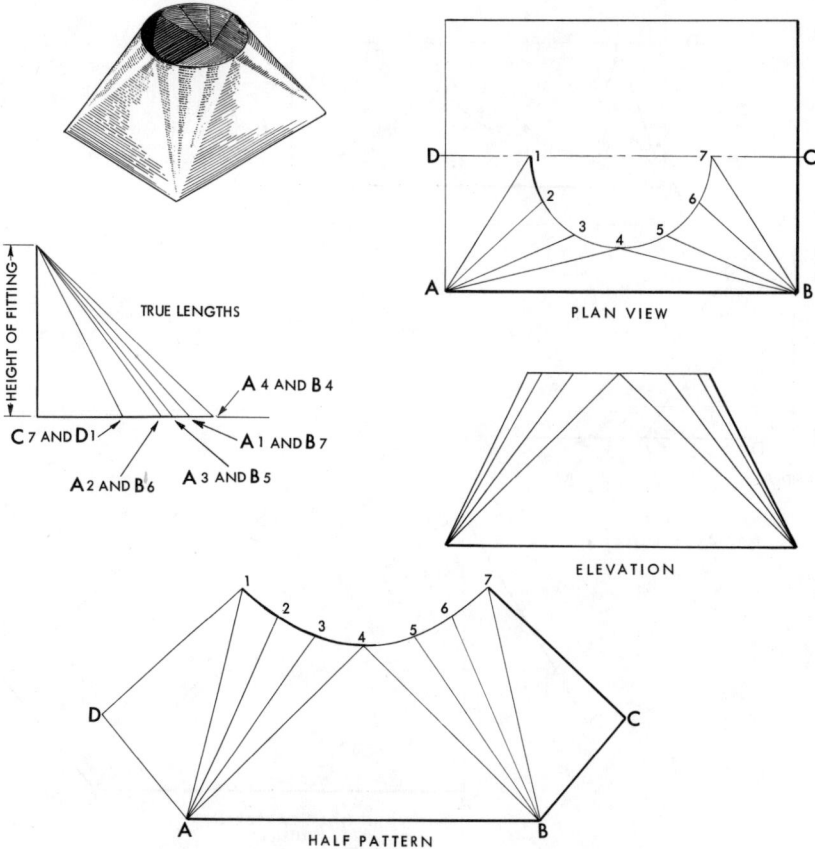

Figure 14. Developing a square to round fitting by triangulation.

tion of another common type of fitting. These are commonly called *square-to-rounds* even though the shape may be rectangular-to-round, or even triangular-to-round.

As in previous problems, the method of layout is still that of forming triangles on the plan view and then forming the same triangles on the pattern in their true length.

Since this is a symmetrical fitting, only one-fourth of the plan view is necessary. However, one-half is marked with measuring lines to make the layout clearer. The true lengths of the measuring lines are found in the usual way, as shown.

Again, the method of starting the pattern of the square to round is from the center out. To start the pattern,

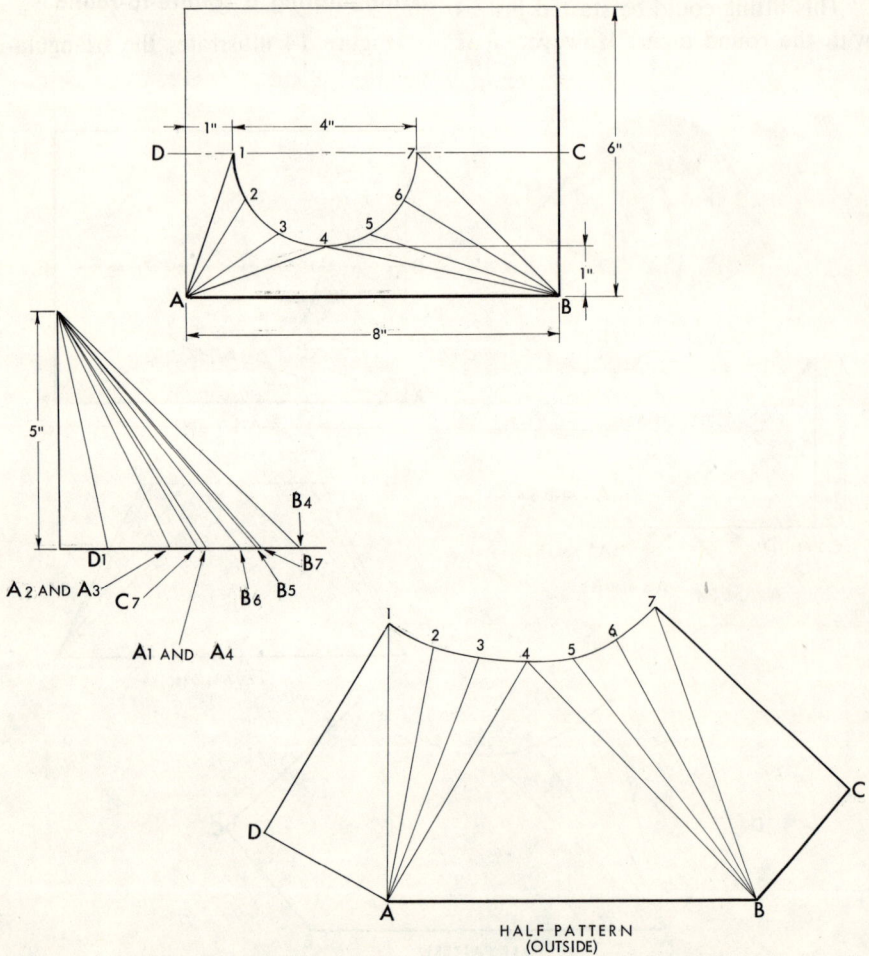

Figure 15. Developing an offset square to round fitting by triangulation.

draw true length line *AB*, which can be taken from the plan view. Next locate point *4* by swinging the true length of *A4* from *A*, and by swinging the true length of *B4* from *B*. After *4* is located, next find point *3*. This is done by swinging the true length of *A3* from *A* and by swinging the distance *4-3* from *4* (*4-3* can be taken directly from the plan view).

Point *2* is found next and then point *1*. After this, the other side of the pattern curve is laid out by locating points *5, 6,* and *7* in that order. After the curve points from *1* to *7* are located, then points *C* and *D* must be found to complete the half-pattern. To find *C* take the distance *BC* from the plan view and swing it from *B* on the pattern. Then take the true length of *C-7* and swing it from *7*. The intersection of these two arcs gives point *C* and the lines *7C* and *BC* can be drawn in. Point *D* is located in the same way. Take *AD* from the plan view and swing it from point *A*. Then take the true length of *D-1* and swing it from *1*. This locates *D* and the lines can be drawn in.

Practicing laying out a square-to-round fitting by triangulation

Figure 15 shows a slightly different square-to-round. This fitting is rectangular on one end and the circle is off center from the rectangle. This, however, makes no difference in the layout of the problem except that the true lengths will all be different rather than being duplicates of corresponding lines. Notice also that no elevation view is drawn of this fitting. In actual shop practice the elevation is seldom drawn unless it is needed in order find some of the true length lines. In most cases the only use for the elevation view is to show the height of the fitting, and this can be done by a note on the plan view as shown.

Lay out the pattern for this fitting to check your understanding of triangulation.

Review Questions

1. Describe the types of object on which triangulatioin is used.
2. How is a true length found?
3. Explain how to identify a line is a true length on the plan view.
4. List the basic steps in triangulation that are used in every problem.
5. Under what circumstances is it only necessary to draw half a plan view of a fitting?

15

RADIAL LINE DEVELOPMENTS

Under what circumstances are radial line developments used? How is a radial line layout similar to parallel line and triangulation? How is a pattern laid out by means of radial line development?

Radial line layouts are the third means by which the sheet metal worker develops patterns. This method is discussed last in this sequence describing sheet metal pattern developments for two reasons. First, radial line developments employ many of the procedures of parallel line development *and* triangulation with which you have been presented in the preceding two chapters. Second, radial line developments are used least of the three methods.

In order for the radial line method to be effective, all lines must radiate from a common center. In addition, the amount of slant of those lines must be relatively large since most radial line developments begin by drawing the side view and then extending the side lines until they meet the peak. Arcs are then projected from this point. If the side taper is so slight

that the peak is several feet from the fitting, it is obviously impractical to use radial lines since the radius needed to swing the arc is long and consequently difficult to use. Because of these limiting circumstances then, the conditions under which radial line developments may be effectively employed are necessarily limited.

Fig. 1 shows some typical objects which could be laid out using radial line development. Remember, however, that such objects *must* be centered, that is equally tapered on all sides. Although these objects could also be laid out by the triangulation method described in the preceding chapter, in these particular cases, radial lines provide a quicker method.

Developing the pattern for a cone by radial lines

Fig. 2 shows the layout of a pattern

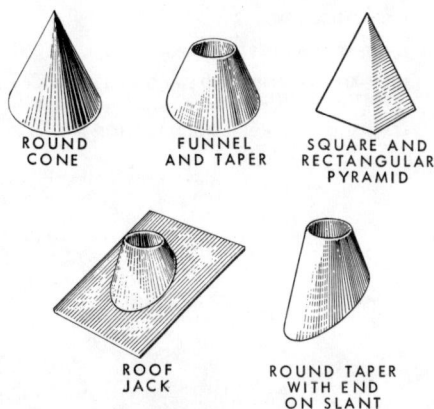

ROUND CONE   FUNNEL AND TAPER   SQUARE AND RECTANGULAR PYRAMID

ROOF JACK   ROUND TAPER WITH END ON SLANT

Figure 1. Some typical fittings and shapes which may be laid out by radial line development.

ous elements in the pattern being constructed.

The pattern for the cone in Fig. 2 is developed in the following manner.

1. The elevation view, showing the true height of the apex, and the plan view, from which the length of the stretchout is determined, are drawn first.
2. The stretchout arc is drawn with a radius equal to the true length of the side or edge of the object.
3. The stretchout arc is drawn of sufficient length to contain each

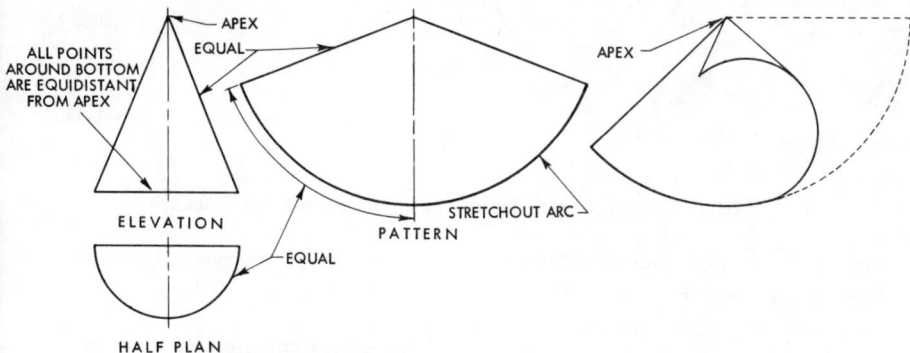

Figure 2. Laying out the pattern for a cone by radial line development.

for a cone. This typical radial line development serves to illustrate some of the principles employed in such layouts.

You will notice that radial line developments have several similarities to the pattern layout methods presented in the preceding two chapters. As with many of the examples presented in those chapters, it is necessary here to have the essential views and to determine true lengths of vari-

space in the plan view and in the same order.

4. The true lengths of the elements are obtained from the elevation view and are placed on the stretchout to complete the pattern.

Developing the patterns for a round taper

Any round taper, *provided that it is equally tapered on all sides,* can be

1. DRAW SIDE VIEW

2. EXTEND SIDE LINES UP TO APEX

3. USE APEX AS CENTER AND SWING ARCS FROM TOP AND BOTTOM OF FITTING

4. MEASURE STRETCHOUT AROUND BOTTOM ARC

PATTERN

APEX

CIRCUMFERENCE OF BOTTOM DIAMETER

SIDE VIEW

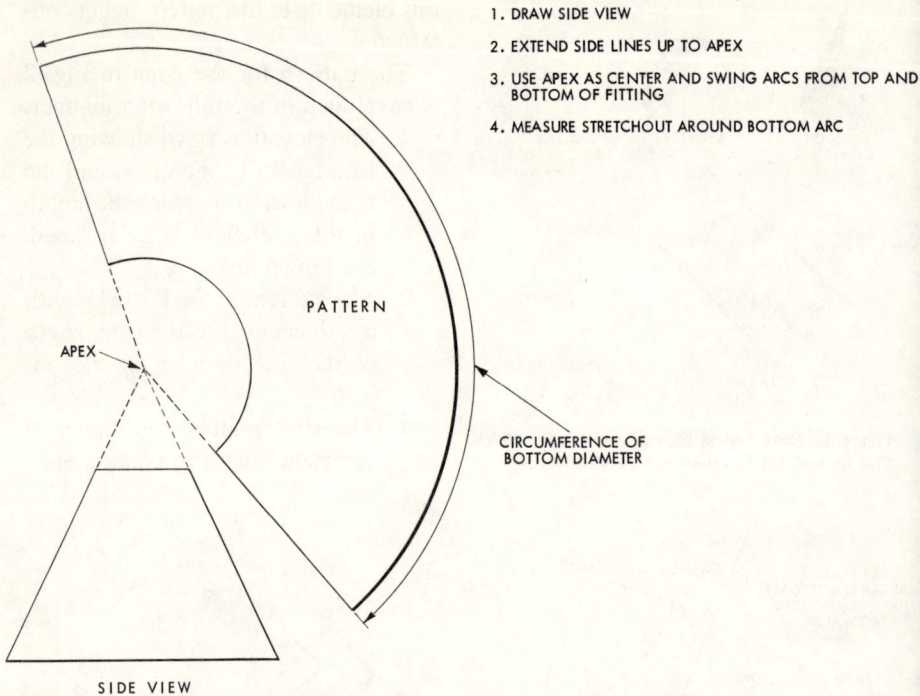

Figure 3. Centered round tapers may be laid out with radial lines.

laid out by radial line development. The round taper shown in Fig. 3 is essentially the same as the cone in Fig. 2 except that the top is cut off. In describing the centered round taper in Fig. 3, follow these steps.

1. Draw the side view of the taper.
2. Extend the side lines until they meet. This forms the apex.
3. Use the apex as the center and project arcs from the top and bottom corners of the taper.
4. The stretchout arc is drawn. In this case, the stretchout is the circumference of a circle whose diameter is the bottom of the taper.
5. Draw lines from the apex to the

ends of the stretchout on the bottom arc.

Developing the patterns for a pyramid with a square base

Pyramids with a square or rectangular base may also be laid out by radial line development, *provided that the sides are equally tapered*. Fig. 4 shows a typical example of such a pyramid. This example employs the principles in determining true lengths which were discussed in Chapter 14 and utilizes the steps in the preceding two examples. Here, however, the chords (the segment of a line between two points of its intersection with the curve) are measured around the arc

TRUE LENGTH
OF AB

H

H ⟵ A B ⟶

TRUE LENGTH OF A B

⟵ 2" ⟶

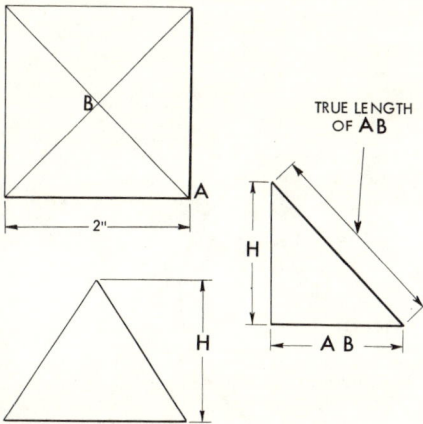

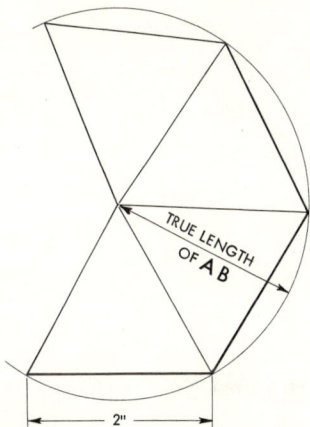

Figure 4. Pyramids with rectangular bases may be laid out by radial line developments when the sides are equally tapered.

equal to the length of the bottom side of the pyramid.

Developing patterns for tapers on a pitch

Though radial line developments are used for the simple tapered objects shown in the preceding examples in this chapter, their greatest use is in

laying out more complex fittings to which their characteristics may be applied. The sheet metal worker often speaks of objects being "on the pitch." What he means here is that one or both ends of the object are slanted rather than in a plane square to the center line. For objects of this kind, the same basic steps previously outlined are followed. However, new applications of them are applied.

Fig. 5 shows a round taper with the bottom pitched up at a 30° angle. The first step is to draw the side view shown by *1-A-B-7'*. Then extend the side line *B-7'* down to point *7* to make the complete cone described by *1-A-B-7*. Remember that one of the prime requisites of a radial line development is that all sides *must* be equally tapered. Therefore, *A-1* and *B-7* must have the same slant.

The profile is drawn next. If you will review Chapters 13 and 14, *Parallel Line Development* and *Triangulation,* you will note that this operation is the same here as in those methods. After the profile is drawn and equal spaces are stepped off, project the spaces to line *1-7* and from these points draw lines up to the apex *O* to form equally spaced, tapering lines around the surface of the cone.

You will note that this operation is similar to that you used in parallel line developments. In parallel lines, the profile is drawn to obtain equally spaced *parallel measuring lines* on the surface. In this example of radial lines, the profile is drawn to obtain equally spaced *tapering lines* on the surface.

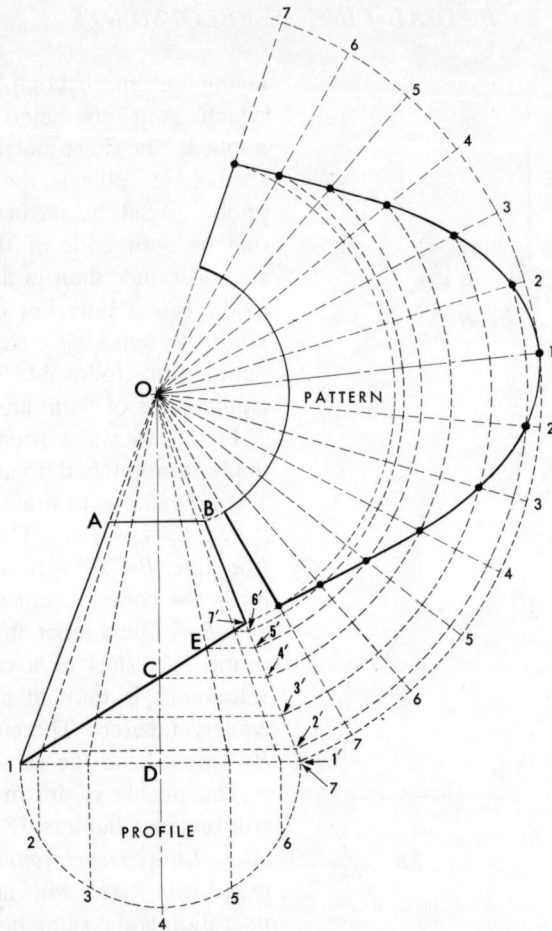

Figure 5. How to lay out the pattern for a round taper on a pitch.

Since the measuring lines are tapering lines, they are obviously *not* true lengths on the side view. True lengths for them may be found by the method described in Chapter 14, *Triangulation*.

However, since the sides of the fitting all slant the same amount, all the lines which indicate the sides must slant the same amount. This means that the lengths of all the lines can

be projected over to the side line to obtain their true length. This is because the side lines are on a plane perpendicular to the line of vision (see Fig. 2, Chapter 14) and are therefore true lengths on the drawing.

As an example, in Fig. 5 follow point *4* on the profile through the operation. Point *4* is projected up to line *1-7* to locate point *D*. A measuring line is drawn from *D* to *O*. Line

DO crosses the bottom of the fitting at point *C.* From *C,* project a line at right angles to the center line over to the side line *B7.* This gives you point *4'.* The distance *O-4'* is the true length of *OC.* Note that all of the points on the side view are projected at right angles to the center line— that is parallel to line *1-7.* All of the points are projected in this manner. Distance *O-5',* for example, is the true length of line *OE.*

When all of the true lengths are located along the side line *B-7,* arcs are swung from each of these points with apex *O* as the center. The stretchout of the profile is then measured around the bottom. Spaces are then stepped off for the measuring lines in duplication of the spaces around the profile. When these spaces are located, lines are drawn from them up to apex *O.*

After the radial lines from the stretchout and the arcs from the true lengths are drawn, then the intersection of the corresponding lines gives the points on the pattern. For example, where the arc whose radius is *O-7'* crosses radial line *O-7* is a point on the pattern. The arc whose radius is *O-6'* and radial line *O-6* gives us another point. After all of the points are drawn in, the bottom curve is drawn through these points to form that portion of the pattern. The upper curve of the pattern is an arc swung from point *B.*

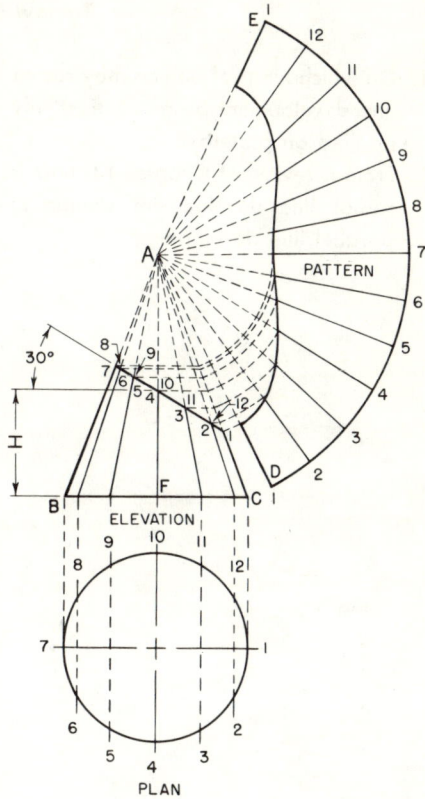

Figure 6. Developing the pattern for a truncated right cone cut at an angle. Base diameter is 6" and height from base to apex is 8".

Practicing developing a pattern for a truncated right cone cut at an angle

Another round taper with the slant at the top is shown in Fig. 6. Check your understanding of radial line development by laying out the pattern for this fitting.

(Review questions on the following page)

Review Questions

1. On which kinds of objects may radial line development be most effectively applied on patterns?

2. From a review of Chapter 13, how is radial line development similar to parallel line development?

3. From a review of Chapter 14, how is radial line development similar to triangulation?

4. What one characteristic must any object have in order for it to be laid out by radial line development?

16

PLASTICS

What are plastics? What are the two major divisions of plastics? What are the common uses of plastics? What are the characteristics of the common plastics? What type of plastic is generally used in the sheet metal shop? What is PVC plastic, and what are its limitations? How is PVC plastic fabricated? What are some of the products made from PVC plastic in the sheet metal shop? What other plastics are used in the sheet metal shop?

One of the new materials with which the sheet metal craftsman works is plastics. For certain uses such as exposure to corrosive fumes and excessive moisture, some types of plastics are superior to sheet metal. Many of the tools and equipment used to lay out, form, and assemble plastics are similar to those used to fabricate sheet metal. Since there has been an increasing demand for plastics, many sheet metal shops have installed the additional equipment needed to fabricate sheet plastics. It is essential for the student who intends to become thoroughly familiar with the sheet metal trade to learn about all plastics, and PVC (polyvinyl chloride) in particular.

Types of plastics

Plastics are man-made materials. They are made from such raw materials as cotton, water, air, coal, salt, crude oil, and natural gas. They are endless in variety. Basically, however, they consist of substances that are solid in their end use but are either granular, liquid, or very soft at some time during their manufacturing process. In this soft state, most plastics may be formed by heat or pressure, or both, followed by a cooling or *setting* cycle.

Because plastics are essentially products of chemistry, the combinations and varieties of plastics possible are unlimited. In general, they are classified in one of 14 different family

217

TABLE I

TYPES OF PLASTIC

Family Group	Thermosetting or Thermoforming	Properties	Typical Uses
AMINOS	THERMOSETTING	1. Solvent–oil grease resisting 2. Great surface hardness 3. Mar resistant 4. Good electric insulation	1. Adhesive for plywood 2. Housing for food mixers 3. Plastic dinnerware
POLYESTERS	THERMOSETTING	1. Easily handled liquids that can be quickly changed to solid material 2. Can be reinforced with fiber glass cloth layers 3. Can be molded into complex shapes with fiber glass reinforcing 4. High impact strength 5. Lightweight, stable	1. Electrical equipment parts 2. Auto bodies 3. Chairs 4. Luggage
ALKYDS	THERMOSETTING	1. Will retain shape and dimensions 2. Tough finish	1. Auto ignition parts 2. Tube bases
PHENOLICS	THERMOSETTING	1. Heat resistant 2. Resists most solvents 3. Nonconductor of electricity 4. Strong and stiff	1. Light plugs, switch boxes, etc. 2. Camera cases 3. Washing machines 4. Adhesives for plywood 5. Manufacture of brake bands
POLYSTYRENE	THERMOSETTING	1. Lightweight 2. Colors well 3. No taste or odor 4. Not poisonous	1. Disposable packages 2. Toys 3. Wall tile 4. Displays (styrofoam balls and sheets) 5. Pipe fittings 6. Helmets 7. Typewriter cases

groups. Some of the most important groups are shown in Table I. These 14 family groups can be divided into two main categories—the *Thermosetting Plastics* and the *Thermoforming Plastics*. Since *thermo* means heat, *thermosetting* means "heat setting." THERMOSETTING PLASTICS set or

TABLE I — Continued

TYPES OF PLASTIC

Family Group	Thermosetting or Thermoforming	Properties	Typical Uses
ACRYLICS	THERMOFORMING	1. Very clear 2. Resists sunlight, weather and most chemicals 3. High impact strength	1. Radar plotting boards 2. Signs and display 3. Auto taillight 4. Knobs, dials, and handles 5. Manufacture of paints and adhesives
CELLULOSICS	THERMOFORMING	1. Very tough 2. High impact strength	1. Extruded pipe 2. Toys 3. Knife handles 4. Women's shoe heels 5. Costume jewelry 6. Packaging material 7. Tape
POLYETHYLENE	THERMOFORMING	1. Flexible 2. Resists almost all chemicals 3. Long lasting	1. Film and sheet for construction, agriculture, and packaging 2. Squeeze bottles and tubes
VINYL	THERMOFORMING	1. Colorless 2. Resists, water, alcohol acids, and alkalies	1. Electrical insulation 2. Shower curtains, 3. Inflatable toys, and other inflatable goods 4. Upholstery 5. Floor covering 6. Substitute for sheet metal duct and other objects
NYLON	THERMOFORMING	1. Stiff 2. Strong and tough 3. Light 4. Abrasion resistant	1. Molded gears and bushings 2. Aerosol bottles 3. Jacket for wire and cable 4. Cloth

harden when heated. Once they have *set,* their shape is permanent. They cannot be reheated and changed to another shape. Heating may soften the shape, but the plastic will never flow into another shape.

THERMOFORMING PLASTICS are shaped by the application of heat.

When heat is applied, the plastic softens and is formed in the shape of the mold. Unlike thermosetting plastics, however, reheating will allow the thermoforming plastics to be re-formed. Thermoforming plastics can be heated and formed and reheated and re-formed many times.

Though we will be concerned primarily with PVC (polyvinyl chloride) plastic, since this thermoforming type is commonly used in the sheet metal shop, you should have some knowledge of the types and uses of all the common plastics. Table I shows the common plastics, their properties, and their uses. When you study this chart, you will recognize many of the products you use at home and at work. You should understand that plastics are used extensively in our lifetime and the uses will undoubtedly increase.

Chemical substances in plastic formulas

Before processing, most raw plastics are chemically formulated to attain certain desired physical and chemical characteristics. One or more of the following substances may be added to the plastic formula to achieve the desired characteristics.

PLASTICIZERS — Plasticizers soften the plastic and make it more flexible.
STABILIZERS — Stabilizers prevent breakdown of the plastic when it is exposed to heat or light.
FILLERS—Fillers add bulk and reduce overall costs.
COLORS — Dyes and pigments are added to achieve the desired color in the plastic.

FIBERS — Fibers are reinforcing elements which add strength to the plastic.
SOLVENTS—Solvents are added to increase the liquidity and adaptability to processes such as, molding, extruding, dipping, brushing, and spraying.
CATALYSTS—Catalysts speed up the hardening process of the plastic.

The raw bulk plastic compounding manufacturer supplies the compounded plastic to either the intermediate manufacturer (one that makes standard products, such as sheets and pipes or ducts) or the molding manufacturer (also called the end use manufacturer) in one of three forms: liquid, granular, or powdered.

Granular or powdered type plastics are usually softened by the application of heat and are generally formed by molding, casting, or by extrusion. Some of these types can also be used to roll sheets or thin films of plastic.

Liquid plastics may be cast into sheets. They are also used in liquid applications such as spray-on and brush-on coatings or added to paints and adhesives. The base from which plastic foam is made is a liquid type plastic. Examples of other products made from liquid plastics are: insulation, cushioning, and styrofoam balls and sheets used for decorative purposes.

Plastic product manufacturing processes

There are basic manufacturing processes such as *molding—vacuum forming—extrusion—casting* and *laminating*. Variations of these basic processes

Figure 1. Light diffuser—product produced by injection molding process. E. I. du Pont de Nemours Co., Inc., Wilmington, Delaware.

are many and too numerous to mention here. Molding processes are the most widely used to produce plastic products. There are three basic molding processes: (1) injection molding, (2) compression molding, and (3) vacuum forming.

INJECTION MOLDING consists of feeding granular or powdered plastic into a cylinder. A unit in the cylinder heats the plastic to a liquid state. At the start of the molding cycle, a ram feeds into the cylinder and compresses the liquid plastic, forcing it out of the nozzle on the end. The nozzle is connected to the mold. The hot plastic is forced into the mold under pressure and quickly fills all the cavities of the mold. The plastic then hardens as the mold is cooled. Figure 1 shows a product of injection molding.

COMPRESSION MOLDING is generally the process used for most thermosetting plastics. In this process, the plastic (usually in a preformed cake or granular state) is put into the mold. The mold and plastic are heated and, at the same time, the two parts of the mold are pressed together. The combination of heat and pressure softens the plastic and forces it into all the cavities of the mold. During this cycle of the molding process, a chemical reaction also takes place, and the plastic

Figure 2. Handle and knobs—products produced by compression molding process. Union Carbide Corp., New York, N.Y.

is permanently *set* to the shape of the mold. Figure 2 shows a product of compression molding.

VACUUM FORMING sheet plastic is also accomplished with a mold. However, in this process usually only one side of a mold is used. The plastic sheet is formed by creating a vacuum under it in the mold. First the plastic sheet is heated to soften it. Then it is clamped over the mold in such a manner that the mold surface is sealed from the atmosphere above. Then, holes in the mold are used to pump all the air from the space between the mold contour and the hot plastic sheet. The resulting vacuum in the mold cavity below, and the atmospheric air pressure above the plastic sheet force it into the mold, where it is held until it cools and hardens. Vacuum forming is used to produce many products such as the one shown in Figure 3.

CASTING. The casting process can be used with either thermosetting or thermoforming plastics. As in molding, casting employs a mold that determines the shape of the plastic product. The major difference between casting and molding is that no pressure is used in casting. The plastic is liquefied either by heat or chemical change. It is then poured into, or heated in, the mold where it usually cools and hardens. Figure 4 illustrates an example of casting.

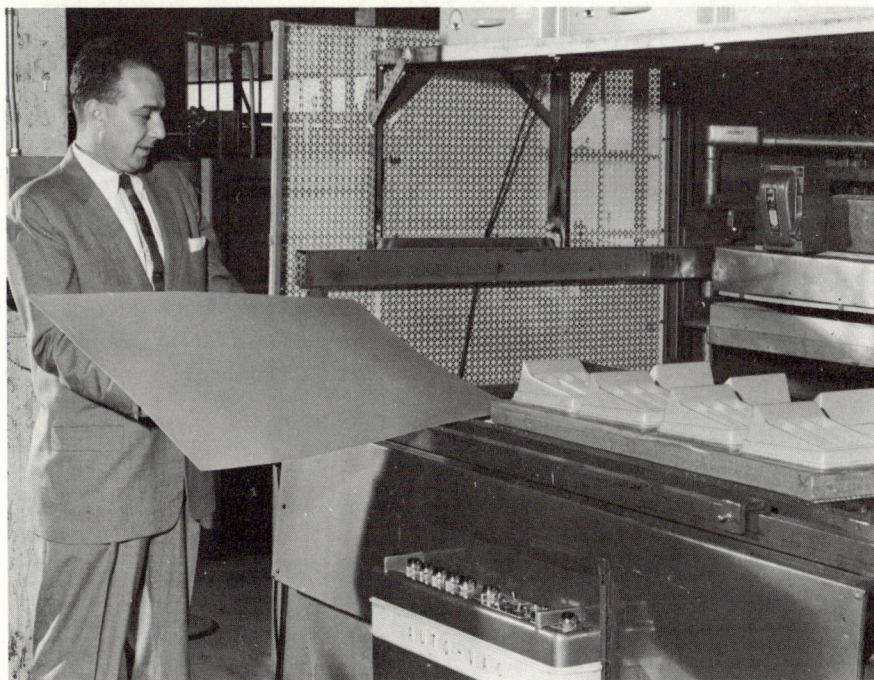

Figure 3. Display trays—products produced by vacuum forming process. Union Carbide Corp., New York, N.Y.

Figure 4. Architectural facia panels—product produced by casting process. Rohm and Haas Co., Philadelphia, Pa.

LAMINATES. There are many types of laminating processes. Figure 5 is one example of a laminated plastic product. Laminating is basically a process that combines resin impregnated sheets. This is usually accomplished by putting the resin impregnated sheets in a press. Pressure and/or heat are then applied. The sheets are bonded into a single sheet called a laminate. A variety of sheet materials such as paper, fiber board, cloth, fiberglas cloth, etc. are laminated. These sheet materials are usually plastic resin impregnated by dipping or roller coating them with a resin which has been liquified. They are then usually dried and stored prior to laminating.

Another common process used to laminate *fiberglas* type products is described here. First, a plaster mold is made to the exact shape required. Then a coat of plastic is sprayed or brushed on the mold. Then, successive coats of plastic and layers of *fiberglas* cloth are added. In this manner, the plastic is gradually increased to the shape and thickness required. Some car bodies, boat hulls, duct components, and plastic lawn furniture are examples of *fiberglas* laminated products.

PVC plastics

The preceding section described the scope of plastics and how they are generally processed. Now we shall concentrate on a type of plastic that will be most important to you in the sheet metal shop. This is polyvinyl chloride, commonly called PVC, or rigid vinyl.

When PVC first became widely

Figure 5. Blower outlet and blower drive housing fabricated from fiberglas laminated sheet. du Verre, Inc., Arcade, N.Y.

known, there was a tendency for sheet metal workers to regard it as a new "wonder material" that would soon replace sheet metal. The fact is that for certain applications PVC has advantages, but it also has limitations. Where there is a volume of industrial work, large sheet metal shops will usually have a PVC fabrication section. A skilled sheet metal worker can soon learn to master all the techniques of PVC fabrication, since they are quite similar to the skills of the sheet metal trade. However, equally important to learning the skills, is learning the char-

acteristics and properties, advantages and limitations of PVC. In the future, there will be a great need for sheet metal workers who understand PVC. Not only will they fabricate it, but they will advise applications for which it is suited, and discourage its misapplication.

Characteristics of PVC

PVC is old, as modern materials go, because it was developed during the year 1934 in Germany. The shortage of metals in Germany during the war, caused PVC to be developed quickly, though it was not until 1940 that it was used to any great extent in the U.S.A.

PVC is a thermoforming plastic. As explained in the previous section, this means it can be heated and re-formed over and over again. This is an advantage in the sheet metal shop, since bends can be adjusted and mistakes can be corrected. It is available in either solid sheets or in laminated or layered sheets. Generally, the sheets under ¼ inch are solid sheets. Thicker sheets are laminated. Plastic sheets are measured by fractional thickness rather than by sheet metal gage. Plastic sheets are available from as thin as $\frac{3}{64}$ of an inch, to 2 inches thick. PVC is also widely used in manufactured pipes which can be ordered as large as 14 inches in diameter.

There are two basic types of PVC sheets in common use. These are called Type I and Type II. The major difference is that Type I is unplasticized, while Type II is plasticized. If you will remember our discussion in the previous section, *Chemical Substances in Plastic Formulas,* you will remember that plasticizer softens the plastic and makes it more flexible. Type II, therefore, is more flexible than Type I, and can be worked more easily. Usually, Type II is not plasticized over 50%, since a sheet plasticized to this extent is about as flexible as sheet rubber. Most Type II sheets are 25% plasticized. At this percentage it is very difficult to shatter the plastic. Because Type I is unplasticized, it is more rigid than Type II. Type I also has greater chemical and

temperature resistance than Type II. Because of these factors, Type I is the type most generally used in the sheet metal shop, especially for duct work. However, Type II is used where job conditions require its use.

PVC is not a strong material when compared to steel. The tensile strength of steel is around 80,000 pounds per square inch, while PVC at room temperature is about 8,000 pounds per square inch—only about one-tenth the strength of steel. Also, as the temperature increases, PVC becomes weaker (at 140° F its strength is only 4,000 psi). Type I PVC is about as brittle as cast iron. A hard blow from a heavy hammer is capable of shattering it. It is comparatively light in weight. Sheets ⅛″ thick weigh approximately one pound per square foot, as compared to ⅛″ steel sheet which weighs approximately five pounds per square foot.

As mentioned above, PVC becomes weaker as the temperature increases. Manufacturers specify that it should not be used where temperatures exceed 180° F. It will start to sag at this temperature. Actually, most shops never use PVC beyond temperature limits of 150° F. They have found that even at this temperature the plastic will sag or the laminations will start to peel after a period of use. A comparison shows that steel does not even begin to weaken until approximately 800° F, and serious weakening does not occur until considerably higher temperatures are reached.

Despite these apparent limitations, PVC does have many desirable quali-

TABLE II

Comparison Chart on Chemical Resistance of Sheet Materials

This chart is based upon the results of laboratory tests on pure chemicals. On-the-job conditions will vary considerably, so that no application involving chemicals should be based entirely upon any chart but should also be based upon tests on the job. The ratings are necessarily only approximate and varying rates of resistance can be expected.

Code: R----resistant
PR---partially resistant
A----attacked
N---No data available

Figures given are for 68° F

Consult manufacturers' charts for more detailed information

Substance	Stainless Steel Type 316	PVC Type 1	Aluminum	Copper
Acetic acid 80%	R	R	R	R
Aluminum hydroxide	R	R	R	A
Ammonium chloride	R	R	A	R
Antimony trichloride	R	R	N	N
Boric acid	R	R	R	R
Calcium Carbonate	PR	R	N	N
Chlorobenzine	R	A	N	N
Citric Acid	R	R	R	R
Gasoline	R	R	R	R
Hydrochloric acid	A	R	A	A
Hydroflouric acid	A	R	A	A
Iodine	A	A	N	N
Methyl alcohol	R	R	R	R
Milk	R	R	R	R
Photographic solutions Regular	R	R	N	
Sea water	R	R	R	R
Stannic chloride	A	R	N	N
Sulfuric acide up to 96% solution	A	R	A	R
Zinc Chloride	R	R	R	R

TABLE III

POLYVINYL CHLORIDE PROPERTIES

Type I	Type II 25% plasticized	Type II 50% plasticized
1. Most rigid	1. Not as rigid as Type I	1. Pliable as rubber
2. Highest corrosion resistance	2. Slightly less corrosion resistance than Type I	2. Used for gaskets only
3. Impact strength equal to cast iron	3. Higher impact strength than Type I	
4. Grey in color	4. Grey in color but different shade from Type I	
5. 160° F highest safe temperature	5. 120° highest safe temperature	
6. Easily formed and fabricated	6. Easier to form and fabricate than Type I	

ties. It has become a material of considerable importance in the sheet metal shop because it is highly resistant to almost all types of corrosion. Under very corrosive conditions, where even stainless steel has corroded in a short time, PVC was installed and has lasted indefinitely. When PVC is used for ductwork or tanks where chemicals such as hydrochloric acid, sulfuric acid, and calcium carbonate are present, it will last for an undetermined long period of time. If sheet metal were used under these same conditions, it would corrode and deteriorate in a relatively short period of time. Table II shows a comparison of corrosion resistance between PVC plastic sheet, Type I, and the basic sheet metals.

Another desirable quality of PVC is that it is a low conductor of heat. This means that when PVC is used for ductwork, there is no need to add extra insulation to prevent heat loss which may be required on sheet metal duct work. The savings in materials and labor help offset the extra cost of PVC. Another advantage of the low heat conductor characteristic of PVC is the absence of moisture condensation inside the ductwork. This occurs in a sheet metal duct due to temperature differences on opposite sides of the sheet.

In addition to these characteristics, PVC is affected very little by the elements. It is unaffected by water or sunlight. It does not support combustion. While it can be ignited, this is accomplished only with great difficulty, and PVC will stop burning by itself almost immediately, when flame or the source of ignition is removed. Table III summarizes the most important features of PVC.

Figure 6. This type of an oven is required to soften PVC sheet so that it may be formed to specifications. Plastics generally are not good heat conductors, so the ovens are thermostatically controlled and have circulating fans and mesh metal shelves to aid heat transfer. Oven temperatures are usually set at 225° to 250°.

Fabricating PVC plastic in the sheet metal shop

PVC must be heated in order to bend or form it. It must also be held in place until it cools and sets. The joints and sections may be joined by adhesives, bolts, or rivets. However, the hot air welding process is more commonly used. Welding is generally accomplished by heating the plastic joint with a hot iron torch until it softens. At the same time, a plastic rod is heated and pressed into the seam to make a welded joint. The forming and joining of plastics will be explained in more detail in the following sections. An important factor in the fabrication of PVC is: the skill you gain through experience which makes it possible for you to estimate the amount of shrinkage which will occur during the fabrication process. Plastic will shrink more than metal, and the plastic welder must be able to estimate the allowance for this shrinkage. Since plastic fabricating is comparatively new in sheet metal shops, there are no standard allowances for shrinkage such as there are for metals. Each sheet metal man who welds plastics has his own method of allowing for shrinkage — much of which is based upon his judgment and experience.

In addition to the usual sheet metal tools and equipment, the shop should have an oven such as the one shown in Fig. 6. The oven is usually made in the shop and is generally gas fired. It is controlled by a thermostat so that the heat may be set at the proper temperature to form the plastic (about 160° F). The oven is usually equipped with shelves made of heavy expanded metal so that the plastic sheet may be

PVC SHEET

SLOT ABOUT 2" WIDE
FOR LENGTH OF TABLE

PLASTIC HEATS AND SOFTENS
ALONG NARROW STRIP
OVER TABLE SLOT

HEAT REFLECTOR

TABLE

ELECTRIC HEATING ELEMENT
RUNS LENGTH OF TABLE

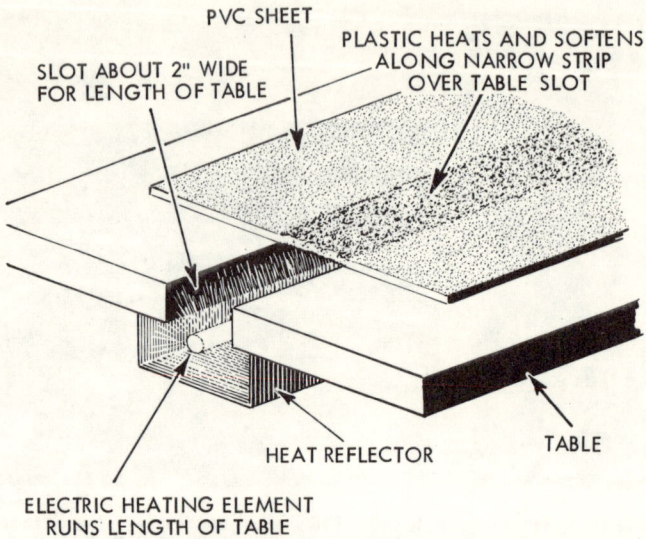

Figure 7A. Closeup of strip heater table.

Figure 7B. Strip heaters are used to heat plastic sheets for bending operations.

laid flat and heated equally on both sides. The strip heater shown in Figs. 7A and 7B is another heating device. The strip heater is used to apply heat to a narrow strip of the plastic sheet so that it can be bent in the sheet metal brake.

Other tools needed to work PVC plastic sheet are: a hot air welding torch as shown in Fig. 8, and wood-working tools such as a table saw to cut the plastic, and a hand router to bevel the edges prior to welding.

Shops that fabricate PVC in volume also have forms on which to shape the hot plastic. These are heavy sheet metal forms made to the contour and size required for the plastic product to be formed. Fig. 9 shows some typical shapes of forms.

Forming a round pipe from PVC plastic

To illustrate how PVC is formed, Fig. 10 shows the full sequence of operations required to make a round pipe from PVC plastic sheet. You can produce many other shapes by following the same procedure and using the appropriate forms. In rectangular duct fabrication, the plastic sheet is heated in the strip heater and is then bent in the sheet metal brake. After the bend

Figure 8. Hot air welding torches are used to weld joints on PVC sheet. Plastic rod of the same type as the sheet is used for filler rod. Courtesy: Joseph T. Ryerson & Son, Inc.

Figure 9. Sheet metal forms such as these are used to form PVC sheet into special shapes. Hot plastic sheet is held in position around the form until the PVC cools. Forms for round tapers and cones are adaptable to a variety of diameters. Courtesy: Heating and Air Conditioning Contractor Magazine.

STEP 1

STEP 3

Step 1. After cutting sheets to size, the edges are beveled to provide a butt weld with included angle of 60°. In the illustration, a wood router is being used with a tapered bit. A wood jointer may also be used for the same operation. Before this beveling operation, the sheet was cut on a table saw. For sheets up to $\frac{3}{16}$" thick, an ordinary sheet metal squaring shear may be used. Some shops cut $\frac{1}{4}$" sheet using a squaring shear. However, there is danger that this sheet thickness will crack.

Step 2. After the sheet is cut to the proper size and shape, it is heat softened. The sheets are placed in the oven and held at a temperature between 225°-250° F. until they become pliable. Note that the operator wears gloves to prevent burns from the hot sheet.

STEP 4

Step 4. Hot PVC sheet is shaped around the sheet metal form.

Step 3. When the sheets are thoroughly heated, they become soft and pliable. The form to be used is placed close to the oven opening, so that the sheet may be shaped quickly while still hot.

Step 5. The plastic is pulled tightly against the form by means of a light gage sheet metal draw band. The draw band is necessary in order to bring all the surface area of the sheet into contact with the fixture.

STEP 2

STEP 5

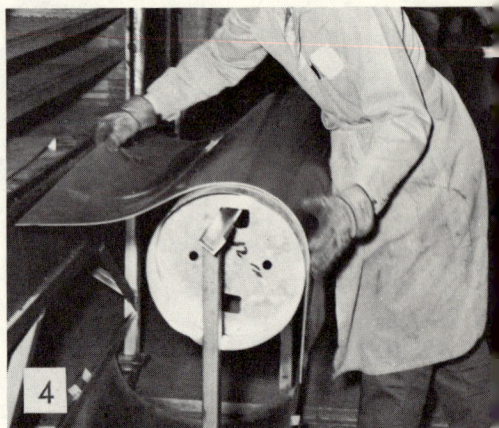

HOW POLYVINYL CHLORIDE PLASTIC SHEET IS FORMED IN THE SHEET METAL SHOP

Figure 10. Steps 1 through 9.

Courtesy: Heating and Air Conditioning Contractor Magazine.

STEP 6

STEP 8

Step 6. When the draw band is in position, it is clamped tightly over the plastic until the sheet has cooled. When several lengths of plastic pipe are to be made, cold air or water is usually circulated through the inside of the sheet metal form in order to accelerate cooling.

Step 8. The seam of the pipe is then welded with a hot air torch and plastic welding rod. Before using the welding rod, the operator closes the seam by making one pass over it with the tacking tip on the torch.

Step 7. After the plastic has cooled thoroughly, it is removed from the fixture. There is always a small amount of spring-back as shown in the illustration.

Step 9. The final weld on a straight seam is made by using a high-speed welding tip on the hot air torch. The tip should straddle the seam and, as it is moved along, the rod feeds down through the torch into the seam.

STEP 7

STEP 9

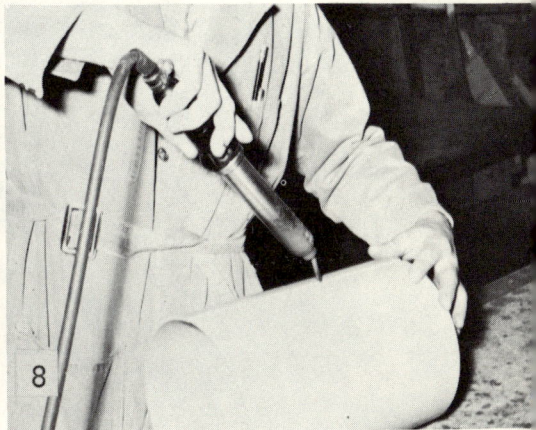

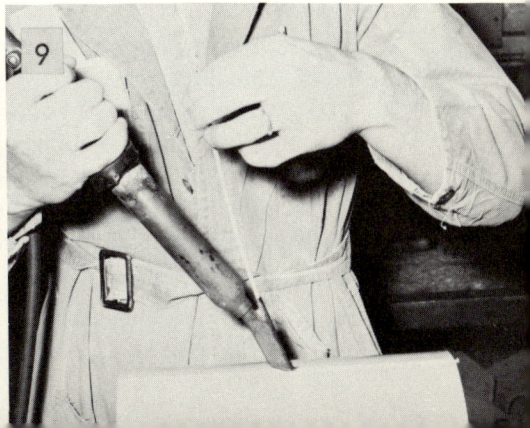

Figure 11. A typical hot air welding operation showing products fabricated from PVC sheet. Courtesy: Heating and Air Conditioning Contractor Magazine.

has been made, the brake bending leaf must be clamped in position until the plastic cools enough to hold the bend.

Welding plastics

Welding as stated before, is one of the most common processes used to fabricate PVC plastic. Fig. 11 shows a typical PVC welding operation. Although anyone skilled in welding can learn to run a presentable plastic weld in a few minutes, it takes considerable practice to run consistently strong welds that will withstand normal use. One of the reasons is that plastic does not become a liquid puddle like metal, in metal welding. The plastic softens only enough to form a bond between the rod and the sheets.

Another reason is that PVC has only one-tenth the strength of steel. By comparison, an imperfect steel weld may have only a fraction of the strength of a perfect weld, but will still hold and have more than enough strength for the particular application. By comparison, a PVC plastic weld, must be close to 100% of its potential strength, since this strength is generally being utilized to the limit.

Plastic welding is a combination of heat and pressure. The plastic sheets to be joined, and the welding rod are heated with a stream of hot air. The rod is pressed down into the softened plastic "V" joint and fuses with the sheets. To learn how to weld plastic correctly, it is necessary to practice until you learn the correct temperature, the proper angle at which to hold the rod, the right amount of pressure to use on the rod and the suitable speed at which to weld. These are the four essentials of plastic welding: temperature, heat, pressure, and speed.

PREPARING THE JOINT. When a butt weld is specified in steel welding fabrication, the edges of the steel plates are usually beveled. This joint design combined with a good weld makes the strongest and best appearing type. This practice is also true in plastic welding.

In the majority of plastic welding operations, the edges of the sheets should be beveled so that when they are butted together they form a maximum angle of 60° shown in Fig. 12. Sometimes this gap is made 5 or 10° less so that fewer beads are needed to

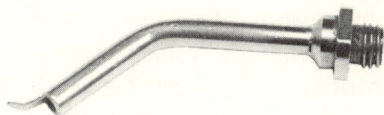

Figure 13. The tacking tip used to make tack welds. Courtesy: Laramy Products Co., Inc.

make the finished weld.

TACK WELDING THE JOINT. After the sheets are beveled and positioned, they are usually tackwelded. Tackwelding holds the sheets in true alignment and prevents them from overlapping. The easiest way to accomplish a good joint is by the use of a tacking tip shown in Fig. 13. This is a special tip that heats the plastic and allows pressure to be applied to the joint. Pressure and heat cause the edges of the plastic sheets to fuse together. The tack weld is run the full length of the joint. Since its purpose is to align or set up the components for the finished weld, the tack weld is not strong, and can be broken,

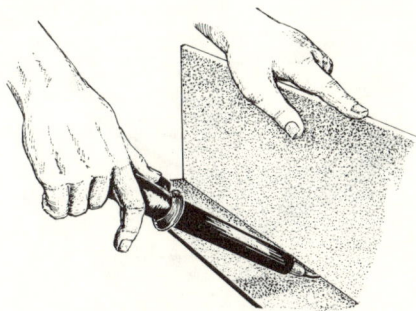

Figure 14. The tacking tip operation.

if necessary. Figure 14 shows a tackwelding operation.

SETTING THE TORCH FOR HEAT. After

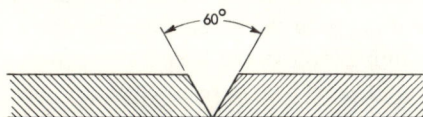

Figure 12. The edges of the sheets are beveled at 30°. When they are butted together, they form a maximum angle of 60°.

the joint is tackwelded, it is ready for the finished welding operation. Temperature setting is usually a matter of experience and the speed at which the operator welds. The air temperature of the torch can be adjusted by increasing or decreasing the flow of air through the heating coils. Type I PVC is welded at 500° to 550° F, while Type II welds at 475° to 525° F. The temperature is more accurately set by the use of a thermometer, until the welder gains enough experience to recognize the proper heat. A good rule of thumb by which to set the heat is: hold the torch ¼ inch away from the plastic for four seconds. After four seconds have elapsed, the PVC should show a trace of yellow color from the heat.

WELDING. The round welding tip should be put on the torch to do the actual welding. The torch should be held at an angle of approximately 30° to and about ½ inch away from the joint. The rod is held at 90° to the sheet, as shown in Fig. 15. Heat both

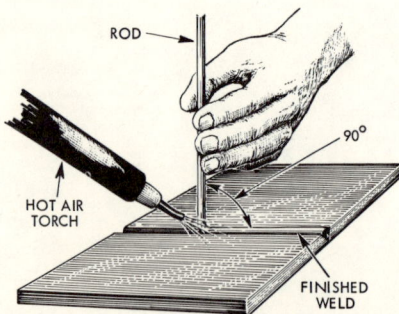

Figure 16. Move the torch over the joint as shown.

the sheets and rod are at the proper heat, the rod will stick to the sheets. At this time, it is important to maintain the proper temperature on both the rod and the sheets without overheating. Overheating either the rod or sheets will weaken the joint. They will wrinkle and turn brown if overheated. To maintain the proper heat on both the rod and the sheet, the torch should be moved in a vertical fanning motion as indicated by the dotted lines in Fig. 16. Since the sheet has a much larger cross section than the rod, more heat should be directed to it. When both the rod and the edges of the sheets are hot enough, they will become slightly shiny. A little pressure downward on the rod will force it into the joint. About three pounds of pressure on the rod is all that is needed when the heat is correct. As the rod is pushed down, it will curve as shown in Figs. 15 and 16 and will begin to move in the direction of the weld. Continuous heating with the torch using the same fanning motion will keep the rod moving. If the rod is overheated, it will bend too soon or in too large a curve, making it impossible to continue a firm, even pressure on it.

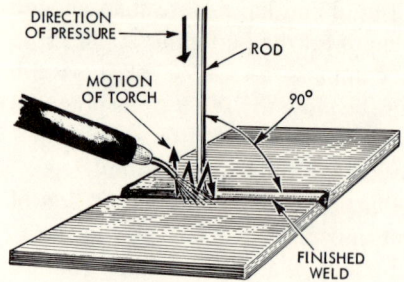

Figure 15. Welding rods are held 90° to the joint.

the starting area on the sheet, and the rod at the same time until the sheets becomes shiny and sticky. When both

In the finished weld, the rod should be approximately the same diameter as it was before the weld. The lines of contact with the sheet on either side of the rod should show a closed, smooth blend of plastic. If the rod lays on the sheet without blending at the lines of contact, or if the rod flattens out or stretches, the weld will be weak. A good check on the quality of the weld is to see if the rod in the weld is the same length as it was before the weld. If it has stretched more than 10% of its original length, the weld is weak. *The average welding speed* for this type of welding *should be 6 to 8 inches per minute.*

It is important to keep continuous pressure on the rod during the entire weld. If the hand holding the rod must be changed as the rod is fed down, place the third and fourth fingers of the changing hand on the finished weld just behind the point at which the rod curves into the plastic joint. Apply pressure here while you grasp the rod with your thumb and forefinger. It is possible to touch the rod at the weld due to the low heat conductivity of this plastic and because the rod is heated only on the underside.

To finish the weld, heat the area of contact between the rod and the sheet quickly. Stop the weld direction movement of the rod. Remove the heat and keep a downward pressure on the rod until the weld cools. Then twist the rod until it breaks.

To join one rod to another on a long weld, stop the weld before the rod is too short to hold. Then cut the rod off with a sharp knife at the point of contact between the rod and the sheet. Make the cut at a 60° angle. Cut the new rod at a 60° angle and start the weld by joining the two rods at the 60° angles with the application of hot air.

On a good PVC weld, there should be no evidence of brown coloration or wrinkles which indicate overheating. The weld should show that the rod has fused with the sheets all along the lines of contact. The rod should not be drawn thinner or compressed much wider than its original form. The weld bead should appear flattened somewhat by comparison to the original round shape of the rod. However, if the rod appears to be lying on the sheet without any fusion, and appears in its exact original round form, in all probability, there was a lack of heat. The rod may be pulled off the weld with little effort. A good weld will show small flow lines or ripples on either side of the weld where the pressure and heat have actually caused the plastic rod to soften and fuse with the sheets.

USING THE SPEED TIP. The speed tip is used on long, straight joints. While the process is essentially the same as the welding just described, this tip affords much greater speeds (about 6 times faster) than when the rod is hand fed. The speed tip preheats the plastic sheets ahead of the weld, and is designed to apply pressure on the rod. The need for hand pressure on the rod is thereby eliminated. After the weld is started, the rod will feed through the tip automatically. Fig. 17 shows a speed welding tip in use and de-

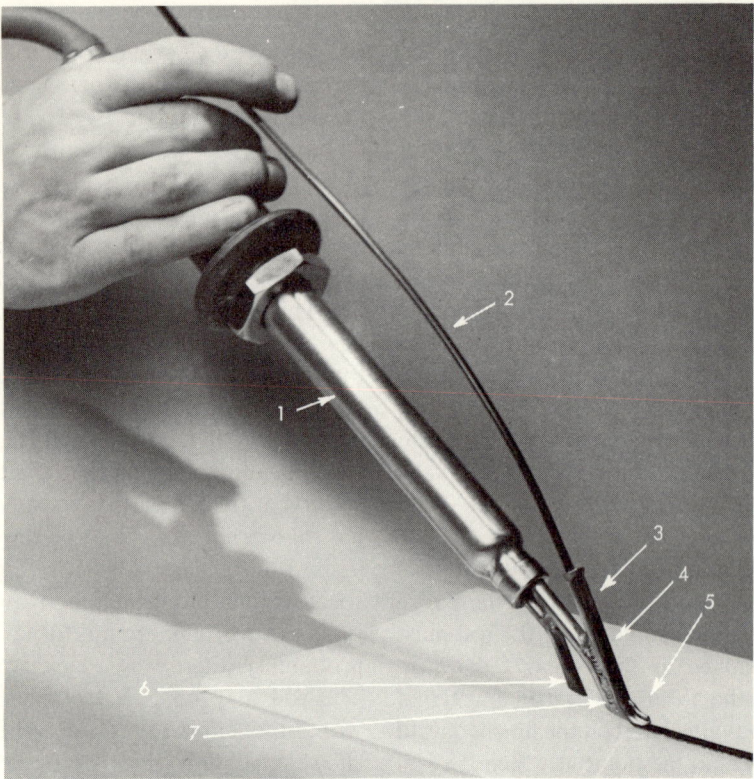

1. TORCH	4. ROD IS PRE-HEATED IN TUBE	6. ORIFICE PREHEATS AREA TO BE WELDED
2. WELDING ROD		
3. SPEED TIP	5. SHOE PROVIDES PRESSURE	7. HEAT FOR WELD

Figure 17. A speed welding tip used to make a production weld. Courtesy: Laramy Products Co., Inc.

scribes details of the tip. When using the speed tip, the torch is first held at 90° to the surface of the sheet. Then the rod is inserted in the tip until it contacts the sheet. The tip is then placed in the weld position on the joint. The rod is pushed into the tip for the first inch or two of the weld. After this starting method, it will feed in automatically. Only the weight of the torch is used for pressure on the weld as it is moved along the joint.

Riveting

PVC plastic sheets may be riveted in some applications. However, the ordinary tinner's rivet should never be used to rivet PVC plastic. Steel rivets are too hard and expand the plastic. This results in a joint of low quality. Plastic rivets are recommended for this application. However, aluminum tinner's rivets, or split brass rivets, or solid copper rivets may be used.

Plastic rivets are one piece, self-expanding type that can be installed from one side of the sheet. These are installed with a special pneumatic gun.

Bolting

In some cases, PVC may be bolted. Standard steel or aluminum bolts may be used. It is necessary to have a flat washer on both sides of the PVC sheet in order to prevent the bolt head or nut from cutting into the material. When bolting PVC, drill holes with proper care. Avoid drilling holes in areas where there is a great deal of strain, and avoid tightening the bolts excessively.

Cementing

PVC sheets may also be cemented. At the present time, welding is the most common and most desirable process used to join PVC sheets. With the development of new techniques in the future, the use of solvent cemented joints may become more widely used than welding. At the present time, more round PVC pipe is cemented rather than welded. To fabricate cemented joints, a special PVC cement is used. The cement is applied to both pieces of the joint. The pieces are then quickly connected. The joined pieces must be clamped and held in position for about thirty minutes. The full strength of a cemented joint is developed after 24 hours has elapsed.

Other types of plastics used for duct work

In this chapter considerable space has been devoted to PVC sheet as a material which can be substituted in spe-cial cases for sheet metal. In some specific product applications, it has characteristics that are particularly desirable. There are other plastics for special requirements. We shall look at some of the other plastics and fabrication methods employed in duct work for industry. The following data is included in this chapter, so that you may have some understanding and knowledge of the advancing technology of our industry. The solutions to new problems required by industry are many. The use of plastics in duct work has provided solutions to some of these problems.

New chemical compounds and fumes are the result of the development of new products, processes, and manufacturing methods. Clean air, health, and safety laws require fumes and dust to be conducted out of the manufacturing building. This is accomplished by the installation of piping or duct work and fans or blowers. Many of the fumes derived from industrial chemistry corrode, erode, or start chemical reactions in sheet metal duct work. The need for materials that are capable of withstanding these chemical reactions is obvious.

In addition to PVC sheet, some of the other types of plastic material used in the fabrication of piping and duct-work in air conditioning, exhaust, and processing systems are: *fiberglas, fiberglas* reinforced polyester (poly-type plastics reinforced with glass fibers, also known as epoxy types), polyethylene, polypropolene, and others. Many of these are fabricated in a manner similar to PVC.

HOW TO WORK WITH
FIBERGLAS TUBING

Figure 18. Steps 1 through 6.

Every skilled occupation including sheet metal work is changing rapidly. The successful craftsman of the future is the one who continues to study the materials of the future.

FIBERGLAS. In sheet metal shops *fiberglas* is generally purchased from a manufacturer in the preformed shape such as duct, pipe, or tank. The reason is: *fiberglas* plastic sheet cannot be easily shaped with the usual tools in the sheet metal shop. However, flat sheets are sometimes cut and assembled, when no forming or bending is necessary. The preformed shapes are also cut and cemented to form many special assemblies.

Fiberglas cannot be welded. PVC plastic can be welded. However fiber glass can be easily cut with a saw and cemented with resins to make a joint equal to or stronger than a PVC weld. The advantage of *fiberglas* over PVC plastic is its greater resistance to abrasion and its greater mechanical strength (about twice as strong as PVC). It is also about equal to PVC plastic in corrosion resistance. Another advantage of *fiberglas* is that it is rigid and lightweight. If it were used for the same installation as sheet metal, *fiberglas* would require less supports, such as angle irons, braces, straps, and hangers.

Using preformed shapes, *fiberglas* is very easy to assemble and install. Custom ductwork can be made on the job

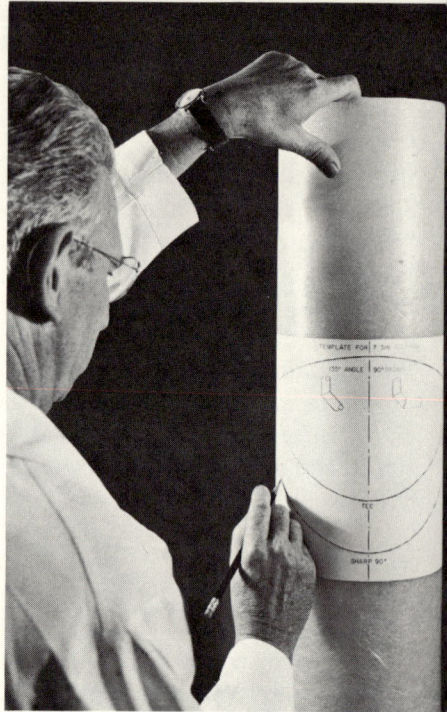

STEP 1

Step 1. Trace ready-to-use template supplied by manufacturer, or make paper template for fast pattern layout.

Step 2. Use a hacksaw to start the cut.

STEP 2

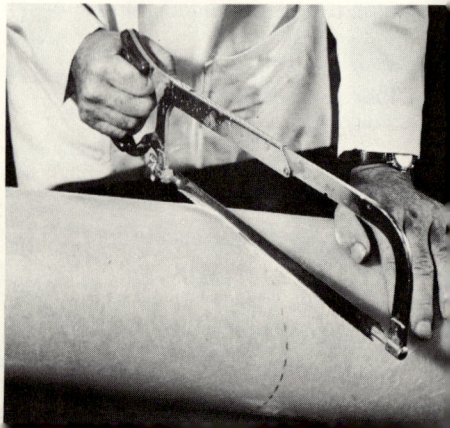

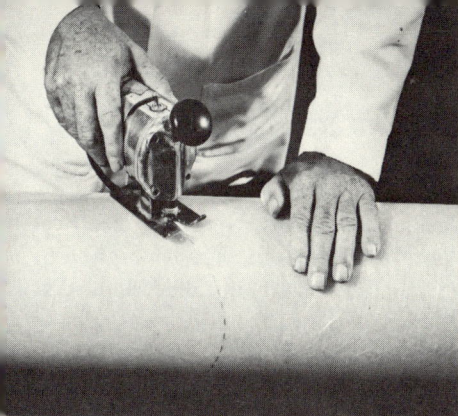

STEP 3

Step 3. Complete the cut with a saber saw.

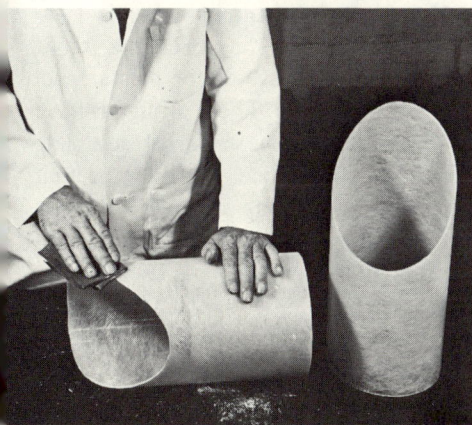

STEP 4

Step 4. Rough the surface area about 1" in width around the cut with coarse sandpaper and clean it with lacquer thinner or naphtha.

Step 5. Mix resin and a hardener together with a smooth, fold-over action to avoid trapping air bubbles.

STEP 5

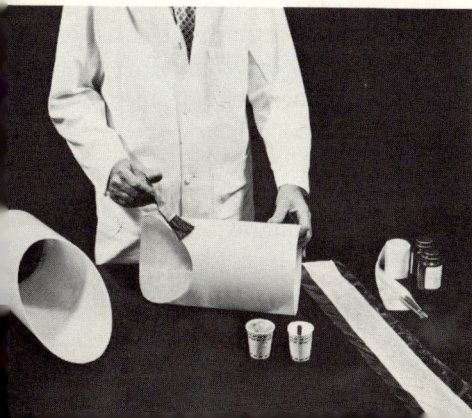

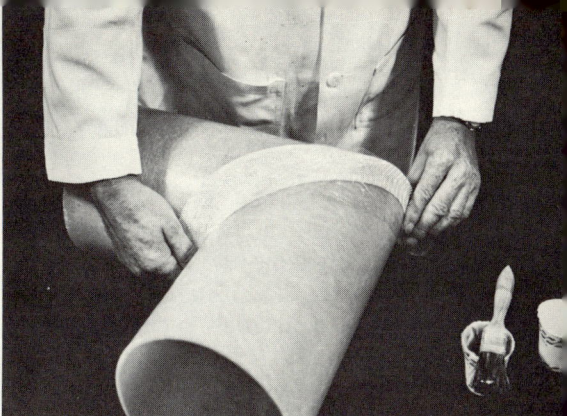

STEP 6

Step 6. Cut a strip of fiberglas cloth large enough to completely cover the joint. Apply the hardening mixture to the tape, wrap it around the joint, and press it with a wood spatula to insure proper resin impregnation. You can achieve more smoothness and even impregnation if you place a strip of cellophane or polyethylene film over the tape before you press it with a spatula. The resin will cure in a few hours at room temperature. The curing process can be speeded up to 15 minutes by the use of an infra-red heat lamp placed no closer than 18" to the joint. After curing, the joint may be sanded, feather edged, primed, and painted. It is worked as though it were wood or metal.

All photos courtesy of Apex Fibre-Glass Products Division of White Consolidated Industries, Inc., Cleveland, Ohio.

by using the templates supplied with the pipe. With these, a variety of fittings can be made such as tees, angles, elbows, branches, and Y's. The photos in Figure 18 show the steps required to fabricate a 90 degree elbow using preformed *fiberglas* pipe. A hacksaw, saber saw, spatula, coarse sandpaper, small brush, and scissors are the only tools needed.

One of the problems that limited the use of *fiberglas* was the comparatively long period required for the cemented joint to harden and gain sufficient strength for further handling. New resins with an extremely short hardening period are now on the market. These will undoubtedly increase the use of *fiberglas* in duct work.

The increasing use of *fiberglas* in the development of new products and processing industries are reasons why the capable sheet metal worker studies the use of materials such as plastics. POLYESTERS. *Polyester epoxy types* of plastic sheet (usually gray colored) are generally used for round or rectangular ducts, stacks, and tanks, in metal and chemical processing systems. The major advantage of these types of plastics is their resistance to alkalies and solvents. They also make possible fabrication of large structures and exhaust components. Fabrication is similar to PVC. However, cementing the joints is the general practice.

POLYETHYLENE. *Polyethylene sheet* is more flexible than the other plastics. It is generally used for components in process systems such as metal plating tanks and vats, ducts, and fan housings. These usually are reinforced with plastic covered steel girths or stiffener ribs. Fabrication is similar to PVC. The joints are usually cemented.

POLYPROPOLENE. *Polypropolene sheet* is used for specific components in chemical processing and laboratory exhaust systems. Some of these components are tanks, fume hoods, and laboratory sinks. Resistance to bleaches and chemical fumes is a major factor in its application. Fabrication is similar to PVC, and the joints are usually cemented.

ADVANTAGES AND DISADVANTAGES. The most desirable characteristics of the plastics used for duct work and piping in exhaust or processing systems are: 1. Corrosion and moisture resistance. 2. Resistance to most chemical vapors and fumes. 3. Low heat conductivity. 4. Low electrical conductivity. 5. Lightweight. 6. Strength. 7. Easily installed. Some disadvantages are: 1. Lower resistance to heat than sheet metal. 2. Slightly more hand labor to assemble in the shop or in the field (cementing joints).

Plastic component products in exhaust and processing systems

Handling chemicals and chemical vapors in industry has been the major factor in the advance of plastic duct work and piping. These problems have contributed to the need for complete exhaust and processing systems that are unaffected by chemical vapors. Following is a list of many of the plastic components that are used by industry in exhaust, chemical, and other processing systems: ducts (round or rectangular)—stacks—exhaust hoods — weather caps — tees — cross fittings — collars — reducers — fume hoods—tanks (round or rectangular) — trays — pans — vats — fan housings—impellers. Figs. 19 A to F show some of the above components.

Industrial users

The application of plastic ducting is growing, now that industrial engineers and management are learning it can be used to solve many of their exhaust, vapor, and processing problems. Some industries that have installed plastic ducting and/or plastic components in processing and exhaust systems are: aerospace—chemical—steel mill—metal treating—paper mill—fertilizer — plastic — pharmaceutical — paint

Figure 19-A. Stacks 42" in diameter and 50' high at pickling plant of large steel mill, fabricated from polyester type plastic. Heil Process Equipment Corporation, Cleveland, Ohio.

Figure 19-B. Round duct exhaust system in plating room, fabricated from polyester type plastic. Heil Process Equipment Corporation, Cleveland, Ohio.

Figure 19-C. Exhaust system used to conduct chemical vapors out of tanks and room area. Duct work is fabricated from polyester type plastic. Heil Process Equipment Corporation, Cleveland, Ohio.

Figure 19-D. Hood to exhaust sulphuric acid fumes at a steel mill, fabricated from solid polyester type plastic. Heil Process Equipment Corporation, Cleveland, Ohio.

Figure 19-E. Duct section of large centrifugal type fan housing fabricated from metal reinforced polyester type plastic. Heil Process Equipment Corporation, Cleveland, Ohio.

Figure 19-F. Reinforced plastic tank for mixed acid service, fabricated from polyester type plastic. Heil Process Equipment Corporation, Cleveland, Ohio.

—crude oil refining—brine and salt.

In conclusion

Plastic ducting is sometimes used with sheet metal ducting just as each may be used independently of one another. Each has advantages that the other does not have. Sheet metal can withstand higher temperatures than most plastics. However, plastics have more resistance to corrosion by chemicals than sheet metal. Each has its own particular advantages for specific applications and solutions to industrial problems. Some of these are exhaust systems, ventilating ducts, hoods, tanks and components necessary to manufacture and process products.

Review Questions

1. What are the raw materials from which plastics are made?
2. Explain the difference between thermosetting and thermoforming plastics.
3. List four plastic products in your home. From the material in the chapter and from Table I, name the types of plastic of which you think they are made.
4. Define the following terms:
   a. Plasticizers
   b. Solvents
   c. Catalysts
5. Describe the process of injection molding.
6. Describe vacuum forming.
7. Explain the difference between molding and casting.
8. What is meant by laminates?
9. What do the letters PVC signify?
10. List some of the limitations of PVC.
11. List some of the advantages of PVC.
12. What is the difference between Type I and Type II PVC?
13. In outline form, list the steps required to make a round pipe from PVC plastic.
14. What are the four essentials for a good plastic weld?
15. What are the differences between plastic welding and metal welding?
16. What is the "speed tip" used in plastic welding?

Projects

Project 16-1. Practicing stringer welds on PVC sheet

1. Cut a piece of ⅛″ PVC plastic sheet about 12″ × 12″.
2. Obtain a piece of ⅛″ diameter PVC plastic welding rod of the same material composition as sheet to be welded.
3. Cut the tip of the welding rod at a 60° angle.
4. Run a bead with the welding rod the length of the sheet, as described in this chapter. At the end of the weld, leave about 1″ of welding rod sticking up in a vertical position.
5. After the weld has thoroughly cooled, try to pull the welding rod away from the sheet with a pair of pliers. If the rod sepa-

rates from the sheet, it indicates an improper bond. Compare your bead with the cross sections in Fig. 20 to determine the reason for failure.

6. Continue running stringer beads until they show the proper fusion between rod and sheet. With proper fusion, the rod will break at the end of the weld, not pull away from the sheet.

Project 16-2. Checking elongation of the welding rod when welding plastic sheet

1. Measure exactly 5″ from one end of the welding rod and make a small scratch at this point.

same as the marked rod before welding. A 10% difference in the two is the maximum allowable. In 5″, 10% would be ½″.

Project 16-3. Practicing manipulation of the welding rod and hot air torch

1. Cut a sheet of ⅛″ PVC plastic approximately 12″ × 12″.
2. With a pair of dividers, draw a circle approximately 7″ in diameter on the sheet.
3. Run a stringer bead with ⅛″ welding rod around this circle and continue the bead in a spiral inside the circle by joining new rod. Do not move the sheet. The purpose of this circular welding is to have you practice

	CONDITIONS		APPEARANCE	RESULTS
	ROD	SHEET		
A	COLD	COLD	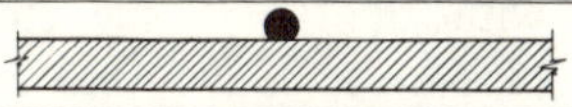	NO BOND
B	HOT	COLD		POOR BOND ON SHEET
C	COLD	HOT		POOR BOND ON ROD
D	HOT	HOT		ROD AND SHEET OVERHEATED–DECOMPOSED
E	OK	OK		GOOD WELD

Figure 20. Analysis of "stringer" bead trial welds.

2. Run a stringer bead on a sheet of plastic using only the marked 5″ of the rod.
3. Measure the distance of the stringer bead on the sheet.
4. If the stringer bead is longer than 5″, the rod has elongated during the welding.
5. Continue practicing in this manner until the length of the finished stringer bead measures the

manipulating the torch and the rod in any manner required of you in order to weld a variety of components.

Project 16-4. Running straight welds

1. Cut four pieces of 3⁄16″ plastic sheet 4″ wide and 6″ long.
2. Bevel the 6″ edges of each piece to 30°. This means that when the beveled edges of both sheets

are butted together the total included angle will be 60° maximum.

3. Clamp the two sheets together so that the beveled edges form a butt joint with a gap of approximately $\frac{1}{64}''$.

4. Set and adjust a hot air welding torch so that the temperature $\frac{1}{4}''$ from the nozzle is 550°.

5. Tackweld the seam. Next, run one bead in the bottom of the 60° groove using a $\frac{1}{8}''$ diameter rod.

6. Using a $\frac{5}{32}''$ diameter rod, run two welds side by side over the first weld. No gap or groove should be visible where the welding rod fuses with the sheets.

7. Compare your weld with the cross sections in Fig. 21.

8. When the weld cools, carefully try to break it with your hands. If the weld does not break, it is a solid weld. If the weld

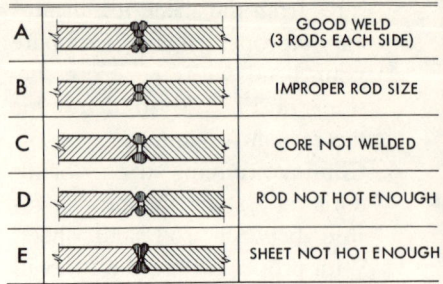

A		GOOD WELD (3 RODS EACH SIDE)
B		IMPROPER ROD SIZE
C		CORE NOT WELDED
D		ROD NOT HOT ENOUGH
E		SHEET NOT HOT ENOUGH

Figure 21. Cross sections of PVC welds.

breaks, examine the break for indications of the reasons for a poor bond. Normally, the reason for breaking, is a poor bond between the sheet and the rod.

9. If the weld does not break, cut the sheet into two pieces using a bandsaw. Make the cut at right angles to the weld. File the cut surface smooth at the weld and examine it for traces of poor bonding.

10. Repeat this practice of welding and testing with the other test pieces.

17

EXOTIC METALS

What are "exotic metals?" What are the uses for beryllium, cadmium, and titanium? What are the names and uses for other less-used exotic metals?

Recent developments in atomic energy and space technology have created a demand for metals with new characteristics appropriate to their new uses. For example, the missile shown in Fig. 1 requires metals which are both light and able to withstand the extremes of temperature which such projectiles encounter. Other metals have received increased attention because of their ability to resist atomic radiation while satisfactorily performing their intended functions. To meet such needs as these, newer exotic metals have come into increased use. Many of these metals have been known for years but have had uses limited to experiments in the metallurgical laboratory because of their cost and scarcity. Such metals are termed "exotic" to distinguish them from metals in common use. In addition, one of the meanings of the word *exotic* is "strange" and, since generally these are metals we know little about in terms of fabrication and uses, this is an apt term.

These are not metals used in the typical sheet metal shop at the present time. However, no sheet metal student should consider his training complete until he has some knowledge of the exotic metals and their uses. As methods of producing these metals become more efficient, some of them may be among the common metals of the future. But the most important reason for sheet metal workers to be familiar with them is the increasing number of workers employed in industries using exotic metals. Therefore, this chapter could not hope to acquaint the student with *all* exotic metals because new types are constantly being developed. However it does aim to acquaint the student with those exotic metals whose present uses suggest even greater future applications.

Figure 1. This Minuteman missile makes extensive use of "exotic" metals, many of which were unknown a few years ago. Courtesy: Allison Division, General Motors Corp.

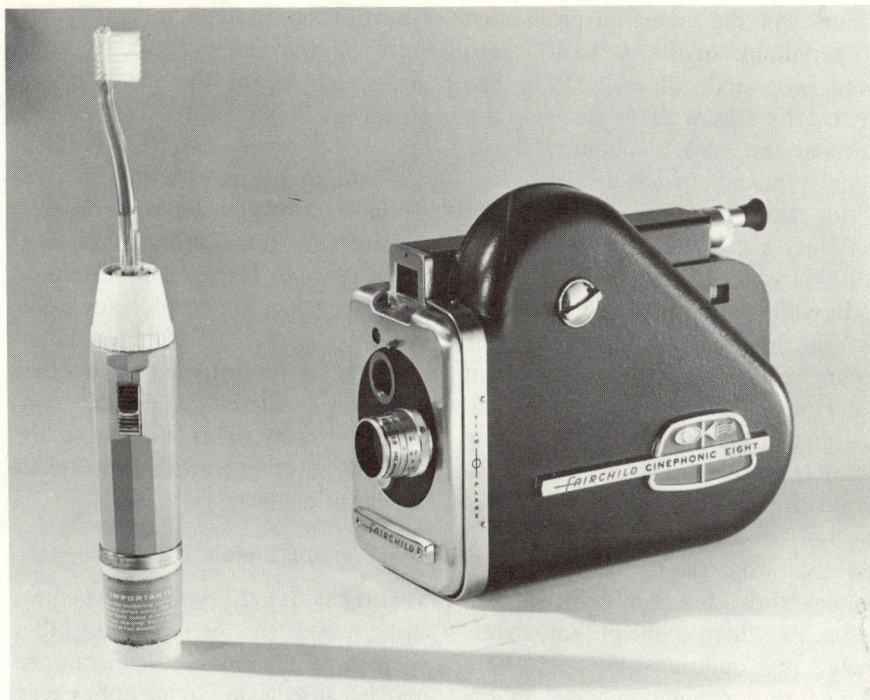

Figure 2. Products such as these have been made possible because of the development of nickel-cadmium batteries. Courtesy: International Nickel Co.

Cadmium

Hardly a "new" metal, cadmium was first discovered in 1817. It is obtained as a by-product in zinc and lead smelting and is closely related to zinc in many of its properties. Cadmium has been used extensively as an electroplating coating on steel because of its corrosion resistance and good luster, as shown by the products illustrated in Fig. 2. Sheet metal screws, for example, may be cadmium plated.

With the development of atomic energy, cadmium has become increasingly important because it has the ability to absorb some of the nuclear radiation in a reactor and in this way

controls the rate of the reaction. However, since cadmium has a comparatively low melting point (610°F), other materials with less absorption power but high melting points are sometimes used.

Beryllium

Beryllium is an example of an exotic metal which, though known since 1798, was never developed commercially because of the high cost of separating and refining it. However, with the advent of the Space Age, the need for beryllium has increased and, with this increased need have come refined processing techniques. As an example of the increased production of beryllium, in 1960, 10,400 tons were processed, while in 1930 less than 2 tons were. This increase has lowered the cost to about $50 per pound. Indications are that improved production techniques will lower beryllium's cost to a point where it will find wider commercial uses.

Beryllium's present use, however, is principally in the area of space technology because it is light—about half the weight of aluminum—and has great heat resistance. Its melting point is 2343°F. The greatest problem with beryllium has been in learning how to fabricate it. It is evident however, that as its uses increase, better fabrication methods will develop. Beryllium is one of those exotic metals that quite possibly could be a comparatively common metal in the future.

Titanium

Titanium is another metal which, though known since 1789, has achieved its greatest importance since the development of space vehicles. This is because of its toughness combined with a high melting point (3074°F). Titanium-bearing ores are plentiful, but it is extremely difficult to separate from other elements in the ore. This processing problem adds to its cost.

As shown in Fig. 3, titanium is used extensively in the various components of space vehicles. It has an excellent strength-to-weight ratio between 300°F and 700°F. Above 800°F its strength drops rapidly.

Above 1200°F titanium readily absorbs oxygen and nitrogen from the air, which makes the metal brittle. However, it is expected that new titanium alloys may solve this problem.

Titanium is almost completely resistant to corrosion. However when it is subject to corrosion the rate is usually very rapid. It is the only structural metal that does not corrode any faster in salt water than it does in air. Titanium should be insulated from other metals by a material that does not conduct electricity. This is because the titanium severely corrodes other metals that it contacts.

Other exotic metals

STAINLESS STEEL. Although stainless steel has been discussed in other chapters of this book, it is mentioned here because its development has been relatively recent. In 1918 stainless steel was truly an "exotic metal" and in a short time has become an accepted part of our ordinary life. In addition, as Fig. 4 shows, the application possibilities for stainless steel are constantly increasing. Stainless steels include over 30 different alloys—each designed for specific advantages. In general, stainless steel contains 74% iron, 18% chromium, and 8% nickel. However these percentages are varied and small amounts of other metals added to provide the different characteristics of the many stainless steel alloys. Although originally developed for large gun barrels during World War I, stainless has found thousands of architectural and engineering applications because of its beauty and corrosion resistance.

Figure 3. The second-stage rocket motor case shown here is constructed entirely of titanium. Courtesy: Allison Division, General Motors Corp.

Figure 4. This modern building exterior is constructed entirely of nickel stainless steel, another example of how exotic metals are used today. Courtesy: International Nickel Co.

URANIUM. Since it is an essential metal in many nuclear energy operations, uranium has become one of the most important metals in modern times, although it was first discovered in 1789. Uranium is a lustrous white metal resembling steel in appearance and is chemically present in fourteen states. Its radioactivity, first discovered in 1896, was responsible for uranium's first increase in importance and, as is well known, its most important use has been in nuclear or atomic energy ever since the first chain reaction sustained by uranium and plutonium isotopes in 1942. Two different forms of uranium U^{235} (uranium) and Pu^{239} (plutonium) can be used as the explosive ingredients in nuclear (atomic) weapons.

ZIRCONIUM. Zirconium, which like uranium was first isolated in 1789, is used extensively in the construction of atomic reactors. It is often used in sheet form with welded joints. Zirconium is slightly harder than aluminum and has a tensile strength somewhat higher than cold-rolled steel. It is also about the same weight as steel. An important quality of zirconium is its high corrosion resistance to most chemicals.

HAFNIUM. Hafnium was discovered in 1923 and is still a rare metal used for control rods in atomic reactors.

SCANDIUM. Scandium is a very rare metal and is slightly lighter than aluminum but has a melting point of nearly 3000°F. It offers many possibilities, however it is so scarce that only recently was the first piece of scandium available in a one-pound piece. This is in spite of the fact that scandium was first discovered in 1879.

TUNGSTEN. Tungsten has become so commonly used since its discovery in 1783 that it can scarcely be called an exotic metal in the sense in which some others can. However, new applications of tungsten using its heavy weight, high strength, and toughness have made tungsten an important metal in nuclear reactor work.

MOLYBDENUM. Like tungsten, molybdenum, which was discovered in 1782, has seen extensive use as an alloy. Some steels have a small percentage of molybdenum added for strength, corrosion resistance, and toughness. An example is the commonly termed "chrome-moly steel" used where toughness and resistance to twisting are desirable.

As an exotic metal, molybdenum is used in comparatively pure form where advantage can be taken of its high melting point (molybdenum retains its hardness up to 4600°F) and great hardness.

Review Questions

1. Where have exotic metals found their principal uses?
2. What factors generally cause a metal to be considered "exotic" as opposed to those in more common use?
3. What metals resist corrosion?
4. What are the advantages of cadmium, beryllium, and titanium?
5. Name several exotic metals having the advantage of light weight.
6. Name several exotic metals having the advantage of high melting points.

18

SHORT METHOD OF PATTERN DEVELOPMENT

When is the short or "rollation" method of layout most effective? How does the sheet metal worker solve the problem of the time consumed in constructing the templates used in the short method? How is the short method applied to such fittings as T joints and Y fittings?

In sheet metal work, as in most trades, there are practical short cuts which are used in the shop to save time and facilitate the operations. The short method of pattern development, often called the "rollation" method, is one of these working aids. No extensive knowledge of geometry, drafting, or mathematics is involved in the short method of pattern development; it may be employed by apprentices and craftsmen alike. However, it must be considered as a supplement to regular drafting procedures rather than as a substitute for them. Through experience, the sheet metal worker learns the layout approach which is best suited to a particular problem and uses that method for the job.

The short method of pattern development is most valuable in jobs where a high degree of accuracy will *not* be required in the resulting pattern and where speed is a major consideration.

Fundamentals of short method pattern development

Most sheet metal patterns employ such geometric forms as squares, rectangles, cylinders, and funnels. Therefore, let us examine the short method by applying it to one such form, a simple funnel of the type shown in Fig. 1.

SHORT METHOD DEVELOPMENT OF A SIMPLE FUNNEL PATTERN. Viewing the funnel as the outside of a cone, it is obvious that a pattern for half of the funnel will be the other half in reverse.

The short method may then be said

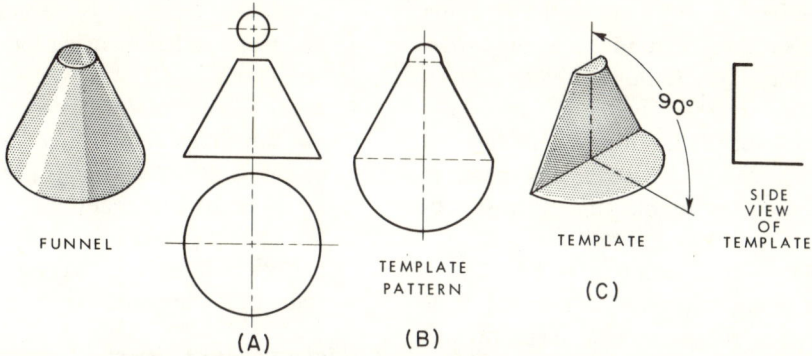

Figure 1. Template and template pattern for "rolling" a simple funnel pattern.

to consist of making a template for half of the pattern, "rolling" this half-pattern on paper, then reversing the paper and matching it to obtain the full-pattern. This procedure is illustrated in Fig. 2.

It should be here noted that the absence of symmetry in the object to be made is not a limiting factor in using the short method. A template may be designed from an off-center pattern, a number of templates may be used, or the template pattern may be used for only one-half of the whole layout and another template used for the other half. However "rollation" is generally used on symmetrical objects, since off-center patterns can usually be developed as fast by other methods.

The essence of the short method, therefore, is the design of the half-pattern template. Once ability to visualize the finished product and express it in these terms has been developed, even the most complex job can be laid out quickly and accurately. An example of this is shown in the half-pattern template used for the layout of the funnel in Fig. 1. *A* shows a cross-section of the funnel with circles above and below which correspond to the diameters of the funnel

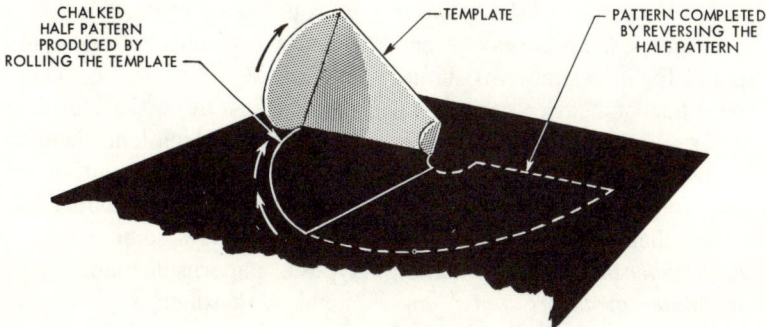

Figure 2. "Rolling" the template to obtain the funnel pattern.

opening. In *B*, half of the opening circles have been added to the cross-section. *This is the template pattern as cut on sheet metal.* *C* shows the completed half-pattern template in which the half-circles are bent at right angles to the funnel cross-section.

Once this template is completed, the edges are chalked and the template is rolled over a sheet of soft black building paper, leaving a clear white outline as shown in Fig. 2. The outline is then reversed and matched as indicated by the dotted lines. This gives the complete funnel pattern. An alternate method by which a clear pattern may be obtained is to dip the edge of the template in oil and roll it over the paper.

Important points to remember when using the short method

1. *Patterns developed by the short method do not include allowance for seams or for soldering.* Be sure to take this into account and make the necessary additions before cutting the metal.
2. *In order to produce an accurate pattern, the ends of the template must be angled accurately.* Templates for larger patterns should be made of heavier gage metal and reinforced with metal braces or blocks of wood. This is also true for lighter or smaller templates that will be used often.
3. *Remember that the short method template produces only one-half of the pattern for the final product.* If a full pattern is de-

sired template must be reversed and matched before using for the stretchout.

4. *Some more complex patterns do not have clearly indicated lines at the points where bends are to be made.* Be sure that these lines are clearly marked on the final pattern during the process of rolling the template.

A brief review of the short method process

The finished sheet metal object is visualized by the worker in terms of its geometric construction. The basic geometric form is graphically shown in halves and these halves are combined to make the template. This is shown in Fig. 1. The template is then chalked on its edges and rolled over a piece of building paper, as shown in Fig. 2. Finally, the half-pattern which results from these operations is reversed and matched, producing the whole pattern.

Some representative applications

At the outset, it is strongly recommended that you try to develop some of your own patterns from beginning to end while studying those illustrated in Figs. 3, 4, 5, and 6. This is the best means by which to determine those forms which lend themselves to the short method of pattern development. The illustrations in Figs. 3, 4, 5, and 6 show some representative types of patterns encountered in sheet metal work which may be developed by the short method. They are more complex than the layout for the sim-

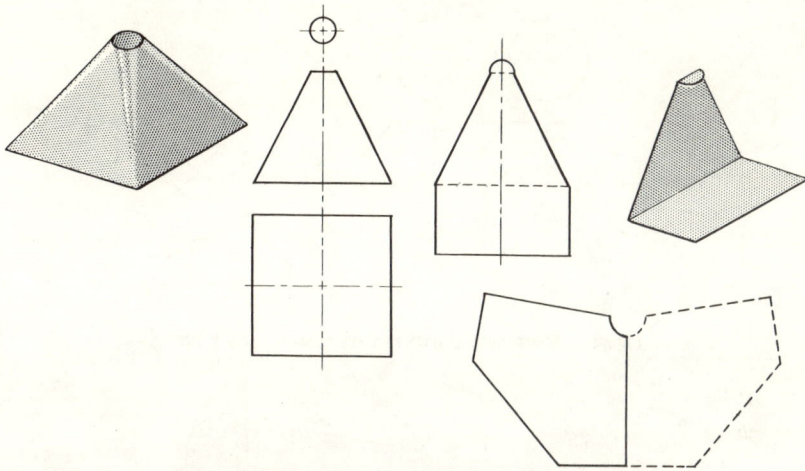

Figure 3. Short method pattern development for a square-to-round fitting.

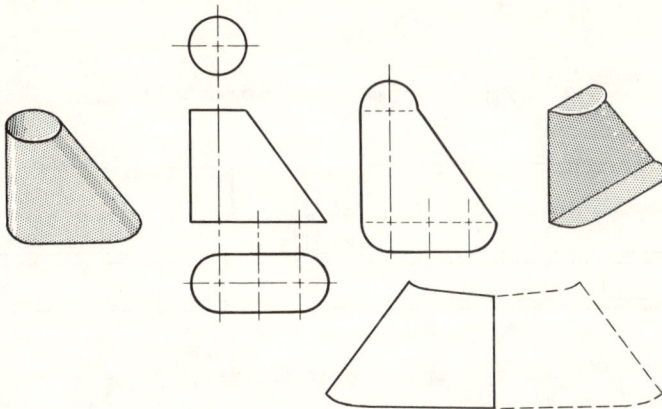

Figure 4. Short method pattern development for an off-center oval-to-round fitting.

ple funnel, but apply the same operations previously described. You will then be able to understand them and develop your own patterns.

Y fitting

1. Since the two prongs are symmetrical, it is only necessary to make a template for one prong and then reverse it.

2. Any experienced sheet metal worker can quickly and accurately add the band.

Making an adjustable template holder

An adjustable template holder, such as the one shown in Fig. 6 will save a great deal of time when making short method templates. A large variety of

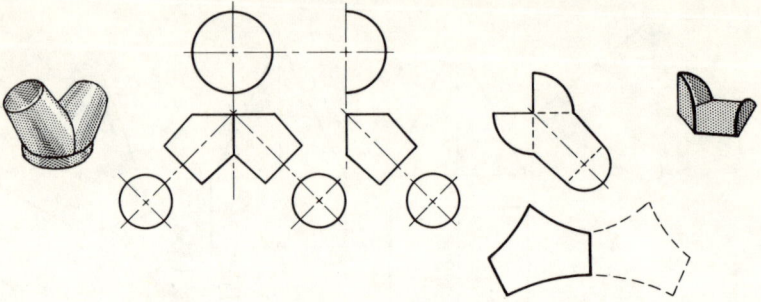

Figure 5. Short method pattern development for a Y fitting.

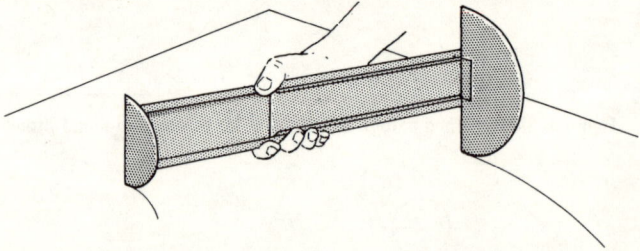

Figure 6. Using an adjustable template holder.

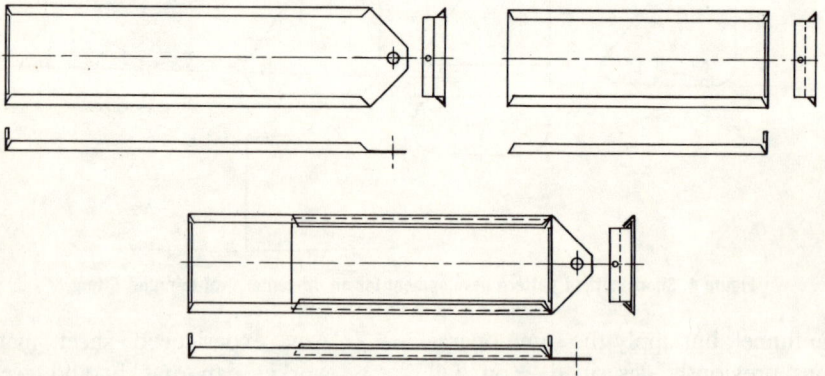

Figure 7. Plan for an adjustable template holder.

templates can be attached and changed for a variety of different sizes and shapes. The body is a two-piece slide to provide for different lengths.

For work involving templates up to 12″ in diameter, a good holder is a 24″ × 4″ with an 18″ slide. It should be made of at least 24-gage galvanized metal. For templates measuring more than 12″ in diameter, a bigger and heavier holder is recommended.

Three important points to remember when using an adjustable template holder

1. *The templates must be securely in place.* To prevent slipping, holes should be made in the body and template so that the templates are held by metal screws.

2. *Make sure that the master templates are flat.* Slight variations will result in large inaccuracies.

3. *The master templates are at right angles to the holder during the "rolling" process.*

Review Questions

1. How much of the final pattern is usually obtained by rolling the template?
2. At what angle are the ends of a template ordinarily bent prior to rolling?
3. How is the template pattern transferred to paper?
4. Why should larger templates be reinforced?

SUPPLEMENTARY PROJECTS

Project 1. Tool tray

OPERATIONS

1. The dimensions of the tray can be made to any size desired.
2. Determine the dimensions.
3. On paper, draw a full size end view to the dimensions desired. If the dimensions chosen prove to be of pleasing proportions, turn the drawing in to the instructor for his approval. Suggested dimensions for a standard tray are: Length 16″; Width 8″; Height 4″; and Top 3.
4. Lay out the end pattern on 16 gage galvanized iron. Mark a second pattern from the first. Cut and notch both pieces.
5. Lay out the pattern for the bottom and sides using 26 gage galvanized iron. Cut out and notch.
6. Bend the ¼″ edges of the ends. Make the bends in the following order: side, bottom side.
7. Bend the bottom and side pattern. Bend in the following order: Pittsburgh seams, double hems, side bends.
8. Set ends into Pittsburgh seams and knock over the seam edge.
9. Lay out the handle pattern, cut out, punch rivet holes and bend. Bend the long bends on the brake. Bend the short end bends with pliers or on a pan brake.
10. Solder the seams of the tool tray on the inside of the tray.
11. Clamp the handle into position; mark and drill the rivet holes through the ends of the tray.
12. Insert the rivets from the outside and rivet the handle in place.

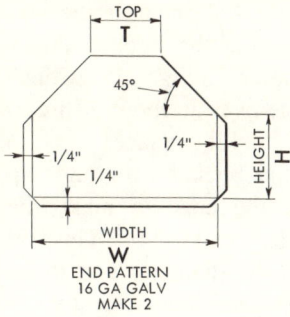

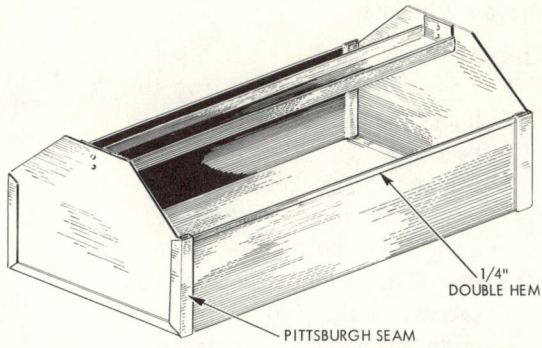

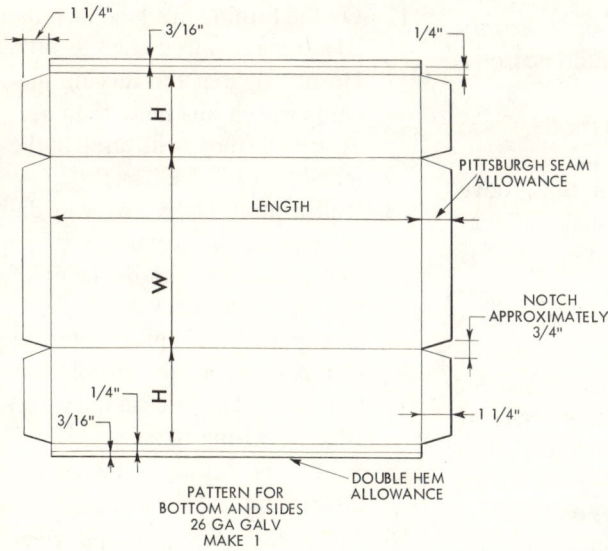

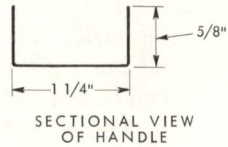

TOP
T

45°

1/4"

1/4"

HEIGHT H

1/4"

WIDTH
W

END PATTERN
16 GA GALV
MAKE 2

1/4"
DOUBLE HEM

PITTSBURGH SEAM

1 1/4"

3/16"

1/4"

H

PITTSBURGH SEAM
ALLOWANCE

LENGTH

W

NOTCH
APPROXIMATELY
3/4"

1/4"

H

3/16"

1 1/4"

DOUBLE HEM
ALLOWANCE

PATTERN FOR
BOTTOM AND SIDES
26 GA GALV
MAKE 1

5/8"

1 1/4"

SECTIONAL VIEW
OF HANDLE

NOTES:

1. ENDS OF 16 GAGE GALVANIZED IRON

2. BOTTOM AND SIDES OF 26 GAGE GALVANIZED IRON

3. HANDLE OF 16 GAGE GALVANIZED IRON

1"

1 1/4"

1"

5/8"

5/8"

LENGTH MINUS 1/8"

HANDLE PATTERN
16 GA GALV
MAKE 1

RIVET
HOLES

ROUND THE EDGES
WITH A FILE

1"

DETAIL OF
END OF HANDLE

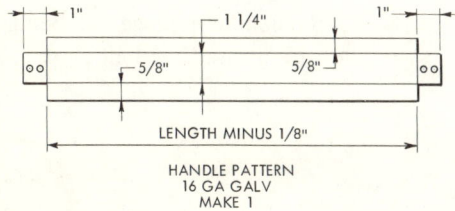

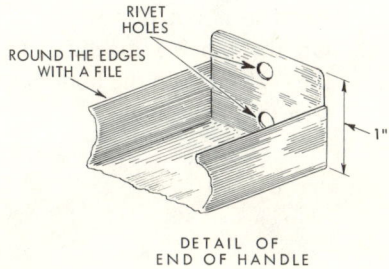

Figure 1. Making a tool tray.

Project 2. Bucket

OPERATIONS

1. Lay out the pattern for the bucket bottom. Dimensions must be exact.
2. Cut out the bucket bottom pattern. Cut roughly about ½″ away from the line for the first time. Then trim on the line. The success of this project depends upon accuracy in patterns and in cutting. Be sure that the distance from *A* to *B* is *exactly* equal to the circumference of a 8¼″ circle.
3. Lay out the pattern for the sides. Cut out and notch.
4. Bend ¼″ edges for the groove seam. Note that though ⅜″ was allowed for the seam only ¼″ is bent.
5. Form sides on rolls and complete groove seam.
6. Solder groove seam on inside, but leave the last ½″ at each end of the seam unsoldered so that the solder does not interfere with the burring machine operation.
7. On burring machine, turn the $\frac{3}{16}$″ edge on the 8¼″ diameter. Bend to the outside. *Do not* bend to a complete 90° angle. Bend to about 60°.
8. On the burring machine, bend the $\frac{5}{32}$″ edge on the bottom pattern to a 90° angle.
9. Hook the bottom over the bottom edge of the side, as shown in Chapter 7, Fig. 31C. Clinch the edge over at about 2″ intervals to hold it in place.
10. Turn the bucket over and tap around the edge to make the $\frac{3}{16}$″ edge bend to 90°. This will expand the diameter and make the two pieces match tightly.
11. Finish clinching the edge and complete the double seam.
12. On the turning machine turn the edge for the wired edge to 90°. Do not tighten the turning machine wheels any more than necessary or they will stretch the metal.
13. Roll a piece of ⅛″ wire in the grooves of the forming rolls so that it matches the diameter of the top of the bucket.
14. Clamp the wire in place with vise clamps and tap the metal over to hold in place. Finish the wired edge on wiring rolls.
15. Solder the inside seams of the bucket and test for leaks.
16. Make the bail ears and rivet them in place.
17. Roll the $\frac{3}{16}$″ wire for the handle. The curve of this handle should match the curve of the top diameter of the bucket.
18. Set the handle in place and bend the wire around the bail ears.

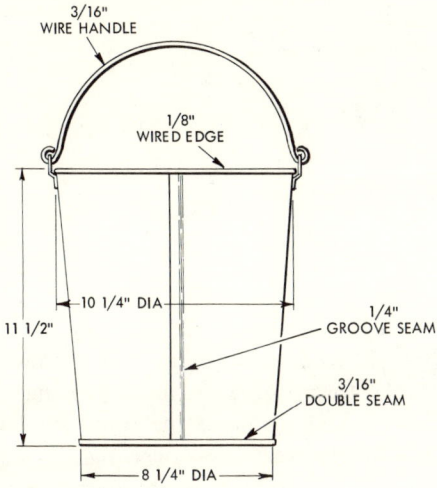

NOTES:

1. BUCKET FROM 26 GAGE GALVANIZED IRON

2. BUCKET BAIL FROM 3/16" DIAMETER WIRE

3. BAIL EARS FROM 16 GAGE GALVANIZED IRON

4. BUCKET BAIL WILL COINCIDE WITH BUCKET RIM WHEN LAID DOWN

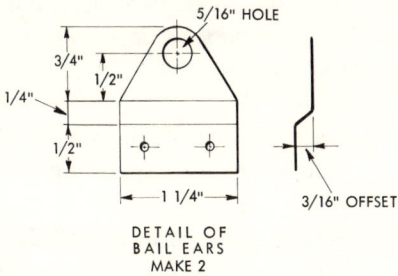

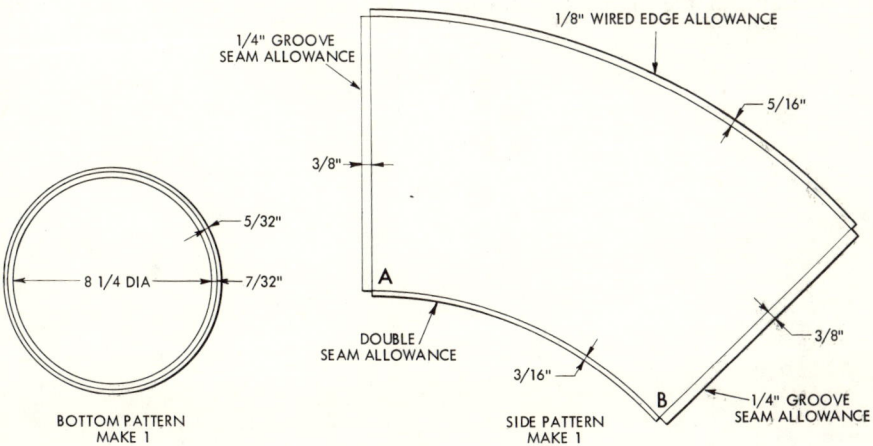

3/16" WIRE HANDLE

1/8" WIRED EDGE

10 1/4" DIA

1/4" GROOVE SEAM

3/16" DOUBLE SEAM

11 1/2"

8 1/4" DIA

5/16" HOLE

3/4"

1/2"

1/4"

1/2"

1 1/4"

3/16" OFFSET

DETAIL OF BAIL EARS MAKE 2

1/4" GROOVE SEAM ALLOWANCE

1/8" WIRED EDGE ALLOWANCE

5/16"

3/8"

A

5/32"

8 1/4 DIA

7/32"

DOUBLE SEAM ALLOWANCE

3/16"

B

3/8"

1/4" GROOVE SEAM ALLOWANCE

BOTTOM PATTERN MAKE 1

SIDE PATTERN MAKE 1

Figure 2. Making a bucket with double seam bottom.

Project 3. Funnel

Operations

1. Lay out the pattern for the funnel, and cut it out.
2. Turn the $3/16''$ hem with the burring machine.
3. Turn the $1/4''$ edges for the groove seam.
4. Roll the funnel as much as possible on the forming rolls, and finish forming on the stakes. Be careful to leave the $1/4''$ edges straight with no bow or bend.
5. Hook the $1/4''$ edges and finish the groove seam.
6. Lay out the spout pattern and cut it out.
7. Roll on forming rolls as much as possible and finish forming on stakes. Shape the spout so that the $1/4''$ laps over tightly and smoothly. It is *not* important to have the spout perfectly round at this time since it will be easy to round up after the $1/4''$ lap is soldered.
8. Solder the lap of the spout.
9. Round up the spout on the stakes.
10. Set the spout in place and tack solder. Check for straightness and finish soldering.
11. Solder the groove seam on the inside.

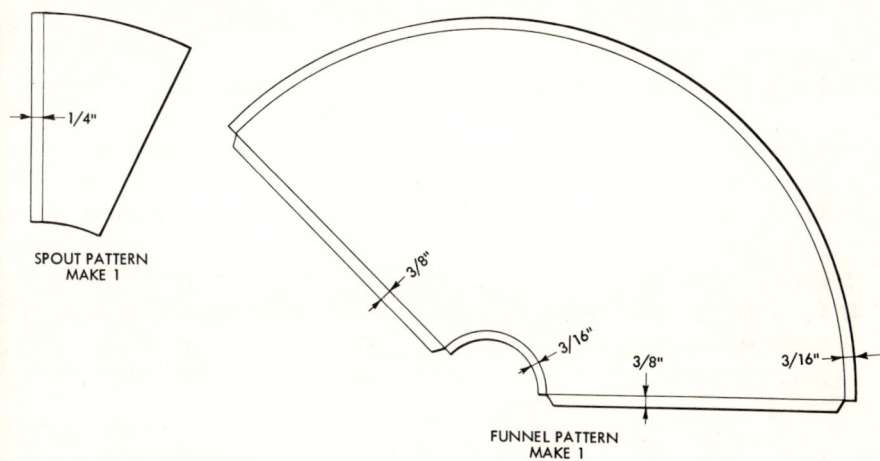

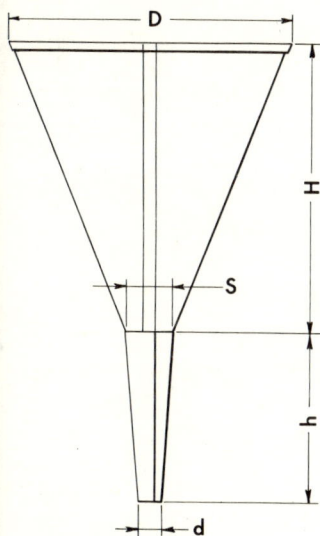

1/4"

SPOUT PATTERN
MAKE 1

3/8"

3/16"

3/8"

3/16"

FUNNEL PATTERN
MAKE 1

D

H

S

h

d

1/4"
GROOVE SEAM

3/16"
HEM

1/4"
LAP AND SOLDER

NOTES:

1. MATERIAL 26 GAGE GALVANIZED

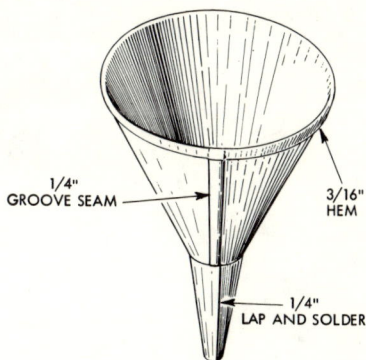

Figure 3. Making a galvanized funnel.

Project 4. Waste basket

OPERATIONS

1. Lay out the pattern for the sides. Cut out and notch.
2. Bend the Pittsburgh seam.
3. Bend the bottom edges of the side pattern to the inside by pounding over the edge of the brake with a wooden mallet. Bend all the way over as with a hem, but do not smash down tightly.
4. Bend the ¼″ edge for the Pittsburgh seam.
5. Bend the corners.
6. Bend the edges around the bottom pattern.
7. Make up the Pittsburgh seam, and set the bottom in place.
8. Tack solder the bottom into place. Solder all the seams on the inside.
9. Cut miters on the split pipe. Set in place and tack weld the corners of the pipe. Remove and weld the miters. (A double hem or wired edge may be used if split pipe is not available.)
10. Place the split pipe in place and tack solder underneath.

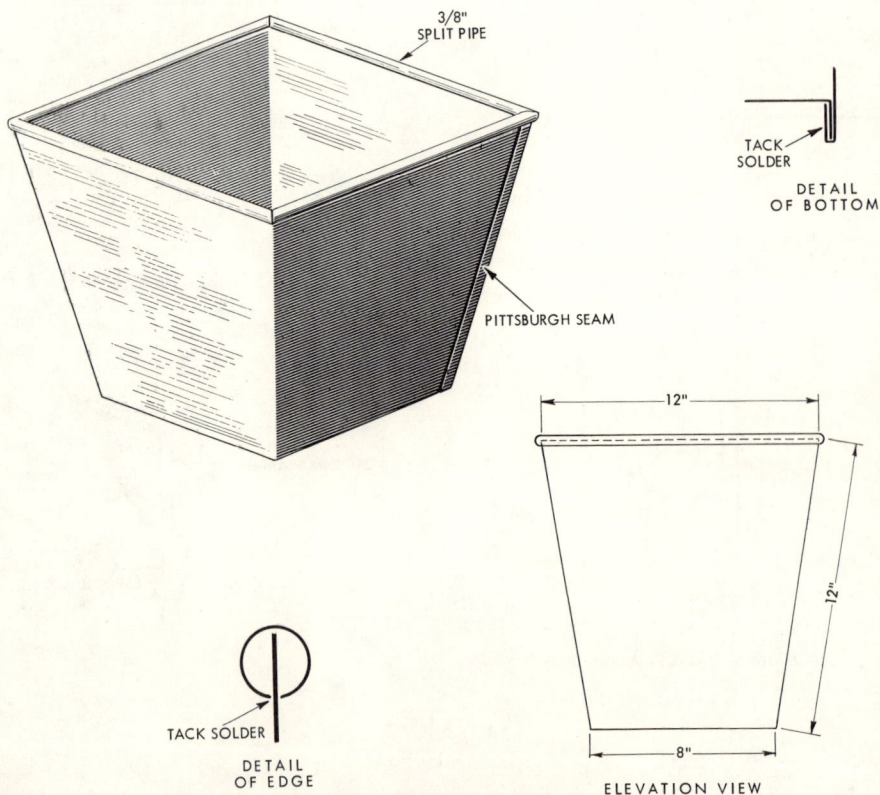

Figure 4. Making a waste basket.

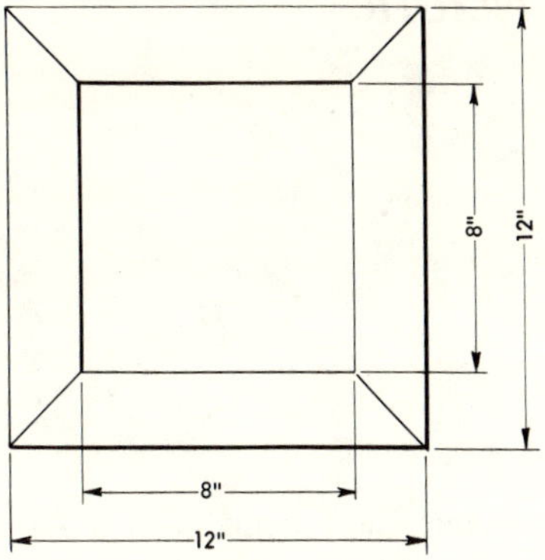

PLAN VIEW

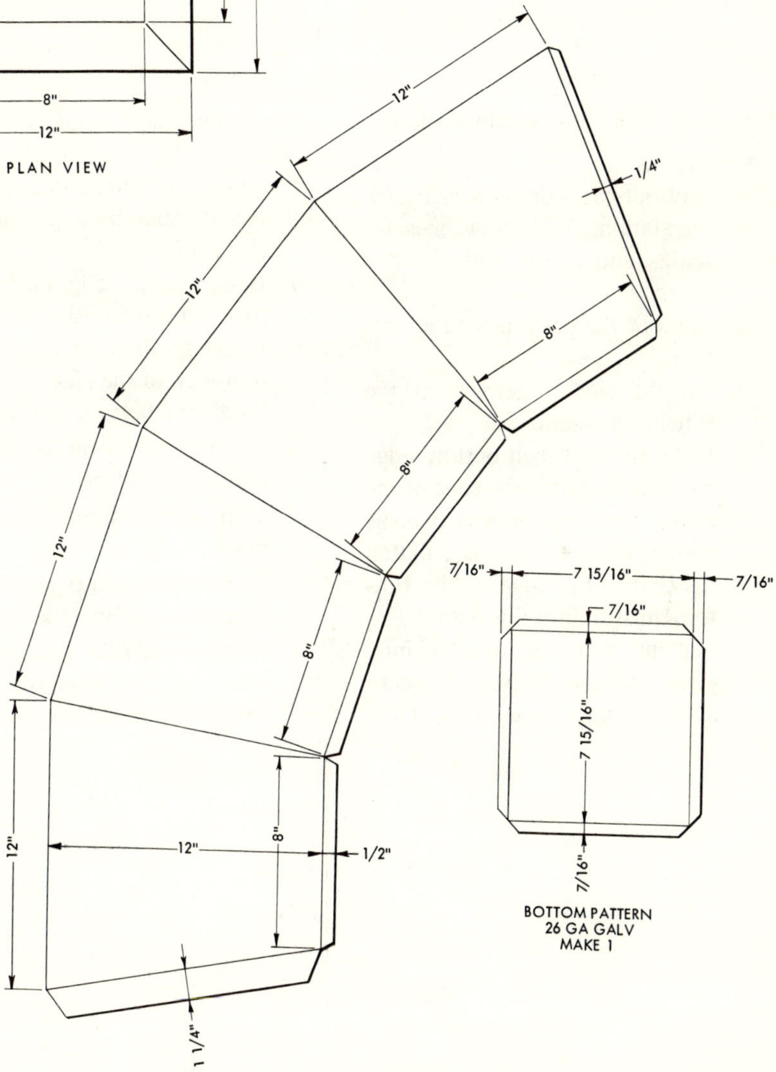

SIDE PATTERN
26 GA GALV
MAKE 1

BOTTOM PATTERN
26 GA GALV
MAKE 1

Figure 4. (continued)

Project 5. Free form waste basket

OPERATIONS

1. Lay out the side pattern by triangulation. Add allowances for seams and edges. Cut out and notch.
2. Lay out the pattern for the bottom.
3. On the side pattern form the Pittsburgh seam.
4. Form the half inch bottom edge by pounding over the edge of the brake. Bend all the way over as with a hem, but do not flatten tight since the edge of the bottom must fit into this hem.
5. Starting with the quarter inch edge for the Pittsburgh seam start bending the corners of the basket. Each bend is to a 45° angle.
6. Insert the quarter inch edge into the Pittsburgh seam and finish the seam.
7. Bend the $7/16''$ edges on the bottom pattern to 90°.
8. Insert the bottom into the bottom lock of the side.
9. Solder the bottom in place.
10. Cut 45° miters on the split pipe and fit into place.
11. Tack weld each miter of the split pipe.
12. Remove the split pipe frame and complete welding the miters.
13. Replace the split pipe and tack solder on the under side on the inside of the basket.

3/8"
SPLIT PIPE

PITTSBURGH SEAM
ON ONE CORNER

SOLDER

1/2"

DETAIL
OF BOTTOM

ELEVATION VIEW

12"

BOTTOM VIEW

8" 8"

12"

12"

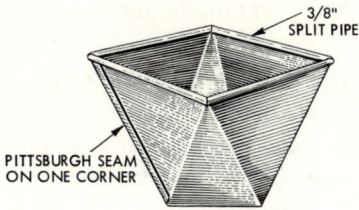

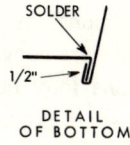

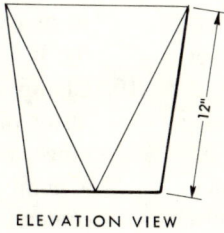

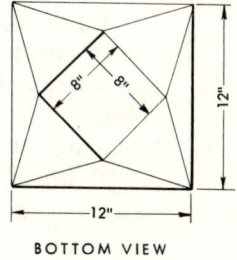

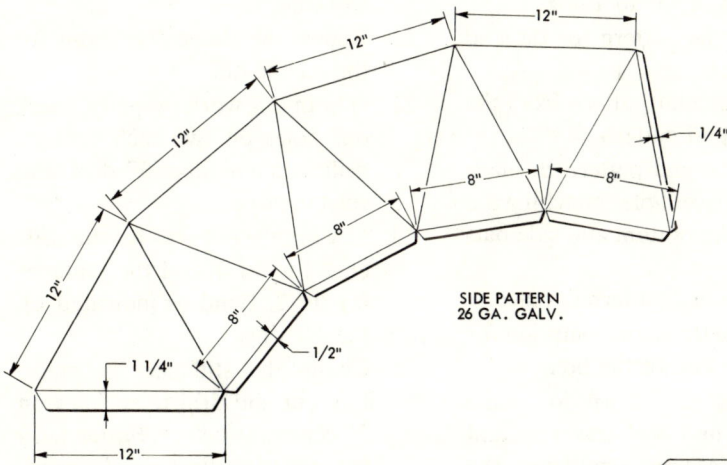

SIDE PATTERN
26 GA. GALV.

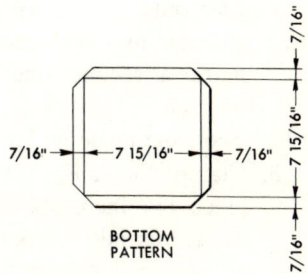

12"

12"

12"

12"

12"

8"

8"

8"

8"

1/4"

1/2"

1 1/4"

12"

BOTTOM
PATTERN

7/16" 7 15/16" 7/16"

7/16"

7 15/16"

7/16"

Figure 5. Making a free form waste basket.

Project 6. Tool box

1. The dimensions shown for the tool box are suggested only. Dimensions may be made to any size desired. However if different dimensions are used draw a full scale end view of the tool box to see whether the dimensions are in pleasing proportions.
2. Lay out the pattern for the bottom and sides including the rivet holes.
3. Drill the rivet holes with a number 30 drill.
4. Bend the three quarter inch edges on each end of the pattern to a 90° angle.
5. On a pan brake make the quarter bends to complete the bottom and sides of the tool box.
6. Lay out the pattern for the end of the box.
7. Mark a similar pattern from the original end pattern.
8. Clamp the end pattern in place and drill rivet holes matching the ones in the bottom and side pattern.
9. Rivet the end pattern in place.
10. Complete the same operation for the other end of the box.
11. Lay out the pattern for angle stiffener and tool tray rest and mark a second one from the original.
12. Bend the angle stiffener.
13. Clamp the angle stiffener in place 1¼ inches below the top of the box side. Mark rivet holes at two inch centers, drill, and rivet the angle in place.
14. Repeat for the angle on the other side of the box.
15. Lay out the pattern for lid 1 and lid 2.
16. Bend the half inch edges on each end of the pattern to 90°.
17. Bend the corner lines of the lid to a 45° angle.
18. Cut two lengths of piano hinge to fit exactly into the inside of the box.
19. Clamp the piano hinge to the inside of the box. Make sure the hinge works freely. Drill with a number 30 drill on two inch centers, and rivet in place.
20. Fasten the lid to the other side of the piano hinge with two sheet metal screws and test for proper working.
21. Repeat the above operations for the second lid.
22. If both lids work properly, mark out holes on two inch centers, drill with a number 30 drill, and rivet in place.
23. Lay out the patterns for the stiffener for lid 1 and the stiffener for lid 2. Bend as indicated on the drawings.
24. Clamp the stiffeners in place. Lay out and drill rivet holes on 2″ centers as before. Fasten temporarily with sheet metal screws. Test the lid for working operation, and rivet the stiffeners in place.
25. Lay out the patterns for the tool tray and assemble. See the instructions for Project 1 for more detailed instructions.

26. Fasten the suitcase latches and handle in place temporarily with sheet metal screws.

27. If latches and handle are working properly rivet or bolt into place.

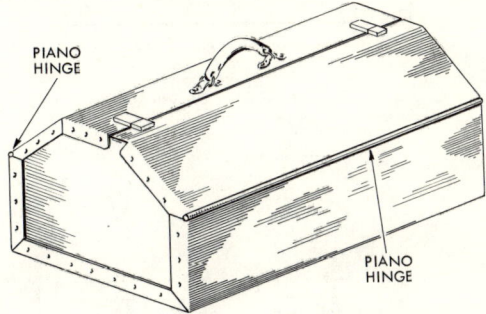

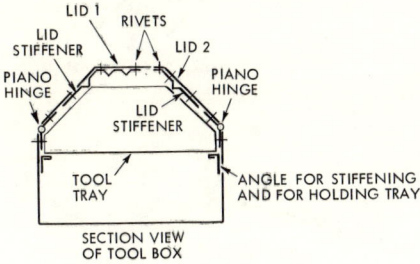

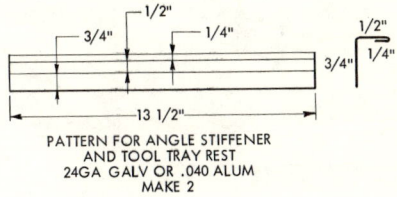

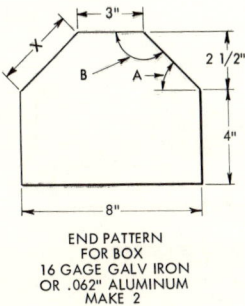

PIANO HINGE

PIANO HINGE

LID 1
LID STIFFENER
RIVETS
LID 2
PIANO HINGE
PIANO HINGE
LID STIFFENER
TOOL TRAY
ANGLE FOR STIFFENING AND FOR HOLDING TRAY

SECTION VIEW OF TOOL BOX

1/2"
3/4"
1/4"
1/2"
1/4"
3/4"
13 1/2"

PATTERN FOR ANGLE STIFFENER AND TOOL TRAY REST
24GA GALV OR .040 ALUM
MAKE 2

3"
X
2 1/2"
B
A
4"
8"

END PATTERN FOR BOX
16 GAGE GALV IRON OR .062" ALUMINUM
MAKE 2

Figure 6. Making a tool box.

STIFFNER FOR LID 1
24 GA GALV OR .040 ALUM

STIFFENER FOR LID 2
24 GA GALV OR .040 ALUM

SEE PROJECT 1
SEE HANDLE DETAIL

DETAIL OF LID STIFFENER

DOUBLE HEM
TO OUTSIDE

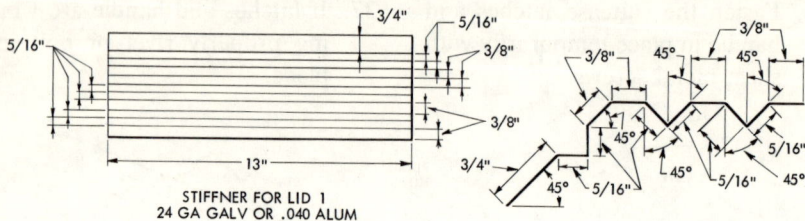

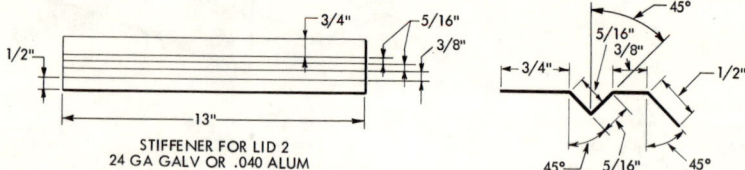

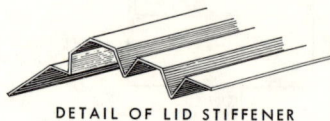

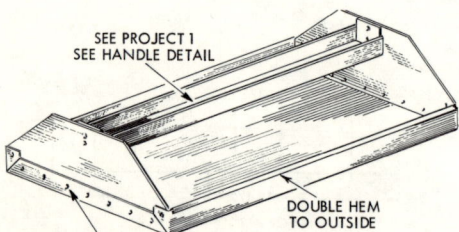

RIVETED AT APPROX 1" CENTERS
WITH 1/8" DIA RIVETS 1/4" LONG

TRAY CONSTRUCTION

NOTE:
X' = 1/8" LESS THAN DIMENSION X
ON END PATTERN
A' = ANGLE A ON END PATTERN
B' = 1/2 OF ANGLE B ON END PATTERN

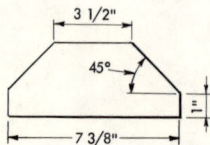

END PATTERN FOR TRAY
18 GA GALV OR .062 ALUM
MAKE 2

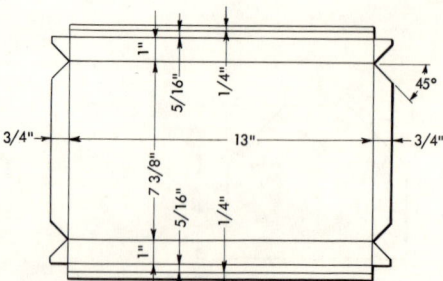

BOTTOM AND SIDE PATTERN
FOR TRAY
26 GA GALV OR .040 ALUM
MAKE 1

Figure 6. (continued)

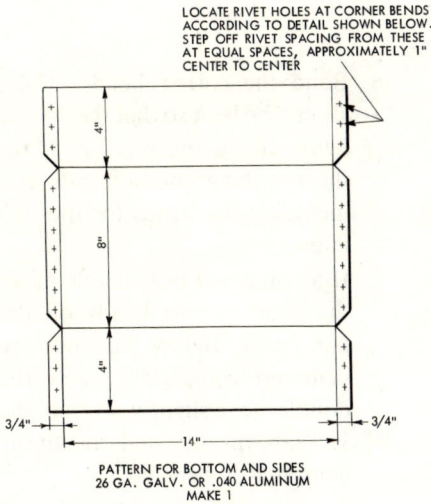

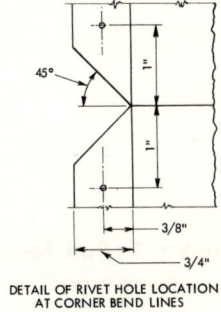

LOCATE RIVET HOLES AT CORNER BENDS
ACCORDING TO DETAIL SHOWN BELOW.
STEP OFF RIVET SPACING FROM THESE
AT EQUAL SPACES, APPROXIMATELY 1"
CENTER TO CENTER

DETAIL OF RIVET HOLE LOCATION
AT CORNER BEND LINES

PATTERN FOR BOTTOM AND SIDES
26 GA. GALV. OR .040 ALUMINUM
MAKE 1

N O T E :

1. DIMENSIONS SUGGESTED MAY BE CHANGED
   FOR INDIVIDUAL NEEDS

2. MATERIAL IS 26 GAGE GALVANIZED FOR
   BOTTOM AND SIDES, AND 16 GAGE
   GALVANIZED FOR ENDS. EQUIVALENT
   THICKNESS IN ALUMINUM MAY BE USED.

3. TOOL TRAY SETS INSIDE OF BOX

4. RIVETS—ALUMINUM 1/8" DIA., 1/4" LONG
   BRAZIER HEAD

PATTERN FOR LID 1
26 GA GALV OR .040 ALUM
MAKE 1

PATTERN FOR LID 2
26 GA GALV OR .040 ALUM

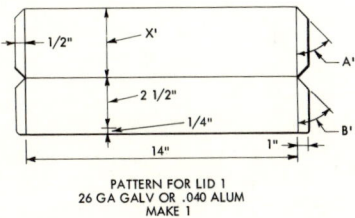

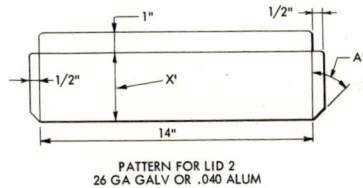

Figure 6. (continued)

Project 7. Pan for small jars to fit between garage studs

OPERATIONS

1. The length of the pan will be approximately 14¼ inches. However this dimension must be verified by measurement taken at the spot where the pan will fit. Make the length of the pan ¼ inch shorter than the actual distance between the studs.
2. Lay out the pattern.
3. Cut and notch the pattern, including prick marking the center holes for punching holes.
4. Punch all holes including the cleanout holes on the bottom.
5. Bend the double hems to the outside.
6. Bend the corner bends. These should be bent so that the double hems are to the outside. Make the two long corner bends first including the bends for the ½" flap.
7. If a pan brake is available make the short corner bends on the pan brake. Before the ends are bent up completely open the double hem slightly so that the ½" lap will slide underneath the hem as it is bent up.
8. If a pan brake is not available, clamp a board on each side of the metal even with the bend line and tap the metal around with a wooden mallet.
9. Solder the corner laps.

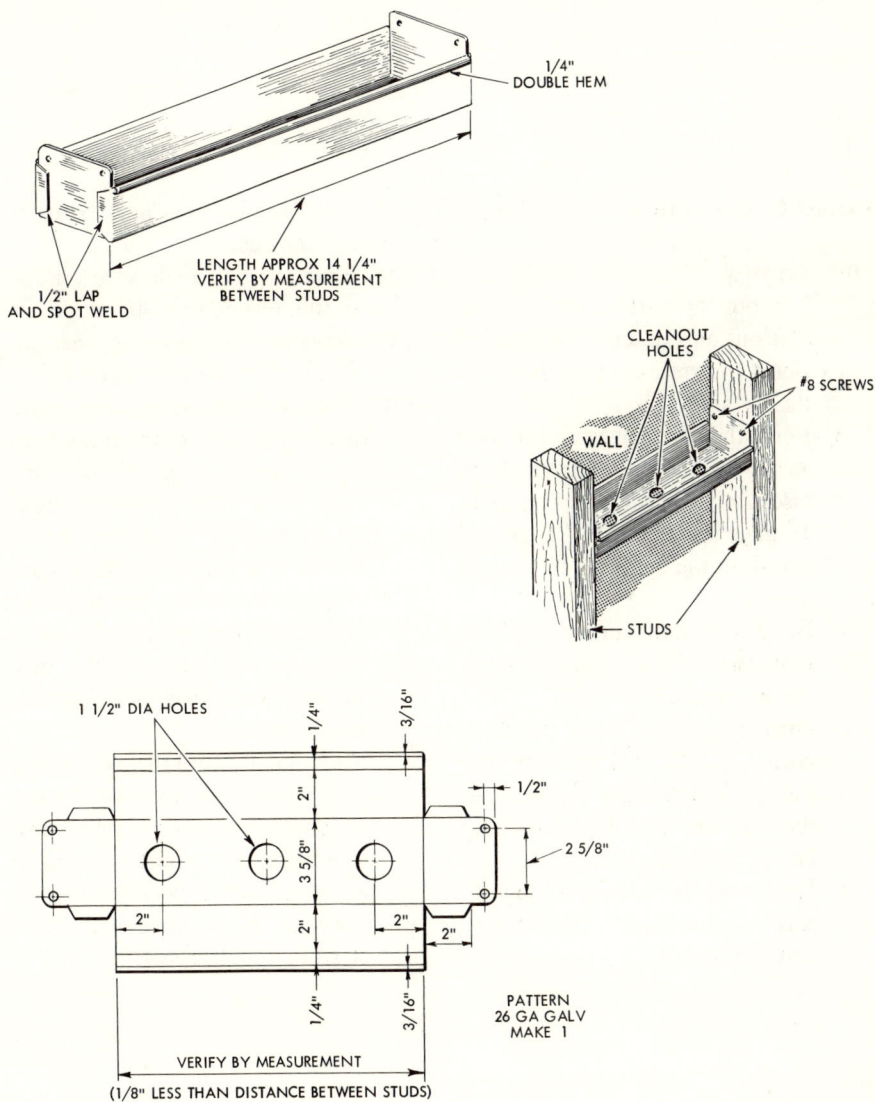

1/4"
DOUBLE HEM

1/2" LAP
AND SPOT WELD

LENGTH APPROX 14 1/4"
VERIFY BY MEASUREMENT
BETWEEN STUDS

CLEANOUT
HOLES

#8 SCREWS

WALL

STUDS

1 1/2" DIA HOLES

1/4"

3/16"

2"

1/2"

3 5/8"

2 5/8"

2"

2"

2"

2"

1/4"

3/16"

PATTERN
26 GA GALV
MAKE 1

VERIFY BY MEASUREMENT
(1/8" LESS THAN DISTANCE BETWEEN STUDS)

Figure 7. Making a pan for small jars.

Project 8. Box with a sliding top

OPERATION

1. Lay out the pattern for the box. Cut out and notch as shown.
2. Bend the quarter inch hems to the outside.
3. Bend the ⅜" edges as far over as is possible in the brake. Then insert a steel rule or a strip of 16 gage under the ⅜" edge and smash in the brake so that a gap is left.
4. Bend both long corner bends so that the ½ "lap is bent with the corner bends.
5. On a pan brake bend the short corner bends, making sure that the ½" laps slide in place to the outside. The ½" laps may be on the inside if desired.
6. Spot weld the half inch laps.
7. Lay out the pattern for the top. Cut and notch.
8. Bend the quarter inch hems to the outside.
9. Bend the half inch edge on end to the outside to a 90° angle.
10. Bend the ⅜" edge on one side of the top to the inside.
11. Flatten down in the same manner as the ⅜" edges on the box.
12. Bend the ½" edge on the same side to the inside to a 90° angle. Leave the ⅜" edge outside the brake so it is not smashed tight.
13. Repeat the above operation for the other edge of the top, making sure that none of the previously bent edges are smashed in the brake.
14. Slide the top into the lock of the box. If the top and box do not fit properly tap the edges with a hammer to adjust. Putting a small amount of beeswax or candle wax on the slide will make it work much easier.

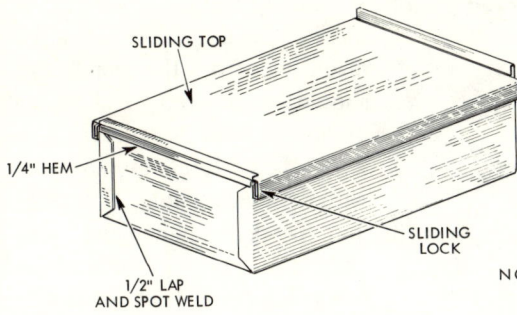

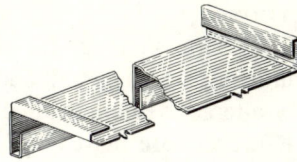

SLIDING TOP

1/4" HEM

1/2" LAP
AND SPOT WELD

SLIDING
LOCK

DETAIL OF TOP

NOTES:

1. MATERIAL 26 OR 28 GAGE GALVANIZED

2. MAKE DIMENSIONS TO SUIT

TOP

DETAIL OF
SIDE FOR TOP

BOX

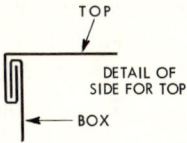

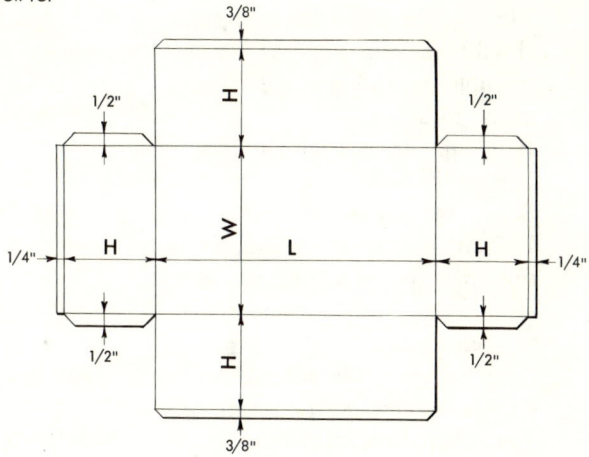

PATTERN FOR BOX

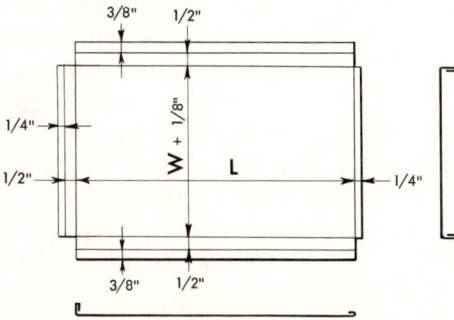

PATTERN FOR TOP

Figure 8. Making a box with a sliding top.

Project 9. Planter with perforated metal jacket

OPERATIONS

1. The dimensions given on the drawing are suggested and may be altered to suit individual taste. However care must be taken to choose dimensions that are of pleasing proportions.
2. Lay out the pattern for the box. Cut and notch.
3. Bend only the *end* $5/16''$ hems to the outside, and smash down tightly in the brake. Do not mar with a hammer.
4. The $5/16''$ hems on the long side should be bent over as far as possible in the brake but not smashed down.
5. Bend up the box with the $3/8''$ laps on the inside.
6. Solder the box.
7. Rub the outside of the box with fine emery paper in long, straight strokes to give a brushed effect to the outside.
8. Paint or spray the outside with a clear lacquer, clear enamel, or any other clear protective material.
9. Lay out the pattern for the perforated metal sides. Be sure that there are no sharp edges on the ends of the pattern as these will be exposed. It is well to try to cut the perforated metal so that the ends are a complete straight line instead of jagged edges. If this is not possible, file all edges to prevent cutting or snagging.
10. Bend the $3/4''$ edge of the metal side to a 90° angle.
11. With masking tape cover part of the $3/4''$ bend. A strip about $3/8$ of an inch from the metal edge should be covered to allow an unpainted edge for soldering.
12. Spray the perforated metal sides with flat black paint.
13. Slip the perforated metal sides under the open $5/16''$ edge of the box being careful not to scratch the lacquered surface of the box. If the $3/4''$ edge does not fit flat against the bottom of the box cut a small amount from the top of the perforated metal side.
14. Cover the $5/16''$ edge with a rag to prevent scarring the metal and squeeze the $5/16''$ edge down flat with tongs. Be very careful not to scar or dent the metal. After this flattening operation the $5/16''$ hem may have to be sprayed again with a clear lacquer. If this is necessary lay a piece of metal over the perforated metal sides to protect them from spray. Also spray the inside of the box, especially near the top.
15. After the $5/16''$ edges are smashed down turn the box over and tack solder the metal sides to the box. Be sure that the soldering is done at a point where it cannot be seen when the box is upright. Wash off all soldered joints carefully to remove any trace of acid.
16. If desired, four small rubber feet may be attached to the bottom of the planter to prevent scarring table. An alternative method is to glue felt to the bottom of the box.

5/16"

3/8"

2"

3 1/2"

2"

3/8"

5/16"

5/16" 2" 9" 2" 5/16"

PATTERN FOR BOX
(COPPER OR BRASS)
MAKE 1

1 7/8"

3/4" 9"

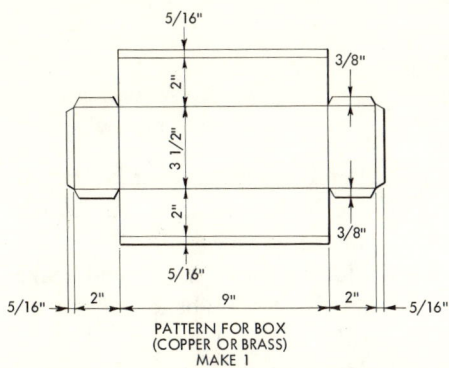

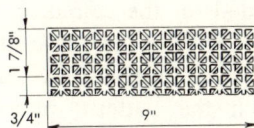

PATTERN FOR
PERFORATED METAL SIDES
MAKE 2
(MAKE OF ANY DESIRED DESIGN)

PERFORATED OR
DECORATIVE METAL
(EXTENDS UNDER HEM)

PLANTER
BOX

TACK SOLDER

DETAIL OF BOX
AND PERFORATED METAL

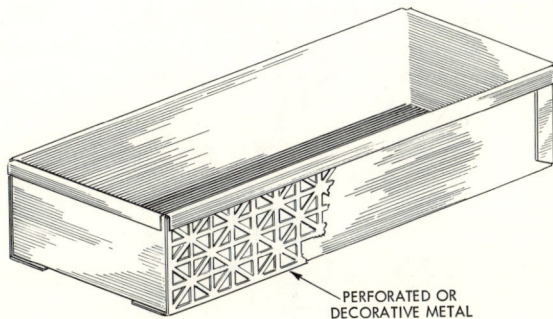

PERFORATED OR
DECORATIVE METAL

Figure 9. Making a planter with a perforated metal jacket.

Project 10. Trash bag holder for inside a kitchen cabinet door

OPERATIONS

1. The dimensions shown are suggested only and these may be altered to fit individual circumstances. Recommended material is 26 gage galvanized iron.
2. Lay out the pattern for the sides including the center marks needed for the tear drop holes. See the detail for the center location on these holes. Cut and notch the pattern; punch the holes and file the edges to make the tear drop holes.
3. Bend the 1¼″ edge for a Pittsburgh seam.
4. Bend the ¼″ edge to the outside to a 90° by pounding over the front edge of the brake with a wooden mallet. Turn the metal over and bend completely over by pounding the edge over the upper leaf of the brake. Put in the brake and smash flat.
5. Bend the ⅜″ edge to the inside.

Bend this edge over as far as the brake will allow but do not smash down.

6. Starting with the ¼″ bend, make all the corner bends to the inside.
7. Make up the Pittsburgh seam.
8. Bend all of the ½″ edges on the bottom pattern to 90 degrees.
9. Insert the bottom into the side pattern so that the ½″ edge of the bottom is hooked into the ⅜″ edge as shown on the detail.
10. With tongs squeeze down the ⅜″ edge of the side so that it grips the bottom edge tightly.
11. Tack solder the bottom into place from the outside.
12. If desired solder completely around the inside of the bottom and up the side seam. All soldering should be done on the inside where it will not show. Complete soldering on the inside is desirable to prevent any dripping of moisture that may be in the trash.

TOP OF BACK

5/16" HOLE

3/4"

5/32"

3/16" HOLES

3/16"

DETAIL OF
TEAR DROP HOLES

SIDE

BOTTOM

TACK
SOLDER

DETAIL OF
BOTTOM SEAM

PITTSBURGH
SEAM

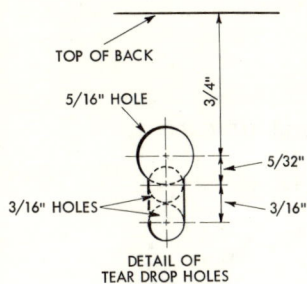

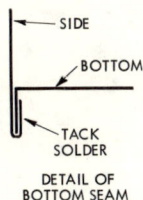

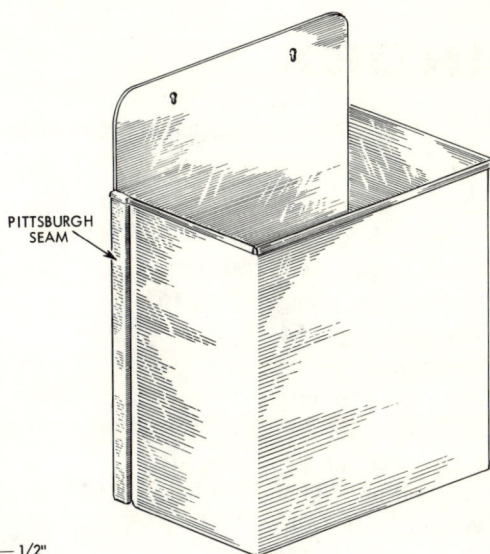

MATERIAL: 26 GAGE GALVANIZED IRON

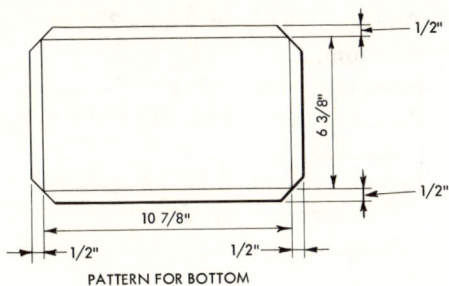

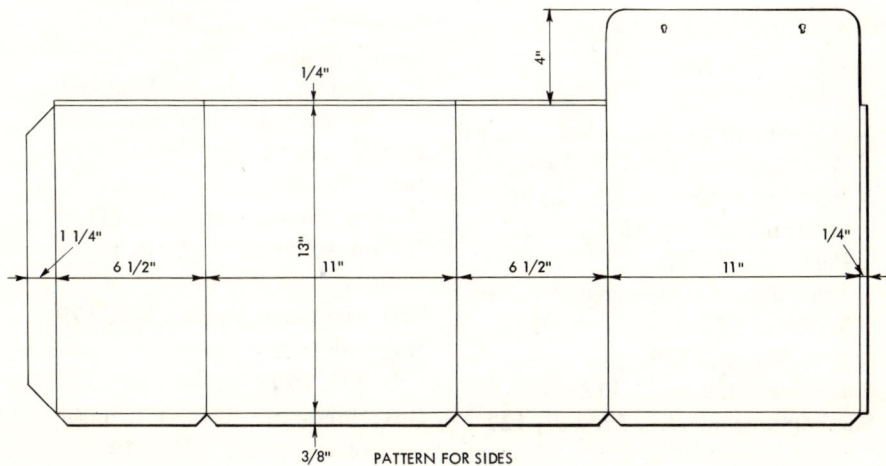

1/2"

6 3/8"

1/2"

10 7/8"

1/2"

1/2"

PATTERN FOR BOTTOM

1/4"

4"

1 1/4"

6 1/2"

13"

11"

6 1/2"

11"

1/4"

3/8"   PATTERN FOR SIDES

Figure 10. Making a kitchen trash bag holder.

INDEX

Numerals which are in **bold face** indicate illustrations.